THE ENGLISH TRADITION:
POETRY

THE ENGLISH TRADITION: POETRY

Marjorie Wescott Barrows
Formerly, General Editor
Macmillan Literary Heritage

Robert P. Bletter
Director, Teachers College Press
New York City

Donald G. Kobler
Chairman, English Department
Housatonic Valley Regional High School
Falls River, Connecticut

Bertrand Evans
Professor Emeritus of English
University of California
Berkeley, California

James E. Frey
Associate Professor of English
California State University
Fresno, California

Matthew Dolkey
Professor of English
Kean College of New Jersey
Union, New Jersey

Nelda B. Kubat
English Coordinator
Lansing High School
Ludlowville, New York

James G. Magill
Formerly, Chairman, English Department
Lincoln High School
Manitowoc, Wisconsin

A revision of *The Early Years of English Literature, Spenser to Goldsmith, Romantic and Victorian Writers,* and *Modern English Prose and Poetry,* previously published by Macmillan Publishing Co., Inc.

MACMILLAN PUBLISHING CO., INC.   New York
COLLIER MACMILLAN PUBLISHERS   London

Acknowledgments

For permission to reprint copyright material in this book, grateful acknowl-edgment is made to the following:

Clarendon Press, Oxford: For "The Blacksmiths" from *Fourteenth-Century Verse and Prose* by Kenneth Sisam. Reprinted by permission of the Clarendon Press, Oxford.

Collins-Knowlton-Wing, Inc.: For "Warning to Children" and "Traveller's Curse" by Robert Graves from *Collected Poems 1955*. Reprinted by per-mission of Collins-Knowlton-Wing, Inc. Copyright © 1955 by Robert Graves.

J. M. Dent & Sons Ltd.: For "Fern Hill," "The Hand That Signed the Paper" from *Collected Poems of Dylan Thomas* by Dylan Thomas. Reprinted by permission J. M. Dent & Sons Ltd. and the Trustees for the Copyrights of the late Dylan Thomas.

Faber and Faber Ltd.: For "Look, Stranger" by W. H. Auden from *Col-lected Shorter Poems 1927-1957*. For "In Memory of W. B. Yeats" by W. H. Auden from *Collected Shorter Poems 1927-1957*. For "Without That Once Clear Aim," by Stephen Spender from *Collected Poems*. For "Mr. Bleaney" by Philip Larkin from *The Whitsun Weddings*. All selections reprinted by permission of Faber and Faber Ltd.

Holt, Rinehart and Winston, Inc.: For "Reveille," "To an Athlete Dying Young" and "Be Still, My Soul" from *A Shropshire Lad*—Authorised Edition —from *The Collected Poems of A. E. Housman*. Copyright 1939, 1940 © 1959 by Holt, Rinehart and Winston, Inc. Copyright © 1967 by Robert E. Symons. For "Oh stay at home, my lad, and plough" from *The Collected Poems of A. E. Housman*. Copyright 1922 by Holt, Rinehart and Winston, Inc. Copy-right 1950 by Barclays Bank Ltd. All selections reprinted by permission of Holt, Rinehart and Winston, Inc.

Macmillan Publishing Co., Inc.: For "In Time of 'The Breaking of Nations,'" "Shelley's Skylark," "The Darkling Thrush," and "The Man He Killed" from *Collected Poems* by Thomas Hardy. Copyright 1925 by Macmillan Pub-lishing Co., Inc. For "The Lake Isle of Innisfree" from *Collected Poems* by

Cover design by William S. Shields

Macmillan Publishing Co., Inc.
866 Third Avenue, New York, New York 10022
Collier-Macmillan Canada, Ltd.

Printed in the United States of America

ACKNOWLEDGMENTS *(continued)*

William Butler Yeats. Reprinted with permission of Macmillan Publishing Co., Inc. Copyright 1906 by Macmillan Publishing Co., Inc., renewed 1934 by William Butler Yeats. For "The Wild Swans at Coole" and "An Irish Airman Foresees His Death" reprinted with permission of Macmillan Publishing Co., Inc. from *Collected Poems* by William Butler Yeats. Copyright 1919 by Macmillan Publishing Co., Inc., renewed 1946 by Bertha Georgie Yeats. For "Easter 1916" reprinted with permission of Macmillan Publishing Co., Inc. from *Collected Poems* by William Butler Yeats. Copyright 1924 by Macmillan Publishing Co., Inc., renewed 1952 by Bertha Georgie Yeats. For "The Coming of Wisdom with Time" reprinted with permission of Macmillan Publishing Co., Inc. from *Collected Poems* by William Butler Yeats. Copyright 1912 by Macmillan Publishing Co., Inc., renewed 1940 by Bertha Georgie Yeats. For "The Song of Wandering Aengus" reprinted with permission of Macmillan Publishing Co., Inc. from *The Collected Poems of W. B. Yeats* by W. B. Yeats. Copyright 1906; renewed 1934. For "A Coat" reprinted with permission of Macmillan Publishing Co., Inc. from *The Collected Poems of W. B. Yeats* by W. B. Yeats. Copyright 1916; renewed 1944 by Bertha Georgie Yeats. For "Sailing to Byzantium" reprinted with permission, Macmillan Publishing Co., Inc. from *The Collected Poems of W. B. Yeats* by W. B. Yeats. Copyright 1928 renewed 1956 by Georgie Yeats. For "Politics" reprinted with permission of Macmillan Publishing Co., Inc. from *The Collected Poems of W. B. Yeats* by W. B. Yeats. Copyright 1940 by Georgie Yeats.

Macmillan & Co., Ltd.: For "In Time of 'The Breaking of Nations,'" "Shelley's Skylark" "The Man He Killed" and "The Darkling Thrush" from *The Collected Poems of Thomas Hardy* by permission of the Trustees of the Hardy Estate, The Macmillan Company of Canada Ltd. and Macmillan & Co., Ltd.

The Marvell Press: For "Places" and "Loved Ones" by Philip Larkin reprinted from *The Less Deceived* by permission of The Marvell Press, Hessle, Yorkshire, England.

William Morris Agency: For "Solo for Ear Trumpet" and "Heart and Mind" from *Collected Poems of Edith Sitwell* by Edith Sitwell. Copyright © 1930 by Edith Sitwell. Reprinted by permission of William Morris Agency.

John Murray Publishers Ltd.: For "Indoor Games Near Newbury" and "Devonshire Street W.1" from *Collected Poems* by John Betjeman.

New Directions: For "Fern Hill," "Do not go gentle. . . ." "And Death Shall Have No Dominion," and "The Hand That Signed the Paper . . ." from *The Collected Poems of Dylan Thomas*. Copyright © 1939 by New Directions; © 1953 by Dylan Thomas. Reprinted by permission of New Directions Publishing Corporation.

Oxford University Press, Inc.: For "Pied Beauty," "God's Grandeur," "Spring," and "I Wake and Feel the Fell of Dark" from *Poems of Gerard Manley Hopkins,* Third Edition, edited by W. H. Gardner. Copyright 1948 by Oxford University Press, Inc. Reprinted by permission. For "The Wanderer" from *An Anthology of Old English Poetry, translated* by Charles W. Kennedy. Copyright © 1960 by Oxford University Press, Inc. Reprinted by permission.

ACKNOWLEDGMENTS *(continued)*

Random House, Inc.: For "Look, Stranger" by W. H. Auden. Copyright 1937 and renewed 1964 by W. H. Auden. From *The Collected Poetry of W. H. Auden.* For "In Memory of W. B. Yeats" by W. H. Auden. Copyright 1940 by W. H. Auden. Reprinted from *The Collected Poetry of W. H. Auden* by permission of Random House, Inc. For "Without That Once Clear Aim" by Stephen Spender. Copyright 1934 and renewed 1961 by Stephen Spender. Reprinted from *Collected Poems 1928-1953* by Stephen Spender. For "Ultima Ratio Regum" by Stephen Spender. Copyright 1942 by Stephen Spender. Reprinted from *Collected Poems 1928-1953* by Stephen Spender. For "Mr. Bleaney" by Philip Larkin. Copyright 1962 by Philip Larkin. Reprinted from *The Whitson Weddings* by Philip Larkin. All selections reprinted by permission of Random House, Inc.

The Society of Authors: For "Reveille," "To an Athlete Dying Young," "Be Still, My Soul, Be Still" and "Oh Stay at Home My Lad and Plough" reprinted by permission of The Society of Authors as the literary representative of the Estate of the late A. E. Housman, and Messrs. Jonathan Cape Ltd., publishers of A. E. Housman's *Collected Poems.*

Vanguard Press, Inc.: For "Heart and Mind" by Dame Edith Sitwell. Reprinted by permission of the publisher, The Vanguard Press, from *The Collected Poems of Edith Sitwell.* Copyright 1946, 1954 by Edith Sitwell.

The Viking Press, Inc.: For "Prologue" and part (2200 words) of "The Pardoner's Tale" from *The Portable Chaucer* translated by Theodore Morrison. Copyright 1949 by Theodore Morrison. Reprinted by permission of The Viking Press, Inc.

A. P. Watt & Son: For "The Lake Isle of Innisfree," "The Wild Swans at Coole," "Easter 1916," "An Irish Airman Foresees His Death" and "The Coming of Wisdom with Time" all from *The Collected Poems of W. B. Yeats.* For "The Song of Wandering Aengus," "A Coat," "Sailing to Byzantium," and "Politics" from *The Collected Poems of W. B. Yeats* by permission of Mr. M. B. Yeats and the Macmillan Co. of Canada Ltd.

Contents

The Great Tradition   1

ANONYMOUS BALLAD
    Sir Patrick Spens   3

WILLIAM SHAKESPEARE
    Juliet's Soliloquy   4

JOHN DONNE
    Death Be Not Proud   5

ANDREW MARVELL
    To His Coy Mistress   6

WILLIAM BLAKE
    The Sick Rose   7

JOHN KEATS
    La Belle Dame Sans Merci   8

ALFRED, LORD TENNYSON
    Break, Break, Break   9

WILLIAM BUTLER YEATS
    The Lake Isle of Innisfree   10

The Anglo-Saxon Period   11

from *Beowulf*   15
    The Building of Heorot   15
    The Coming of Beowulf   17
    Beowulf's Reply to Unferth   20
    The Battle with Grendel   22
    Beowulf's Funeral   26
The Seafarer   30
The Wanderer   33

The Medieval Period   37

Ballads and Lyrics
    The Twa Corbies   43
    Lady Isabel and the Elf Knight   44
    Thomas Rymer   47
    Get Up and Bar the Door   50
    Edward, Edward   52
    Cuckoo Song   55
    Jesu, Swete Sone Dere   56
    I Sing of a Maiden   57
    The Blacksmiths   58

GEOFFREY CHAUCER
    from *The Canterbury Tales*   60
    Prologue   60
    The Pardoner's Tale   87

The Elizabethans   95

SIR PHILIP SIDNEY
    With How Sad Steps, O Moon   101
    My True Love Hath My Heart   102

EDMUND SPENSER
    What Guile Is This   104
    One Day I Wrote Her Name   105

CHRISTOPHER MARLOWE
    The Passionate Shepherd to His Love   107

SIR WALTER RALEIGH
    The Nymph's Reply to the Shepherd   108

WILLIAM SHAKESPEARE
    Shall I Compare Thee to a Summer's Day?   111
    When In Disgrace with Fortune and Men's Eyes 112
    When to the Sessions of Sweet Silent Thought 113
    That Time of Year Thou Mayst in Me Behold   115

Let Me Not to the Marriage of True Minds 116
My Mistress' Eyes Are Nothing Like the Sun 117
Song (from *Twelfth Night*) 118
All the World's a Stage (from *As You Like It*) 119
To Be, or Not to Be (from *Hamlet*) 120
Our Revels Now Are Ended (from *The Tempest*) 122

The Cavaliers and Metaphysical Poets 123

BEN JONSON
Song to Celia 126
On My First Son 127

ROBERT HERRICK
To the Virgins to Make Much of Time 129
Upon Julia's Clothes 131
Corinna's Going A-Maying 131

SIR JOHN SUCKLING
The Constant Lover 136

RICHARD LOVELACE
To Lucasta, on Going to the Wars 137
To Althea, from Prison 138

JOHN DONNE
Sweetest Love, I Do Not Go 141
The Bait 143
The Message 145
At the Round Earth's Imagined Corners 146
Batter My Heart, Three-Personed God 148
A Hymn to God the Father 149

GEORGE HERBERT
Easter Wings 151
The Collar 152
Love 154

The Puritan Poet: John Milton 156

JOHN MILTON
On His Blindness 158
from *Paradise Lost* 160
from Book I 160
Book II 170

The Age of Reason and Common Sense 203

JOHN DRYDEN
Alexander's Feast 207

ALEXANDER POPE
from *An Essay on Man* 216
from *The Rape of the Lock* (Canto I) 220

The Reaction Against Reason 226

THOMAS GRAY
Elegy Written in a Country Churchyard 232
Ode on the Death of a Favorite Cat 237

ROBERT BURNS
To a Mouse 240
A Red, Red Rose 242
Highland Mary 243
John Anderson My Jo 245
To a Louse 246
Is There for Honest Poverty 248

WILLIAM BLAKE
from *Songs of Innocence* 251
Introduction 251
The Lamb 252
Holy Thursday 254

from *Songs of Experience*   255
     The Tyger   255
     Holy Thursday   256
     The Clod and the Pebble   257
     The Chimney-Sweeper   258

The Romantic Poets   260

WILLIAM WORDSWORTH
     Lines Written in Early Spring   267
     Lines Composed a Few Miles
       Above Tintern Abbey   269
     She Dwelt Among the Untrodden Ways   274
     London, 1802   275
     The World Is Too Much with Us   276
     The Solitary Reaper   277
     She Was a Phantom of Delight   279

SAMUEL TAYLOR COLERIDGE
     Kubla Khan   281
     The Rime of the Ancient Mariner   284

GEORGE GORDON, LORD BYRON
     She Walks in Beauty   309
     The Destruction of Sennacherib   310
     The Prisoner of Chillon   312

PERCY BYSSHE SHELLEY
     Song to the Men of England   326
     To Night   328
     Ode to the West Wind   330
     To a Skylark   334

JOHN KEATS
     When I Have Fears That I May Cease to Be   339
     On First Looking into Chapman's Homer   340
     Ode on a Grecian Urn   341
     Ode to a Nightingale   344
     The Eve of St. Agnes   348

The Victorian Poets   362

ALFRED, LORD TENNYSON
   Tears, Idle Tears   368
   Now Sleeps the Crimson Petal   370
   The Lady of Shalott   371
   Ulysses   377
   from *In Memoriam*   380
     Prologue   381
     Dark house, by which once more I stand   383
     I envy not in any moods   384
     Love is and was my lord and king   385

ROBERT BROWNING
   Home-Thoughts, from Abroad   387
   Prospice   389
   My Last Duchess   390
   The Bishop Orders His Tomb
     at Saint Praxed's Church   393

ELIZABETH BARRETT BROWNING
   How Do I Love Thee?   398
   If Thou Must Love Me, Let It Be for Naught   399

MATTHEW ARNOLD
   Self-Dependence   401
   To Marguerite   403
   The Buried Life   404
   Dover Beach   408

ALGERNON CHARLES SWINBURNE
   When the Hounds of Spring   411

Bridging the Centuries   415

GERARD MANLEY HOPKINS
   Spring   419
   God's Grandeur   420

Pied Beauty   422
I Wake and Feel the Fell of Dark   423

THOMAS HARDY
Shelley's Skylark   426
The Darkling Thrush   428
In Time of "The Breaking of Nations"   430
The Man He Killed   431

A. E. HOUSMAN
Reveille   433
To an Athlete Dying Young   435
Be Still, My Soul, Be Still   437
Oh Stay at Home, My Lad, and Plough   438

WILLIAM BUTLER YEATS
The Song of Wandering Aengus   439
A Coat   441
The Wild Swans at Coole   442
An Irish Airman Foresees His Death   444
Easter 1916   445
Sailing to Byzantium   449
The Coming of Wisdom with Time   451
Politics   451

The Moderns   452

EDITH SITWELL
Heart and Mind   457
Solo for Ear-Trumpet   459

ROBERT GRAVES
Warning to Children   461
Traveller's Curse After Misdirection   463

W. H. AUDEN
In Memory of W. B. Yeats   464
Look, Stranger   469

xiii

STEPHEN SPENDER
    Without That Once Clear Aim   471
    Ultima Ratio Regum   472

DYLAN THOMAS
    Fern Hill   474
    The Hand That Signed the Paper Felled a City   477

JOHN BETJEMAN
    Indoor Games Near Newbury   479
    Devonshire Street W.1   481

PHILIP LARKIN
    Places, Loved Ones   483
    Mr. Bleaney   485

    About the Poets   487
    Glossary of Literary Terms   503

THE ENGLISH
TRADITION: POETRY

THE GREAT TRADITION

Before human beings could read they were enjoying poetry. They enjoyed creating it, listening to it, and reciting it. For those who find poetry less appealing than prose, this seemingly innate love of poetry in the human animal is, at first, a mystery. But the fact that poetry is to be found in almost every culture suggests that some very basic pleasures are to be derived from a good poem. The first of these, obviously, has to do with sound. Pleasing combinations of sounds appeal to small children—as anyone who has watched a child babbling nonsense syllables knows. One of the basic pleasures in hearing poetry comes from listening to effective combinations of sounds. And sounds are most effective when they match the sense of the words being used. A poem in which this matching or blending of sound and meaning occurs is much more advanced than magic chants or nonsense rhymes which rely for their appeal on sound alone.

The earliest English poetry now available to us is narrative; that is, it tells a story. Obviously, one appeal of these early poems is to be found in the events which are recounted. In trying to define what makes particular narrative poems "interesting," however, we get to another characteristic of good poetry: it expresses in appropriate sound combinations some situation or emotion which most people have experienced. The subject matter of great poetry, whether narrative or lyrical, is familiar human emotions—love, grief, fear, hate, or

1

joy. A major pleasure in reading a poem on grief, for example, is finding this emotion expressed better than we could express it ourselves, even during personal moments of grief.

But what makes one poem about grief more enduring than another? The greatness of a poem depends upon the intelligent combination of several things: sound, sense, and perceptive selection of vocabulary. Power of expression depends on precision and economy. Saying things fluently is not enough; one must also choose the best of all possible words to say the most in the least space.

Following are a group of poems from different periods of English literature. They have been judged by hundreds of thousands of readers to be among the greatest poems of the English language. You will want to read them primarily because they are a pleasure to read. But, perhaps, as you read you will notice that the pleasure they offer comes from their sounds, the fitting combinations of sound and meaning, and the craft of the poet who expresses what he wants to say with economy and precision, and, therefore, with power.

SIR PATRICK SPENS

The king sits in Dumferling toune,
    Drinking the blude-reid° wine: blood-red
"O whar will I get a guid° sailor,   good
    To sail this schip of mine?"

Up and spak an eldern knicht,°   knight 5
    Sat at the king's richt kne:°   knee
"Sir Patrick Spens is the best sailor
    That sails upon the se."

The king has written a braid° letter,   official
    And signed it wi' his hand,   10
And sent it to Sir Patrick Spens,
    Was walking on the sand.

The first line that Sir Patrick red,°   read
    A loud lauch° lauched he;   laugh
The next line that Sir Patrick red,   15
    The teir blinded his ee.°   eye

"O wha is this has don this deid,°   deed
    This ill deid don to me,
To send me out this time o' the yeir,
    To sail upon the se!   20

"Mak hast, mak hast, my mirry men all,
    Our guid schip sails the morne:"
"O say na sae,° my master deir,   so
    For I feir a deadlie storme.

"Late late yestreen° I saw the new moone,   yesterday
   Wi the auld moone in hir arme,   evening   26
And I feir, I feir, my deir master,
   That we will cum to harme."

O our Scots nobles were richt laith°   right loathe
   To weet° their cork-heild schoone;°   wet; shoes   30
Bot lang owre a' the play wer playd,
   Thair hats they swam aboone.°   about

O lang, lang, may their ladies sit,
   Wi thair fans into their hand,
Or eir they se Sir Patrick Spens   35
   Cum sailing to the land.

O lang, lang, may the ladies stand,
   Wi thair gold kembs° in their hair,   combs
Waiting for their ain deir lords,
   For they'll see thame na mair.   40

Haf owre,° haf owre to Aberdour,   half way
   It's fiftie fadom deip,
And thair lies guid Sir Patrick Spens,
   Wi the Scots lords at his feit.

                         ANONYMOUS BALLAD

JULIET'S SOLILOQUY

Gallop apace, you fiery-footed steeds,
Towards Phœbus' lodging! Such a wagoner
As Phaëton would whip you to the West
And bring in cloudy night immediately.

Spread thy close curtain, love-performing night,   5
That runaway eyes may wink, and Romeo
Leap to these arms untalk'd of and unseen.
Lovers can see to do their amorous rites
By their own beauties; or, if love be blind,
It best agrees with night. Come, civil night,   10
Thou sober-suited matron, all in black,
And learn me how to lose a winning match,
Play'd for a pair of stainless maidenhoods.
Hood my unmann'd blood, bating in my cheeks,
With thy black mantle till strange love, grown bold,   15
Think true love acted simple modesty.
Come, night; come, Romeo; come, thou day in night;
For thou wilt lie upon the wings of night
Whiter than new snow upon a raven's back.
Come, gentle night; come, loving, black-brow'd night;   20
Give me my Romeo; and, when he shall die,
Take him and cut him out in little stars,
And he will make the face of heaven so fine
That all the world will be in love with night
And pay no worship to the garish sun.   25

(FROM *Romeo and Juliet*)
WILLIAM SHAKESPEARE

Death Be Not Proud

Death be not proud, though some have called thee
Mighty and dreadful, for thou art not so;
For those whom thou think'st thou dost overthrow
Die not, poor Death, nor yet canst thou kill me.
From rest and sleep, which but thy picture be,   5
Much pleasure, then from thee much more must flow,
And soonest° our best men with thee do go,   most willingly
Rest of their bones, and souls' delivery.

Thou art slave to fate, chance, kings, and desperate men,
And dost with poison, war, and sickness dwell;   10
And poppy or charms can make us sleep as well
And better than thy stroke; why swell'st thou then?
One short sleep past, we wake eternally,
And Death shall be no more; death, thou shalt die!

JOHN DONNE

TO HIS COY MISTRESS

Had we but world° enough, and time,   space
This coyness, Lady, were no crime.
We would sit down and think which way
To walk and pass our long love's day.
Thou by the Indian Ganges' side   5
Shouldst rubies find; I by the tide
Of Humber would complain. I would
Love you ten years before the Flood,
And you should, if you please, refuse
Till the conversion of the Jews.   10
My vegetable love should grow
Vaster than empires, and more slow;
An hundred years should go to praise
Thine eyes and on thy forehead gaze;
Two hundred to adore each breast,   15
But thirty thousand to the rest;
An age at least to every part,
And the last age should show your heart.
For, Lady, you deserve this state,
Nor would I love at lower rate.   20
   But at my back I always hear
Time's winged chariot hurrying near;
And yonder all before us lie
Deserts of vast eternity.
Thy beauty shall no more be found,   25

Nor, in thy marble vault, shall sound
My echoing song; then worms shall try
That long preserved virginity,
And your quaint honor turn to dust,
And into ashes all my lust: 30
The grave's a fine and private place,
But none, I think, do there embrace.
   Now therefore, while the youthful hue
Sits on thy skin like morning dew,
And while thy willing soul transpires   35
At every pore with instant fires,
Now let us sport us while we may,
And now, like amorous birds of prey,
Rather at once our time devour
Than languish in his slow-chapped° power.   slowly crushing
Let us roll all our strength and all   41
Our sweetness up into one ball,
And tear our pleasures with rough strife
Thorough the iron gates of life:
Thus, though we cannot make our sun   45
Stand still, yet we will make him run.

ANDREW MARVELL

THE SICK ROSE

O Rose thou art sick.
The invisible worm,
That flies in the night
In the howling storm:

Has found out thy bed
Of crimson joy:
And his dark secret love
Does thy life destroy.

WILLIAM BLAKE

LA BELLE DAME SANS MERCI[1]

O what can ail thee, knight-at-arms,
    Alone and palely loitering?
The sedge has withered from the lake,
    And no birds sing.

O what can ail thee, knight-at arms,   5
    So haggard and so woe-begone?
The squirrel's granary is full,
    And the harvest's done.

I see a lily on thy brow,
    With anguish moist and fever dew,   10
And on thy cheeks a fading rose
    Fast withereth too.

"I met a lady in the meads,°   meadows
    Full beautiful—a faery's child;
Her hair was long, her foot was light,   15
    And her eyes were wild.

"I made a garland for her head,
    And bracelets too, and fragrant zone;°   girdle
She looked at me as she did love,
    And made sweet moan.   20

"I set her on my pacing steed,
    And nothing else saw all day long;
For sidelong would she bend, and sing
    A faery's song.

"She found me roots of relish sweet,   25
    And honey wild, and manna-dew;
And sure in language strange she said,
    'I love thee true.'

[1] *La Belle . . . Merci:* The Beautiful Lady Without Pity

"She took me to her elfin grot,
  And there she wept and sighed full sore,   30
And there I shut her wild, wild eyes,
  With kisses four.

"And there she lullèd me asleep,
  And there I dreamed—ah! woe betide!—
The latest dream I ever dreamed   35
  On the cold hill's side.

"I saw pale kings, and princes too,
  Pale warriors, death-pale were they all:
They cried—'La Belle Dame sans Merci
  Hath thee in thrall!   40

"I saw their starved lips in the gloam,
  With horrid warning gapèd wide,
And I awoke, and found me here
  On the cold hill's side.

"And this is why I sojourn here   45
  Alone and palely loitering,
Though the sedge is withered from the lake,
  And no birds sing."

JOHN KEATS

Break, Break, Break

Break, break, break,
  On thy cold gray stones, O Sea!
And I would that my tongue could utter
  The thoughts that arise in me.

O well for the fisherman's boy,   5
  That he shouts with his sister at play!
O well for the sailor lad,
  That he sings in his boat on the bay!

And the stately ships go on
  To their haven under the hill;   10
But O for the touch of a vanished hand,
  And the sound of a voice that is still!

Break, break, break,
  At the foot of thy crags, O Sea!
But the tender grace of a day that is dead   15
  Will never come back to me.

ALFRED, LORD TENNYSON

THE LAKE ISLE OF INNISFREE

I will arise and go now, and go to Innisfree,
And a small cabin build there, of clay and wattles° made: rods
Nine bean-rows will I have there, a hive for the honeybee,
And live alone in the bee-loud glade.

And I shall have some peace there, for peace comes dropping
    slow,   5
Dropping from the veils of the morning to where the cricket
    sings;
There midnight's all a glimmer, and noon a purple glow,
And evening full of the linnet's wings.

I will arise and go now, for always night and day
I hear lake water lapping with low sounds by the shore;   10
While I stand on the roadway, or on the pavements grey,
I hear it in the deep heart's core.

WILLIAM BUTLER YEATS

THE ANGLO-SAXON PERIOD

Great literature, like all great art, so satisfies the human imagination, emotions, and intellect, that it has permanent value for people. For over fifteen hundred years, some of this great literature has come from the small island of England. Why, you might ask, did so much of it originate here? Why has it been read throughout the world, providing cultural inspiration everywhere? As scholars searched for answers to these questions, they discovered a wealth of literary works, as well as the origins of many customs, traditions, laws, and religious beliefs. More important still, they were able to understand the development of the English language and to appreciate its variety and potential beauty.

England's geographical location has played an important part in the development of both its language and its literature. An Englishman's feeling that he is "twice blessed" is voiced by John of Gaunt in Shakespeare's *Richard II:*

This royal throne of kings, this scept'red isle,
This earth of majesty, this seat of Mars,
This other Eden, demiparadise,
This fortress built by nature for herself
Against infection and the hand of war,
This happy breed of men, this little world,
This precious stone set in the silver sea,

Which serves it in the office of a wall
Or as a moat defensive to a house
Against the envy of less happier lands;
This blessed plot, this earth, this realm, this England. . . .

It is not surprising that less fortunate people across the
English Channel shared these feelings, and that the early
history of England is one of invasions and conquest. The island's first inhabitants were probably Celtic tribes, believed
to have come originally from Central Asia. In 55 B. C., under
Julius Caesar, the Romans unsuccessfully attempted an invasion of the island. About one hundred years later, under
the Emperor Claudius, forty thousand Roman troops made a
successful landing; and for the next four hundred years England was a Roman province. The Romans, as "benevolent
protectors," established a way of life similar to that of Rome.
But, after four centuries, Rome herself grew weak, and recalled her legions, needing them at home. The Celts, grown
peaceful and dependent on Rome for military protection, were
left vulnerable to attacks from the fierce Nordic tribes, the
Angles, Saxons, and Jutes of the Danish peninsula. Soon after
the Romans withdrew, these tribes conquered significant
portions of the island.

The Angles and the Saxons contributed most to its language
and literature. From the Angles—the most numerous tribe—
the country became known as Angle-land, or England, and
from the Angles and the Saxons the language took its name,
Anglo-Saxon. These Anglo-Saxon people were brave, reckless,
adventurous, and barbaric. They brought with them a rich
folk heritage, most of it celebrating the great deeds of heroes,
real and mythical. When they returned from a battle or an
adventure, they spent the night feasting, drinking mead, and
listening to the tales recited and sung by the scops and minstrels, called gleemen. These recitations and songs are the
beginnings of English literature. Eventually they were written down, but for approximately three hundred years they
were passed on by word of mouth.

The invasion which was perhaps the most significant occurred in the year 595 when Pope Gregory I sent St. Augustine from Rome to Christianize England as St. Patrick had earlier Christianized Ireland. St. Augustine and his missionaries made many converts, and before long, monasteries were established as centers of learning. Gradually, the oral language became a written language; clerics collected and recorded the old epics and lyrics, and a written literature began to evolve.

The written literature followed the pattern established by the scop in his chants and recitations. Frequently the subject of the tale or song was North European rather than English. For example, *Beowulf*, the most famous of the extant early tales, has as its setting the seacoast of Denmark and Sweden during the sixth century. Occasionally, however, the scop might give his tale an English setting if it served just as well. He could also add pious Christian sentiments to his story, so as not to offend the devout or fainthearted.

In addition to narrative poetry such as *Beowulf*, some beautiful lyric verses have survived for which we are also indebted to the scops. "The Wanderer" is the mournful reminiscence of an exile who longs for the once happy days under his now-dead lord. "The Seafarer" presents two contrasting points of view on the perils and adventures of the sea. These poems show the Anglo-Saxons' fascination with the sea, their strong feelings for nature, and their loyalty and devotion to lord or leader.

Anglo-Saxon poetry reflects the values and attitudes of those who began the English tradition of literature. Bravery and a willingness to undergo great hardship for its own sake or for the good of others are always typical of the Anglo-Saxon hero. The events of their tales dramatically illustrate their love of adventure, their serious and somewhat melancholy disposition, and their fear of Fate or Wyrd, their life-guiding principle.

Particular poetic devices are also a part of this poetry. In the original versions of poems such as *Beowulf*, for example, each line is divided into two parts, each having two accents, suggesting the points at which the singer or teller might have struck a note on his musical instrument as he performed in the mead hall.

ᚦa of wealle geseah   weard Scildinga,
se ᚦe holmclifu   healdan scolde,
beran ofer bolcan   beorhte randas. . . .

(Then from the wall saw the guard of the Scyldings,
he who had to keep the sea-cliffs, [men] bearing over
the gangplank bright shields. . . .)

The Anglo-Saxon fascination with alliteration is seen, even
in translation, in the repetition of initial consonant sounds.
There is also an obvious delight in the use of figurative language and effective word combinations, especially in descriptive poetical names, called *kennings*, such as "wave-walker"
for "ship," "swan-road" for "sea," and "his word-hoard
unlocked" for "began to speak."

from Beowulf

The Building of Heorot

To Hrothgar was given such glory of war,
such honor of combat, that all his kin
obeyed him gladly till great grew his band
of youthful comrades. It came in his mind
to bid his henchmen a hall uprear,   5
a master mead-house,° mightier far   *drinking-hall*
than ever was seen by the sons of earth,
and within it, then, to old and young
he would all allot that the Lord had sent him,
save only the land and the lives of his men.   10
Wide, I heard, was the work commanded,
for many a tribe this mid-earth round,
to fashion the folkstead. It fell, as he ordered,
in rapid achievement that ready it stood there,
of halls the noblest: Heorot[1] he named it   15
whose message had might in many a land.
Not reckless of promise, the rings he dealt,
treasure at banquet: there towered the hall,
high, gabled wide, the hot surge waiting
of furious flame.[2] Not far was that day   20
when father and son-in-law stood in feud
for warfare and hatred that woke again.
   With envy and anger an evil spirit[3]
endured the dole° in his dark abode,   *gift-giving*
that he heard each day the din of revel   25
high in the hall: there harps rang out,
clear song of the singer. He sang who knew
tales of the early time of man,

[1]*Heorot:* Hart Hall, so called because of the stags' antlers fixed above the gables of the building
[2]*furious flame:* the fire burning at one end of the hall
[3]*evil spirit:* the monster Grendel

15

how the Almighty made the earth,
fairest fields enfolded by water,   30
set, triumphant, sun and moon
for a light to lighten the land-dwellers,
and braided bright the breast of earth
with limbs and leaves, made life for all
of mortal beings that breathe and move.   35
   So lived the clansmen in cheer and revel
a winsome life, till one began
to fashion evils, that fiend of hell.
Grendel this monster grim was called,   39
march-riever° mighty, in moorland living,   border-raider
in fen and fastness, fief° of the giants   hereditary domain
the hapless wight° a while had kept   fellow
since the Creator his exile doomed.
On kin of Cain was the killing avenged
by sovran God for slaughtered Abel.   45
Ill fared his[4] feud, and far was he driven,
for the slaughter's sake, from sight of men.
Of Cain awoke all that woeful breed,
Etins° and elves and evil-spirits,   giants
as well as the giants that warred with God   50
weary while: but their wage was paid them!
Went he[5] forth to find at fall of night
that haughty house, and heed° wherever   note
the Ring-Danes, outrevelled, to rest had gone.
Found within it the atheling° band   noble
asleep after feasting and fearless of sorrow,   56
of human hardship. Unhallowed wight,
grim and greedy, he grasped betimes,°   at once
wrathful, reckless, from resting-places,
thirty of the thanes,° and thence he rushed   clansmen 60
fain° of his fell° spoil, faring homeward,   glad; deadly
laden with slaughter, his lair to seek.

    [4]*his:* Cain's
    [5]*he:* Grendel

Then at the dawning, as day was breaking,
the might of Grendel to men was known;   64
then after wassail° was wail uplifted,   merry-making
loud moan in the morn. The mighty chief,
atheling° excellent, unblithe° sat,   nobleman; unhappy
labored in woe for the loss of his thanes,
when once had been traced the trail of the fiend,
spirit accurst: too cruel that sorrow,   70
too long, too loathsome. Not late° the respite;   long
with night returning, anew began
ruthless murder; he recked no whit,°   cared not at all
firm in his guilt, of the feud and crime.
They were easy to find who elsewhere sought   75
in room remote their rest at night,
bed in the bowers, when that bale° was shown,   evil
was seen in sooth,° with surest token,—   truth
the hall-thane's[6] hate. Such held themselves
far and fast who the fiend outran!   80
Thus ruled unrighteous and raged his fill
one against all; until empty stood
that lordly building, and long it bode so.

The Coming of Beowulf

Finally, word of Grendel's deeds reaches the far country of the
Geats. Beowulf, with the keenest of warriors, goes to Hrothgar's
aid.

This heard in his home Hygelac's thane,[7]
great among Geats, of Grendel's doings.
He was the mightiest man of valor
in that same day of this our life,
stalwart and stately. A stout wave-walker°   ship 5

---

[6]*the hall-thane's:* Grendel's
[7]*Hygelac's thane:* Beowulf, the chief thane of Hygelac, king of the Geats,
who dwelt in southern Sweden

he bade make ready. Yon battle-king, said he,
far o'er the swan-road° he fain would seek,   sea
the noble monarch who needed men!
The prince's journey by prudent folk
was little blamed, though they loved him dear;   10
they whetted° the hero, and hailed good omens.   stimulated
And now the bold one from bands of Geats
comrades chose, the keenest of warriors
e'er he could find; with fourteen men
the sea-wood° he sought, and, sailor proved,   ship 15
led them on to the land's confines.
 Time had now flown; afloat was the ship,
boat under bluff. On board they climbed,
warriors ready; waves were churning
sea with sand; the sailors bore   20
on the breast of the bark their bright array,
their mail° and weapons: the men pushed off,   armor
on its willing way, the well-braced craft.
Then moved o'er the waters by might of the wind
the bark like a bird with breast of foam,   25
till in season due, on the second day,
the curvèd prow such course had run
that sailors now could see the land,
sea-cliffs shining, steep high hills,
headlands broad. Their haven was found,   30
their journey ended. Up then quickly
the Weders'[8] clansmen climbed ashore,
anchored their sea-wood, with armor clashing
and gear of battle: God they thanked
for passing in peace o'er the paths of the sea.   35
 Now saw from the cliff a Scylding[9] clansman,
a warden° that watched the water-side,   sentinel
how they bore o'er the gangway glittering shields,
war-gear in readiness; wonder seized him
to know what manner of men they were.   40

 [8]*Welder:* Geats
 [9]*Scylding:* descendant of Scyld, founder of the Danish Royal House

Straight to the strand° his steed he rode,   beach
Hrothgar's henchman; with hand of might
he shook his spear, and spake in parley.°   conference
"Who are ye, then, ye armèd men,
mailèd° folk, that yon mighty vessel   armor-clad 45
have urged thus over the ocean ways,
here o'er the waters? A warden I,
sentinel set o'er the sea-march here,
lest any foe to the folk of Danes
with harrying° fleet should harm the land.   raiding 50
No aliens ever at ease thus bore them,
linden-wielders:° yet word-of-leave   spearmen
clearly ye lack from clansmen here,
my folk's agreement. — A greater ne'er saw I
of warriors in world than is one of you, —   55
yon hero in harness! No henchman he
worthied by weapons, if witness his features,
his peerless presence! I pray you, though, tell
your folk and home, lest hence ye fare
suspect to wander your way as spies   60
in Danish land. Now, dwellers afar,
ocean-travellers, take from me
simple advice: the sooner the better
I hear of the country whence ye came."
To him the stateliest[10] spake in answer;   65
the warriors' leader his word-hoard unlocked: —
"We are by kin of the clan of Geats,
and Hygelac's own hearth-fellows we.
To folk afar was my father known,
noble atheling, Ecgtheow named.   70
Full of winters, he fared away
agèd from earth; he is honored still
through width of the world by wise men all.
To thy lord and liege in loyal mood
we hasten hither, to Healfdene's son,   75
people-protector: be pleased to advise us!

[10]*the stateliest:* Beowulf

To that mighty-one come we on mickle° errand,   *mighty*
to the lord of the Danes; nor deem I right
that aught be hidden. We hear—thou knowest
if sooth it is—the saying of men,   80
that amid the Scyldings a scathing monster,
dark ill-doer, in dusky nights
shows terrific rage unmatched,
hatred and murder. To Hrothgar I
in greatness of soul would succor° bring."   *aid* 85

BEOWULF'S REPLY TO UNFERTH

    Beowulf and his men are most heartily welcomed by Hrothgar, who greets Beowulf as the son of an old and dear friend and also as a possible deliverer of Heorot. In the course of the celebrations, a jealous thane, Unferth, accuses Beowulf of showing foolhardiness in a youthful seven-day contest with his friend Breca. He also foretells defeat for Beowulf at the hands of Grendel: "So ween I for thee a worse adventure . . . if Grendel's approach thou dar'st await through the watch of the night!" Undaunted, Beowulf not only refutes Unferth's accusations but also exposes his former friend's true character.

    Beowulf spake, bairn° of Ecgtheow:—   *son*
"What a deal hast uttered, dear my Unferth,[11]
drunken with beer, of Breca now,
told of his triumph! Truth I claim it,
that I had more of might in the sea   5
than any man else, more ocean-endurance.
We twain° had talked, in time of youth,   *two*
and made our boast,—we were merely boys,
striplings still,—to stake our lives
far at sea: and so we performed it.   10
Naked swords, as we swam along,
we held in hand, with hope to guard us

[11]*Unferth:* prominent orator at the Danish court

against the whales. Not a whit from me
could he float afar o'er the flood of waves,
haste o'er the billows; nor him I abandoned.   15
Together we twain on the tides abode
five nights full till the flood divided us,
churning waves and chillest weather,
darkling night, and the northern wind
ruthless rushed on us: rough was the surge.   20
Now the wrath of the sea-fish rose apace;
yet me 'gainst the monsters my mailèd coat,
hard and hand-linked, help afforded,—
battle-sark° braided my breast to ward,   armor
garnished with gold. There grasped me firm   25
and haled me to bottom the hated foe,
with grimmest gripe.° 'Twas granted me, though,   grip
to pierce the monster with point of sword,
with blade of battle: huge beast of the sea
was whelmed by the hurly° through hand of mine.   confusion
   "Me thus often the evil monsters   31
thronging threatened. With thrust of my sword,
the darling, I dealt them due return!
Nowise had they bliss from their booty then
to devour their victim, vengeful creatures,   35
seated to banquet at bottom of sea;
but at break of day, by my brand sore hurt,
on the edge of ocean up they lay,
put to sleep by the sword. And since, by them
on the fathomless sea-ways sailor-folk   40
are never molested.—Light from east,
came bright God's beacon; the billows sank,
so that I saw the sea-cliffs high,
windy walls. For Wyrd° oft saveth   Fate
earl undoomed if he doughty° be!   valiant 45
And so it came that I killed with my sword
nine of the nicors.° Of night-fought battles   sea monsters
ne'er heard I a harder 'neath heaven's dome,
nor adrift on the deep a more desolate man!

Yet I came unharmed from that hostile clutch,   50
though spent with swimming. The sea upbore me,
flood of the tide, on Finnish land,
the welling waters. Nowise of thee
have I heard men tell such terror of falchions,°   short swords
bitter battle, Breca ne'er yet,   55
not one of you pair, in the play of war
such daring deed has done at all
with bloody brand,—I boast not of it!—
though thou wast the bane° of thy brethren dear,   murderer
thy closest kin, whence curse of hell   60
awaits thee, well as thy wit may serve!"

The Battle With Grendel

    When the welcoming celebrations are over, Hrothgar and his
thanes retire from the hall. Beowulf and his warriors remain to
await the arrival of the monster Grendel.

Then from the moorland, by misty crags,
with God's wrath laden, Grendel came.
The monster was minded of mankind now
sundry° to seize in the stately house.   various
Under welkin° he walked, till the wine-palace there,   sky 5
gold-hall of men, he gladly discerned,
flashing with fretwork.° Not first time, this,   decorative carving
that he the home of Hrothgar sought,—
yet ne'er in his life-day, late or early,
such hardy heroes, such hall-thanes, found!   10
To the house the warrior walked apace,
parted from peace;° the portal opened,   doomed to hell
though with forged bolts fast, when his fists had struck it,
and baleful° he burst in his blatant° rage,   with evil intent;
                                                    clamorous
the house's mouth. All hastily, then,   15
o'er fair-paved floor the fiend trod on,
ireful he strode; there streamed from his eyes

fearful flashes, like flame to see.
He spied in hall the hero-band,
kin and clansmen clustered asleep,   20
hardy liegemen. Then laughed his heart;
for the monster was minded, ere morn should dawn,
savage, to sever the soul of each,
life from body, since lusty banquet
waited his will! But Wyrd forbade him   25
to seize any more of men on earth
after that evening. Eagerly watched
Hygelac's kinsman[12] his cursèd foe,
how he would fare in fell attack.
Not that the monster was minded to pause!   30
Straightway he seized a sleeping warrior
for the first, and tore him fiercely asunder,
the bone-frame bit, drank blood in streams,
swallowed him piecemeal: swiftly thus
the lifeless corse° was clear devoured,   corpse   35
e'en feet and hands. Then farther he hied;°   sped
for the hardy hero with hand he grasped,
felt for the foe with fiendish claw,
for the hero reclining,—who clutched it boldly,
prompt to answer, propped on his arm.   40
Soon then saw that shepherd-of-evils
that never he met in this middle-world,
in the ways of earth, another wight
with heavier hand-gripe; at heart he feared,
sorrowed in soul,—none the sooner escaped!   45
Fain would he flee, his fastness seek,
the den of devils: no doings now
such as oft he had done in days of old!
Then bethought him the hardy Hygelac-thane
of his boast at evening: up he bounded,   50
grasped firm his foe, whose fingers cracked.
The fiend made off, but the earl close followed.

[12]*Hygelac's kinsman:* Beowulf

The monster meant—if he might at all—
to fling himself free, and far away
fly to the fens,—knew his fingers' power   55
in the gripe of the grim one. Gruesome march
to Heorot this monster of harm had made!
Din filled the room; the Danes were bereft,°   deprived
castle-dwellers and clansmen all,
earls, of their ale. Angry were both   60
those savage hall-guards: the house resounded.
Wonder it was the wine-hall firm
in the strain of their struggle stood, to earth
the fair house fell not; too fast it was
within and without by its iron bands   65
craftily clamped; though there crashed from sill
many a mead-bench—men have told me—
gay with gold, where the grim foes wrestled.
So well had weened° the wisest Scyldings   planned
that not ever at all might any man   70
that bone-decked, brave house break asunder,
crush by craft,—unless clasp of fire
in smoke engulfed it.—Again uprose
din redoubled. Danes of the North
with fear and frenzy were filled, each one,   75
who from the wall that wailing heard,
God's foe sounding his grisly song,
cry of the conquered, clamorous pain
from captive of hell. Too closely held him
he who of men in might was strongest   80
in that same day of this our life.
Not in any wise would the earls'-defence[13]
suffer° that slaughterous stranger to live,   allow
useless deeming° his days and years   judging
to men on earth. Now many an earl   85
of Beowulf brandished blade ancestral,
fain the life of their lord to shield,

---

[13]*earls'-defence:* Beowulf

their praisèd prince, if power were theirs;
never they knew,—as they neared the foe,   90
hardy-hearted heroes of war,
aiming their swords on every side
the accursed to kill,—no keenest blade,
no fairest of falchions fashioned on earth,
could harm or hurt that hideous fiend!   95
He was safe, by his spells, from sword of battle,
from edge of iron. Yet his end and parting
on that same day of this our life
woeful should be, and his wandering soul
far off flit to the fiends' domain.   100
Soon he found, who in former days,
harmful in heart and hated of God,
on many a man such murder wrought,
that the frame of his body failed him now.
For him the keen-souled kinsman of Hygelac   105
held in hand; hateful alive
was each to other. The outlaw dire
took mortal hurt; a mighty wound
showed on his shoulder, and sinews cracked,
and the bone-frame burst. To Beowulf now   110
the glory was given, and Grendel thence
death-sick his den in the dark moor sought,
noisome° abode; he knew too well   foul-smelling
that here was the last of life, an end
of his days on earth.—To all the Danes   115
by that bloody battle the boon had come.
From ravage had rescued the roving stranger
Hrothgar's hall; the hardy and wise one
had purged it anew. His night-work pleased him,
his deed and its honor. To Eastern Danes   120
had the valiant Geat his vaunt° made good,   boast
all their sorrow and ills assuaged,
their bale of battle borne so long,
and all the dole they erst endured,
pain a-plenty.—'Twas proof of this,

when the hardy-in-fight a hand laid down,   125
arm and shoulder,—all, indeed,
of Grendel's gripe,—'neath the gabled roof.

BEOWULF'S FUNERAL

Beowulf's victory over Grendel and the freeing of the hall are
again followed by a great celebration, and to show his gratitude
Hrothgar bestows many gifts upon Beowulf. Their joy is short-
lived, however, for Grendel's mother, seeking revenge, attacks the
hall and carries off to her lair one of Hrothgar's thanes. Beowulf
tracks her to her cave beneath the water and, in a bloody battle,
slays her. He returns to Heorot for more celebrations and gift-
giving, and then departs with his men for his homeland, where he
rules for "fifty" years. Finally, to rid his land of a great dragon,
Beowulf challenges it to battle. With the help of a young thane he
slays the dragon, but in doing so he receives a mortal wound.

Then fashioned for him the folk of Geats
firm on the earth a funeral-pile,
and hung it with helmets and harness of war
and breastplates bright, as the boon he asked;
and they laid amid it the mighty chieftain,   5
heroes mourning their master dear.
Then on the hill that hugest of balefires
the warriors wakened. Wood-smoke rose
black over blaze, and blent° was the roar,   blended
of flame with weeping (the wind was still),   10
till the fire had broken the frame of bones,
hot at the heart. In heavy mood
their misery moaned they, their master's death.
Wailing her woe, the widow[14] old,
her hair upbound, for Beowulf's death   15
sung in her sorrow, and said full oft

[14]*widow:* Beowulf's wife

she dreaded the doleful days to come,
deaths enow, and doom of battle,
and shame. — The smoke by the sky was devoured.

   The folk of the Weders fashioned there   20
on the headland a barrow° broad and high,   grave-mound
by ocean-farers far descried:°   detected
in ten days' time their toil had raised it,
the battle-brave's beacon. Round brands of the pyre
a wall they built, the worthiest ever   25
that wit could prompt in their wisest men.
They placed in the barrow that precious booty,
the rounds and the rings they had reft° erewhile,   seized
hardy heroes, from hoard in cave,[15] —
trusting the ground with treasure of earls,   30
gold in the earth, wherever it lies
useless to men as of yore it was.

   Then about that barrow the battle-keen rode,
atheling-born, a band of twelve,
lament to make, to mourn their king,   35
chant their dirge, and their chieftain honor.
They praised his earlship, his acts of prowess
worthily witnessed: and well it is
that men their master-friend mightily laud,
heartily love, when hence he goes   40
from life in the body forlorn away.

   Thus made their mourning the men of Geatland,
for their hero's passing his hearth-companions:
quoth that of all the kings of earth,
of men he was mildest and belovèd,   45
to his kin the kindest, keenest for praise.

[15]*hoard in cave:* treasures buried in olden days which the dragon had guarded for three hundred winters. When a peasant stole one of the cups, the dragon, in revenge, burned Beowulf's hall. This was the dragon which Beowulf fought and slew before he died.

1. From your own reaction to these selected episodes from *Beowulf*, tell why you think this early narrative poem was kept alive so many centuries before it was written down, and why it continues to give pleasure in a printed translation. Why does each episode hold your interest? Are the characters well-portrayed and convincing? Are you able to picture the setting of each important event? Does the setting add to the mood of the event and to the pleasure of reading about it? Support your answers to these questions with specific references to the episodes included here.

2. Why does Grendel begin his attacks on Heorot? How is his attack related to the cause of his exile and the building of Heorot? What has led Hrothgar to build this hall? From the details in lines 1-38, what impression do you gain of Hrothgar, the relationship between him and his thanes, and the "winsome life" at Heorot?

3. To what "woeful breed" does Grendel belong? Why is his first attack on "the haughty house" so successful? How do Hrothgar and his men react? What efforts do they make to oppose Grendel? In what mood does the first episode end?

4. In the first thirty lines of "The Coming of Beowulf," what evidence are you given that Beowulf is the one person who might rid Danish land of the monster? Do not overlook the reaction of the Geats and the way Beowulf prepares for the journey.

5. Why does the Danish sentinel challenge the arrival of Beowulf and his warriors? When Beowulf "his word-hoard" unlocks, does he merely recount what the reader or hearer already knows or does he supply new information? Explain.

6. What is the purpose of the third episode? In his defense against Unferth's unjust accusations, what explanation does Beowulf give of the seven-day contest? Despite his statement, "I boast not of it," what impression does he convey?

7. How do you interpret lines 44 and 45? At the close of Beowulf's speech (lines 56-61), of what does he accuse Unferth? Is the phrase "dear my Unferth" (line 2) meant to be satirical, or is Beowulf trying to smooth over an awkward situation? Explain.

8. Why is Grendel so confident that a "lusty banquet" awaits him at Heorot and that he will succeed as before in his attack? In what lines is his failure foreshadowed (see page 23)? From the description of his behavior and of his entrance into the hall, what mental picture do you have of him?

9. Why does Beowulf watch Grendel, even while he murders one one of the sleeping warriors? Describe the tactics Beowulf then uses in order to overpower Grendel, and the struggle that follows. What reason can you see for the rather lengthy description of the indestructibility of Heorot? What details suggest what happens as "the grim foes wrestled"? How does Grendel react?

10. Why are Beowulf's earls powerless to help him? If Grendel is safe from the "keenest blade," how do you explain lines 106-109? What is the purpose of lines 96-103?

11. In what lines in this episode does the sequence of events reach a climax? Point out the various ways in which suspense is created. Were you ever in doubt that Beowulf would be the victor? What held your interest until the bloody battle was over?

12. Why is Grendel allowed to return alive to his den? What visible proof does Beowulf have that he has made good his boast? Tell why the ending of this episode is such a dramatic one.

13. Before his death, what "boon" does Beowulf ask of his countrymen? What gives the cremation scene such dramatic intensity? Point out specific words, phrases, and details. What is the significance of the statement in line 19?

14. Describe the two ways in which Beowulf's people pay honor to their king. What qualities do they admire? Why is it well that men praise "their master-friend"? How do you interpret the last phrase, "keenest for praise"?

15. As with most folk literature, the listeners were probably well acquainted with the events recounted. In what do you think they found most enjoyment—the scenes pictured, the heroism of the main characters, the drama of the battles and the breathtaking adventures, the language in which all were expressed? Cite examples from the preceding episodes to support your opinion.

16. Only the great poets of England or of any country have created works equal to many passages in this narrative. Select several passages which seem especially beautiful in imagery and sound. Point out the poetic devices—figurative language, kennings, alliteration, rhythm—which contribute to their effectiveness.

The Seafarer

This poem appears to be about two different people, yet the speaker in each part is the same person, expressing his thoughts and feelings at a different period in his life.

THE OLD SAILOR

True is the tale that I tell of my travels,
Sing of my seafaring sorrows and woes;
Hunger and hardship's heaviest burdens,
Tempest and terrible toil of the deep,   5
Daily I've borne on the deck of my boat
Fearful the welter° of waves that encompassed me,   tumbling
Watching at night on the narrow bow,
As she drove by the rocks, and drenched me with spray.
Fast to the deck my feet were frozen,   10
Gripped by the cold, while care's hot surges
My heart o'erwhelmed, and hunger's pangs
Sapped the strength of my sea-weary spirit.
Little he knows whose lot is happy,
Who lives at ease in the lap of the earth,   15
How, sick at heart, o'er icy seas,
Wretched I ranged the winter through,
Bare of joys, and banished from friends,
Hung with icicles, stung by hailstones.
Nought I heard but the hollow boom   20
Of wintry waves, or the wild swan's whoop.
For singing I had the solan's° scream;   sea gull's
For peals of laughter, the yelp of the seal;
The sea-mew's cry, for the mirth of the mead° hall.   drinking
Shrill through the roar of the shrieking gale   25
Lashing along the sea-cliff's edge,
Pierces the ice-plumed petrel's° defiance,   sea bird's
And the wet-winged eagle's answering scream.
Little he dreams that drinks life's pleasure,

By danger untouched in the shelter of towns,
Insolent and wine-proud, how utterly weary   30
Oft I wintered on open seas.
Night fell black, from the north it snowed
Harvest of hail.

THE YOUTH

                    Oh, wildly my heart
Beats in my bosom and bids me to try   35
The tumble and surge of seas tumultuous,
Breeze and brine and the breakers' roar.
Daily, hourly, drives me my spirit
Outward to sail, far countries to see.
Liveth no man so large in his soul,   40
So gracious in giving, so gay in his youth,
In deeds so daring, so dear to his lord,
But frets his soul for his sea adventure,
Fain° to try what fortune shall send.   eager
Harping he needs not, nor hoarding of treasure;   45
Nor woman can win him, nor joys of the world.
Nothing does please but the plunging billows;
Ever he longs, who is lured by the sea.
Woods are abloom, the wide world awakens.
Gay are the mansions, the meadows most fair;   50
These are but warnings, that haste on his journey
Him whose heart is hungry to taste
The perils and pleasures of the (pathless deep.)

              THE OLD SAILOR

Dost mind the cuckoo mournfully calling?
The summer's watchman sorrow forebodes.   55
What does the landsman that wantons° in luxury,   indulges
What does he reck° the rough sea's foe,   know of
The cares of the exile, whose keel has explored
The uttermost parts of the ocean ways!

THE YOUTH   *Land*

Sudden my soul starts from her prison house,   60
Soareth afar o'er the sounding main;
Hovers on high, o'er the home of the whale;
Back to me darts the bird sprite and beckons,
Winging her way o'er woodland and plain,
Hungry to roam, and bring me where glisten   65
Glorious tracts of glimmering foam.
This life on land is lingering death to me,
Give me the gladness of God's great sea.

1. What mood is expressed in lines 1-4 and, primarily, by what words? The Old Sailor recalls his seafaring years as ones of sorrow and woe. What picture do you gain of the boat, and of the kind of life endured by the seafarers?

2. Point out the various ways in which the Old Sailor contrasts his past life with the life of the land-dwellers. Why do you think he makes so much of what he missed and endured? Discuss.

3. Describe the change in mood beginning with line 34. What details in this part illustrate the Youth's eagerness? When a man is "lured by the sea," how is his life affected? How do you interpret line 51? What do you learn from this part about the relationship between the common man and "his lord"?

4. How do you interpret the Old Sailor's warning in lines 54-59? What purpose do you think he has in giving it?

5. The Youth's attitude toward "life on land" could hardy be more different from that of the Old Sailor. Do you think that this difference is one of age or of experience? Give reasons for whatever conclusion you think is justified by the poem itself.

6. What characteristics of Anglo-Saxon poetry are evident in this poem—even in the modern translation? (See the comments on page 13.) Point out lines, phrases, and words which you consider good examples of each of these characteristics.

7. This poem is unusually lyrical in sound and in feeling. As you read aloud lines 34 through 53, try to convey the emotion felt by the speaker in the poem. Also try to convey the "singing quality" created by the rhythm of the lines and by the sounds of the words within the lines.

The Wanderer

Oft to the Wanderer, weary of exile,
Cometh God's pity, compassionate love,
Though woefully toiling on wintry seas
With churning oar in the icy wave,
Homeless and helpless he fled from Fate.   5
Thus saith the Wanderer mindful of misery,
Grievous diasters, and death of kin:
"Oft when the day broke, oft at the dawning,
Lonely and wretched I wailed my woe.
No man is living, no comrade left,   10
To whom I dare fully unlock my heart.
I have learned truly the mark of a man
Is keeping his counsel and locking his lips,
Let him think what he will! For, woe of heart
Withstandeth not Fate; a failing spirit   15
Earneth no help. Men eager for honor
Bury their sorrow deep in the breast.
So have I also, often, in wretchedness
Fettered my feelings, far from my kin,
Homeless and hapless, since days of old,   20
When the dark earth covered my dear lord's face,
And I sailed away with sorrowful heart,
Over wintry seas, seeking a gold-lord,
If far or near lived one to befriend me
With gift in the mead-hall and comfort for grief.   25
Who bears it, knows what a bitter companion,
Shoulder to shoulder, sorrow can be,
When friends are no more. His fortune is exile,
Not gifts of fine gold; a heart that is frozen,
Earth's winsomeness° dead. And he dreams   attractiveness
   of the hallmen,   30
The dealing of treasure, the days of his youth,
When his lord bade welcome to wassail° and feast.   drink

But gone is that gladness, and never again
Shall come the loved counsel of comrade and king.
Even in slumber his sorrow assaileth,   35
And, dreaming, he claspeth his dear lord again,
Head on knee, hand on knee, loyally laying,
Pledging his liege as in days long past.
Then from his slumber he starts lonely-hearted,
Beholding gray stretches of tossing sea,   40
Sea-birds bathing, with wings outspread,
While hail-storms darken, and driving snow.
Bitterer then is the bane° of his wretchedness,   ruin
The longing for loved one: his grief is renewed.
The forms of his kinsmen take shape in the silence;   45
In rapture he greets them; in gladness he scans
Old comrades remembered. But they melt into air
With no word of greeting to gladden his heart.
Then again surges his sorrow upon him;
And grimly he spurs on his weary soul   50
Once more to the toil of the tossing sea.
No wonder therefore, in all the world,
If a shadow darkens upon my spirit
When I reflect on the fates of men —
How one by one proud warriors vanish   55
From the halls that knew them, and day by day
All this earth ages and droops unto death.
No man may know wisdom till many a winter
Has been his portion. A wise man is patient,
Not swift to anger, nor hasty of speech,   60
Neither too weak, nor too reckless, in war,
Neither fearful nor fain,° nor too wishful of wealth,   eager
Nor too eager in vow — ere he know the event.
A brave man must bide when he speaketh his boast
Until he know surely the goal of his spirit.   65
A wise man will ponder how dread is that doom
When all this world's wealth shall be scattered and waste —
As now, over all, through the regions of earth,

Walls stand rime-covered° and swept by the winds.   frost-
The battlements crumble, the wine-halls decay;   covered
Joyless and silent the heroes are sleeping   71
Where the proud host fell by the wall they defended.
Some battle launched on their long, last journey;
One a bird bore o'er the billowing sea;
One the gray wolf slew; one a grieving earl   75
Sadly gave to the grave's embrace.
The Warden of men[1] hath wasted this world
Till the sound of music and revel is stilled,
And these giant-built structures stand empty of life.
He who shall muse on these mouldering ruins,   80
And deeply ponder this darkling life,
Must brood on old legends of battle and bloodshed,
And heavy the mood that troubles his heart:
'Where now is the warrior? Where is the warhorse?
Bestowal of treasure, and sharing of feast?   85
Alas! the bright ale-cup, the byrny-clad° warrior,   armor-clad
The prince in his splendor—those days are long sped
In the night of the past, as if they never had been!'
And now remains only, for warriors' memorial,
A wall wondrous high with serpent shapes carved.   90
Storms of ash-spears have smitten the earls,
Carnage of weapon, and conquering Fate.
Storms now batter these ramparts of stone;
Blowing snow and the blast of winter
Enfold the earth; night-shadows fall   95
Darkly lowering, from the north driving
Raging hail in wrath upon men.
Wretchedness fills the realm of earth,
And Fate's decrees transform the world.
Here wealth is fleeting, friends are fleeting,   100
Man is fleeting, maid is fleeting;
All the foundation of earth shall fail!"
Thus spake the sage in solitude pondering.

   [1]*The Warden of men:* God

Good man is he who guardeth his faith.
He must never too quickly unburden his breast   105
Of its sorrow, but eagerly strive for redress;
And happy the man who seeketh for mercy
From his heavenly Father, our fortress and strength.

1. This poem is considered by some critics one of the loveliest, ancient or modern. Why is the Wanderer deserving of "God's pity, compassionate love"? Why must he keep his counsel, "locking his lips"? With whom does he compare himself? In what ways is his fate and behavior similar to that person's?
2. Why did the Wanderer sail away? Why is his only companion a bitter one? What does he mean by "Earth's winsomeness [is] dead"?
3. When he awakes from his slumber, why is he lonely-hearted? What guidance is given? Why does his sorrow "surge upon him"?
4. As he reflects on the fates of men, he discovers some of the great truths about life which are limited to no time or place. What are these? In what ways are they as meaningful today as when he spoke them centuries ago?
5. What does the Wanderer mean by line 77? How does he justify his accusations? What deep feelings are conveyed in the questions he asks and the answers he gives (lines 84-102)?
6. When the scop or minstrel has finished his heart-stirring song of the Wanderer, he (or the recorder of that song) adds a few comments of his own. In your opinion, are they in keeping with the rest of the poem? Support your answer by referring to specific lines, to the over-all tone of the poem, and to the mood created by the Wanderer's tale.
7. Both scholarship and artistry were required to retain, in this modern English version of the poem, the characteristics of the Anglo-Saxon original. Discuss these characteristics, pointing out lines, phrases, and words which you consider unusually effective examples. Comment on the rhythm of the lines and on the many variations which make this poem different from those written in the last hundred years.

THE MEDIEVAL PERIOD

Five hundred years after the Anglo-Saxon invasion, England was again overrun by warriors and seafarers from the northern coast of Europe. By 870 the new invaders, called Danes, laid claim to practically all of England except the southern kingdom of Wessex, which King Alfred the Great stoutly defended. Before his death, Alfred succeeded in bringing part of the Danish lands under English rule, and his descendants completed the task. Unfortunately this rule was sufficiently weak to permit easy conquest, and the Danes were quick to see it. In 991 they began a series of invasions so formidable that by 1017 all of England was under Danish control and a Danish king sat on the English throne. Twenty-five years passed before English rule was restored.

The years between 1017 and 1066 were relatively peaceful and prosperous. Commerce with the Continent increased and towns grew in importance, but England continued to be an essentially agricultural nation. Its class structure was much as it had been in Anglo-Saxon times: a nobility, consisting of hereditary earls; landed proprietors, called thanes; serfs, originally free peasants but increasingly dependent upon large landowners; and bond-slaves, most of whom had no legal rights. In addition, each nobleman had a sworn band of re-

37

tainers who considered loyalty in battle the highest virtue. This structure paved the way for the feudal state that was, in large part, responsible for the transformation of England after the Norman Conquest.

The person responsible for this Conquest was William, Duke of Normandy, who crossed the English Channel in 1066 to enforce his claim to the throne of England. Normandy was a province in northwestern France and had acquired its name from the "North-men" who invaded France at the time the Danes invaded England. These "North-men" had readily adopted the language, feudal institutions, and Roman Catholic religion of France, but they had retained the fierce, driving energy and daring spirit of their Scandinavian ancestors. From this union of the Nordic and Latin came a new energetic civilization which was to make the Duchy of Normandy a powerful force in medieval Europe.

With well-disciplined forces and shrewd military tactics, William met the newly crowned King of England at the Battle of Hastings and defeated him. Within a few months, William had seized control of the southwestern half of England and had had forced the king's council to elect him William the Conqueror, King of England. Systematically he "took over" England as his own, suppressing any revolt against his authority and establishing a new language, a new culture, and a new ruling class.

William's power was based on feudalism, the social-political system currently prevalent in Europe and under which William himself held the Duchy of Normandy. Taking advantage of the feudal relation already existing in England, he confiscated all land as the property of the king. He then gave the use of it to those he could trust or to whom he was indebted, principally Normans. The chief tenants of the land were the barons, who were bound by oaths of fealty to provide the king with money and armed soldiers, and to attend his Great Council at stated times. Each baron distributed parts of his land to lesser nobility upon terms of service to himself and to the king. The serfs or villeins — about ninety per cent of the population — were little more than slaves. They worked the soil in exchange for produce and gifts and had no legal rights against the overlord. Such serfs as were allowed to become merchants were subject to a heavy tax and also to capture and punishment. English feudalism under William was a great pyramid structure: a Norman king and barons at the top and the English common people at the base. The power and strength of this feudalism rested on the sacred obligations of loyalty and homage, each man to his overlord and all men to the king himself.

The English people, like their Norman rulers, were Roman Catholics, and William readily accepted the position and spiritual authority of the English church. He was quick to see, however, that this church needed a strong and righteous hand. He therefore appointed as Archbishop of Canterbury a man well qualified to serve the Church Universal yet willing to make such changes as William considered essential. Under English feudalism, church land also belonged to the king, and those who administered it were responsible to him. Naturally, the king felt he had a right to dictate who held high church offices. The barons held a similar view of appointments to lesser ecclesiastical posts. Inevitably, many men serving the church — from lowly summoners to exalted bishops — were without true spiritual vocation, and sometimes without morals. Most of the changes urged by William strengthened the church and increased its influence, both culturally and spiritually. Monasteries were enriched as well as purified; cathedrals were erected that still are admired for their stonework and Romanesque style. A new emphasis was placed on the knowledge of Latin, later of French, and promising young men of English and Norman ancestry were sent to study in continental schools.

As William was forced to demonstrate his mastery of England, it was inevitable that more and more positions of power should be occupied by Normans and Frenchmen, who knew little if any English. Thus French became the language of the court, of society, and of official business and diplomacy. Moreover, French was becoming so popular throughout civilized Europe that its use was cultivated at courts outside France. Not until 1204, when Normandy was seized by France, did English kings and nobles look upon England as their first concern. After that, French continued in use, but English made steady enough advances to be widely used among the upper classes by 1300. The English spoken after 1300, however, was a different language from the English spoken before William's day. Almost half the words in the Englishman's vocabulary were of French origin.

The people of medieval England had little part in the written literature that flourished there during the fourteenth and fifteenth centuries. It was composed for the wealthier classes by priests and professional writers; it was read by that small section of the population who had learned to read and who had access to the few copies — hand-written or hand-printed — that were available. Yet the people were not without a literature of their own. It was an oral literature and, for the most part, grew up independently of either manuscript or printed book. Composed by unknown but gifted poets, storytellers, and minstrels, this literature was transmitted from generation to generation of unlettered common folk. How much of it was lost before or after it was copied down is not known. Nor is it known how closely the surviving lyrics and ballads resemble the original creations. Any composition that descends from age to age by word of mouth is constantly being modified and, in time, comes to represent the feeling and taste of the community that preserves it, not of the unknown poet who composed it.

Medieval lyrics and ballads had their origin in the vast store of popular song accumulated in England during the twelfth century. Much of this store was brought from France by courtly singers and wandering worldly clerics for the entertainment of the aristocracy. Some of it was the creation of English songsters who more or less imitated French and Latin models. There were carols and rounds that sprang from folk dances; there were songs of love, of work, and of nature. There were also songs of religious devotion, including the sacred lullaby.

The ballads of medieval England were most truly the literature of the people, for they belonged neither to the church nor to the court. Of these ballads, some three hundred have been preserved in various English and Scottish dialects, most of them written down as late as the seventeenth and eighteenth centuries. The impulse to create ballads seems to have been strongest during the fifteenth century, but several ballads are known to have existed much earlier. At one time it was thought that these ballads were the spontaneous and joint composition of a group of people. More likely they were composed by individuals of common origin—yeomen, serfs, minstrels—who spoke for the group.

Originally these early ballads were accompanied by music, but they are now enjoyed as narrative poems. Some are based on historical incidents, on deeds of legendary heroes, or on extraordinary or supernatural events. Many are tales of family relationships and of romantic love and death. The story is told in the language of the people and with the most straightforward simplicity. It is usually centered in a single situation—sometimes a single scene—with a few carefully selected details which allow the reader to infer all he must know. The action is swift and compressed; the appeal is to the emotions and the imagination. Rarely does the poet comment or philosophize; almost never does he pass judgment. Unmarked by current events, the old ballads are timeless, the products of imaginations unsophisticated enough to voice the most basic human concerns.

Toward the latter part of the medieval period, two new classes were rising that by their very importance in English life would help to recover for the English language its former prestige. One of these—a substantial middle class—was composed of independent workers. Another was composed of craftsmen and merchants who, for their own protection and advantage, banded together into commercial fraternities and guilds. Members of this second class enjoyed a higher social position and exercised considerable influence in the cultural and political life of the town. The "Black Death" of 1348-49, which reduced the population of England by one-third, increased the economic importance of both classes and with it the importance of the language they spoke. One indication of the general adoption of the English language by *all* classes was its establishment in 1385 as the language of the schools.

Another was its use in writing, and especially in writing of outstanding literary quality.

GEOFFREY CHAUCER, was England's first master poet. The kindly understanding and amused tolerance of human weakness that he brought to his poetry have seldom been matched in English literature. Critics have described him as "a one-man Renaissance," for his works foreshadow the familiarity with foreign literature, the brilliant skill with words, the technical ability with versification, and the joyful curiosity about life which were to "burst out" two centuries later in the English Renaissance.

Born the son of a wealthy wine merchant, Chaucer had a busy and varied career which enabled him to observe the whole range of medieval life, both in England and on the Continent. He served as a page and squire in courtly circles, fought with the English army in France, held several important civil-service posts, and traveled to France, Italy, and Flanders to carry out special government negotiations. Surprisingly, this busy man of affairs—for whom writing was only an avocation—created a number of superior poetic works.

Chaucer's first poems were free translations of French works and resembled those works in rhythm, rhyme, and poetic style. The poems of his middle years, though influenced somewhat by Italian writers such as Dante and Boccaccio, showed Chaucer's growing independence. The works of his concluding years were his finest and most independent, the most original of all being the last, *The Canterbury Tales*. Here Chaucer revealed more clearly than anywhere else the two qualities which made his poetry great. The first was his ability to perceive with startling clarity the physical appearance, behavior, and attitudes of his contemporaries. The second was his genius in communicating these perceptions through exact, telling details, and through surprising comparisons and contrasts. A wise and knowing observer of life, he was as detached, good-humored, and gently ironic when describing a saint as when portraying a scoundrel. He observed life and rejoiced in it; he did not judge it.

Ballads

THE TWA CORBIES

As I was walking all alane,
I heard twa corbies° making a mane;°   ravens; moan
The tane° unto the t'other did say,   one
"Where sall° we gang° and dine today?"   shall; go

"O down beside yon auld fail dyke,°   turf wall 5
I wot° there lies a new-slain knight;   know
And naebody kens° that he lies there,   knows
But his hawk, his hound, and lady fair.

"His hound is to the hunting gane,
His hawk to fetch the wild-fowl hame,   10
His lady's ta'en another mate,
So we may mak our dinner sweet.

"Ye'll sit on his white hause-bane,°   neck-bone
And I'll pike° out his bonny blue een;°   pick; eyes
Wi' ae lock o' his gowden° hair   golden 15
We'll theek° our nest when it grows bare.   thatch

"Mony a ane for him makes mane,
But nane sall ken where he is gane;
O'er his white banes,° when they are bare,   bones
The wind sall blaw for evermair."   20

1. What situation furnishes the background of this story? What is the over-all mood of the ballad? What lines are especially effective in establishing the mood?
2. If the lady knew where the knight was lying, why didn't she give him proper burial? What hints suggest the cause of his death?
3. How do you interpret the last stanza? Are all the stanzas equally necessary to the telling of the story? One characteristic of the ballad is that the speaker's personality is not important. Is this fact true of this ballad? Who tells the story?
4. The version printed here is intended to suggest Scottish dialect, not Middle English. As you read the ballad aloud, try to reproduce the sound and the rhythm, at the same time maintaining the rhyme. What is the predominant rhythm pattern?

LADY ISABEL AND THE ELF KNIGHT

There came a bird out o a bush,
    On water for to dine,
An sighing sair,° says the king's daughter,   sore
    "O wae's° this heart o mine!"   woe's

He's taen° a harp into his hand,   taken 5
    He's harped them all asleep,
Except it was the king's daughter,
    Who one wink couldna get.

He's luppen° on his berry-brown steed,   leaped
    Taen 'er on behind himsell,   10
Then baith rede° down to that water   rode
    That they ca° Wearie's Well.   call

"Wide° in, wide in, my lady fair,   wade
    No harm shall thee befall;
Oft times I've watered my steed   15
    Wi the waters o Wearie's Well."

The first step that she stepped in,
   She stepped to the knee;
And sighend says this lady fair,
   "This water's nae for me."   20

"Wide in, wide in, my lady fair,
   No harm shall thee befall;
Oft times I've watered my steed
   Wi the water o Wearie's Well."

The next step that she stepped in,   25
   She stepped to the middle;
"O," sighend says this lady fair,
   "I've wat° my gowden° girdle."   wet; golden

"Wide in, wide in, my lady fair,
   No harm shall thee befall;   30
Oft times have I watered my steed
   Wi the water o Wearie's Well."

The next step that she stepped in,
   She stepped to the chin;
"O," sighend says this lady fair,   35
   "They sud gar twa loves twin."[1]

"Seven king's-daughters I've drownd there,
   In the water o Wearie's Well,
And I'll make you the eight o them,
   And ring the common bell."   40

"Since I am standing here," she says,
   "This dowie° death to die,   wretched
One kiss o you comely mouth
   I'm sure wad comfort me."

---

[1]*They . . . twin:* They should cause two lovers to part.

He louted° him oer his saddle bow,   leaned 45
    To kiss her cheek and chin;
She's taen him in her arms twa,
    And thrown him headlong in.

"Since seven king's daughters ye've drowned there,
    In the water o Wearie's Well,
I'll make you bridegroom to them a',   50
    An ring the bell mysell."

And aye she warsled,° and aye she swam,   wrestled
    And she swam to dry lan;
She thanked God most cheerfully   55
    The dangers she oercame.

1. The ballad of "Lady Isabel and the Elf Knight" is one of the most widespread in Europe and exists in some form in almost every European country. What reasons could explain its remarkable and broad appeal?

2. In more recent versions of this ballad, the knight is no longer supernatural and has become an evil nobleman or a false priest. What effects would such changes have on the ballad? Do you think changing the elf to a man improves or damages the story? Why?

3. In the German version of this ballad, the maiden returns home with the head of the elf in her hand; her father gives a great banquet to celebrate her victory over her abductor. What does the ballad gain by this kind of ending? What advantages does the present version have?

4. Stanzas 4-9 are especially typical of the ballad: the same stanzas are repeated several times with one or two lines changed. Of course this gradual change made the words easier for the singer to remember. But what other effects are achieved through such repetition and modification?

THOMAS RYMER

True Thomas lay oer yond grassy bank,
   And he beheld a ladie° gay,   lady
A ladie that was brisk and bold,
   Come riding oer the fernie brae.°   green hill

Her skirt was of the grass-green silk,   5
   Her mantel of the velvet fine,
At ilka tett° of her horse's mane   each lock
   Hung fifty silver bells and nine.

True Thomas he took off his hat,
   And bowed him low down till his knee: 10
"All hail, thou mighty Queen of Heaven!
   For your peer on earth I never did see."

"O no, O no, True Thomas," she says,
   "That name does not belong to me;
I am but the queen of fair Elfland,   15
   And I'm come here for to visit thee.

. . . .

"But ye maun° go wi me now, Thomas,   must
   True Thomas, ye maun go wi me,
For ye maun serve me seven years,
   Thro weel° or wae° as may chance to be."   wealth; woe 20

She turned about her milk-white steed,
   And took True Thomas up behind,
And aye wheneer her bridle rang,
   The steed flew swifter than the wind.

For forty days and forty nights   25
   He wade thro red blude° to the knee,   blood
And he saw neither sun nor moon,
   But heard the roaring of the sea.

O they rade° on, and further on,   rode
   Until they came to a garden green: 30
"Light down, light down, ye ladie free,
   Some of that fruit let me pull to thee."

"O no, O no, True Thomas," she says,
   "That fruit maun not be touched by thee,
For a' the plagues that are in hell   35
   Light on the fruit of this countrie.

"But I have a loaf here in my lap,
   Likewise a bottle of claret wine,
And now ere we go farther on,
   We'll rest a while, and ye may dine."   40

When he had eaten and drunk his fill,
   "Lay down your head upon my knee,"
The lady sayd, "ere we climb yon hill,
   And I will show you fairlies° three.   wonders

"O see not ye yon narrow road,   45
   So thick beset wi thorns and briers?
That is the path of righteousness,
   Tho after it but few enquires.

"And see not ye that braid° braid road,   broad
   That lies across yon lillie leven?°   lovely lawn 50
That is the path of wickedness,
   Tho some call it the road to heaven.

"And see not ye that bonny road,
   Which winds about the fernie brae?
That is the road to fair Elfland,   55
   Where you and I this night maun gae.

"But Thomas, ye maun hold your tongue,
   Whatever you may hear or see,
For gin° ae word you should chance to speak,   if
   You will neer get back to your ain countrie."   60

He has gotten a coat of the even cloth,
   And a pair of shoes of velvet green,
And till seven years were past and gone
   True Thomas on earth was never seen.

1. The subject matter of a folk ballad is either a common, simple experience or else a dream (or nightmare) which has occurred to many people. It is interesting, therefore, to notice how frequently supernatural beings appear in folk tales and ballads. "Thomas Rymer," for example, is "Lady Isabel" in reverse, with the supernatural creature a woman. Compare these two ballads. How else are they alike and different?

2. Thomas the Rhymer, or Thomas of Erceldoune, actually lived at some time between 1210 and 1297. He was famous throughout England and Scotland for his prophetic powers, and was still venerated by the common folk of Scotland—who continued to quote his sayings—as late as 1870. Supposedly Thomas's poetic and prophetic powers were given to him by the Queen of Elfland. The ballad describes how Thomas received such gifts. What elements in the poem create or increase the atmosphere of mystery, wonder, and awe?

3. Several details in "Thomas Rymer" seem more related to conventional religion than to fantasies. What are the religious elements in the ballad? How can you account for their presence in this fairy tale?

GET UP AND BAR THE DOOR

It fell about the Martinmas time,[1]
  And a gay time it was then,
When our goodwife got puddings° to make,   sausages
  And she's boild them in the pan.

The wind sae could° blew south and north,   so cold 5
  And blew into the floor;
Quoth our goodman to our goodwife,
  "Gae° out and bar the door."   go

"My hand is in my hussyfskap,°   kneading-trough
  Goodman, as ye may see;   10
An° it should nae be barrd this hundred year,   if
  It's no be barrd for me."

They made a paction° tween them twa,°   agreement; two
  They made it firm and sure,
That the first word whaeer° shoud speak,   whoever 15
  Shoud rise and bar the door.

Then by there came two gentlemen,
  At twelve oclock at night,
And they could neither see house nor hall,
  Nor coal nor candle-light.   20

"Now whether is this a rich man's house,
  Or whether is it a poor?"
But neer a word wad ane o' them speak,
  For barring of the door.

[1]*Martinmas time:* November 11

And firt they ate the white puddings,   25
    And then they ate the black;
Tho muckle° thought the goodwife to hersel,   much
    Yet neer a word she spake.

Then said the one unto the other,
    "Here, man, tak ye my knife;   30
Do ye tak aff the auld man's beard,
    And I'll kiss the goodwife."

"But there's nae water in the house,
    And what shall we do than?"
"What ails thee at the pudding-broo,°   broth 35
    That boils into the pan?"

O up then started our goodman,
    An angry man was he:
"Will ye kiss my wife before my een,
    And scad° me wi pudding-bree?"   scald 40

Then up and started our goodwife,
    Gied three skips on the floor:
"Goodman, you've spoken the foremost word,
    Get up and bar the door."

1. Few of the old ballads are humorous. Why would the story in this ballad have amused the common people? What situation presented in stanzas 1-4 creates a conflict? How do the two gentlemen become involved in this conflict and in its resolution? Does the goodman have more reason to be angry than the goodwife does? What subtle and humorous implications might be drawn from the goodman's being defeated by the goodwife?

2. The ballad-maker omitted several details probably already known to his audience. How do you explain the gentlemen's inability to tell whether the house belongs to a rich or a poor man? What reason would they have for taking off "the auld man's beard"? What does the goodwife think to herself? Would the addition of such details have made the ballad more interesting or humorous? Tell why or why not.

EDWARD, EDWARD

"Why dois your brand° sae drap wi' bluid,°   sword; blood
   Edward, Edward?
Why dois your brand sae drap wi' bluid,
 And why sae sad gang° yee O?"   go
"O, I hae killed my hauke sae guid,   5
   Mither, mither,
O, I hae killed my hauke sae guid,
 And I had nae mair° bot hee O."   more

"Your haukis° bluid was nevir sae reid,°   hawk's; red
   Edward, Edward,   10
Your haukis bluid was nevir sae reid,
 My deir son, I tell thee O."
"O, I hae killed my reid-roan steid,°   red-roan steed
   Mither, mither,
O, I hae killed my reid-roan steid,   15
 That erst° was sae fair and frie O."   once

"Your steid was auld, and ye hae gat mair,
   Edward, Edward,
Your steid was auld, and ye hae gat mair,
 Sum other dule° ye drie° O."   sorrow; endure 20

"O, I hae killed my fadir° deir,   father
  Mither, mither,
O, I hae killed my fadir deir,
  Alas, and wae° is mee O!"   woe

"And whatten penance wul ye drie for that,   25
  Edward, Edward?
And whatten penance wul ye drie for that?
  My deir son, now tell me O."
"Ile set my feit in yonder boat,
  Mither, mither,   30
Ile set my feit in yonder boat,
  And Ile fare ovir the sea O."

"And what wul ye doe wi' your towirs and your ha',°   hall
  Edward, Edward?
And what wul ye doe wi' your towirs and your ha',   35
  That were sae fair to see O?"
"Ile let thame stand tul they doun fa',°   fall
  Mither, mither,
Ile let thame stand tul they doun fa',
  For here nevir mair maun° I bee O."   must 40

"And what wul ye leive to your bairns° and your wife,
  Edward, Edward?   children
And what wul ye leive to your bairns and your wife,
  When ye gang ovir the sea O?"
"The warldis° room, late them beg thrae° life,   world's; 45
                                                             through
  Mither, mither,
The warldis room, late them beg thrae life,
  For thame nevir mair wul I see O."

"And what wul ye leive to your ain° mither deir,   own
  Edward, Edward?   50
And what wul ye leive to your ain mither deir?

My deir son, now tell me O."
"The curse of hell frae me sall° ye beir,   shall
     Mither, mither,
The curse of hell frae me sall ye beir,   55
     Sic° counseils ye gave to me O."   such

1. The last line of "Edward, Edward" is unique among ballads in the way it implicates Edward's mother. What is implied about the mother in this line? How does the last stanza change the whole ballad?
2. A will which bequeaths a curse as its final gift appears in many ballads in almost the identical form you find it in "Edward, Edward." Analyze lines 33-56 carefully and see if you can find why the use of a will has been so appealing. Why would it be added at the end of so many sad stories?
3. How many details of this poem remind you that it was designed to be sung. Find the devices that especially create a musical effect.
4. "Edward, Edward" is considered among England's most dramatic ballads. How is the form of this ballad dramatic? What makes the form not typical of ballads generally?

Lyrics

CUCKOO SONG

Sumer is icumen in,
Lhude° sing cuccu!   loud
Groweth sed and bloweth med°   bloometh
                                                                    meadow
And springth the wode nu.°   now
Sing cuccu!   5

Awe° bleteth after lomb   ewe
Lhouth° after calve cu,°   lows; cow
Bulluc sterteth,° bucke verteth.°   leaps up;
                                                                     snorts
Murie° sing cuccu!   merry
Cuccu, cuccu,   10
Wel singes thu,° cuccu.   thou
Ne swik° thu naver nu!   nor ceaseth

Sing cuccu nu, Sing cuccu!
Sing cuccu, Sing cuccu nu!

1. Written before 1250, this lyric is probably the oldest medieval lyric in existence. The version printed here is in the Middle English of Chaucer's time. Why does the poet urge the cuckoo to sing "murie"? What feelings do you think he wants to express? Tell why you do, or do not, think the lyric is about the cuckoo's song.
2. This lyric was written to be sung as a round. Thus the metrical rhythm of the lines is especially important. Chart the rhythm pattern of the first two stanzas. Then discuss the ways in which they are alike and different. Which of the final -*e's* need to be sounded lightly? Where would you place the accents in the final couplet?

JESU, SWETE SONE DERE

Jesu, swete sone dere!
   On porful° bed liest thou here,   pitifully poor
And that me greveth sore;
For thy cradel is as a bere,°   cattle stall
Oxe and asse beth thy fere;°   companions 5
   Weepe ich° may therefore.   I

Jesu, swete, beo not wroth,
Tho ich nabbe° clout ne cloth   have not
   Thee on° for to folde,   in
   Thee on to folde ne to wrappe,   10
For ich nabbe clout ne lappe;°   robe
Bute lay thou thy fet to my pappe,°   breast
And wite° thee from the colde.   protect

1. Here, on facing pages, are two lyrics of devotion that were probably written in Chaucer's time. In "Jesu, Swete Sone Dere" who
   is the speaker? What scene and situation are suggested? Why is
   this lyric called a sacred lullaby? What emotions are conveyed in
   it? What is the over-all mood of the lyric?
2. "I Sing of a Maiden" is a religious lyric of adoration. Who is the
   maiden? How do you interpret these repeated lines: He cam also
   stille As dew in Aprille"? What effect do they have on the mood
   created in the poem? What is this mood? What emotion is conveyed in the lyric, especially in the last stanza?
3. The "tunefulness" of these lyrics must be heard to be appreciated.
   Therefore, try to read them aloud, using the chart on the opposite
   page as a guide to the pronunciation of the vowels. The conso-
   nants are, for the most part, pronounced as they are today. The
   th in *thu* is unvoiced, as in *thin;* the *ch* in *ich* is pronounced like
   k. In most instances the *-e* and *-es* endings are pronounced. The
   two lyrics have different rhythm patterns. The first has four accents to the line. The second has two accents to the line or three,
   depending on how you read this lyric. When you have worked out
   the tunefulness of these lyrics, do the same for the "Cuckoo Song."

I SING OF A MAIDEN

I sing of a maiden
    That is makeles;°   matchless
King of alle kinges
    To here sone che ches.°   she chose

He came also° stille   as 5
    Ther° his moder° was,   where; mother
As dew in Aprille
    That fallith on the gras.

He cam also stille
    To his moderes bowr,   10
As dew in Aprille
    That fallith on the flowr.

He cam also stille
    Ther his moder lay,
As dew in Aprille   15
    That fallith on the spray.

Moder and maiden
    Was never non but che;°   she
Wel may swich° a lady   such
    Godes moder be.   20

	Sounds	Middle English Examples
a	like *a* in *father*	*nabbe, fallith*
e	like *a* in *day*	*swete, che*
	or like *a* in *care*	*dere, sterteth*
i	like *e* in *me*	*in, his*
o	like *o* in *so*	*sone, moder*

	or like *o* in *hot*	*wroth, non*
u	like *oo* in *boot*	*bute, sumer*
ou or ow	like *ou* in *about*	*lhouth, flowr*

THE BLACKSMITHS

This fourteenth-century lyric is too fine a poem to be omitted but too difficult to be given in the original. Fortunately, the modern translation has preserved the feeling and detail of the original.

Swart, sweaty smiths, smutched with smoke,
Drive me to death with din of their dints.°   blows
Such noise a-nights heard a man never:
What criminal cries, what clatter and clanging!
The cursed cow-carpenters cry after "Coal! coal!"   5
And blow their bellows till their brains burst.
"Huff puff," says the one, "Hoff poff," the other.
They spit and sprawl and spell many spells;
They gnaw and gnash, they groan together,
And hold hot at it with hard hammers.   10
Of a bull's hide is their bellies' covering;
Their shanks are shackled for the spattering sparks;
Heavy hammers they have, that are handled hard.
Stark strokes they strike on a steel-stock
And batter out a burden:° "Loos boos! las das!"   refrain 15
Such a damnable din is due only the devil.
The master lays into the links, lashing with his hammer,
Twists them together, and taps out a treble:
"Tic tock, hic hock, tiket taket, tic tock—
Loos boos, las das!" *This* is the life they lead,   20
These mare-clothers. Christ give them curses!
Not a man these nights can have his rest!

1. In medieval times, a military expedition involved horses and armor. What part did the "cow-carpenters" play in these preparations? Why would they cry "Coal! coal!"? what impression does the poet create of the men and of the scene? What are his feelings and why?
2. Note the Anglo-Saxon influence in the aliteration and balanced lines. Note also the poet's use of graphic details and of onomatopoeia. How are these related to one another and to the total effect of the lyric? What is that effect? Discuss and cite examples.

Geoffrey Chaucer

The scope and variety of Chaucer's *The Canterbury Tales* inspired one poet to exclaim, "Here is God's plenty!" Virtually every type of writing in medieval literature is represented here, including sermons, beast-fables, medieval romances, and even bawdy jokes. To present his twenty tales, Chaucer uses an ancient narrative device, the frame-story; that is, a story within a story. He introduces this device in "The Prologue," where he describes how a number of people from all walks of life gather at an inn for the purpose of going on a pilgrimage to Canterbury. Chaucer describes the time, the place, and the people, each in vivid detail. This is the general setting or "frame" within which the various pilgrims tell stories along the way to Canterbury. "The Prologue" is more than a "frame," however, for the stories in *The Canterbury Tales.* It is in itself a richly various and humorous picture of life in the Middle Ages, filled with human beings who are vividly alive. Since the general reader often has trouble with the archaic words and spellings of Chaucer's time, what follows is a modern verse translation.

FROM The Canterbury Tales

Prologue

As soon as April pierces to the root
The drought of March, and bathes each bud and shoot
Through every vein of sap with gentle showers
From whose engendering liquor spring the flowers;
When zephyrs[1] have breathed softly all about   5

[1]*zephyrs:* the west winds

Inspiring every wood and field to sprout,
And in the zodiac the youthful sun
His journey halfway through the Ram[2] has run;
When little birds are busy with their song
Who sleep with open eyes the whole night long   10
Life stirs their hearts and tingles in them so,
On pilgrimages people long to go
And palmers[3] to set out for distant strands
And foreign shrines renowned in many lands.
And specially in England people ride   15
To Canterbury[4] from every countyside
To visit there the blessed martyred saint
Who gave them strength when they were sick and faint.
   In Southwark at the Tabard[5] one spring day
It happened, as I stopped there on my way,   20
Myself a pilgrim with a heart devout
Ready for Canterbury to set out,
At night came all of twenty-nine assorted
Travelers, and to that same inn resorted,
Who by a turn of fortune chanced to fall   25
In fellowship together, and they were all
Pilgrims who had it in their minds to ride
Toward Canterbury. The stable doors were wide,
The rooms were large, and we enjoyed the best,
And shortly, when the sun had gone to rest,   30
I had so talked with each that presently
I was a member of their company
And promised to rise early the next day
To start, as I shall show, upon our way.
   But none the less, while I have time and space,   35
Before this tale has gone a further pace,
I should in reason tell you the condition

---

[2]*the Ram:* the zodiac sign for the period beginning March 21
[3]*palmers:* pilgrims, so called because of the palm branches they frequently carried
[4]*Canterbury:* site of the cathedral where St. Thomas à Becket was murdered in 1170. Canterbury is about sixty miles from London.
[5]*Tabard in Southwark:* inn on the outskirts of London

Of each of them, his rank and his position,
And also what array they all were in;
And so then, with a knight I will begin.   40
  A Knight was with us, and an excellent man,
Who from the earliest moment he began
To follow his career loved chivalry,
Truth, openhandedness, and courtesy.
He was a stout man in the king's campaigns   45
And in that cause had gripped his horse's reins
In Christian lands and pagan through the earth,
None farther, and always honored for his worth.
He was on hand at Alexandria's[6] fall.
He had often sat in precedence to all   50
The nations at the banquet board in Prussia.
He had fought in Lithuania and in Russia,
No Christian knight more often; he had been
In Moorish Africa at Benmarin,
At the siege of Algeciras in Granada,   55
And sailed in many a glorious armada
In the Mediterranean, and fought as well
At Ayas and Attalia when they fell
In Armenia and on Asia Minor's coast.
Of fifteen deadly battles he could boast,   60
And in Algeria, at Tremessen,
Fought for the faith and killed three separate men
In single combat. He had done good work
Joining against another pagan Turk
With the king of Palathia. And he was wise,   65
Despite his prowess, honored in men's eyes,
Meek as a girl and gentle in his ways.
He had never spoken ignobly all his days
To any man by even a rude inflection.
He was a knight in all things to perfection.   70
He rode a good horse, but his gear was plain,
For he had lately served on a campaign.

[6]*Alexandria:* city in Egypt

His tunic was still spattered by the rust
Left by his coat of mail, for he had just
Returned and set out on his pilgrimage.   75
    His son was with him, a young Squire, in age
Some twenty years as near as I could guess.
His hair curled as if taken from a press.
He was a lover and would become a knight.
In stature he was of a moderate height   80
But powerful and wonderfully quick.
He had been in Flanders, riding in the thick
Of forays in Artois and Picardy,
And bore up well for one so young as he,
Still hoping by his exploits in such places   85
To stand the better in his lady's graces.
He wore embroidered flowers, red and white,
And blazed like a spring meadow to the sight.
He sang or played his flute the livelong day.
He was as lusty as the month of May.   90
His coat was short, its sleeves were long and wide.
He sat his horse well, and knew how to ride,
And how to make a song and use his lance,
And he could write and draw well, too, and dance.
So hot his love that when the moon rose pale   95
He got no more sleep than a nightingale.
He was modest, and helped whomever he was able,
And carved as his father's squire at the table.
    But one more servant had the Knight beside,
Choosing thus simply for the time to ride: 100
A Yeoman, in a coat and hood of green.
His peacock-feathered arrows, bright and keen,
He carried under his belt in tidy fashion.
For well-kept gear he had a yeoman's passion.
No draggled feather might his arrows show,   105
And in his hand he held a mighty bow.
He kept his hair close-cropped, his face was brown,
He knew the lore of woodcraft up and down.
His arm was guarded from the bowstring's whip

By a bracer, gaily trimmed. He had at hip   110
A sword and buckler, and at his other side
A dagger whose fine mounting was his pride,
Sharp-pointed as a spear. His horn he bore
In a sling of green, and on his chest he wore
A silver image of St. Christopher,[7]   115
His patron, since he was a forester.
   There was also a Nun, a Prioress,
Whose smile was gentle and full of guilelessness.
"By St. Loy!" was the worst oath she would say.
She sang mass well, in a becoming way,   120
Intoning through her nose the words divine,
And she was known as Madame Eglantine.
She spoke good French, as taught at Stratford-Bow,
For the Parisian French she did not know.
She was schooled to eat so primly and so well   125
That from her lips no morsel ever fell.
She wet her fingers lightly in the dish
Of sauce, for courtesy was her first wish.
With every bite she did her skillful best
To see that no drop fell upon her breast.   130
She always wiped her upper lip so clean
That in her cup was never to be seen
A hint of grease when she had drunk her share.
She reached out for her meat with comely air.
She was a great delight, and always tried   135
To imitate court ways, and had her pride,
Both amiable and gracious in her dealings.
As for her charity and tender feelings,
She melted at whatever was piteous.
She would weep if she but came upon a mouse   140
Caught in a trap, if it were dead or bleeding.
Some little dogs that she took pleasure feeding
On roasted meat or milk or good wheat bread
She had, but how she wept to find one dead

---

[7]*Christopher:* image of St. Christopher, the patron saint of foresters

Or yelping from a blow that made it smart,   145
And all was sympathy and loving heart.
Neat was her wimple in its every plait,
Her nose well formed, her eyes as gray as slate.
Her mouth was very small and soft and red.
She had so wide a brow I think her head   150
Was nearly a span broad, for certainly
She was not undergrown, as all could see.
She wore her cloak with dignity and charm,
And had her rosary about her arm,
The small beads coral and the larger green,   155
And from them hung a brooch of golden sheen,
On it a large A and a crown above;
Beneath, "All things are subject unto love."
    A Priest accompanied her toward Canterbury,
And an attendant Nun, her secretary.   160
    There was a Monk, and nowhere was his peer,
A hunter, and a roving overseer.
He was a manly man, and fully able
To be an abbot. He kept a hunting stable,
And when he rode the neighborhood could hear   165
His bridle jingling in the wind as clear
And loud as if it were a chapel bell.
Wherever he was master of a cell
The principles of good St. Benedict,
For being a little old and somewhat strict,   170
Were honored in the breach, as past their prime.
He lived by the fashion of a newer time.
He would have swapped that text for a plucked hen
Which says that hunters are not holy men,
Or a monk outside his discipline and rule   175
Is too much like a fish outside his pool;
That is to say, a monk outside his cloister.
But such a text he deemed not worth an oyster.
I told him his opinion made me glad.
Why should he study always and go mad,   180
Mewed in his cell with only a book for neighbor?

Or why, as Augustine commanded, labor
And sweat his hands? How shall the world be served?
To Augustine be all such toil reserved!
And so he hunted, as was only right.   185
He had greyhounds as swift as birds in flight.
His taste was all for tracking down the hare,
And what his sport might cost he did not care.
His sleeves I noticed, where they met his hand,
Trimmed with gray fur, the finest in the land.   190
His hood was fastened with a curious pin
Made of wrought gold and clasped beneath his chin,
A love knot at the tip. His head might pass,
Bald as it was, for a lump of shining glass,
And his face was glistening as if anointed.   195
Fat as a lord he was, and well appointed.
His eyes were large, and rolled inside his head
As if they gleamed from a furnace of hot lead.
His boots were supple, his horse superbly kept.
He was a prelate to dream of while you slept.   200
He was not pale nor peaked like a ghost.
He relished a plump swan as his favorite roast.
He rode a palfrey brown as a ripe berry.
   A Friar was with us, a gay dog and a merry,
Who begged his district with a jolly air.   205
No friar in all four orders[8] could compare
With him for gallantry; his tongue was wooing.
Many a girl was married by his doing,
And at his own cost it was often done.
He was a pillar, and a noble one,   210
To his whole order. In his neighborhood
Rich franklins° knew him well, who served good food,   landowners
And worthy women welcomed him to town;
For the license that his order handed down,
He said himself, conferred on him possession   215
Of more than a curate's power of confession.

   [8]*all four orders:* the four principal orders of friars, which were the Augustinians, Carmelites, Dominicans, and Franciscans

Sweetly the list of frailties he heard,
Assigning penance with a pleasant word.
He was an easy man for absolution
Where he looked forward to a contribution,   220
For if to a poor order a man has given
It signifies that he has been well shriven,°   absolved from sin
And if a sinner let his purse be dented
The Friar would stake his oath he had repented.
For many men become so hard of heart   225
They cannot weep, though conscience makes them smart.
Instead of tears and prayers, then, let the sinner
Supply the poor friars with the price of dinner.
For pretty women he had more than shrift.
His cape was stuffed with many a little gift,   230
As knives and pins and suchlike. He could sing
A merry note, and pluck a tender string,
And had no rival at all in balladry.
His neck was whiter than a fleur-de-lis,
And yet he could have knocked a strong man down.   235
He knew the taverns well in every town.
The barmaids and innkeepers pleased his mind
Better than beggars and lepers and their kind.
In his position it was unbecoming
Among the wretched lepers to go slumming.   240
It mocks all decency, it sews no stitch
To deal with such riffraff; but with the rich,
With sellers of victuals, that's another thing.
Wherever he saw some hope of profiting,
None so polite, so humble. He was good,   245
The champion beggar of his brotherhood.
Should a woman have no shoes against the snow,
So pleasant was his *"In principio"*
He would have her widow's mite before he went.
He took in far more than he paid in rent   250
For his right of begging within certain bounds.
None of his brethren trespassed on his grounds!
He loved as freely as a half-grown whelp.

On arbitration-days he gave great help,
For his cloak was never shiny nor threadbare   255
Like a poor cloistered scholar's. He had an air
As if he were a doctor or a pope.
It took stout wool to make his semicope
That plumped out like a bell for portliness.
He lisped a little in his rakishness   260
To make his English sweeter on his tongue,
And twanging his harp to end some song he'd sung
His eyes would twinkle in his head as bright
As the stars twinkle on a frosty night.
Hubert this gallant Friar was by name.   265
   Among the rest a Merchant also came.
He wore a forked beard and a beaver hat
From Flanders. High up in the saddle he sat,
In figured cloth, his boots clasped handsomely,
Delivering his opinions pompously,   270
Always on how his gains might be increased.
At all costs he desired the sea policed
From Middleburg in Holland to Orwell.[9]
He knew the exchange rates, and the time to sell
French currency, and there was never yet   275
A man who could have told he was in debt
So grave he seemed and hid so well his feelings
With all his shrewd engagements and close dealings.
You'd find no better man at any turn;
But what his name was I could never learn.   280
   There was an Oxford Student too, it chanced,
Already in his logic well advanced.
He rode a mount as skinny as a rake,
And he was hardly fat. For learning's sake
He let himself look hollow and sober enough.   285
He wore an outer coat of threadbare stuff,
For he had no benefice° for his enjoyment   endowed church job
And was too unworldly for some lay employment.

[9]*Orwell:* an English port

He much preferred to have beside his bed
His twenty volumes bound in black or red   290
All packed with Aristotle from end to middle
Than a sumptuous wardrobe or a merry fiddle.
For though he knew what learning had to offer
There was little coin to jingle in his coffer.
Whatever he got by touching up a friend   295
On books and learning he would promptly spend
And busily pray for the soul of anybody
Who furnished him the wherewithal for study.
His scholarship was what he truly heeded.
He never spoke a word more than was needed,   300
And that was said with dignity and force,
And quick and brief. He was of grave discourse,
Giving new weight to virtue by his speech,
And gladly would he learn and gladly teach.
    There was a Lawyer, cunning and discreet,   305
Who had often been to St. Paul's porch to meet
His clients. He was a Sergeant of the Law,
A man deserving to be held in awe,
Or so he seemed, his manner was so wise.
He had often served as Justice of Assize   310
By the king's appointment, with a broad commission,
For his knowledge and his eminent position.
He had many a handsome gift by way of fee.
There was no buyer of land as shrewd as he.
All ownership to him became fee simple.   315
His titles were never faulty by a pimple.
None was so busy as he with case and cause,
And yet he seemed much busier than he was.
In all cases and decisions he was schooled
That were of record since King William ruled.   320
No one could pick a loophole or a flaw
In any lease or contract he might draw.
Each statute on the books he knew by rote.
He traveled in a plain, silk-belted coat.
    A Franklin° traveled in his company.   landowner, not   325
                                                       of noble birth

Whiter could never daisy petal be
Than was his beard. His ruddy face gave sign
He liked his morning sop of toast in wine.
He lived in comfort, as he would assure us,
For he was a true son of Epicurus[10]   330
Who held the opinion that the only measure
Of perfect happiness was simply pleasure.
Such hospitality did he provide,
He was St. Julian[11] to his countryside.
His bread and ale were always up to scratch.   335
He had a cellar none on earth could match.
There was no lack of pasties in his house,
Both fish and flesh, and that so plenteous
That where he lived it snowed of meat and drink.
With every dish of which a man can think,   340
After the various seasons of the year,
He changed his diet for his better cheer.
He had coops of partridges as fat as cream,
He had a fishpond stocked with pike and bream.
Woe to his cook for an unready pot   345
Or a sauce that wasn't seasoned and spiced hot!
A table in his hall stood on display
Prepared and covered through the livelong day.
He presided at court sessions for his bounty
And sat in Parliament often for his county.   350
A well-wrought dagger and a purse of silk
Hung at his belt, as white as morning milk.
He had been a sheriff and county auditor.
On earth was no such rich proprietor!
    There were five Guildsmen, in the livery   355
Of one august and great fraternity,
A Weaver, a Dyer, and a Carpenter,
A Tapestry-maker and a Haberdasher.
Their gear was furbished new and clean as glass.
The mountings of their knives were not of brass   360

[10]*Epicurus:* Greek philosopher
[11]*St. Julian:* patron saint of hospitality

But silver. Their pouches were well made and neat,
And each of them, it seemed, deserved a seat
On the platform at the Guildhall, for each one
Was likely timber to make an alderman.
They had goods enough, and money to be spent,   365
Also their wives would willingly consent
And would have been at fault if they had not.
For to be "Madamed" is a pleasant lot,
And to march in first at feasts for being well married,
And royally to have their mantles carried.   370
    For the pilgrimage these Guildsmen brought their own
Cook to boil their chicken and marrow bone
With seasoning powder and capers and sharp spice.
In judging London ale his taste was nice.
He well knew how to roast and broil and fry,   375
To mix a stew, and bake a good meat pie,
Or capon creamed with almond, rice, and egg.
Pity he had an ulcer on his leg!
    A Skipper was with us, his home far in the west.
He came from the port of Dartmouth, as I guessed.   380
He sat his carthorse pretty much at sea
In a coarse smock that joggled on his knee.
From his neck a dagger on a string hung down
Under his arm. His face was burnished brown
By the summer sun. He was a true good fellow.   385
Many a time he had tapped a wine cask mellow
Sailing from Bordeaux while the owner slept.
Too nice a point of honor he never kept.
In a sea fight, if he got the upper hand,
Drowned prisoners floated home to every land.   390
But in navigation, whether reckoning tides,
Currents, or what might threaten him besides,
Harborage, pilotage, or the moon's demeanor,
None was his like from Hull to Cartagena.
He knew each harbor and the anchorage there   395
From Gotland to the Cape of Finisterre
And every creek in Brittany and Spain,

And he had called his ship the *Madeleine*.
   With us came also an astute Physician.
There was none like him for a disquisition   400
On the art of medicine or surgery,
For he was grounded in astrology.
He kept his patient long in observation,
Choosing the proper hour for application
Of charms and images by intuition   405
Of magic, and the planets' best position.
For he was one who understood the laws
That rule the humors, and could tell the cause ⟍
That brought on every human malady,
Whether of hot or cold, or moist or dry.   410
He was a perfect medico, for sure.
The cause once known, he would prescribe the cure,
For he had his druggists ready at a motion
To provide the sick man with some pill or potion—
A game of mutual aid, with each one winning.   415
Their partnership was hardly just beginning!
He was well versed in his authorities,
Old Aesculapius, Dioscorides,
Rufus, and old Hippocrates, and Galen,
Haly, and Rhazes, and Serapion,   420
Averroës, Bernard, Johannes Damascenus,
Avicenna, Gilbert, Gaddesden, Constantinus.
He urged a moderate fare on principle,
But rich in nourishment, digestible;
Of nothing in excess would he admit.   425
He gave but little heed to Holy Writ.
His clothes were lined with taffeta; their hue
Was all of blood red and of Persian blue,
Yet he was far from careless of expense.
He saved his fees from times of pestilence,   430
For gold is a cordial, as physicians hold,
And so he had a special love for gold.
   A worthy woman there was from near the city
Of Bath, but somewhat deaf, and more's the pity.

For weaving she possessed so great a bent   435
She outdid the people of Ypres and of Ghent.
No other woman dreamed of such a thing
As to precede her at the offering,
Or if any did, she fell in such a wrath
She dried up all the charity in Bath.   440
She wore fine kerchiefs of old-fashioned air,
And on a Sunday morning, I could swear,
She had ten pounds of linen on her head.
Her stockings were of finest scarlet-red,
Laced tightly, and her shoes were soft and new.   445
Bold was her face, and fair, and red in hue.
She had been an excellent woman all her life.
Five men in turn had taken her to wife,
Omitting other youthful company —
But let that pass for now! Over the sea   450
She had traveled freely; many a distant stream
She crossed, and visited Jerusalem
Three times. She had been at Rome and at Boulogne,
At the shrine of Compostella, and at Cologne.
She had wandered by the way through many a scene.   455
Her teeth were set with little gaps between.
Easily on her ambling horse she sat.
She was well wimpled, and she wore a hat
As wide in circuit as a shield or targe.
A skirt swathed up her hips, and they were large.   460
Upon her feet she wore sharp-roweled spurs.
She was a good fellow; a ready tongue was hers.
All remedies of love she knew by name,
For she had all the tricks of that old game.
   There was a good man of the priest's vocation,   465
A poor town Parson of true consecration,
But he was rich in holy thought and work.
Learned he was, in the truest sense a clerk
Who meant Christ's gospel faithfully to preach
And truly his parishioners to teach.   470
He was a kind man, full of industry,

Many times tested by adversity
And always patient. If tithes were in arrears,
He was loth to threaten any man with fears
Of excommunication; past a doubt   475
He would rather spread his offering about
To his poor flock, or spend his property.
To him a little meant sufficiency.
Wide was his parish, with houses far asunder,
But he would not be kept by rain or thunder,   480
If any had suffered a sickness or a blow,
From visiting the farthest, high or low,
Plodding his way on foot, his staff in hand.
He was a model his flock could understand,
For first he did and afterward he taught.   485
That precept from the Gospel he had caught,
And he added as a metaphor thereto,
"If the gold rusts, what will the iron do?"
For if a priest is foul, in whom we trust,
No wonder a layman shows a little rust.   490
A priest should take to heart the shameful scene
Of shepherds filthy while the sheep are clean.
By his own purity a priest should give
The example to his sheep, how they should live.
He did not rent his benefice for hire,   495
Leaving his flock to flounder in the mire,
And run to London, happiest of goals,
To sing paid masses in St. Paul's for souls,
Or as chaplain from some rich guild take his keep,
But dwelt at home and guarded well his sheep   500
So that no wolf should make his flock miscarry.
He was a shepherd, and not a mercenary.
And though himself a man of strict vocation
He was not harsh to weak souls in temptation,
Not overbearing nor haughty in his speech,   505
But wise and kind in all he tried to teach.
By good example and just words to turn
Sinners to heaven was his whole concern.

But should a man in truth prove obstinate,
Whoever he was, of rich or mean estate,   510
The Parson would give him a snub to meet the case.
I doubt there was a priest in any place
His better. He did not stand on dignity
Nor affect in conscience too much nicety,
But Christ's and his disciples' word he sought   515
To teach, and first he followed what he taught.
   There was a Plowman with him on the road,
His brother, who had forked up many a load
Of good manure. A hearty worker he,
Living in peace and perfect charity.   520
Whether his fortune made him smart or smile,
He loved God with his whole heart all the while
And his neighbor as himself. He would undertake,
For every luckless poor man, for the sake
Of Christ to thresh and ditch and dig by the hour   525
And with no wage, if it was in his power.
His tithes on goods and earnings he paid fair.
He wore a coarse, rough coat and rode a mare.
   There also were a Manciple, a Miller,
A Reeve, a Summoner, and a Pardoner,   530
And I—this makes our company complete.
   As tough a yokel as you care to meet
The Miller was. His big-beefed arms and thighs
Took many a ram put up as wrestling prize.
He was a thick, squat-shouldered lump of sins.   535
No door but he could heave it off its pins
Or break it running at it with his head.
His beard was broader than a shovel, and red
As a fat sow or fox: A wart stood clear
Atop his nose, and red as a pig's ear   540
A tuft of bristles on it. Black and wide
His nostrils were. He carried at his side
A sword and buckler. His mouth would open out
Like a great furnace, and he would sing and shout
His ballads and jokes of harlotries and crimes.   545

He could steal corn and charge for it three times,
And yet was honest enough, as millers come,
For a miller, as they say, has a golden thumb.
In white coat and blue hood this lusty clown,
Blowing his bagpipes, brought us out of town.   550
    The Manciple° was of a lawyers' college,   steward
And other buyers might have used his knowledge
How to be shrewd provisioners, for whether
He bought on cash or credit, altogether
He managed that the end should be the same: 555
He came out more than even with the game.
Now isn't it an instance of God's grace
How a man of little knowledge can keep pace
In wit with a whole school of learned men?
He had masters to the number of three times ten   560
Who knew each twist of equity and tort;
A dozen in that very Inn of Court
Were worthy to be steward of the estate
To any of England's lords, however great,
And keep him to his income well confined   565
And free from debt, unless he lost his mind,
Or let him scrimp, if he were mean in bounty;
They could have given help to a whole county
In any sort of case that might befall;
And yet this Manciple could cheat them all!   570
    The Reeve° was a slender, fiery-tempered man.   overseer
He shaved as closely as a razor can.
His hair was cropped about his ears, and shorn
Above his forehead as a priest's is worn.
His legs were very long and very lean.   575
No calf on his lank spindles could be seen.
But he knew how to keep a barn or bin,
He could play the game with auditors and win.
He knew well how to judge by drought and rain
The harvest of his seed and of his grain.   580
His master's cattle, swine, and poultry flock,

Horses and sheep and dairy, all his stock,
Were altogether in this Reeve's control.
And by agreement, he had given the sole
Accounting since his lord reached twenty years.   585
No man could ever catch him in arrears.
There wasn't a bailiff, shepherd, or farmer working
But the Reeve knew all his tricks of cheating and shirk-
   ing.
He would not let him draw an easy breath.
They feared him as they feared the very death.   590
He lived in a good house on an open space,
Well shaded by green trees, a pleasant place.
He was shrewder in acquisition than his lord.
With private riches he was amply stored.
He had learned a good trade young by work and will.   595
He was a carpenter of first-rate skill.
On a fine mount, a stallion, dappled gray,
Whose name was Scot, he rode along the way.
He wore a long blue coat hitched up and tied
As if it were a friar's, and at his side   600
A sword with rusty blade was hanging down.
He came from Norfolk, from nearby the town
That men call Bawdswell. As we rode the while,
The Reeve kept always hindmost in our file.

   A Summoner in our company had his place.   605
Red as the fiery cherubim his face.
He was pocked and pimpled, and his eyes were narrow.
He was lecherous and hot as a cock sparrow.
His brows were scabby and black, and thin his beard.
His was a face that little children feared.   610
Brimstone or litharge° bought in any quarter,   oxide
Quicksilver, ceruse, borax, oil of tartar,
No salve nor ointment that will cleanse or bite
Could cure him of his blotches, livid white,
Or the nobs and nubbins sitting on his cheeks.   .615
He loved his garlic, his onions, and his leeks.

He loved to drink the strong wine down blood-red.
Then would he bellow as if he had lost his head,
And when he had drunk enough to parch his drouth,
Nothing but Latin issued from his mouth.   620
He had smattered up a few terms, two or three,
That he had gathered out of some decree—
No wonder; he heard law Latin all the day,
And everyone knows a parrot or a jay
Can cry out "Wat" or "Poll" as well as the pope;   625
But give him a strange term, he began to grope.
His little store of learning was paid out,
So *"Questio quod juris"*[12] he would shout.
He was a goodhearted bastard and a kind one.
If there were better, it was hard to find one.   630
He would let a good fellow, for a quart of wine,
The whole year round enjoy his concubine
Scot-free from summons, hearing, fine, or bail,
And on the sly he too could flush a quail.
If he liked a scoundrel, no matter for church law.   635
He would teach him that he need not stand in awe
If the archdeacon threatened with his curse—
That is, unless his soul was in his purse,
For in his purse he would be punished well.
"The purse," he said, "is the archdeacon's hell."   640
Of course I know he lied in what he said.
There is nothing a guilty man should so much dread
As the curse that damns his soul, when, without fail,
The church can save him, or send him off to jail.[13]
He had the young men and girls in his control   645
Throughout the diocese; he knew the soul
Of youth, and heard their every last design.
A garland big enough to be the sign

[12]*Questio quad juris:* The question is what is the law.
[13]These lines attempt to render the sense and tone of a passage in which Chaucer says literally that a guilty man should be in dread "because a curse will slay just as absolution saves, and he should also beware of a Significavit." This word, according to Robinson, was the first word of a writ remanding an excommunicated person to prison.

Above an alehouse balanced on his head,
And he made a shield of a great round loaf of bread.   650
   There was a Pardoner of Rouncivalle
With him, of the blessed Mary's hospital,
But now come straight from Rome (or so said he).
Loudly he sang, "Come hither, love, to me,"
While the Summoner's counterbass trolled out pro-
     found —   655
No trumpet blew with half so vast a sound.
This Pardoner had hair as yellow as wax,
But it hung as smoothly as a hank of flax.
His locks trailed down in bunches from his head,
And he let the ends about his shoulders spread,   660
But in thin clusters, lying one by one.
Of hood, for rakishness, he would have none,
For in his wallet he kept it safely stowed.
He traveled, as he thought, in the latest mode,
Disheveled. Save for his cap, his head was bare,   665
And in his eyes he glittered like a hare.
A Veronica° was stitched upon his cap,   religious talisman
His wallet lay before him in his lap
Brimful of pardons from the very seat
In Rome. He had a voice like a goat's bleat.   670
He was beardless and would never have a beard.
His cheek was always smooth as if just sheared.
I think he was a gelding or a mare;
But in his trade, from Berwick down to Ware,
No pardoner could beat him in the race,   675
For in his wallet he had a pillow case
Which he represented as Our Lady's veil;
He said he had a piece of the very sail
St. Peter, when he fished in Galilee
Before Christ caught him, used upon the sea.   680
He had a latten cross embossed with stones
And in a glass he carried some pig's bones,
And with these holy relics, when he found
Some village parson grubbing his poor ground,

He would get more money in a single day   685
Than in two months would come the parson's way.
Thus with his flattery and his trumped-up stock
He made dupes of the parson and his flock.
But though his conscience was a little plastic
He was in church a noble ecclesiastic.   690
Well could he read the Scripture or saint's story,
But best of all he sang the offertory,
For he understood that when this song was sung,
Then he must preach, and sharpen up his tongue
To rake in cash, as well he knew the art,   695
And so he sang out gaily, with full heart.
    Now I have set down briefly, as it was,
Our rank, our dress, our number, and the cause
That made our sundry fellowship begin
In Southwark, at this hospitable inn   700
Known as the Tabard, not far from the Bell.
But what we did that night I ought to tell,
And after that our journey, stage by stage,
And the whole story of our pilgrimage.
But first, in justice, do not look askance   705
I plead, nor lay it to my ignorance
If in this matter I should use plain speech
And tell you just the words and style of each,
Reporting all their language faithfully.
For it must be known to you as well as me   710
That whoever tells a story after a man
Must follow him as closely as he can.
If he takes the tale in charge, he must be true
To every word, unless he would find new
Or else invent a thing or falsify.   715
Better some breadth of language than a lie!
He may not spare the truth to save his brother.
He might as well use one word as another.
In Holy Writ Christ spoke in a broad sense,
And surely his word is without offense.   720

Plato,[14] if his are pages you can read,
Says let the word be cousin to the deed.
So I petition your indulgence for it
If I have cut the cloth just as men wore it,
Here in this tale, and shown its very weave.   725
My wits are none too sharp, you must believe.
  Our Host gave each of us a cheerful greeting
And promptly of our supper had us eating.
The victuals that he served us were his best.
The wine was potent, and we drank with zest.   730
Our Host cut such a figure, all in all,
He might have been a marshal in a hall.
He was a big man, and his eyes bulged wide.
No sturdier citizen lived in all Cheapside,
Lacking no trace of manhood, bold in speech,   735
Prudent, and well versed in what life can teach,
And with all this he was a jovial man.
And so when supper ended he began
To jolly us, when all our debts were clear.
"Welcome," he said. "I have not seen this year   740
So merry a company in this tavern as now,
And I would give you pleasure if I knew how.
And just this very minute a plan has crossed
My mind that might amuse you at no cost.
  "You go to Canterbury—may the Lord   745
Speed you, and may the martyred saint reward
Your journey! And to while the time away
You mean to talk and pass the time of day,
For you would be as cheerful all alone
As riding on your journey dumb as stone.   750
Therefore, if you'll abide by what I say,
Tomorrow, when you ride off on your way,
Now, by my father's soul, and he is dead,
If you don't enjoy yourselves, cut off my head!

[14]*Plato:* Greek philosopher

Hold up your hands, if you accept my speech."   755
   Our counsel did not take us long to reach.
We bade him give his orders at his will.
"Well, sirs," he said, "then do not take it ill,
But hear me in good part, and for your sport.
Each one of you, to make our journey short,   760
Shall tell two stories, as we ride, I mean,
Toward Canterbury; and coming home again
Shall tell two other tales he may have heard
Of happenings that some time have occurred.
And the one of you whose stories please us most,   765
Here in this tavern, sitting by this post
Shall sup at our expense while we make merry
When we come riding home from Canterbury.
And to cheer you still the more, I too will ride
With you at my own cost, and be your guide.   770
And if anyone my judgment shall gainsay
He must pay for all we spend along the way.
If you agree, no need to stand and reason.
Tell me, and I'll be stirring in good season."
   This thing was granted, and we swore our pledge   775
To take his judgment on our pilgrimage,
His verdict on our tales, and his advice.
He was to plan a supper at a price
Agreed upon; and so we all assented
To his command, and we were well contented.   780
The wine was fetched; we drank, and went to rest.
   Next morning, when the dawn was in the east,
Up sprang our Host, who acted as our cock,
And gathered us together in a flock,
And off we rode, till presently our pace   785
Had brought us to St. Thomas' watering place.
And there our Host began to check his horse.
"Good sirs," he said, "you know your promise, of course.
Shall I remind you what it was about?
If evensong and matins don't fall out,   790

We'll soon find who shall tell us the first tale.
But as I hope to drink my wine and ale,
Whoever won't accept what I decide
Pays everything we spend along the ride.
Draw lots, before we're farther from the Inn.   795
Whoever draws the shortest shall begin.
Sir Knight," said he, "my master, choose your straw.
Come here, my lady Prioress, and draw,
And you, Sir Scholar, don't look thoughtful, man!
Pitch in now, everyone!" So all began   800
To draw the lots, and as the luck would fall
The draw went to the Knight, which pleased us all.
And when this excellent man saw how it stood,
Ready to keep his promise, he said, "Good!
Since it appears that I must start the game,   805
Why then, the draw is welcome, in God's name.
Now let's ride on, and listen, what I say."
And with that word we rode forth on our way,
And he, with his courteous manner and good cheer,
Began to tell his tale, as you shall hear.   810

1. As a group, the pilgrims represent nearly the whole range of
   life in Chaucer's England. Rank the pilgrims according to their
   social status. Does the order in which Chaucer presents them
   aid you in any way? Who represents the highest and who the
   lowest levels? Among those associated with the church, which
   are religious and which are worldly? Which professional, business, guild, and vocational groups are represented, and by
   whom?
2. When the narrator tells you about each of the pilgrims, is he
   basing his impressions on (a) his meeting with them at the inn,
   or (b) his journey with them to Canterbury? Cite specific details
   which depict manners, behavior, reactions, and the like.
3. How do you account for the high interest appeal of the sketches
   in the Prologue? Does this interest arise from the kinds of people

who are described? From the kind of information you are given about each person? Is it because of the way in which the information is presented? Is it because people are, by nature, curious about other people? As you discuss these possible explanations, support your opinions with specific references to the Prologue.

4. The Prologue to *The Canterbury Tales* establishes the frame Chaucer uses for his tales. What situation brings all the pilgrims together? When do you learn what season of the year it is? Why is the season stressed?

5. What about the Knight confirms the narrator's opinion that he is "a Knight in all things to perfection"? In what ways is the young Squire like his father or very different from him? Compare their interests, histories, and habits. Does the comparison suggest anything about chivalry?

6. By what manners and accomplishments does the Prioress hope to be considered worthy of respect? Do you think she is "putting on airs" or is she naturally genteel? What evidence does the narrator give that she "melted at whatever was piteous"? What impresses him about her appearance? Is he being lightly satirical about the luxuries she enjoys and about her imitation of court behavior? Do her mannerisms seem appropriate for a nun? Support your answers to these questions.

7. Neither the Monk nor the Friar represent the ideals of the Catholic Church in Chaucer's time. What "old-fashioned things" does the Monk let go? To what "new-fangled ideas" does he devote himself, and how are these ideas evident in his appearance? The Friar is also a very merry man. What theories does he have about dealing with the rich and the poor, and how does he apply his theories to his work? What kind of person does the narrator picture him to be? Tell how you know that Chaucer is is being somewhat satirical in his portraits of these two men. What details keep them distinctly individualized?

8. The order of the next four pilgrims—the Merchant, Clerical Student, Lawyer, and Franklin—indicates their importance in English society. What evidence are you given that the Merchant represents a very rich and powerful class? Why is the Student so thin, solemn, and poor? What interests and talents does he have? How has the Lawyer earned the wide reputation he enjoys? What evidence can you find that the narrator is being satirical in each of these descriptions? The Franklin, despite his riches, is described last. Why might this be due to the fact that that he is a sub-vassal? What proof are you given that he lives for pleasure?

9. Each of the five Guildsmen belongs to a different trade; therefore, the uniform that each wears must be that of a social or
religious guild. To which of the new classes do they belong?
How do they and their wives show their enjoyment of their new
position and power? Would their behavior seem surprising today? Are any comparisons with people in our society possible?
Explain.

10. Although the Cook is mentioned only briefly, many have found
his characterization among the most memorable of the Canterbury pilgrims. Through it, Chaucer makes comments on the
Cook, the Guildsmen, and their society. What ironic points does
Chaucer make?

11. One would hardly expect to find a Skipper among the pilgrims,
particularly one who refused to keep "too nice a point of honor."
The narrator calls him a "good fellow," which in Chaucer's day
could mean "a rascal." From the information you are given, what
opinion did you form of him as a person and a sailor?

12. From the narrator's description of the Physician, you are told as
much about the medieval practice of medicine as about the man
himself. A knowledge of astrology was considered necessary
then, since the physician administered treatment during the
hours when the position of the stars and planets was most favorable to the patient. Images representing both the patient and
the signs of the zodiac were widely manufactured and used.
Physicians also assumed that human beings were governed by
four humours: blood (hot), black bile (cold), phlegm (moist),
and yellow bile (dry). When all of these humours were balanced
equally, the individual was the picture of health. Physical and
mental disease could result, however, if one of the humours
began to dominate the other three.

   Generally, physicans were believed to have more faith in
ancient science than in the Bible. What reason do you have for
believing that the Physician described here was, or was not, as
learned and honest as most fourteenth-century physicians?

13. In Chaucer's day, a pilgrimage was a favorite form of traveling
for pleasure, and provisions were made for the pilgrims' safety
and comfort. Consequently, one who had been on a great many
pilgrimages might be either extremely devout or extremely
frivolous. Why do you think the Wife of Bath joined the pilgrimage to Canterbury? In what accomplishments does she take
pride? From the details about her appearance and behavior,
what kind of person do you suspect her of being?

14. How are both the parish Priest and his brother, the Plowman,

different from any other pilgrims described so far? In what ways does each demonstrate that he loves God with all his heart? Do you think Chaucer does, or does not, intend to represent the Priest as an "ideal Christian"? Explain.

15. In Chaucer's day a person's physiognomy—the features of the face or the form of the body—was believed to indicate his character or personality. In the case of the Miller, his big-boned, stocky body, his beard, and his flat nose indicate a shameless, talkative, and quarrelsome fellow. If you had been the narrator, what—if anything—would you have found worthy of admiration?

16. Both the Manciple and the Reeve know how to use their talents to their own profit. What impression do you gain of the Manciple and of the narrator's attitude toward him? Why is the Reeve trusted by his lord and feared by those who are under him? What character or personality do you think is indicated by his physiognomy?

17. Of all the pilgrims, the Summoner and the Pardoner are probably the greatest rascals. How does each take advantage of his connection with the church to fill his own purse? How are the two rascals alike and different in appearance and behavior? Tell why you do, or do not, think that the narrator is being satirical in his portrayal of either the Summoner or the Pardoner.

18. Instead of telling the reader about himself, the narrator makes several requests. What are they? How does it happen that the Host joins the pilgrims? To what plan do they all agree? Why is the Host well qualified to serve as manager of the pilgrimage and as judge of the tales recounted?

THE PARDONER'S TALE

There was a company of young folk living
One time in Flanders, who were bent on giving
Their lives to follies and extravagances,
Brothels and taverns, where they held their dances
With lutes, harps, and guitars, diced at all hours,   5
And also ate and drank beyond their powers,
Through which they paid the devil sacrifice
In the devil's temple with their drink and dice,
Their abominable excess and dissipation.
They swore oaths that were worthy of damnation;   10
It was grisly to be listening when they swore. . . .
   These three young roisterers of whom I tell
Long before prime had rung from any bell
Were seated in a tavern at their drinking,
And as they sat, they heard a bell go clinking   15
Before a corpse being carried to his grave.
One of these roisterers, when he heard it, gave
An order to his boy: "Go out and try
To learn whose corpse is being carried by.
Get me his name, and get it right. Take heed."   20
   "Sir," said the boy, "there isn't any need.
I learned before you came here, by two hours.
He was, it happens, an old friend of yours,
And all at once, there on his bench upright
As he was sitting drunk, he was killed last night.   25
A sly thief, Death men call him, who deprives
All the people in this country of their lives,
Came with his spear and smiting his heart in two
Went on his business with no more ado.
A thousand have been slaughtered by his hand   30
During this plague. And, sir, before you stand
Within his presence, it should be necessary,
It seems to me, to know your adversary.

Be evermore prepared to meet this foe.
My mother taught me thus; that's all I know." 35
    "Now by St. Mary," said the innkeeper,
"This child speaks truth. Man, woman, laborer,
Servant, and child the thief has slain this year
In a big village a mile or more from here.
I think it is his place of habitation. 40
It would be wise to make some preparation
Before he brought a man into disgrace."
    "God's arms!" this roisterer said. "So that's the case!
Is it so dangerous with this thief to meet?
I'll look for him by every path and street, 45
I vow it, by God's holy bones! Hear me,
Fellows of mine, we are all one, we three.
Let each of us hold up his hand to the other
And each of us become his fellow's brother.
We'll slay this Death, who slaughters and betrays. 50
He shall be slain whose hand so many slays,
By the dignity of God, before tonight!"
    The three together set about to plight
Their oaths to live and die each for the other
Just as though each had been to each born brother, 55
And in their drunken frenzy up they get
And toward the village off at once they set
Which the innkeeper had spoken of before,
And many were the grisly oaths they swore.
They rent Christ's precious body limb from limb— 60
Death shall be dead, if they lay hands on him!
    When they had hardly gone the first half mile,
Just as they were about to cross a stile,
An old man, poor and humble, met them there.
The old man greeted them with a meek air 65
And said, "God bless you, lords, and be your guide."
    "What's this?" the proudest of the three replied.
"Old beggar, I hope you meet with evil grace!
Why are you all wrapped up except your face?

What are you doing alive so many a year?"   70
    The old man at these words began to peer
Into this gambler's face. "Because I can,
Though I should walk to India, find no man,"
He said, "in any village or any town,
Who for my age is willing to lay down   75
His youth. So I must keep my old age still
For as long a time as it may be God's will.
Nor will Death take my life from me, alas!
Thus like a restless prisoner I pass
And on the ground, which is my mother's gate,   80
I walk and with my staff both early and late
I knock and say, 'Dear mother, let me in!
See how I vanish, flesh, and blood, and skin!
Alas, when shall my bones be laid to rest?
I would exchange with you my clothing chest,   85
Mother, that in my chamber long has been
For an old haircloth rag to wrap me in.'
And yet she still refuses me that grace.
All white, therefore, and withered is my face.
    "But, sirs, you do yourselves no courtesy   90
To speak to an old man so churlishly
Unless he had wronged you either in word or deed.
As you yourselves in Holy Writ may read,
'Before an aged man whose head is hoar
Men ought to rise.' I counsel you, therefore,   95
No harm nor wrong here to an old man do,
No more than you would have men do to you
In your old age, if you so long abide.
And God be with you, whether you walk or ride!
I must go yonder where I have to go."   100
    "No, you old beggar, by St. John, not so,"
Said another of these gamblers. "As for me,
By God, you won't get off so easily!
You spoke just now of that false traitor, Death,
Who in this land robs all our friends of breath.   105

Tell where he is, since you must be his spy,
Or you will suffer for it, so say I
By God and by the holy sacrament.
You are in league with him, false thief, and bent
On killing us young folk, that's clear to my mind." 110
    "If you are so impatient, sirs, to find
Death," he replied, "turn up this crooked way,
For in that grove I left him, truth to say,
Beneath a tree, and there he will abide.
No boast of yours will make him run and hide. 115
Do you see that oak tree? Just there you will find
This Death, and God, who bought again mankind,
Save and amend you!" So said this old man;
And promptly each of these three gamblers ran
Until he reached the tree, and there they found 120
Florins of fine gold, minted bright and round,
Nearly eight bushels of them, as they thought.
And after Death no longer then they sought.
Each of them was so ravished at the sight,
So fair the florins glittered and so bright, 125
That down they sat beside the precious hoard.
The worst of them, he uttered the first word.
    "Brothers," he told them, "listen to what I say.
My head is sharp, for all I joke and play.
Fortune has given us this pile of treasure 130
To set us up in lives of ease and pleasure.
Lightly it comes, lightly we'll make it go.
God's precious dignity! Who was to know
We'd ever tumble on such luck today?
If we could only carry this gold away, 135
Home to my house, or either one of yours—
For well you know that all this gold is ours—
We'd touch the summit of felicity.
But still, by daylight that can hardly be.
People would call us thieves, too bold for stealth, 140
And they would have us hanged for our own wealth.

It must be done by night, that's our best plan,
As prudently and slyly as we can.
Hence my proposal is that we should all
Draw lots, and let's see where the lot will fall,   145
And the one of us who draws the shortest stick
Shall run back to the town, and make it quick,
And bring us bread and wine here on the sly,
And two of us will keep a watchful eye
Over this gold; and if he doesn't stay   150
Too long in town, we'll carry this gold away
By night, wherever we all agree it's best."
   One of them held the cut out in his fist
And had them draw to see where it would fall,
And the cut fell on the youngest of them all.   155
At once he set off on his way to town,
And the very moment after he was gone
The one who urged this plan said to the other:
"You know that by sworn oath you are my brother.
I'll tell you something you can profit by.   160
Our friend has gone, that's clear to any eye,
And here is gold, abundant as can be,
That we propose to share alike, we three.
But if I worked it out, as I could do,
So that it could be shared between us two,   165
Wouldn't that be a favor, a friendly one?"
   The other answered, "How that can be done,
I don't quite see. He knows we have the gold.
What shall we do, or what shall he be told?"
   "Will you keep the secret tucked inside your head?   170
And in a few words," the first scoundrel said,
"I'll tell you how to bring this end about."
   "Granted," the other told him. "Never doubt,
I won't betray you, that you can believe."
   "Now," said the first, "we are two, as you perceive,   175
And two of us must have more strength than one.
When he sits down, get up as if in fun

And wrestle with him. While you play this game
I'll run him through the ribs. You do the same
With your dagger there, and then this gold shall be   180
Divided, dear friend, between you and me.
Then all that we desire we can fulfill,
And both of us can roll the dice at will."
Thus in agreement these two scoundrels fell
To slay the third, as you have heard me tell.   185
   The youngest, who had started off to town,
Within his heart kept rolling up and down
The beauty of these florins, new and bright.
"O Lord," he thought, "were there some way I might
Have all this treasure to myself alone,   190
There isn't a man who dwells beneath God's throne
Could live a life as merry as mine should be!"
And so at last the fiend, our enemy,
Put in his head that he could gain his ends
If he bought poison to kill off his friends.   195
Finding his life in such a sinful state,
The devil was allowed to seal his fate.
For it was altogether his intent
To kill his friends, and never to repent.
So off he set, no longer would he tarry,   200
Into the town, to an apothecary,
And begged for poison; he wanted it because
He meant to kill his rats; besides, there was
A polecat living in his hedge, he said,
Who killed his capons; and when he went to bed   205
He wanted to take vengeance, if he might,
On vermin that devoured him by night.
   The apothecary answered, "You shall have
A drug that as I hope the Lord will save
My soul, no living thing in all creation,   210
Eating or drinking of this preparation
A dose no bigger than a grain of wheat,
But promptly with his death-stroke he shall meet.

Die, that he will, and in a briefer while
Than you can walk the distance of a mile,   215
This poison is so strong and virulent."
    Taking the poison, off the scoundrel went,
Holding it in a box, and next he ran
To the neighboring street, and borrowed from a man
Three generous flagons. He emptied out his drug   220
In two of them, and kept the other jug
For his own drink; he let no poison lurk
In that! And so all night he meant to work
Carrying off the gold. Such was his plan,
And when he had filled them, this accursed man   225
Retraced his path, still following his design,
Back to his friends with his three jugs of wine.
    But why dilate upon it any more?
For just as they had planned his death before,
Just so they killed him, and with no delay.   230
When it was finished, one spoke up to say:
"Now let's sit down and drink, and we can bury
His body later on. First we'll be merry,"
And as he said the words, he took the jug
That, as it happened, held the poisonous drug,   235
And drank, and gave his friend a drink as well,
And promptly they both died. But truth to tell,
In all that Avicenna ever wrote
He never described in chapter, rule, or note
More marvelous signs of poisoning, I suppose,   240
That appeared in these two wretches at the close.
Thus they both perished for their homicide,
And thus the traitorous poisoner also died. . . .

1. When the old man sends the three rioters to the oak tree, do you
   think he knows what is there and what the outcome will be? How
   do you explain his knowing where Death is and what Death will
   do? Is the old man a real person or an apparition? What does he
   contribute to the plot of the tale and to the mood?

2. What leads the three rioters to pledge their faith together and to rush off toward the village mentioned by the tavern keeper? What possible reasons might they have?

3. Why do they accuse the old man of being Death's spy? What favor does his "mother" refuse him though he knocks with his stick? Who is this "mother"? What information does he give the three rioters that ends their search for Death? Tell why you think he is, or is not, the messenger of Death.

4. What reason does the worst of the three rioters give for drawing straws? When the youngest leaves, what do the others agree to do? By what trick does the youngest hope to accomplish the same wicked deed? Why is the outcome of all this intrigue especially ironic?

5. What kinds of wickedness would this tale serve to illustrate? How is the ending of the story related to the rioters' pledge of faith at the tavern and their determination to "slay this false traitor Death"? What general truth or commentary on life and people do you think was brought out through this tale?

6. This tale has been called the best short story in existence. If this is true, then it should have the following characteristics: compactness, skillful creation of mood and character, swift rising action, high suspense, and dramatic climax. Discuss and evaluate each of these traits and then tell whether you think this tale merits such high praise.

7. Why is the pledge of faith among the three rioters ironic? What is ironic about their finding gold when they expect to find Death, and about the youngest rioter's intention to get all the treasure by poisoning the other two? Why is the ending especially ironic? In your opinion is the irony in this tale humorous or satirical, or both? Discuss.

THE ELIZABETHANS

The Renaissance did not take root in England until the 1500's, but for more than a century thereafter, that country enjoyed one of the most brilliant periods in its history. The crowning artistic achievement of the English Renaissance was its literature, which expressed the national spirit in a voice that was popular and, at the same time, versatile and mature. The number of gifted writers, fired by enthusiasm for their own time, would do credit to any period. Towering above them all was William Shakespeare, supremely representative of his age yet unique in his own genius.

The term *Renaissance*, which means "rebirth," is a convenient historical label for describing the revival of interest in the classical ideas of ancient Greece and Rome. Actually, the Renaissance was a natural outgrowth of the medieval period but with traditions which reached far back into the past. Thus, the Renaissance combined an awakening of old interests with the cultivation of new ones.

In England, there had been a brief flurry of the Renaissance spirit as early as the fourteenth century, when Geoffrey Chaucer returned from his visit to Italy full of excitement about the new literature. At that time, the Renaissance in Italy was, in fact, well advanced. The literary works of Dante,

Petrarch, and Boccaccio commanded as much popular interest as Italy's outstanding achievements in painting and sculpture. Chaucer created in *The Canterbury Tales* a work equal to that of any of his Italian contemporaries, but conditions in England did not encourage the continued growth of the Renaissance. After Chaucer's death in 1400, England was plagued by civil war for almost a century. Coming hard upon England's war with France, this civil war left the English people neither time, wealth, nor inclination to pursue those cultural interests that were occupying people on the Continent. Not until 1485, when many differences were settled and the Tudor line was established on the throne, could Englishmen begin to catch up with the rapidly changing world.

Even then, it took England over a hundred years to reach its place in the sun. When the first Tudor king, Henry VII, came to power, he began to repair his country's situation. His willful son, Henry VIII, in many respects a typical "man of the Renaissance," further consolidated England's position. The religious controversy that marked his rule and led to the establishment of the Church of England continued under his Catholic daughter Mary, and then under his Protestant daughter Elizabeth. Although the early years of Elizabeth's reign sometimes bogged down in seemingly insoluble problems, the defeat of the Spanish Armada in 1588 brought England to a position of pre-eminence in the Renaissance world. Not only had the country arrived as an economic leader and a great sea power; it had also developed an intellectual and cultural life unrivaled anywhere in Europe at that time.

The heady feeling of living in a "brave new world" had many sources, some in the glories of the past, others in the potentialities of the future. The classical world of the past began to unfold as the study of Greek and Latin was brought back to England by university scholars who had studied on the Continent. There they had profited by instruction from Greek scholars who had fled to Italy after Constantinople fell to the Turks in 1453. An international community of scholars made the Renaissance the great age of translation. This art of translation served not only to revive the past but also to prepare for the future. Religious reformers used their knowledge of Greek to produce more accurate renditions of the Scriptures. The habit of study, because it searched out answers to the fundamental questions that concerned men at the time, fostered the intellectual and moral courage that was an outstanding trait of Renaissance man.

The horizons of the sixteenth century were also broadened geographically by discoveries and explorations that enriched the coffers of England and satisfied men's highest sense of adventure. The nature of this economic expansion was particularly congenial to a seafaring people like the English, who used fair means and foul to win supremacy at sea. Their success fed a growing nationalism. When, by a combination of seamanship and luck, England defeated the Spanish Armada, Englishmen were bursting with pride in their country and in their queen. Elizabeth, though her ways at court were often devious and cruel, did not disappoint her subjects. Through her patronage of the arts, she gave material and political support to one of the most creative periods in history. She also did honor to herself; for, since her reign, the whole sweep of the Renaissance in England has come to be known as the Elizabethan period.

Renaissance writers, unlike those of some other periods, seemed always to be in the mainstream of life. Shakespeare's opinions on many subjects may not be clear from his plays, but there is never any question about the wide range of his interests as a man of affairs. The acquisition of learning became more possible in the sixteenth century with the widespread use of the printing press. Travel, and the books which travelers wrote about their experiences, helped prevent Englishmen from being narrow-minded and provincial. The opening of new trade routes around the world introduced fresh ideas as well as a new source of income into English life. Advances in science, especially the Copernican theory upsetting the old notion that the sun revolved around the earth, gave new dimensions to man's universe.

At first, Renaissance poetry in England was strictly amateur —written for the love of it—and began as "translation, imitation, and emulation" of Italian and French favorites. Two poets deserving special mention were the young courtiers,

Sir Thomas Wyatt and Henry Howard, Earl of Surrey, who popularized the Italian or Petrachan sonnet form in England. Their poems, with those of several other gentlemen, were printed in 1557 in *The Book of Songs and Sonnets* that became known, after the name of its publisher, as *Tottel's Miscellany*. Previously these poems had circulated among friends in manuscript only, but they were so popular—the book went through eight printings—that numerous collections followed. The writing of lyric verse became so fashionable that a lyric outburst occurred, unparalleled in the history of English literature for both the quantity and quality of the poetry. When given appropriate musical setting—a common occurrence—the language of lyric poetry sang as it had never sung before.

One of the first in a long line of distinguished poets was SIR PHILIP SIDNEY, in many ways the living model of the Renaissance ideal. Besides being a distinguished poet, he was a helpful patron of poets, a discerning critic, and a stout defender of poetry. Sidney wrote the first sonnet sequence in the English language, *Astrophel and Stella*, which recounted the progress of a "mainly imaginary but partly real" love affair. After Wyatt and Surrey had introduced the sonnet form into England, it had fallen into some neglect. Sidney revived it, going directly to Petrarch's works for his model and, in turn, providing a model for Spenser, whose sonnets were written some years after Sidney's.

EDMUND SPENSER has been variously described as a "poet's poet," the "magic mirror of the English Renaissance," the "greatest non-dramatic poet of the Elizabethan Period." Although he came from a modest family, he had an excellent education that included study of the Greek philosophers, the Italian and French poets, and Chaucer. Spenser's most famous work, *The Faerie Queen*, is an elaborate allegory. For this work he developed a new stanza form—subsequently known as the Spenserian stanza—which was a favorite with several distinguished poets. But though *The Faerie Queen* was much admired and deeply influential in his day, and his "sensuous imagery and verbal magic" still delight literary scholars, modern readers find greater enjoyment in Spenser's excellent sonnets.

CHRISTOPHER MARLOWE made good use of poetry to celebrate love and immortality. Despite his short and stormy life — he died at the age of twenty-nine — he wrote several important plays in which he "made blank verse a flexible and powerful speech." A later Renaissance writer, Ben Jonson, paid tribute to "Marlowe's mighty line," and Shakespeare is considered indebted to Marlowe, with whom he may have collaborated. Marlowe also translated Ovid's *Amores* and composed a love poem of his own, *Hero and Leander.*

Another poet who could never be accused of having an "earth-creeping mind" was SIR WALTER RALEIGH. His life was longer than Marlowe's and filled with even greater extremes of fortune. In those lyrics definitely traced to him is a note of bitterness, probably the result of his experiences. Although he was looked upon as an ideal Renaissance courtier and adventurer, he did not, like Sidney, die a hero. James I had him executed in 1618 on a charge of conspiracy.

Of course, the greatest figure of the Elizabethan period — and perhaps of all English literature — was WILLIAM SHAKESPEARE. Poet, actor, and playwright, Shakespeare would not have been human if, during the first ten to fifteen years after his arrival in London, he had not experienced loves and hates, moments of exhilaration and moments of despair, doubts, jealousies, attractions, revulsions. In those same years he wrote his 154 sonnets, using a form which his age and country borrowed from Italy and which was devised for the purpose of expressing the personal feelings of the poet. For many, however, Shakespeare's greatest poetry is the blank verse to be found in his plays. Here the full range of his interests and powerful imagination becomes dramatically evident.

Thus, from beginning to end, the English Renaissance in literature was characterized by a respect for classical learning that was combined with a boldness of experimentation. Renaissance writers seemed always to be in the act of discovering themselves and the world. They made of the English language a superb instrument for expressing the full man. What was most precious to them was not a freedom to withdraw from life or to rebel against it. It was a freedom to experience life and to participate in it as fully as possible.

Approximately two hundred poets have been identified

with the Elizabethan Period, a number that attests to the widespread popularity and practice of the art. Love, patriotism,
comradeship, the joys of the pastoral life — all were favorite
themes, but love was the most popular. The period produced
other kinds of writing as well — plays, travel accounts, satirical
pamphlets, and religious tracts — but the outstanding achievement of early Renaissance literature was the development of
lyric poetry.

Sir Philip Sidney

The first of these two sonnets is from *Astrophel and Stella*, Sidney's sonnet sequence supposedly inspired by Penelope Devereux, whom the poet had known since she was thirteen and who was married in 1581 to an elderly man, Lord Rich. Partially because of the influence of this sonnet sequence, unrequited love became in Elizabethan poetry the most familiar theme for the sonnet. The second poem appeared in *Arcadia*, a novel which exerted on English prose as strong an influence as *Astrophel and Stella* had on English poetry.

WITH HOW SAD STEPS, O MOON

With how sad steps, O Moon, thou climb'st the skies!
How silently, and with how wan a face!
What, may it be that even in heav'nly place
That busy archer° his sharp arrows tries?   Cupid
Sure, if that long-with-love-acquainted eyes   5
Can judge of love, thou feel'st a lover's case.
I read it in thy looks; thy languished grace,   shows
To me that feel the like, thy state descries.°
Then, ev'n of fellowship,[1] O Moon, tell me,
Is constant love deemed there but want of wit?°   good sense 10
Are beauties there as proud as here they be?
Do they above love to be loved, and yet
Those lovers scorn whom that love doth possess?
Do they call virtue there ungratefulness?

[1] *even of fellowship:* equal as we friends are

1. Analyze in what respects Sidney observes the conventions of the Petrarchan sonnet, both in form and content.
2. By addressing the Moon as though it could hear and understand him, what poetic device is Sidney using? What other human attributes does he assign to the Moon?
3. What similarities does Sidney see between his own feelings and state and those of the Moon? Does he find any comfort in this "fellowship"? Explain.
4. Note that the sestet is comprised of a series of questions. What feeling about his own situation apparently prompts the poet to ask these questions? Are they merely rhetorical questions, or do you think he expects to find answers to them? If the latter, what answers might the Moon give him—assuming it could speak?

MY TRUE LOVE HATH MY HEART

My true love hath my heart, and I have his,
By just exchange one to the other given:
I hold his dear, and mine he cannot miss,
There never was a better bargain driven:
His heart in me keeps him and me in one,   5
My heart in him his thoughts and senses guides:
He loves my heart, for once it was his own,
I cherish his because in me it bides:
His heart his wound receivèd from my sight;
My heart was wounded with his wounded heart;   10
For as from me, on him his hurt did light,
So still methought in me his hurt did smart:
    Both equal hurt, in this change sought our bliss,
    My true love hath my heart, and I have his.

1. This love song displays the kind of play on words that intrigued writers of the English Renaissance. Within the central idea or conceit—the exchange of hearts—Sidney explores the many facets that this idea suggests. What words in line 4 reinforce the idea expressed in line 2?

2. How does this exchange bind the lovers intellectually and emotionally? Why is pain involved in this exchange? In what way does this pain make the exchange "just"?

3. A close analysis of Sidney's language can do much to explain the involved feeling which the poem conveys. Count the number of times the word *heart* is used. Tell why you think the repetition is, or is not, more effective than the use of synonyms. Note the other words Sidney used. Describe the impression conveyed by the words.

4. This poem suggests the intricacy of a puzzle, primarily because of Sidney's manipulation of the language. How many sentences are there in the entire poem? What is the structure of each line? Is the sense of an idea ordinarily completed within a line or is it carried over to succeeding lines? Are the lines within the total sentence pattern logically independent of each other? Discuss.

5. Who is the speaker in this sonnet? What idea do you think the poet intended to bring out? What attitude does the poem convey toward the person about whom he is writing?

Edmund Spenser

Although Spenser was a profoundly moral and serious man, his short poems reveal his love of physical as well as of spiritual beauty. His sonnets illustrate the richness, subtlety, and sustaining power of Spenser's poetic gifts. Following are two of the eighty-eight sonnets that comprise the *Amoretti*, Spenser's sequence of love poems addressed to Elizabeth Boyle, who later became his wife.

WHAT GUILE IS THIS

What guile is this, that those her golden tresses,
    she doth attire under a net of gold:
    and with sly skill so cunningly them dresses,
    that which is gold or hair, may scarce be told?
Is it that men's frail eyes, which gaze too bold,   5
    she may entangle in that golden snare:
    and being caught may craftily enfold,
    their weaker hearts, which are not well aware?
Take heed therefore, mine eyes, how ye do stare
    henceforth too rashly on that guileful net,   10
    in which, if ever ye entrappèd are,
    out of bands ye by no means shall get.
Fondness° it were for any being free,   foolishness
    to covet fetters,° though they golden be,   chains

104

1. Renaissance poetry is noted for its use of conceits. (See page 506.) On what conceit is this sonnet based? Who is guilty of the guile? What does the speaker in the poem think that "she" hopes to accomplish by it? To what does *them* refer in line 3? Of what are "weaker hearts" not well aware? What double meaning is suggested by the word *net*?
2. Make a list of the words in the octave which are closely associated with the meaning of the poem and at the same time contribute to the poem's conceit, such as *sly* and *entangle*. What attitude on the part of the speaker do they suggest?
3. To whom is the sestet addressed? What is its purpose? What observation is expressed in the closing couplet? Is the tone of the sestet similar to that of the octave? If not, how has it changed?
4. Do you think the poet is serious about not wanting to be fettered? Or is his warning to "take heed" merely part of the conceit? Support your opinion by referring to words and lines in the sonnet.

ONE DAY I WROTE HER NAME

One day I wrote her name upon the strand,
    but came the waves and washèd it away:
    Again I wrote it with a second hand,
    but came the tide, and made my pains his prey.
Vain man, said she, that dost in vain assay°   attempt 5
    a mortal thing so to immortalize,
    for I myself shall like to this decay,
    and eek° my name be wipèd out likewise.   also
Not so, (quoth I) let baser things devise°   be left
    to die in dust, but you shall live by fame: 10
    my verse your virtues rare shall eternize,°   make eternal
    and in the heavens write your glorious name.
Where whenas death shall all the world subdue,
    our love shall live, and later life renew.

1. What theme do you think the poet intends the poem to convey? State the theme in your own words. What relationship can you see

between the theme and the excitement about language which is characteristic of the Renaissance period?

2. Note that the quality of the language in this sonnet is different from that of the preceding sonnet. Make separate lists of the adjectives and adverbs in each of the two poems. Then compare the two lists, noting the number and kind of words they contain. You can learn much about both poems from such a comparison.

3. Now look at the nouns and verbs in this sonnet. Would you describe them as plain or fancy, soft or hard, long or short? Discuss the effect that the poet's choice of words has on the meaning and the tone.

4. Alliteration can also add to the effect by emphasizing a particular sound, such as the *w* sound in this line: "But came the *w*aves and *w*ashèd it a*w*ay." Point out other examples of alliteration.

5. The same line also illustrates the poet's use of assonance, in the repetition of the long and short *a* sounds: "But c*a*me the w*a*ves *a*nd w*a*shèd it aw*a*y." In what other lines did he use assonance to enrich the melodiousness of the poem?

THE PASSIONATE SHEPHERD
TO HIS LOVE

CHRISTOPHER MARLOWE

These companion pieces illustrate both the romantic and realistic strains in Renaissance poetry. Marlowe's poem inspired several replies. Sir Walter Raleigh's was one of the best.

Come live with me, and be my love;
And we will all the pleasures prove
That hills and valleys, dales and fields,
Woods, or steepy mountain yields.

And we will sit upon the rocks,   5
Seeing the shepherds feed their flocks
By shallow rivers, to whose falls
Melodious birds sing madrigals.°   melodies

And I will make thee beds of roses,
And a thousand fragrant posies;   10
A cap of flowers, and a kirtle°   skirt
Embroidered all with leaves of myrtle;

A gown made of the finest wool
Which from our pretty lambs we pull;
Fair-lined slippers for the cold,   15
With buckles of the purest gold;

A belt of straw and ivy-buds,
With coral clasps and amber studs;
And if these pleasures may thee move,
Come live with me, and be my love.   20

The shepherd-swains shall dance and sing
For thy delight each May morning;
If these delights thy mind may move,
Then live with me, and be my love.

The Nymph's Reply to the Shepherd

SIR WALTER RALEIGH

If all the world and love were young,
And truth in every shepherd's tongue,
These pretty pleasures might me move
To live with thee and be thy love.

Time drives the flocks from field to fold, 5
When rivers rage and rocks grow cold,
And Philomel[1] becometh dumb;
The rest complains of cares to come.

The flowers do fade, and wanton fields
To wayward winter reckoning yields; 10
A honey tongue, a heart of gall,
Is fancy's spring, but sorrow's fall.

Thy gowns, thy shoes, thy beds of roses,
Thy cap, thy kirtle,° and thy posies   skirt
Soon break, soon wither, soon forgotten, 15
In folly ripe, in reason rotten.

[1]*Philomel:* the nightingale; in Greek mythology, an Athenian princess who, after her tongue was cruelly torn out, was changed into a nightingale

Thy belt of straw and ivy buds,
Thy coral clasps and amber studs,
All these in me no means can move
To come to thee and be thy love.   20

But could youth last and love still breed,
Had joys no date nor age no need,
Then these delights my mind might move
To live with thee and be thy love.

The Passionate Shepherd

1. Pastoral poems like Marlowe's reflect the intense interest of Renaissance writers in classical poetry of the same type. Such poems picture an idealized countryside, inhabited by shepherds and shepherdesses as lovely as their surroundings. What pretty inducements does the shepherd offer his loved one if she will share her life with him?
2. Which of these proffered gifts might be less desirable than they, at first, appear to be? Which are not so easily obtainable as the "passionate shepherd" seems to assume?
3. Although the poem can be easily criticized as impossibly romantic, it has nevertheless exerted a very real charm for several centuries. Movement, for one thing, enhances the poem's musical quality. Scan the first quatrain to discover the metrical length of each line. How does this length differ from the pentameter of all the preceding poems? Which line moves faster, the longer or the shorter?
4. The rhyme scheme, one of the simplest, depends on eye rhymes in some instances and on both masculine and feminine rhymes. Point out examples of each.
5. Do you think that the poet used feminine rhymes intentionally about halfway through the poem? What does this change in accent add to, or detract from, the total effect of the poem?

The Nymph's Reply

1. In his reply, do you think Raleigh assumed Marlowe's poem was sincere? Support your answer with evidence from the poem.

2. Compare the form of this poem with that of Marlowe's. In what respects do they parallel each other? Point out any variation, however slight.
3. Look closely at Raleigh's point-by-point answer to the shepherd's appeal. Discuss each point. Did Raleigh overlook anything? Cite examples where he paraphrased Marlowe's lines.
4. What is the central idea on which Raleigh has the nymph base her refusal of the shepherd's proposal?
5. "Imitation is the sincerest flattery." In what respects does Raleigh's poem flatter Marlowe's?
6. What merits does Raleigh's poem possess independently of the poem which inspired it? In your opinion, could it stand by itself?

William Shakespeare

Shakespeare's sonnets, when considered as a group, appear to tell a kind of story. The early ones express his strong feelings of regard for a nameless friend, a young man, presumably of the nobility, who may have been Shakespeare's benefactor. This young friend is urged to marry and have children, so that in them his physical beauty and his admirable personal qualities will be preserved. These sonnets also reveal Shakespeare's hope that "in black ink" — that is, in verse — he himself may help to preserve his friend's qualities for future ages. For a time the friendship between the two young men is interrupted by a mysterious rival poet who came between them. Shakespeare then made a journey — perhaps a brief return to Stratford. The sonnets of this period suggest a rivalry between Shakespeare and his friend over a nameless lady. A note of cynicism is now evident as Shakespeare experienced, and gave magnificent expression to, the "ups and downs" of life. He alternated between a zest for life and a disgust with it and with himself. The later sonnets in the series are addressed to a woman — the famous and mysterious "dark lady of the sonnets."

Shall I Compare Thee to a Summer's Day?

SONNET 18

Shall I compare thee to a summer's day?
Thou art more lovely and more temperate.
Rough winds do shake the darling buds of May,
And summer's lease hath all too short a date.°   term
Sometime too hot the eye of heaven shines,   5

111

And often is his gold complexion dimned;
And every fair° from fair sometime declines,   beauty
By chance, or nature's changing course, untrimmed.
But thy eternal summer shall not fade
Nor lose possession of that fair thou ow'st°,   own 10
Nor shall Death brag thou wand'rest in his shade
When in eternal lines to time thou grow'st.
  So long as men can breathe or eyes can see,
  So long lives this, and this gives life to thee.

1. This is the first of the sonnets in which the poet expresses bold confidence in the power of his own verse. What tremendous feat does he assert that it will accomplish? Do you think the poet's claim has been justified over the intervening centuries?
2. From what familiar field of activity is the image in line 4 drawn? What does this line mean?
3. In line 9, what is the meaning of "eternal summer"? What does "summer" itself stand for, figuratively, in this context? Explain the significance of "eternal" for the whole poem.
4. In line 11, Death is personified as a braggart. What, literally, would it mean to wander in Death's shade?
5. Rhythm and rhyme are certainly a part of the "magic" of this unusually musical sonnet. Comment on the poet's choice of words for their vowel and consonant sounds and on his arrangement of the words.

WHEN IN DISGRACE WITH FORTUNE AND MEN'S EYES

SONNET 29

When, in disgrace with Fortune and men's eyes,
I all alone beweep my outcast state,
And trouble deaf heaven with my bootless° cries,   useless
And look upon myself and curse my fate,
Wishing me like to one more rich in hope,   5
Featured like him, like him with friends possessed,

Desiring this man's art, and that man's scope,
With what I most enjoy contented least;
Yet in these thoughts myself almost despising,
Haply° I think on thee, and then my state,   by chance 10
Like to the lark at break of day arising
From sullen earth, sings hymns at heaven's gate;
   For thy sweet love remembered such wealth brings
   That then I scorn to change my state with kings.

1. This is probably the best known and most frequently reprinted of all Shakespeare's sonnets. Yet it is no richer in imagery, color, or the music of poetry than any one of fifty or more. What, then, do you think accounts for its favored place?
2. What condition of mind and spirit does the poet describe in the first eight lines? How can one be in disgrace with "fortune" and with "men's eyes"? What other details strikingly reveal the poet's mood?
3. In lines 5-7, how many persons does the poet envy—one, two, three or more?
4. What change in the poet's spirit or "state" is indicated in lines 10-12? What is responsible for this change?
5. The English lark flies so high, singing as it rises, that the song can be heard though its source cannot be seen. With this fact in mind, tell why the image, "sings hymns at heaven's gate," is perfectly suited to the meaning the poet wanted to convey. State the theme of the sonnet in your own words.

WHEN TO THE SESSIONS
OF SWEET SILENT THOUGHT

SONNET 30

When to the sessions of sweet silent thought
I summon up remembrance of things past,
I sigh the lack of many a thing I sought,
And with old woes new wail my dear time's waste.

Then can I drown an eye (unused to flow) 5
For precious friends hid in death's dateless night,
And weep afresh love's long since cancelled woe,
And moan th' expense of many a vanished sight.
Then can I grieve at grievances foregone,° past
And heavily from woe to woe tell o'er 10
The sad account of fore-bemoanèd° moan, previously
Which I new pay as if not paid before. lamented
  But if the while I think on thee, dear friend,
  All losses are restored and sorrows end.

1. The theme in this sonnet is the same as that in Sonnet 29, but the two poems differ in the way in which the theme is developed. At what point in this sonnet does the turning point—the change of mood—occur? Where does it occur in Sonnet 29? Which sonnet do you think gives greater impact to the resolution, or "point," of the sonnet?
2. From what field of activity is the image of "sessions" and "summons" drawn? How is this image appropriate to the thought of the poem?
3. Why is death's night "dateless"? What is "love's long since cancelled woe"? Is love itself a "woe"? How can a "vanished sight" be considered an "expense"? The word *expense* sometimes means "waste." Does it here?
4. The poem is especially noteworthy for its use of alliteration. Point out examples of this particular poetic device and tell why you do, or do not, think it effective.
5. Note the repetition of the long "o" sound throughout the poem. Why is this sound appropriate to the mood? Do the vowel sounds in the final couplet suggest a different mood?

THAT TIME OF YEAR
THOU MAYST IN ME BEHOLD

SONNET 73

That time of year thou mayst in me behold
When yellow leaves, or none, or few, do hang
Upon those boughs which shake against the cold,
Bare ruined choirs where late the sweet birds sang.
In me thou see'st the twilight of such day   5
As after sunset fadeth in the west,
Which by and by black night doth take away,
Death's second self, that seals up all in rest.
In me thou see'st the glowing of such fire
That on the ashes of his youth doth lie,   10
As the death-bed whereon it must expire,
Consumed with that which it was nourished by.
   This thou perceiv'st, which makes thy love more strong,
   To love that well which thou must leave ere long.

1. To identify the specific period of life about which the poet is
   writing, what three principal images does he use?
2. Note that the first image is doubly indirect. The poet is not really
   speaking of a "time of year" or season. Neither does he tell you
   directly what this "time of year" is. What details used in developing the image indicate the "time of year"?
3. Tell why you do, or do not, think that the other two principal
   images have the "double indirectness" of the first image.
4. From the evidence given in the sonnet, would you say that the
   poet's main purpose is to tell what time of life he has reached?
   If not, what do you think his purpose is?
5. In many of his sonnets, Shakespeare reveals his concern for the
   passing of his friend's youth and beauty and his hope that he
   might be able to prevent their ultimate destruction. Point out the
   ways in which this sonnet differs both in what concerns the poet
   and what he hopes.

Let Me Not to the Marriage of True Minds

SONNET 116

Let me not to the marriage of true minds
Admit impediments.° Love is not love   obstructions
Which alters when it alteration finds
Or bends with the remover to remove.
O, no! It is an ever-fixed mark°   point of
                                                          reference   5
That looks on tempests and is never shaken;
It is the star to every wand'ring bark,°   ship
Whose worth's unknown, although his height
    be taken.°   determined
Love's not Time's fool,° though rosy lips   plaything
    and cheeks   10
Within his bending sickle's compass° come.   reach
Love alters not with his brief hours and weeks,
But bears it out even to the edge of doom.
    If this be error and upon me proved,
    I never writ, nor no man ever loved.

1. What is meant by a "marriage of true minds"?
2. How do you interpret "alters when it alteration finds" and "bends
   with the remover to remove"?
3. Lines 5-8 develop an image drawn from what field of activity?
   What tribute is paid to love by calling it the "star to every wan-
   d'ring bark"? Of what importance is it to a "wand'ring bark" that
   stars are "ever-fixed"?
4. In many of the sonnets, Shakespeare deplores the waste that Time
   makes of youth and beauty. He finds the seasons of the year, the
   growing things of nature, and even life itself transitory, imperma-
   nent. Keeping these in mind, tell what you believe to be the essential point of this sonnet.
5. Often Shakespeare's mood in the sonnets is playful; his images
   suggest a "tongue-in-cheek" attitude. In the manner in which he
   affirms the power of love in this sonnet, is he jesting and whim-
   sical, or is he serious? What evidence in the poem supports your
   opinion?

My Mistress' Eyes Are Nothing Like the Sun

SONNET 130

My mistress' eyes are nothing like the sun;
Coral is far more red than her lips' red;
If snow be white, why then her breasts are dun;
If hairs be wires, black wires grow on her head.
I have seen roses damasked,° red and white,   variegated 5
But no such roses see I in her cheeks;
And in some perfumes is there more delight
Than in the breath that from my mistress reeks.
I love to hear her speak, yet well I know
That music hath a far more pleasing sound.   10
I grant I never saw a goddess go:
My mistress, when she walks, treads on the ground.
    And yet, by Heaven, I think my love as rare
    As any she belied with false compare.

1. In the tradition of the "conceit," or extravagant image, Elizabethan poets vied with one another in praising the beauty of their real or imaginary beloveds. Shakespeare also indulged in this poetic pastime, both in his sonnets and in his plays. Thus Romeo calls Juliet "fair sun," and likens her eyes to the stars—to the disadvantage of the heavenly lights. Is this poem as unflattering as it seems?
2. Remembering that Shakespeare regularly makes his summarizing point in the sonnet's final couplet, explain how the poet actually gets ahead of all others who strive for the most potent way of praising their ladies.
3. Compare the tone of this sonnet with that of the preceding sonnets. May a poem have a playful manner, yet a serious point? What choices of detail in word or phrase particularly suggest the poet's attitude toward the lady and toward the poem he is composing?
4. Would you expect the mysterious dark-haired lady to be pleased or displeased by this little masterpiece? What details might offend her? Would the ending be powerful enough to placate her?

The poetry of Shakespeare's plays is of two kinds: the lyrics, or songs, sung as musical interludes or to help create a mood, and the stately and often magnificent blank verse spoken by the characters. Shakespeare's songs are noted for their lively grace and delicate musical quality. The extraordinary power of his unrhymed blank verse depends on internal musical devices, original or striking metaphors, and rolling rhythms. Perhaps better than any other English poet, Shakespeare writes lines which are both natural and dignified, and also have great emotional impact.

SONG

O mistress mine, where are you roaming?
O, stay and hear! your true-love's coming,
   That can sing both high and low.
Trip no further, pretty sweeting;
Journeys end in lovers meeting,   5
   Every wise man's son doth know.

What is love? 'Tis not hereafter;
Present mirth hath present laughter;
   What's to come is still unsure:
In delay there lies no plenty;   10
Then come kiss me, sweet and twenty!
   Youth's a stuff will not endure.

FROM *Twelfth Night*

1. Beneath the delightful melody of this little song is a philosophical view of life. Describe that view. What does the singer think of the future? What does he advocate for the present? Why?
2. What is the singer like? How does he woo his sweetheart? Does he make her any promises? Why or why not?

ALL THE WORLD'S A STAGE

All the world's a stage,
And all the men and women merely players.
They have their exits and their entrances,
And one man in his time plays many parts,
His acts being seven ages. At first, the infant   5
Mewling and puking in the nurse's arms.
Then the whining schoolboy, with his satchel
And shining morning face, creeping like snail
Unwillingly to school. And then the lover,
Sighing like furnace, with a woful ballad   10
Made to his mistress' eyebrow. Then a soldier,
Full of strange oaths and bearded like the pard,
Jealous in honour, sudden and quick in quarrel,
Seeking the bubble reputation
Even in the cannon's mouth. And then the justice,   15
In fair round belly with good capon lin'd,
With eyes severe and beard of formal cut,
Full of wise saws and modern instances;
And so he plays his part. The sixth age shifts
Into the lean and slipper'd pantaloon,   20
With spectacles on nose and pouch on side;
His youthful hose, well sav'd, a world too wide
For his shrunk shank, and his big manly voice,
Turning again toward childish treble, pipes
And whistles in his sound. Last scene of all,   25
That ends this strange eventful history,
Is second childishness and mere oblivion,
Sans teeth, sans eyes, sans taste, sans everything.

FROM *As You Like It*

1. Is this speech essentially an optimistic or a pessimistic description of human life? Give reasons why you think it is or is not an accurate picture? Which of the seven "ages" of man seems most attractive or desirable? Why?

2. Does the last line seem a fitting conclusion to this speech or is it unexpectedly blunt? Support your opinion by referring to specific lines in the speech.
3. If you were writing a "stages-of-life" speech would you have more or fewer than seven parts? What would they be?
4. This speech provides an excellent example of an extended metaphor. What is effective about such an elaborate figure of speech? What is dangerous about such a device?
5. When the world is compared to a stage, what does the comparison imply about the world? About life in the world? In what ways is the world like a stage?

TO BE, OR NOT TO BE

To be, or not to be: that is the question:
Whether 'tis nobler in the mind to suffer
The slings and arrows of outrageous fortune,
Or to take arms against a sea of troubles,
And by opposing end them? To die: to sleep;   5
No more; and, by a sleep to say we end
The heart-ache and the thousand natural shocks
That flesh is heir to, 'tis a consummation
Devoutly to be wish'd. To die, to sleep;
To sleep: perchance to dream: ay, there's the rub;   10
For in that sleep of death what dreams may come
When we have shuffled off this mortal coil,
Must give us pause. There's the respect
That makes calamity of so long life;
For who would bear the whips and scorns of time,   15
The oppressor's wrong, the proud man's contumely,° contempt
The pangs of dispriz'd love, the law's delay,
The insolence of office, and the spurns
That patient merit of the unworthy takes,
When he himself might his quietus° make   finishing stroke
With a bare bodkin?° who would fardels° bear, dagger; burdens

To grunt and sweat under a weary life,
But that the dread of something after death,
The undiscover'd country from whose bourn°   boundary
No traveller returns, puzzles the will,   25
And makes us rather bear those ills we have
Than fly to others that we know not of?
Thus conscience° does make cowards of us all;   consciousness
And thus the native hue of resolution
Is sicklied o'er with the pale cast of thought,   30
And enterprises of great pith and moment
With this regard their currents turn awry,
And lose the name of action.

FROM Hamlet

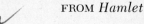

1. What precisely is Hamlet debating with himself in this famous soliloquy? What two alternative ways of living seem possible to him?

2. When Hamlet compares his troubles to a sea, what does he suggest about those troubles? Why are they sea-like? What would happen to anyone who tried to fight a sea with conventional weapons or arms? How would that fight end his troubles?

3. Hamlet traps himself in his own metaphor when he compares death to sleep. What aspects of sleep does he begin to fear that death will duplicate?

4. To what is Hamlet comparing man in the phrase "shuffle off this mortal coil"? What does this line tell you about Hamlet's view of man?

5. Within this speech, Hamlet lists all the disadvantages of living. What evidence do you find in lines 13-22 that he is speaking as a commoner rather than a prince? Why would Shakespeare have given him such an apparently inappropriate speech?

6. Test the rule of behavior Hamlet formulates in lines 26-27. In your experience, are these lines true or untrue? Give examples to support your opinion.

7. After studying this speech thoroughly, explain what Hamlet means when he says "conscience does make cowards of us all." Paraphrase, in your own words, Hamlet's conclusion in lines 28-33. What pair of opposites does he contrast in these lines?

OUR REVELS NOW ARE ENDED

Our revels now are ended. These our actors,
As I foretold you, were all spirits and
Are melted into air, into thin air;
And, like the baseless fabric of this vision,
The cloud-capp'd towers, the gorgeous palaces,   5
The solemn temples, the great globe itself,
Yea, all which it inherit, shall dissolve,
And, like this insubstantial pageant faded,
Leave not a rack behind. We are such stuff
As dreams are made on, and our little life   10
Is rounded with a sleep.

FROM *The Tempest*

1. This speech comes near the end of the last play Shakespeare
   wrote alone. Many have loved the speech as a summary not only
   of *The Tempest*, but also of Shakespeare's dramatic career. What
   is the basic comparison on which the speech is built?
2. How does the speaker view the "revels" which have been completed? Do the memories please or hurt him? Were the "dreams"
   sweet or nightmarish? When he compares life to a dream, do you
   feel he liked or hated life?
3. As in Hamlet's soliloquy, the speaker here compares death to
   sleep. Is his point of view similar to Hamlet's in any other way?

THE CAVALIERS AND
METAPHYSICAL POETS

Lyric poetry continued to flourish in the seventeenth century and, in many ways, even survived those political and religious upheavals that by midcentury had divided Englishmen into hostile camps. Based originally on imitation — either of ancient classical models or of the more recent works of the Italian and French Renaissance — poetry in England had acquired a definitely national character during the reign of Queen Elizabeth. After she died and James I came to the throne as the first Stuart king, the art of poetry did not decline. Nor was it any less English; but changes were occurring in English poetry that should be noted.

For one thing, James I did not inspire the same kind of national enthusiasm that Elizabeth had. Proud of his erudition, he often failed to act in a humanistic spirit; nor did his morals inspire love or respect. His insistence on the divine right of kings indicated his vanity as a person and his insecurity as a ruler; consequently, the great poetry written during his reign did not reflect the same unity and patriotism that characterized the poetry written under Elizabeth. It grew more cynical, ironic, and intellectual in mood.

For another thing, as the Puritan movement grew in strength and popularity, Englishmen identified themselves either with those who supported Puritan reform or those who supported

Royalist rights. Writers also tended to move toward extremes in defense of their respective points of view. Young poets criticized the subject matter and techniques that had won praise during the early years of the Renaissance. Young playwrights found fault with the conventions of the theater within which Shakespeare worked with such genius. To some seventeenth-century writers, the style that had resulted from an exciting experiment with language now seemed heavy and tired. The time was ripe for a literary reform which, before the end of the Renaissance, would reflect the wide interests and varied talents of some of England's most gifted writers.

A leader in this reform was the dramatist and poet BEN JONSON. He had worked closely with Shakespeare and greatly admired him, even though he deplored some of his methods as a playwright and, especially, his many inaccuracies. A self-taught scholar of great learning, Jonson advocated a strict adherence to classical principles. Writers who found him persuasive became members of the "tribe of Ben," and looked to him as the literary arbiter of his day.

By temperament a satirist, Jonson attempted, through his plays, to give a realistic picture of life, but his characters tended to be types rather than real people. He was at his best in such satires as *The Alchemist, Volpone,* and *Bartholomew Fair.* His poetic imagination found freer rein in the masque, a special kind of entertainment presented at court and in the homes of noblemen. His lyric poetry, also, was not stifled by that classicism which, largely because of his efforts, persisted into the eighteenth century. Above all he was a poet of logic, judgment, and control.

Among the "tribe of Ben," no poet agreed more wholeheartedly with Jonson's insistence on classical standards than ROBERT HERRICK. Nor was any English poet more successful than Herrick in infusing poetry with the restrained grace and classical form of the Latin poets, whom he and Jonson admired. Even after Herrick became an Anglican clergyman, he did not outgrow this "pagan" influence. He lived through seventy-five years of the turbulent seventeenth century, singing sweetly of shepherds and maidens in their idyllic pastoral existence. While England was being turned upside down, he went his serene way, writing poetry "both human and divine."

SIR JOHN SUCKLING and RICHARD LOVELACE inherited the view of poetry elaborated by Robert Herrick. As Cavaliers, or followers of King Charles I, they despised the moral and social rigidity which they felt characterized the Puritans — Charles's powerful opposition. Expressing their pleasure in the moment without worrying about either a temporal or an eternal future, they voiced their love of wine, women, king, and song with both wit and charm.

JOHN DONNE, a contemporary of Ben Jonson's, reacted in a different way to the literature of his time. His poetry clearly suggests a revolt against the smooth and often elegant lyricism of Elizabethan poetry. Donne's poetry is rough, angular, abrupt, and difficult. In his original way, he made the poetic conceit highly intellectual. A *conceit* is an elaborately worked out comparison between two things which seem to have nothing in common. Two lovers, for example, are compared by Donne to the twin points of a drawing compass. Through this kind of clever comparison, new insights and fresh observations are possible about subjects as old as love, hate, and fear. Donne also found the religious life of the inner man a subject of absorbing interest. He treated his own spiritual condition in an introspective manner which was startlingly new and powerful.

Donne won admirers during his lifetime by circulating his poetry among friends. The posthumous publication of his poems in 1633 attracted a group who later became known as the Metaphysical poets. Their poetry attempted to express the complexities and contradictions of life, and often dealt with death, love, and religious devotion. This poetry was intellectual, analytical, and filled with bold conceits.

The most distinguished Metaphysical poet after Donne was GEORGE HERBERT, who as a boy had known Donne. Herbert was a gentle man whose serene religious poetry contrasts dramatically with Donne's anguished cries. In technical virtuosity, however, Herbert's genius is equal, if not superior, to Donne's.

Ben Jonson

In his effort to improve the literary style of his day, Jonson gave this advice: "For a man to write well, there are required three necessaries—to read the best authors, observe the best speakers, and much exercise of his own style." He disagreed with those who praised Shakespeare for never blotting out a line. "My answer hath been," Jonson wrote, "would he had blotted a thousand . . . ." Nothing was of more crucial importance than conciseness of expression: "A strict and succinct style is that where you can take away nothing without loss." In his own poetry, he attempted to practice what he preached.

Song to Celia

Drink to me only with thine eyes,
　　And I will pledge with mine;
Or leave a kiss but in the cup,
　　And I'll not look for wine.
The thirst that from the soul doth rise   5
　　Doth ask a drink divine;
But might I of Jove's[1] nectar sup,
　　I would not change for thine.

[1]*Jove:* Jupiter, ruler of the gods in Roman mythology

I sent thee, late, a rosy wreath,
   Not so much honoring thee,   10
As giving it a hope, that there
   It could not withered be.
But thou thereon did'st only breathe,
   And sent'st it back to me;
Since when it grows, and smells, I swear,   15
   Not of itself, but thee.

1. Jonson composed this song from prose passages in the work of a Greek letter writer, Philostratus, who lived around 200 A.D. It has been popular ever since — nearly three hundred and fifty years. It illustrates two characteristics of the late Renaissance period: a love of music, especially singing; and an interest in the classics. When sung, the first two stanzas fit the "Old English air" perfectly. The music is then repeated for the last two stanzas. What is logical about this arrangement in view of the total pattern of the poem?
2. What is the central conceit in stanzas 1 and 2? Point out the ways in which Jonson extends it to suggest a comparison between objects which are apparently dissimilar.
3. What is the central conceit of stanzas 3 and 4? How are these conceits extended? Tell why you do, or do not, think these last stanzas have greater unity than the first two. Is the second conceit more effective than the first?
4. By scansion, determine the metrical difference between the rhythm pattern of line 1 and line 2. How are these lines similar to, or different from, the remaining lines of the poem?

ON MY FIRST SON

Farewell, thou child of my right hand, and joy;
   My sin was too much hope of thee, loved boy.
Seven years[1] thou wert lent to me, and I thee pay,
   Exacted by thy fate, on the just day.

[1]*Seven years:* Jonson's first son died of the plague at the age of seven.

Oh, could I lose all father now! For why   5
  Will man lament the state he should envy?
To have so soon 'scaped world's and flesh's rage,
  And if no other misery, yet age!
Rest in soft peace, and asked, say, Here doth lie
  Ben Jonson his best piece of poetry.   10
For whose sake henceforth all his vows be such,
  As what he loves may never like too much.

1. This lament of a father for his son includes, as well, what the father would have the boy say about him. Why do you think that Jonson considered his hopes for his son as sinful? How do lines 3 and 4 support this opinion? How do you interpret the half line, "and I thee pay"?
2. The compactness of poetic language creates a problem in understanding Jonson's cry in line 5. What does he mean by "all father"? Perhaps if you change the line to prose, the meaning will be more clear.
3. The "state" referred to in line 6 is death. What idea do you think he is expressing in his rhetorical question about it? How is this related to the death of his son?
4. Beginning with "Here doth lie" (line 9), Jonson imagines that his son is speaking of him. What is Jonson's "best piece of poetry"?
5. Why would Jonson vow not to "like too much" what he loved?
6. The plague that snuffed out the life of Jonson's little boy was all too familiar in Europe at the time. Ten years earlier Jonson's first daughter, at the age of six months, had also died of a plague. What do you know about life in Jonson's day that indicates that death was a more common experience then than it is today? What differences, if any, in the attitudes toward death are revealed in the literature of Jonson's time and in the literature of today?

Robert Herrick

Robert Herrick was steeped in the classical tradition and wrote as a Latin poet might, had one lived in the seventeeth century. While Herrick accepted Jonson's love of the classics, he surpassed Jonson as a lyrical poet because he was more spontaneous. Many of Herrick's poems were set to music, and, ideally, should be heard rather than read. But though his musical settings have been lost, an imaginative reader can still hear the music of Herrick's words.

To the Virgins
to Make Much of Time

Gather ye rosebuds while ye may,
  Old Time is still a-flying;
And this same flower that smiles to-day,
  To-morrow will be dying.

The glorious lamp of heaven, the sun,   5
  The higher he's a-getting,
The sooner will his race be run,
  And nearer he's to setting.

That age is best, which is the first,
  When youth and blood are warmer;   10
But being spent,° the worse, and worst   passed
  Times, still succeed the former.

Then he not coy, but use your time,
  And while ye may, go marry;
For, having lost but once your prime,   15
  You may forever tarry.

1. This seemingly effortless poem has a clear design, carefully
   worked out in imagery and style. In line 1, Herrick introduces the
   metaphor which is the central image of the poem. What do you
   think *rosebuds* represents? Does Herrick mean literally that
   young maidens should rush out into their gardens or into the
   fields to gather rosebuds?
2. Lines 14-16 add depth to the idea presented figuratively in line 1,
   because they give a reason for gathering rosebuds "while ye
   may." What is that reason?
3. What is the image in stanza 1? What idea does it convey? How
   does the image in stanza 2 reinforce this idea? This second image
   may seem to be a mixed metaphor unless you recall the Greek
   legend explaining how the sun journeys across the heavens.
4. Stanzas 3 and 4 round out the meaning of the preceding stanzas
   in somewhat the same way as lines 2-4 round out line 1 and lines
   6-8 round out line 5. Herrick makes a clear statement of his philosophy, a view of life influenced by the Greek thinker Epicurus.
   Consult a standard reference work for information about Epicurus.
   Then discuss whether or not this poem expresses the Epicurean
   philosophy.
5. In this song, as in many others, lines 2 and 4 of each stanza are
   shorter than lines 1 and 3. An oral reading, however, is likely to
   leave the impression that they are the same length. Read the first
   stanza aloud. Which sounds in lines 2 and 4 seem to draw out
   the lines?
6. In what way are the end rhymes in lines 1 and 3 of each stanza
   different from the end rhymes of lines 2 and 4? What effect might
   this difference have in setting the words of the poem to music?
7. Explain Herrick's attitude toward growing old as expressed by
   "the worse, and worst/Times." Why doesn't he say "worse and
   worse"?

Upon Julia's Clothes

Whenas in silks my Julia goes,
Then, then (methinks) how sweetly flows
The liquefaction of her clothes.

Next, when I cast mine eyes, and see
That brave vibration, each way free,   5
O how that glittering taketh me!

1. Frequently a "big" word is an important clue to the poet's attitude toward his subject. What do you think of *liquefaction?* What is appropriate about its use here? By what word is it echoed in the second stanza?
2. Each stanza in this poem is a tercet. Notice the rhyme scheme. Identify the predominant rhythm and metrical line. How do the rhythm and punctuation of the lines reflect this meaning?
3. Herrick's youthful apprenticeship to his uncle, goldsmith to the king, frequently has been cited as an important influence on his poetry. This little gem of a lyric might be held up as an example, especially in the second tercet. What words in that stanza, consistent with the image created in the first tercet, convey the jewel-like quality of Julia's clothes? Might the girl's name also be suggestive of this quality?

Corinna's Going A-Maying

Herrick's poem about the traditional English observance of May Day has provided an insight into a time-honored custom. This festival, especially popular in England during the medieval period and the Renaissance, stemmed partly from old Druid rites and partly from Roman festivities in honor of Flora. The Puritans tried to suppress it in the seventeenth century. In Herrick's time, May Day was celebrated on May 12. A Puritan writer, Philip Stubbes, described with stern disapproval the behavior of those who helped "fetch in the May." He wrote:

Against May, Whitsonday, or other time, all the yung men and maides, olde men and wives, run gadding over night to the woods, groves, hils, and mountains, where they spend all night in pleasant pastimes; and in the morning they return, bringing with them birch and branches of trees, to deck their assemblies withall . . . the chiefest jewel they bring thence is their maypole, which they bring home with great veneration, as thus. They have twentie or fortie yoke of oxen, every oxe having a sweet nosegay of flowers placed on the tip of his hornes, and these oxen drawe home this may-pole (this stinkyng ydol, rather), which is covered all over with floures and hearbs . . . they straw the ground round about, binde green boughes about it, set up sommer haules, bowers, and arbors hard by it. And then fall they to daunce about it, like as heathen people did at the dedication of the Idols, whereof this is a perfect pattern, or rather the thing itself.[1]

Get up, get up for shame, the blooming morn
Upon her wings presents the god[2] unshorn.
   See how Aurora[3] throws her fair
   Fresh-quilted colors through the air:
   Get up, sweet slug-a-bed, and see   5
   The dew bespangling herb and tree.
Each flower has wept and bowèd toward the east
Above an hour since: yet you not dressed;
   Nay! not so much as out of bed?
   When all the birds have matins° said   morning prayers 10
   And sung their thankful hymns, 'tis sin,
   Nay, profanation, to keep in,
Whenas° a thousand virgins on this day   while
Spring, sooner than the lark, to fetch in May.

Rise, and put on your foliage, and be seen   15
To come forth, like the springtime, fresh and green,
   And sweet as Flora.[4] Take no care

---

[1] Phillip Stubbes, *Anatomie of Abuses* (London, 1583), quoted in James George Frazer, *The Golden Bough* (New York: The Macmillan Company, 1922), p. 123.
[2] *god:* Apollo, mythological god of the sun
[3] *Aurora:* Roman goddess of the dawn
[4] *Flora:* Roman goddess of flowers

For jewels for your gown or hair:
Fear not; the leaves will strew
    Gems in abundance upon you: 20
Besides, the childhood of the day has kept,
Against° you come, some orient pearls unwept;   until
    Come and receive them while the light
    Hangs on the dew-locks of the night:
    And Titan⁵ on the eastern hill   25
    Retires himself, or else stands still
Till you come forth. Wash, dress, be brief in praying:
Few beads are best when once we go a-Maying.

Come, my Corinna, come; and coming, mark
How each field turns a street, each street a park   30
    Made green and trimmed with trees; see how
    Devotion gives each house a bough
    Or branch: each porch, each door ere this
    An ark,⁶ a tabernacle is,
Made up of white-thorn, neatly interwove;   35
As if here were those cooler shades of love.
    Can such delights be in the street
    And open fields and we not see 't?
    Come, we'll abroad; and let's obey
    The proclamation made for May: 40
And sin no more, as we have done, by staying;
But my Corinna, come, let's go a-Maying.

There's not a budding boy or girl this day
But is got up, and gone to bring in May.
    A deal of youth, ere this, is come   45
    Back, and with white-thorn laden home.
    Some have dispatched their cakes and cream
    Before they we have left° to dream: ceased
And some have wept, and wooed, and plighted troth,

⁵*Titan:* Helios, sun god
⁶*ark:* the Ark of the Tabernacle, symbol of God's presence to the Israelites

And chose their priest, ere we can cast off sloth: 50
   Many a green-gown has been given;
   Many a kiss, both odd and even:
   Many a glance too has been sent
   From out the eye, love's firmament;°   residence
Many a jest told of the keys betraying   55
This night, and locks picked, yet we're not a-Maying.

Come, let us go, while we are in our prime;
And take the harmless folly of the time.
   We shall grow old apace, and die
   Before we know our liberty.   60
   Our life is short, and our days run
   As fast away as does the sun,
And, as a vapor or a drop of rain,
Once lost, can ne'er be found again,
   So when or you or I are made   65
   A fable, song, or fleeting shade°   spirit
   All love, all liking, all delight
   Lies drowned with us in endless night.
Then while times serves, and we are but decaying,
Come, my Corinna, come let's go a-Maying.   70

1. With a wealth of detail, Herrick describes the bustle of activity to which his "sweet slug-a-bed" seems indifferent on this "blooming morn." Look closely at these details. What does he mean by saying the god of the sun was "unshorn"? Where are the "fresh-quilted colors" of Aurora to be seen? Why do the flowers bow toward the east"?

2. He describes the bird songs as morning prayers. Is the religious spirit he ascribes to the act of "bringing in the May" Christian or pagan? Against what "religious" duty is failure to participate in the May ritual considered a "profanation"?

3. The reference to Flora is particularly appropriate because several May Day practices have their origin in the Roman rites of spring known as the Floralia. This frequent use of Greek and Roman

mythology in Renaissance poetry is a direct result of the wide-spread revival of ancient classical literature. By classical allusions, as such references to mythology are called, writers could suggest much because their readers were familiar with the mythological figures and the stories about them. Analyze other classical allusions in the poem, pointing out how they represent ideas which would otherwise require considerable explanation.

4. A young lady who bathed her face in the morning dew of May was assured of a lovely complexion. What mention of the dew does Herrick make, especially in connection with Corinna? Why does she not need to spend much time dressing herself?

5. The third stanza gives a vivid glimpse of what happened in the villages. How do the people bring the country back to the village? How do they turn each field into a street, and each street into a park? Whitethorn was considered especially potent in keeping witches away and was usually hung over the doorway of each house. What other activities will Corinna miss if she doesn't get up?

6. In the final stanza, Herrick expands the meaning of his poem so that it has a wider application to life than just the observance of May Day. What is this larger meaning? Is there an underlying note of pessimism? In answering these questions, cite specific evidence found in the poem.

7. Herrick follows a common practice in rhyming each pair of lines. By what variation in length of line, however, does he keep the rhyme scheme from becoming monotonous? Comment especially on the original pattern he gives these variations.

8. This poem is filled with examples of that happy turn of phrase in which Herrick excelled. Point out those you particularly like and tell what makes each one pleasing. Perhaps it is a particular word, unexpected but just right. Or it might be a figure of speech or the use of alliteration or assonance.

Sir John Suckling and Richard Lovelace

The verse of Suckling and Lovelace embodies traits which their enemies scornfully associated with the Cavaliers, or courtiers of Charles I. Such poetry is carefree, witty, and elegant. For present-day readers, however, a sense of humor, a graceful style, and light-hearted good spirits are qualities to be admired, not shunned. The following lyrics reveal that the Cavalier poets were at their best when writing of love and war.

The Constant Lover

SIR JOHN SUCKLING

Out upon it, I have loved
   Three whole days together!
And am like to love three more,
   If it prove fair weather.

Time shall moult away his wings,   5
   Ere he shall discover
In the whole wide world again
   Such a constant lover.

136

But the spite on't is, no praise
   Is due at all to me: 10
Love with me had made no stays,°   *stops*
   Had it any been but she.

Had it any been but she,
   And that very face,
There had been at least ere this   15
   A dozen dozen in her place.

1. This poem is, of course, flippant and ironic. How does line 4 heighten the irony?
2. What comment upon lovers in general is made by stanza 2? To what is Time compared in this stanza?
3. What kind of person is the speaker? What does the title suggest about his character? What pose does he strike in stanza 3?
4. The Cavalier poets reacted against Elizabethan verse in which lovers vowed that their devotion was eternal and complained bitterly when their love was not returned. Compare this poem to those by Spenser and Sidney. What differences do you see in the ways in which the speakers viewed themselves? Their sweethearts? Their lives? What difference in technique, form, and style do you notice? How does the language differ?
5. Although this poem is flippant, it does contain a compliment to the lady. Do you think this type of compliment is or is not as effective as that contained in an Elizabethan lyric? Explain.

To Lucasta, on Going to the Wars

RICHARD LOVELACE

Tell me not, sweet, I am unkind,
   That from the nunnery
Of thy chaste breast and quiet mind
   To war and arms I fly.

True, a new mistress now I chase,   5
  The first foe in the field;
And with a stronger faith embrace
  A sword, a horse, a shield.

Yet this inconstancy is such
  As thou too shalt adore: 10
I could not love thee, dear, so much,
  Loved I not honor more.

1. This poem illustrates the use of paradox evident in much seventeenth-century poetry. What is the paradox expressed in this poem? In your own words, paraphrase the apparent contradiction.
2. What pun on *arms* is in line 4? Who is the "new mistress" mentioned in line 5? What is the "stronger faith" referred to in line 7? To what weaker faith is the stronger faith compared? What does the comparison tell you about the speaker's values? What does he value most highly?
3. How, in stanza 3, does the speaker prove to his sweetheart that she will love his unfaithfulness?
4. At what specific points in this poem do you feel the rhythm of the lines reinforces the meaning particularly well?

TO ALTHEA, FROM PRISON

RICHARD LOVELACE

When Love with unconfinéd wings
  Hovers within my gates,
And my divine Althea brings
  To whisper at the grates;
When I lie tangled in her hair   5
  And fettered° to her eye,   chained
The gods that wanton° in the air   frolic
  Know no such liberty.

When flowing cups run swiftly round
  With no allaying Thames,°   water 10
Our careless heads with roses bound,
  Our hearts with loyal flames;
When thirsty grief in wine we steep,
  When healths and draughts go free,
Fishes that tipple° in the deep   drink 15
  Know no such liberty.

When, like committed° linnets, I   caged
  With shriller throat will sing
The sweetness, mercy, majesty,
  And glories of my king;   20
When I shall voice aloud how good
  He is, how great should be,
Enlarged winds, that curl the flood,
  Know no such liberty.

Stone walls do not a prison make,   25
  Nor iron bars a cage:
Minds innocent and quiet take
  That for an hermitage:
If I have freedom in my love,
  And in my soul am free,   30
Angels alone, that soar above,
  Enjoy such liberty.

1. In the first stanza, freedom is contrasted with bondage. What words reinforce this contrast? As Lovelace develops this comparison, however, it becomes a paradox. Express in your own words the paradox of stanza 1.
2. In stanza 2, rather than being a paradox, the contrast becomes hyperbole, or exaggeration used for a particular effect. What is exaggerated here? What effect is gained by exaggerating?

3. As what does the poet picture himself in stanzas 2 and 3? What kind of person does he feel he is? On what comparison is stanza 3 built?
4. This poem is like a speech which includes three illustrations supporting a major point or generalization. What is the generalization? What are the illustrations? How well do you think the generalization is proved?
5. Define *freedom* as Lovelace would define it.

John Donne

John Donne is recognized today as the greatest of the Metaphysical poets. In his early poetry, he dealt predominantly with the subject of love, which he treated with wit, irreverence, and ingenuity. After he became a famous clergyman in the Anglican Church, however, his poetry became religious in theme. Noted for its intensity and intellectual power, it influenced such later poets as Gerard Manley Hopkins, T. S. Eliot, and W. H. Auden.

SWEETEST LOVE, I DO NOT GO

Sweetest love, I do not go,
   For weariness of thee,
Nor in hope the world can show
   A fitter love for me;
      But since that I   5
Must die at last, 'tis best,
To use myself in jest
   Thus by feigned deaths to die;

Yesternight the sun went hence,
   And yet is here today,   10
He hath no desire nor sense,

Nor half so short a way:
   Then fear not me,
But believe that I shall make
Speedier journeys, since I take   15
   More wings and spurs than he.

O how feeble is man's power,
   That if good fortune fall,
Cannot add another hour,
   Nor a lost hour recall!   20
      But come bad chance,
And we join to it our strength,
And we teach it art and length,
   Itself o'er us to advance.

When thou sighest, thou sighest not wind,   25
   But sighest my soul away,
When thou weepest, unkindly kind,
   My life's blood doth decay.
      It cannot be
That thou lovest me, as thou sayest,   30
If in thine my life thou waste,
   Thou art the best of me.

Let not thy divining heart
   Forethink me any ill,
Destiny may take thy part,   35
   And may thy fears fulfill;
      But think that we
Are but turned aside to sleep;
They who one another keep
   Alive, ne'er parted be.   40

1. In some volumes this poem is entitled "Song." Is the rhythm of
the lines regular enough so that they could be sung to a tune? Are

the stanza forms identical, similar, quite different? What slight irregularity, quite adaptable to music, occurs at the beginning of certain lines? Which lines?

2. Even at his most lyrical, Donne could not resist forming intellectual arguments. He begins (lines 1-4) with a clear declaration and then immediately indulges in some of his characteristically subtle logic. Why would leaving his beloved be a "feigned" death? Why would he be using himself "in jest" by such "feigned deaths"?

3. What analogy does he develop in stanza 2? When you have carefully analyzed it, tell why you do, or do not, think it is credible.

4. In stanza 3, what observations does Donne make about the way man deals with "good fortune" and "bad chance"? Is he implying that his "sweetest love" is dealing with his departure in the same way?

5. In stanza 4, he chides his wife for being "unkindly kind." Why does he encourage her to cease her sighing and weeping? How do you interpret lines 31 and 32? What attitude is Donne pleading with his wife to adopt?

6. What admonition is expressed in lines 33-36? What reassurance is given in lines 37-40?

THE BAIT

Come live with me, and be my love,
And we will some new pleasures prove
Of golden sands, and crystal brooks,
With silken lines, and silver hooks.

There will the river whispering run   5
Warmed by thy eyes, more than the Sun.
And there the enamoured fish will stay,
Begging themselves they may betray.

When thou wilt swim in that live bath,
Each fish, which every channel hath,   10
Will amorously to thee swim,
Gladder to catch thee, than thou him.

If thou, to be so seen, beest loath,
By Sun, or Moon, thou darknest both,
And if myself have leave to see,   15
I need not their light, having thee.

Let others freeze with angling reeds,
And cut their legs, with shells and weeds,
Or treacherously poor fish beset,
With strangling snare, or windowy net: 20

Let coarse bold hands, from slimy nest
The bedded fish in banks out-wrest,
Or curious traitors, sleavesilk flies
Bewitch poor fishes wandring eyes.

For thee, thou needst no such deceit,   25
For thou thyself art thine own bait;
That fish, that is not catched thereby,
Alas, is wiser far than I.

1. This poem is parody of Marlowe's famous poem, "The Passionate Shepherd to His Love." At what point did you become aware of its comic intent?
2. On what far-fetched conceit does Donne base his parody? What clues are you given in lines 3 and 4? By his choice of words, what quality does Donne give to the conceit?
3. Who are the "enamoured fish" who swim to the bait? Who is the bait?
4. Note that in stanza 4 there are six commas in the first two lines. What reason can you see (including the rhyme) for so much punctuation? Rearrange the words in the entire stanza, if necessary, to express the same meaning in language that is easier to read. Notice what happens to the punctuation.
5. How do you interpret stanzas 5 and 6? To whom is the speaker in the poem referring by the word *others*? How do they differ from her? What attitude does he reveal in the way he speaks of them?
6. His descriptions of the methods of fishing show Donne's consider-

able ingenuity and skill. Point out the imagery, sense impressions, and unusual use of words which impress you.

7. In the final stanza, Donne expresses both a summary of the central idea of the poem and a "moral." Is the tone of the "moral" facetious, disillusioned, mocking? Discuss. Do you think the poem is, or is not, a compliment to the lady? Give reasons to support your answer.

THE MESSAGE

Send home my long strayed eyes to me,
Which (Oh) too long have dwelt on thee;
Yet since there they have learned such ill,
    Such forced fashions,
    And false passions,   5
      That they be
      Made by thee
Fit for no good sight, keep them still.

Send home my harmless heart again,
Which no unworthy thought could stain;   10
But if it be taught by thine
    To make jestings
    Of protestings,
      And cross both
      Word and oath,   15
Keep it, for then 'tis none of mine.

Yet send me back my heart and eyes,
That I may know, and see thy lies,
And many laugh and joy, when thou
    Art in anguish   20
    And dost languish
      For some one
      That will none,
Or prove as false as thou art now.

146 ?? *John Donne*

1. Few writers have done as unusual things with the eight-line stanza as Donne. Chart the rhyme scheme for each stanza. Why does the conventional way of indicating rhyme not adequately explain the special quality of lines 4 and 5 and of 6 and 7 in each stanza? What is this special quality?
2. Try to scan the entire poem in order to see the many variations in metrical feet and lines. Then compare the stanzas, pointing out the pattern which Donne follows in these variations.
3. Donne's use of the caesura in several lines affects the rhythm and meaning of the poem. Note the caesura after *yet* in line 3, which calls attention to the use of the word. Reread lines 3-8. What meaning do you think Donne intended *yet* to convey? Is this meaning tied to the last three words "keep them still"? Find other caesuras that affect the meaning.
4. Try to describe in your own words the effects of the rhythmic variations. What do you think is the over-all effect?
5. In stanza 1, after the speaker in the poem asks his false lover to return his "long strayed eyes," why does he then bid her keep them?
6. What does the speaker ask in stanza 2? Why does he again change his mind? Does Donne follow the same "reversal" pattern here as in stanza 1? If so, point out the way he handles it.
7. What does the speaker finally decide in stanza 3? What proof does he think it would provide? What feelings are reflected in the words he uses in speaking of his false lover? What reasons do you have for believing that he intended her to learn a lesson from his "message"?

AT THE ROUND EARTH'S
IMAGINED CORNERS

The following two sonnets are among nineteen Holy Sonnets in which Donne, in his highly original style, revealed his spiritual struggle to find peace with his God—a struggle over which always lurked the somber shadow of death.

At the round earth's imagined corners, blow
Your trumpets, angels, and arise, arise
From death, you numberless infinities
Of souls, and to your scattered bodies go,

All whom the flood did, and fire shall o'erthrow, 5
All whom war, dearth, age, agues,° tyrannies,   fevers
Despair, law, chance, hath slain, and you whose eyes,
Shall behold God, and never taste death's woe.
But let them sleep, Lord, and me mourn a space;
For, if above all these, my sins abound, 10
'Tis late to ask abundance of thy grace,
When we are there; here on this lowly ground,
Teach me how to repent; for that's as good
As if Thou hadst sealed my pardon with thy blood.

1. In the octave, whom is the speaker addressing? What great moment is at hand? The speaker might be the archangel Gabriel, God, or the poet himself. Which do you consider most likely and why?
2. The central image of the octave (introduced in line 1) is apparently based on the following passage from II Peter 3:5-7:

   > For this they willingly are ignorant of, that by the word of God the heavens were of old, and the earth standing out of the water and in the water:
   > Whereby the world that then was, being overflowed with water, perished:
   > But the heavens and the earth, which are now, by the same word are kept in store, reserved unto fire against the day of judgment and perdition of ungodly men.

   Point out the imagery and details which Donne added to the poem and the way in which they heighten the visual and emotional effects of the octave. What word in line 1 reveals that he was conscious of the paradoxical nature of this central image?
3. To whom is the sestet addressed? What evidence in these lines suggests that Donne is speaking for himself? What request does he make? When and where would it be "late to ask abundance"? How do you interpret the closing couplet?
4. Which of the two basic sonnet forms does this poem more closely resemble? (You will need to chart the rhyme scheme.) Which lines are predominantly iambic pentameter? Note that lines 1 and 2 *appear* iambic, but in each the meter must be adjusted to the meaning. Point out the most striking departures from iambic meter—within lines or at the beginning of lines—and tell why you think these add to the meaning or the total effect.

BATTER MY HEART, THREE-PERSONED GOD

Batter my heart, three-personed God, for you
As yet but knock, breathe, shine, and seek to mend;
That I may rise and stand, o'erthrow me; and bend
Your force to break, blow, burn, and make me new.
I, like an usurped° town to another due;   besieged   5
Labor to admit you, but oh, to no end;
Reason, your viceroy° in me, me should defend,   appointed ruler
But is captived, and proves weak or untrue.
Yet dearly I love you, and would be lovèd fain,°   gladly
But am bethrothed unto your enemy: 10
Divorce me, untie or break that knot again;
Take me to you, imprison me, for I
Except you enthrall° me, never shall be free,   enslave
Nor ever chaste, except you ravish° me.   physically possess

1. When Donne addresses God as "three-personed," he refers, of course, to the Christian concept of the Trinity. What quality does "three-personed" have that is different from such a word as "trinitarian," which he might have used? Is "three-personed" the kind of word a man might use in speaking to a remote deity or a close one?

2. Donne based almost every element of his sonnet on this idea of the Trinity. There are, for instance, three images in the poem, the first one presented in lines 1-4. Because modern readers are unfamiliar with the tinker who once traveled about mending pots and pans, the first image may seem obscure. Donne, with bold inventiveness, compares himself to a vessel in need of repair, and likens God to a tinker. "Batter my heart," Donne cries. What three verbs in line 2 describe what he felt God was doing for him at the time?

3. Under what circumstances could Donne be made "new"? That he might "rise and stand" — that is, live again — he asks God to "o'erthrow" him. What does *o'erthrow* mean in this case?

4. Notice the three verbs in line 4. Why three? How are they appro-

priate to the task Donne asks God to perform? What do they have in common with *batter,* the strong initial word of the sonnet?

5. In the second image, developed in lines 5-8, Donne made himself "an usurped town," a walled city which has been conquered by the enemy and which he asks God to storm. How would the images in lines 1-4 also agree with this image? What other words in the octave help to make a transition between the two images?

6. In the first line of the sestet, Donne reaffirms his desire to be made "new." Why can't he himself admit God to the fortess of his soul? What has "usurped" him? Why is "viceroy" an especially appropriate word for "reason"?

7. The third image, of Donne as a lover entreating God to possess him, dominates the sestet. How is the transition to this image achieved? Look for words that continue to suggest the idea of a siege.

8. How do the three verbs in line 11 carry out the idea of the third image?

9. Does the rhyme scheme follow that of the Petrarchan sonnet, the Shakespearean sonnet, or neither? By scanning the lines, study the effects Donne achieves by varying the traditional iambic pentameter of the sonnet.

A HYMN TO GOD THE FATHER

Wilt thou forgive that sin where I begun,
   Which was my sin, though it were done before?
Wilt thou forgive that sin through which I run,
   And do run still, though still I do deplore?
When thou hast done, thou has not done,   5
    For I have more.

Wilt thou forgive that sin which I have won
   Others to sin, and made my sin their door?
Wilt thou forgive that sin which I did shun
   A year or two, but wallowed in a score?   10
When thou hast done, thou has not done,
    For I have more.

I have a sin of fear, that when I have spun
   My last thread, I shall perish on the shore;
But swear by thyself that at my death thy Son   15
   Shall shine as he shines now, and heretofore;
And having done that, thou hast done,
     I fear no more.

1. What sins are implied in the phrases "that sin where I begun" and "that sin through which I run, and do run still"? Why would Donne refrain from specifying his sins in a hymn? What does his admission of guilt reveal about his character?
2. Explain the play on words in line 5. Why would God not have Donne even after forgiving his sins?
3. What other sins are implied in stanza 2? Are they more serious than those implied in stanza 1? Explain. Of what did he have more?
4. In stanza 3, he describes in precise terms what sin besets him most. What was his "sin of fear"? Of what does he ask God to assure him?
5. How does Donne complete his play on words in the final stanza? In your opinion, is this play on words irreverent? Defend your answer.
6. Look for metrical differences which, though minor, help to set the third stanza apart from the other two.

George Herbert

George Herbert proved, by writing in over a hundred different stanzaic patterns, that religious verse does not have to be dull, pious, and boring. Although his themes are exclusively religious, the poems are so intricate, original, intelligent, and intense that they continue to delight the lovers of good poetry who may not share Herbert's religious persuasions. Herbert's verse demonstrates that good poetry can be enjoyed for its evocative power, regardless of whether or not the reader agrees with the theme expressed.

EASTER WINGS

Lord, who createdst man in wealth and store,
　　Though foolishly he lost the same,
　　　　Decaying more and more,
　　　　　　Till he became
　　　　　　　Most poor:　　　　　　5
　　　　　　With thee
　　　　　O let me rise
　　　As larks, harmoniously,
　　And sing this day thy victories:
Then shall the fall further the flight in me.　　10

151

My   tender   age   in   sorrow   did   begin:
And still with sicknesses and shame
Thou didst so punish sin,
That   I   became
Most   thin.   15
With   thee
Let   me combine
And feel this day thy victory:
For, if I imp° my wing on thine,   graft
Affliction shall advance the flight in me.   20

1. Herbert is especially noted for shaped poems such as "Easter Wings." A shaped poem *looks* like its subject. Thus the poem explores an image not only verbally, but also visually. Read "Easter Wings" out loud. Do you find any correspondence between the sense and the length of the lines? Between the sense and the rhythm of the lines?
2. What does line 1 mean? To what biblical account does it refer?
3. Throughout the seventeenth century, a heresy referred to as the "Fortunate Fall" idea had much popularity. Briefly, this theory held that it was a good thing for Adam to have sinned, because his sin made the goodness of God even easier to recognize and comprehend. Further, man could not be good until he was free to be bad. Consequently, man's sinning created the opportunity for virtue. Where do you find traces of this idea in stanza 1?
4. What comparison is there in line 8? Why is it particularly appropriate to this poem? What pattern of imagery is present in both stanzas?
5. What does Herbert's title mean? What does Easter have to do with wings?

THE COLLAR[1]

I struck the board,° and cried, "No more;   table
I will abroad!
What! shall I ever sigh and pine?

---

[1] The collar suggests something which restrains the speaker; for example, a dog collar or a yoke. By extension, it can also mean the clerical collar.

My lines and ~~life are free~~; free as the road,
   Loose as the wind, as large as store.°   abundance 5
     Shall I be still in suit?°   petitioning in
                                          court
  Have I no harvest but a thorn
  To let me blood, and not restore
What I have lost with cordial fruit?
        Sure there was wine   10
Before my sighs did dry it; there was corn
  Before my tears did drown it.
  Is the year only lost to me?
     Have I no bays[2] to crown it,
No flowers, no garlands gay? all blasted,   15
     All wasted?
  Not so, my heart, but there is fruit,
     And thou hast hands.
  Recover all thy sigh-blown age
On double pleasures; leave thy cold dispute   20
Of what is fit and not; forsake thy cage,
    Thy rope of sands,
Which petty thoughts have made; and made
   to thee
  Good cable, to enforce and draw,
     And be thy law,   25
  While thou didst wink and wouldst not see.
    Away! take heed!
    I will abroad.
Call in thy death's-head there, tie up thy fears.
    He that forbears   30
  To suit and serve his need
    Deserves his load."
But as I raved, and grew more fierce and wild
    At every word,
  Methought I heard one calling, "Child";   35
    And I replied, "My Lord."

[2]*bays:* garlands made of bay leaves or laurel, bestowed as prizes

1. Before you study the individual lines of this poem, read the poem out loud, putting in whatever inflection the punctuation demands. What kind of rhythm characterizes the poem? Are the lines smooth and flowing, with regular rhythms? If not, why not? What does Herbert communicate through the rhythm?
2. What is the speaker's mood at the beginning of the poem? What kind of life has he led recently? What kind of life does he think he would prefer?
3. Much of the exceptional merit of this poem comes from its compactness. Herbert tells us a great deal in a few words by using imagery which suggests more than is stated. What does the legal image in line 6 tell you about his relationship to his "Lord"? What is the poet complaining of in lines 7-12? What kind of images does he use in these lines? Explain the hyperbole in lines 10-12.
4. What do lines 13-15 reveal about his aspirations? What kind of image occurs in these lines? Where did Herbert get this image?
5. What does the speaker resolve to do in lines 17-28? What type of person does he dismiss contemptuously in lines 29-32?
6. What happens at the end of the poem?
7. Identify the rhyme scheme of this poem. Does the rhyme contribute to the total impact of the poem? If so, how? If not, why not?
8. Why would readers consider this to be one of Herbert's most dramatic poems? Do you find dramatic movement in the poem? Do you see a beginning, middle, and end? A climax and resolution?

LOVE

Love bade me welcome; yet my soul drew
    back,
      Guilty of dust and sin.
But quick-eyed Love, observing me grow slack
      From my first entrance in,
Drew nearer to me, sweetly questioning,   5
      If I lacked anything.

"A guest," I answered, "worthy to be here:"
      Love said, "You shall be he."
"I, the unkind, ungrateful? Ah, my dear,

[handwritten: God's "God is Love"]

"I cannot look on Thee!"   10
Love took my hand and smiling did reply,
    "Who made the eyes but I?"

"Truth, Lord; but I have marred them; let
    my shame
    Go where it doth deserve."
"And know you not," says Love, "who bore
    the blame?"   15
    "My dear, then I will serve."
"You must sit down," says Love, "and taste
    my meat."
    So I did sit and eat.

[handwritten annotations: "Christ took on the world & suffered for all sins" ; "Sacrament of Communion Eucharist" ; "Take, eat, this is My Body"]

1. This poem is allegorical, which means that each character and place has a literal part in the story, but also represents an abstract quality. What kind of love is this poem about? To what place does Love welcome the speaker? What might the place symbolize allegorically? What Christian sacrament is suggested by the last two lines of the poem? *[handwritten: Communion]*
2. What does "guilty of dust" mean? What connotations does *dust* have? Why is the word effective here?
3. What is the familiar situation on which Herbert bases his poem? In this poem, what are the characteristics of Love? What are the traits of the speaker? How does Love treat the speaker? Why is such treatment given him?
4. Christian theology is concerned with a quality of God called *grace*. As a clergyman, Herbert was familiar with scholarly discussions of grace, yet as a poet he knew such abstract terms could be understood best when illustrated. "Love" explains God's grace so that the untrained worshipper can understand it. After studying the poem, define *grace*.

THE PURITAN POET: JOHN MILTON

Civil war made the seventeenth century one of the most troubled in England's history. The conflict had political and economic causes, but the convictions that prompted Englishmen to fight each other were basically religious. Queen Elizabeth, in a crisis, could persuade her subjects to subordinate religious differences to the national welfare. Her successor James I, however, only provoked trouble by his stubborn insistence on the divine rights of kings and bishops. He and his son Charles I were supported by royalists and by high-ranking officials of the Church of England. They were opposed by many Parliamentary leaders and a wide range of religious dissenters called Puritans.

At their name implies, the Puritans wanted to "purify" the Church of England. They preferred simple worship to ritualistic services and contended that each congregation should be governed by its own minister and lay elders. They adhered with fervor to the Calvinist doctrines of predestination, election, and damnation, and in defense of their convictions they were fined, flogged, imprisoned, and even executed. It was inevitable that their zealous determination should create controversy and involve them in a political struggle that led to full-scale revolution, to the beheading of Charles I in 1649, and to a commonwealth under Oliver Cromwell.

Unfortunately, many of the ideals of the Commonwealth were never realized. The Puritans, having won the right to worship as they pleased, now denied that right to other religious groups. The much-needed political and social reforms urged by leaders of the Commonwealth lacked the support of the people. Cromwell was an able leader of heroic stature, but after his death in 1658 the Commonwealth soon collapsed. By this time, the execution of Charles I was widely held to be an outrage against tradition and decency. In 1660 his exiled son, Charles II, made a triumphant return to England, restoring the monarchy.

During the Restoration period the abuse and persecution suffered by Puritan leaders was as unrestrained as the frivolity and immorality of Charles II and his court. Plots and counterplots were the order of the day. Charles' brother James II, who succeeded him in 1685, aroused widespread revolt by his attempt to restore the Roman Catholic faith to England. Three years of civil strife drove him into exile. His replacement by the joint sovereigns, William and Mary, marked the beginning of a new era. Englishmen agreed to exercise reason and restraint in reconciling their differences. In deciding how best to govern themselves, they embodied in their new government many ideals that had inspired the earnest dissent and conviction of the Puritan Revolution. Most important of all, Parliament clearly emerged as the principal instrument of government.

JOHN MILTON was the grandest literary figure to identify himself with Puritanism. In a very real sense, he was also a product of the Renaissance, yet at the same time a great innovator. He could work within the form of the Petrarchan sonnet without being its slave. He admired Spenser profoundly but was not content to imitate him. He borrowed much from the *Iliad* and the *Odyssey* to adorn his own epic, *Paradise Lost,* but he defied every convention by not using rhyme in the same work. He incorporated in his works quotations from the classics, but to evoke new meanings.

In an age of great learning, Milton was probably the most learned man of his time. He placed his great gifts in the service of both the Puritan Commonwealth and the English literary tradition. In his devotion to "religious humanism in its Protestant form," he served the state under Cromwell, but also served poetic art. Through his masterpiece, *Paradise Lost*, he traced the pilgrimage not only of the individual but also of the whole human race.

Milton regarded the poet's vocation as a sacred calling. To discharge his noble duties, he prepared himself as no other English poet has done, before or since. According to the tradition of his time, Milton first wrote Latin verse as an academic exercise. This discipline has often been credited with producing the sonority and classical elegance of Milton's language. The subject matter of Milton's work reflects the same conscientious preparation and seriousness of purpose. He followed Bacon's example by taking all knowledge for his province, but he did not permit his encyclopedic knowledge to stifle his daring imagination. In the mature work of his old age, he achieved a grandeur of form and theme to which only his grand style could do justice. For many critics, *Paradise Lost* remains the greatest poetic achievement in the English language.

ON HIS BLINDNESS

When I consider how my light is spent,
  Ere half my days, in this dark world and wide,
  And that one talent which is death to hide,
  Lodged with me useless, though my soul
      more bent°   intent
To serve therewith my Maker, and present   5
  My true account, lest he returning chide;
  "Doth God exact day-labor, light denied?"
  I fondly° ask. But Patience, to prevent   foolishly
That murmur, soon replies, "God doth not need

Either man's work or his own gifts; who best   10
   Bear his mild yoke, they serve him best. His state
Is kingly: thousands at his bidding speed
   And post o'er land and ocean without rest:
   They also serve who only stand and wait."

1. In the eighteen sonnets Milton wrote in English, he recorded his
    most deeply felt experiences. What troubled him most deeply
    about the tragedy that had befallen him in mid-life? Is the mood
    of the sonnet despair, shame, resignation, self-pity, confidence
    based on belief? Whatever your answer, give reasons to support it.
2. "That one talent which is death to hide" echoes a parable in the
    New Testament, Matthew 25:14-30, A servant entrusted by his
    master with a talent (coin) chose to hide it in the ground rather
    than put it to work. Later, when the master learned of this, he took
    the talent away from the servant saying, "For unto every one that
    hath shall be given, and he shall have abundance: but from him
    that hath not shall be taken away even that which he hath." Why
    would Milton feel that this parable was applicable to him? What
    double meaning might "talent" have for him?
3. In the question Milton asks (line 7), do you think he is being
    critical of himself, of his fate, or of his Maker? Is the purpose of
    Patience's reply to rebuke him for his attitude or to reveal to him
    what "true account" his Maker would expect and Milton could
    present?
4. The "thousands" in line 12 included, for Milton, not only mortal
    beings who serve God but celestial beings as well. How does this
    larger concept of God's universe both humble and exalt Milton
    as he reflected on his affliction? Do you interpret the last line to
    mean that those who do nothing also serve God? Tell why or
    why not.
5. What conventions of the Petrarchan sonnet does Milton use in
    this poem? What liberty does he take with the customary octave-
    sestet arrangement?

FROM Paradise Lost

BOOK I

THE ARGUMENT

This first book proposes, first in brief, the whole subject, man's disobedience, and the loss thereupon of Paradise wherein he was placed: then touches the prime cause of his fall, the Serpent, or rather Satan in the Serpent; who revolting from God, and drawing to his side many legions of angels, was by the command of God driven out of Heaven with all his crew into the great deep. While action past over, the poem hastes into the midst of things, presenting Satan with his angels now fallen into Hell, described here, not in the center (for Heaven and Earth may be supposed as yet not made, certainly not yet accurst) but in a place of utter darkness, fitliest called Chaos: here Satan with his angels lying on the burning lake, thunder-struck and astonished, after a certain space recovers, as from confusion, calls up him who next in order and dignity lay by him; they confer of their miserable fall. Satan awakens all his legions, who lay till then in the same manner confounded; they rise, numbers, array of battle, chief leaders named, according to the idols known afterwards in Canaan and the countries adjoining. To these Satan directs his speech, comforts them with hope yet of regaining Heaven, but tells them lastly of a new world and new kind of creature to be created, according to an ancient prophecy or report in Heaven; for that angels were long before this visible creation, was the opinion of many ancient fathers. To find out the truth of this prophecy, and what to determine thereon he refers to a full council. What his associates thence attempt. Pandemonium, the palace of Satan, rises, suddenly built out of the deep: The infernal peers there sit in council.

Of man's first disobedience, and the fruit
Of that forbidden tree, whose mortal° taste   deadly
Brought death into the world, and all our woe,
With loss of *Eden*, till one greater Man
Restore us, and regain the blissful seat,°   abode   5

Sing Heav'nly Muse,[1] that on the secret top
Of *Oreb,* or of *Sinai,*[2] didst inspire
That shepherd,[3] who first taught the chosen seed,°   people
In the beginning how the Heav'ns and Earth
Rose out of *Chaos.*[4] Or if *Sion* Hill[5]   10
Delight thee more, and *Siloa's* brook that flow'd
Fast by° the oracle° of God; I thence   close to; temple
Invoke thy aid to my advent'rous song,
That with no middle flight intends to soar
Above th' Aonian Mount,[6] while it pursues   15
Things unattempted yet in prose or rhyme.
And chiefly Thou O Spirit, that dost prefer
Before all temples th' upright heart and pure,
Instruct me, for Thou know'st; Thou from the first
Wast present, and with mighty wings outspread   20
Dove-like satst brooding on the vast abyss
And mad'st it pregnant: What in me is dark
Illumine, what is low raise and support;
That to the highth of this great argument
I may assert° Eternal Providence,   defend 25
And justify the ways of God to men.
    Say first, for Heav'n hides nothing from thy view
Nor the deep tract of Hell, say first what cause
Mov'd our grand° parents in that happy state,   first
Favor'd of Heav'n so highly, to fall off   30
From their Creator, and transgress his will
For one restraint, lords of the world besides?
Who first seduced them to that foul revolt?
Th' infernal Serpent;[7] he it was, whose guile
Stirred up with envy and revenge, deceived   35

[1]*Heav'nly Muse:* Holy Spirit
[2]*the secret . . . Sinai:* mountains on which Moses received the message of God
[3]*shepherd:* Moses
[4]*taught . . . Chaos:* Moses wrote the first five books of the Old Testament.
[5]*Sion Hill:* the hill on which Jersualem was built
[6]*Aonian Mount:* Helicon, the mountain where the Muses dwelled
[7]*infernal Serpent:* Satan

The mother of mankind; what time° his pride   when
Had cast him out from Heav'n, with all his host
Of rebel angels, by whose aid aspiring
To set himself in glory above his peers,°   equals
He trusted to have equalled the most High,   40
If he opposed; and with ambitious aim
Against the throne and monarchy of God
Raised impious war in Heav'n and battle proud
With vain attempt. Him the almighty power
Hurled headlong flaming from th' ethereal sky   45
With hideous ruin and combustion down
To bottomless perdition, there to dwell
In adamantine chains and penal fire,
Who durst defy th' Omnipotent to arms.
    Nine times the space that measures day and night   50
To mortal men, he with his horrid crew
Lay vanquished, rolling in the fiery gulf
Confounded though immortal: But his doom
Reserved him to more wrath; for now the thought
Both of lost happiness and lasting pain   55
Torments him; round he throws his baleful° eyes   sorrowful
That witnessed huge affliction and dismay
Mixed with obdúrate pride and steadfast hate:
At once as far as angels' ken° he views   know
The dismal situation waste and wild,   60
A dungeon horrible, on all sides round
As one great furnace flamed, yet from those flames
No light, but rather darkness visible
Served only to discover sights of woe,
Regions of sorrow, doleful shades, where peace   65
And rest can never dwell, hope never comes
That comes to all; but torture without end
Still urges,° and a fiery deluge, fed   presses on
With ever-burning sulphur unconsumed:
Such place Eternal Justice had prepared   70
For those rebellious, here their prison ordained

In utter° darkness, and their portion set   outer
As far removed from God and light of Heaven
As from the center thrice to th' utmost pole.
O how unlike the place from whence they fell!   75
There the companions of his fall, o'erwhelmed
With floods and whirlwinds of tempestuous fire,
He soon discerns, and welt'ring° by his side   wallowing
One next himself in power, and next in crime,
Long after known in Palestine, and named   80
Beëlzebub. To whom th' Arch-Enemy,
And thence in Heav'n called Satan, with bold words
Breaking the horrid silence thus began.
    "If thou beest he; But O how fall'n! how changed
From him, who in the happy realms of light   85
Clothed with transcendent brightness didst outshine
Myriads though bright: If he whom mutual league,
United thoughts and counsels, equal hope,
And hazard in the glorious enterprise,
Joined with me once, now misery hath joined   90
In equal ruin: into what pit thou seest
From what highth fall'n, so much the stronger proved
He[8] with his thunder: and till then who knew
The force of those dire arms? yet not for those,
Nor what the potent victor in his rage   95
Can else inflict, do I repent or change,
Though changed in outward luster; that fixed mind
And high disdain, from sense of injured merit,
That with the mightiest raised me to contend,
And to the fierce contention brought along   100
Innumerable force of spirits armed
That durst dislike his reign, and me preferring,
His utmost power with adverse power opposed
In dubious battle on the plains of Heav'n,
And shook his throne. What though the field be lost?   105
All is not lost; the unconquerable will,

    [8]*He:* God

And study of revenge, immortal hate,
And courage never to submit or yield:
And what is else not to be overcome?
That glory never shall his wrath or might   110
Extort from me. To bow and sue for grace
With suppliant knee, and deify his power
Who from the terror of this arm so late
Doubted his empire, that were low indeed,
That was an ignominy and shame beneath   115
This downfall; since by fate the strength of gods
And this empyreal° substance cannot fail,   heavenly
Since through experience of this great event
In arms not worse, in foresight much advance
We may with more successful hope resolve   120
To wage by force or guile eternal war
Irreconcilable to our grand foe,
Who now triumphs, and in th' excess of joy
Sole reigning holds the tyranny of Heav'n."
    So spake th' apostate angel, though in pain,   125
Vaunting aloud, but racked with deep despair:
And him thus answered soon his bold compeer.°   companion
    "O Prince, O chief of many thronèd powers,
That led th' imbattled seraphim° to war   highest
                                                    order of angels
Under thy conduct, and in dreadful deeds   130
Fearless, endangered Heav'n's perpetual king;
And put to proof his high supremacy,
Whether upheld by strength, or chance, or fate;
Too well I see and rue the dire event,°   outcome
That with sad overthrow and foul defeat   135
Hath lost us Heav'n, and all this mighty host
In horrible destruction laid thus low,
As far as gods and heav'nly essences°   beings
Can perish: for the mind and spirit remains
Invincible, and vigor soon returns,   140
Though all our glory extinct, and happy state
Here swallowed up in endless misery.

But what if he our conqueror (whom I now
Of force° believe almighty, since no less   necessity
Than such could have o'erpow'rd such force as ours)   145
Have left us this our spirit and strength entire
Strongly to suffer and support our pains,
That we may so suffice° his vengeful ire,   satisfy
Or do him mightier service as his thralls
By right of war, whate'er his business be   150
Here in the heart of Hell to work in fire,
Or do his errands in the gloomy deep;°   chaos
What can it then avail though yet we feel
Strength undiminished, or eternal being
To undergo eternal punishment?"   155
Whereto with speedy words th' Arch-fiend replied.
    "Fall'n cherub,° to be weak is miserable   second highest
Doing or suffering: but of this be sure,   order of angels
To do aught good never will be our task,
But ever to do ill our sole delight,   160
As being the contrary to his high will
Whom we resist. If then his providence
Out of our evil seek to bring forth good,
Our labor must be to pervert that end,
And out of good still to find means of evil;   165
Which oft-times may succeed, so as perhaps
Shall grieve him, if I fail° not, and disturb   mistake
His inmost counsels from their destined aim.
But see the angry victor hath recalled
His ministers of vengeance and pursuit   170
Back to the gates of Heav'n: the sulphurous hail
Shot after us in storm, o'erblown hath laid
The fiery surge, that from the precipice
Of Heav'n received us falling, and the thunder,
Winged with red lightning and impetuous rage,   175
Perhaps hath spent his° shafts, and ceases now   its
To bellow through the vast and boundless deep.
Let us not slip° th' occasion, whether scorn,   miss

Or satiate fury yield it from our foe.
Seest thou yon dreary plain, forlorn and wild,   180
The seat of desolation, void of light,
Save what the glimmering of these livid flames
Casts pale and dreadful? Thither let us tend
From off the tossing of these fiery waves,
There rest, if any rest can harbor there,   185
And reassembling our afflicted° powers,   overthrown
Consult how we may henceforth most offend°   do violence to
Our enemy, our own loss how repair,
How overcome this dire calamity,
What reinforcement we may gain from hope,   190
If not what resolution from despair."
    Thus Satan talking to his nearest mate
With head up-lift above the wave, and eyes
That sparkling blazed, his other parts besides
Prone on the flood, extended long and large   195
Lay floating many a rood,° in bulk as huge   yard
As whom the fables name of monstrous size,
Titanian,[9] or Earth-born, that warred on Jove,
Briareos or Typhon,[10] whom the den
By ancient Tarsus held, or that sea-beast   200
Leviathan,[11] which God of all his works
Created hugest that swim th' ocean stream:
Him haply slumb'ring on the Norway foam
The pilot of some small night-foundered skiff,°   boat
Deeming some island, oft, as seamen tell,   205
With fixed anchor in his scaly rind
Moors by his side under the lee, while night
Invests the sea, and wished morn delays:
So stretched out huge in length the arch-fiend lay
Chained on the burning lake, nor ever thence   210
Had ris'n or heaved his head, but that the will
And high permission of all-ruling Heaven

[9]*Titanian:* The Titans were a race of giant deities.
[10]*Briareos . . . Typhon:* hundred-headed monsters
[11]*Leviathan:* a biblical monster, resembling a whale

Left him at large to his own dark designs,
That with reiterated crimes he might
Heap on himself damnation, while he sought   215
Evil to others, and enraged might see
How all his malice served but to bring forth
Infinite goodness, grace and mercy shown
On man by him seduced,° but on himself   led into evil
Treble confusion, wrath and vengeance poured.   220
Forthwith upright he rears from off the pool
His mighty stature; on each hand the flames
Driv'n backward slope their pointing spires, and rolled
In billows, leave i' th' midst a horrid vale.
Then with expanded wings he steers his flight   225
Aloft, incumbent° on the dusky air   lying
That felt unusual weight, till on dry land
He lights, if it were land that ever burned
With solid, as the lake with liquid fire
And such appeared in hue; as when the force   230
Of subterranean wind transports a hill
Torn from Pelorus, or the shattered side
Of thund'ring Ætna,[12] whose combustible
And fuelled entrails thence conceiving fire,
Sublimed° with mineral fury, aid the winds,   vaporized 235
And leave a singed bottom all involved
With stench and smoke: Such resting found the sole
Of unblest feet. Him followed his next° mate,   nearest
Both glorying to have scaped the Stygian flood
As gods, and by thir own recovered strength,   240
Not by the sufferance° of supernal power.   permission
   "Is this the region, this the soil, the clime,"
Said then the lost arch-angel, "this the seat
That we must change for Heav'n, this mournful gloom
For that celestial light? Be it so, since he   245
Who now is sovran° can dispose and bid   sovereign
What shall be right: fardest° from him is best   farthest

---

[12]*Pelorus . . . Aetna:* mountains in Sicily

Whom reason hath equalled,[13] force hath made supreme
Above his equals. Farewell happy fields
Where joy for ever dwells: hail horrors, hail   250
Infernal world, and thou profoundest° hell   *deepest*
Receive thy new possessor: One who brings
A mind not to be changed by place or time.
The mind is its own place, and in itself
Can make a Heav'n of Hell, a Hell of Heav'n.   255
What matter where, if I be still the same,
And what I should be, all but less than he[14]
Whom thunder hath made greater? Here at least
We shall be free; th' Almighty hath not built
Here for his envy, will not drive us hence: 260
Here we may reign secure, and in my choice
To reign is worth ambition though in Hell:
Better to reign in Hell, than serve in Heav'n.
But wherefore let we then our faithful friends,
Th' associates and copartners of our loss   265
Lie thus astonished° on th' oblivious pool,   *thunderstruck*
And call them not to share with us their part
In this unhappy mansion: or once more
With rallied arms to try what may be yet
Regained in Heav'n, or what more lost in Hell?"   270

[13]*Whom . . . equalled:* Satan believes he is God's equal in everything except power.
[14]*all . . . he:* second only to God

1. In the first twenty-six lines, Milton sets forth his subject, invokes the Heavenly Muse, and makes clear his purpose in writing *Paradise Lost.* Determine the particular lines which fulfill each of these traditional features of the epic.
2. Note that two sentences comprise this opening passage. Because of their complex structure (each contains several clauses) it is important to determine the subjects and verbs. In your opinion do such sentence patterns help to create poetry of epic grandeur? An analysis of other sentences will reveal how their structure affects both tone and movement.
3. From the beginning, the "brilliant tension" between biblical

and classical elements in Milton's poetry is evident. Cite an example from the first twenty-six lines.

4. What fundamental question is raised in lines 27-33? How does Milton answer it, and in what lines?

5. Why have Satan and his followers been cast out of heaven? (Read aloud lines 44-49 to sense the downward movement of this passage describing the fall "to bottomless perdition.") What thought torments Satan and how does he react to his surroundings?

6. In *Paradise Lost,* the images of day and night, light and dark, are extremely important. How do you interpret the phrase, "yet from those flames no light" (lines 62 and 63)? What do the flames reach? Compare "darkness visible" (line 63) with lines 181-183. In what ways is this "dungeon horrible" unlike "The place from which they fell"?

7. Following the tradition of the epic, *Paradise Lost* begins *in medias res* — in the middle of the story. What struggle has Satan lost? Why is he unable to accept defeat?

8. Study Satan's first speech, addressed to Beëlzebub. How does he flatter Beëlzebub? By what reasoning does Satan try to maintain his own pride and self-esteem? In foreshadowing the inevitable struggle between himself and God, what new tactic does he plan to use? By what comments does he reveal his failure to understand God?

9. In Beëlzebub's reply to Satan's speech (lines 128-155), what attitude does he reveal toward Satan and toward the outcome of Satan's defeat? What questions does he raise in lines 143-155? Compare his mood with that of Satan when the latter resolves to wage warfare.

10. What is the statement of evil purpose with which Satan reassures Beëlzebub? (Compare lines 158-168 with lines 650-660 to see how Satan's idea grows.) What changes does Satan point out? Where do they go to consult?

11. What picture does Milton create, through comparisons and details, of the size of Satan (lines 192-208) and of his escape from the "Stygian flood"? How is the setting appropriate to his huge figure?

12. Reread Satan's speech in lines 242-270, paying particular attention to this statement:

> The mind is its own place, and in itself
> Can make a heaven of hell; a hell of heaven.

Is Satan honestly arriving at a truth or is he rationalizing his defeat? Discuss.

BOOK II

THE ARGUMENT

The consultation begun, Satan debates whether another battle be to be hazarded for the recovery of Heaven: some advise it, others dissuade: A third proposal is preferred, mentioned before by Satan, to search the truth of that prophecy or tradition in Heaven concerning another world, and another kind of creature equal or not much inferior to themselves, about this time to be created: Their doubt who shall be sent on this difficult search: Satan their chief undertakes alone the voyage, is honored and applauded. The Council thus ended, the rest betake them several ways and to several employments, as their inclinations lead them, to entertain the time till Satan return. He passes on his journey to Hell Gates, finds them shut, and who sat there to guard them, by whom at length they are opened, and discover to him the great gulf between Hell and Heaven; with what difficulty he passes through, directed by Chaos, the power of that place, to the sight of this new world which he sought.

High on a throne of royal state, which far
Outshone the wealth of Ormus[1] and of Ind,[2]
Or where the gorgeous East with richest hand
Show'rs on her kings barbaric pearl and gold,
Satan exalted sat, by merit raised   5
To that bad eminence; and from despair
Thus high uplifted beyond hope, aspires
Beyond thus high, insatiate to pursue
Vain war with Heav'n, and by success° untaught   experience
His proud imaginations thus displayed.   10
    "Powers and Dominions, Deities of Heav'n,
For since no deep within her gulf can hold
Immortal vigor, though opprest and fall'n,
I give not Heav'n for lost. From this descent
Celestial virtues rising, will appear   15
More glorious and more dread than from no fall

[1]*Ormus:* an island in the Persian Gulf, and a market for jewels
[2]*Ind:* India; Milton conjures up British fantasies about the lavish and exotic East.

And trust themselves to fear no second fate:
Me though just right and the fixed laws of Heav'n
Did first create your leader, next, free choice,
With what besides, in counsel or in fight, 20
Hath been achieved of merit, yet this loss
Thus far at least recovered, hath much more
Established in a safe unenvied throne
Yielded with full consent. The happier state
In Heav'n, which follows dignity, might draw 25
Envy from each inferior; but who here
Will envy whom the highest place exposes
Foremost to stand against the thunderer's aim
Your bulwark, and condemns to greatest share
Of endless pain? where there is then no good 30
For which to strive, no strife can grow up there
From faction; for none sure will claim in Hell
Precedence, none, whose portion is so small
Of present pain, that with ambitious mind
Will covet more. With this advantage then 35
To union, and firm faith, and firm accord,
More than can be in Heav'n, we now return
To claim our just inheritance of old,
Surer to prosper than prosperity
Could have assured us; and by what best way, 40
Whether of open war or covert guile,
We now debate; who can advise, may speak."
   He ceased, and next him Moloch, sceptered king
Stood up, the strongest and the fiercest spirit
That fought in Heav'n; now fiercer by despair: 45
His trust was with th' Eternal to be deemed
Equal in strength, and rather than be less
Cared not to be at all; with that care lost
Went all his fear: of God, or Hell, or worse
He recked not, and these words thereafter spake. 50
   "My sentence is for open war: of wiles,
More unexpert, I boast not: them let those
Contrive who need, or when they need, not now.

For while they sit contriving, shall the rest,
Millions that stand in arms, and longing wait   55
The signal to ascend, sit ling'ring here
Heav'n's fugitives, and for their dwelling place
Accept this dark opprobrious den of shame,
The prison of his tyranny who reigns
By our delay? no, let us rather choose   60
Armed with Hell flames and fury all at once
O'er Heav'n's high tow'rs to force resistless way,
Turning our tortures into horrid° arms   bristling
Against the torturer; when to meet the noise
Of his almightly engine he shall hear   65
Infernal thunder, and for lightning see
Black fire and horror shot with equal rage
Among his angels; and his throne itself
Mixed with Tartarean³ sulphur, and strange fire,
His own invented torments. But perhaps   70
The way seems difficult and steep to scale
With upright wing against a higher foe.
Let such bethink them, if the sleepy drench
Of that forgetful lake benumb not still,
That in our proper motion we ascend   75
Up to our native seat: descent and fall
To us is adverse.⁴ Who but felt of late
When the fierce foe hung on our brok'n rear
Insulting, and pursued us through the deep,
With what compulsion and laborious flight   80
We sunk thus low? Th' ascent is easy then;
Th' event is feared; should we again provoke
Our stronger, some worse way his wrath may find
To our destruction: if there be in Hell
Fear to be worse destroyed: what can be worse   85
Then to dwell here, driv'n out from bliss, condemned

³*Tartarean:* a word derived from Tartarus, or the place of punishment and
torment in classical mythology
⁴Angels supposedly were not subject to natural laws such as gravity. Their
natures dictated that they always strive upwards toward God.

In this abhorred deep to utter woe;
Where pain of unextinguishable fire
Must exercise us without hope of end
The vassals of his anger, when the scourge   90
Inexorably, and the torturing hour
Calls us to penance? More destroyed than thus
We should be quite abolished and expire.
What fear we then? what doubt we to incense
His utmost ire? which to the highth enraged,   95
Will either quite consume us, and reduce
To nothing this essential, happier far
Than miserable to have eternal being:
Or if our substance be indeed divine,
And cannot cease to be, we are at worst   100
On this side nothing; and by proof we feel
Our power sufficient to disturb his Heav'n,
And with perpetual inroads to alarm,
Though inaccessible, his fatal throne:
Which if not victory is yet revenge."   105
   He ended frowning, and his look denounced
Desperate revenge, and battle dangerous
To less than gods. On th' other side up rose
Belial, in act more graceful and humane;
A fairer person lost not Heav'n; he seemed   110
For dignity composed and high exploit:
But all was false and hollow; though his tongue
Dropped manna, and could make the worse appear
The better reason, to perplex and dash
Maturest counsels: for his thoughts were low;   115
To vice industrious, but to nobler deeds
Timorous and slothful: yet he pleased the ear,
And with persuasive accent thus began.
   "I should be much for open war, O peers,
As not behind in hate; if what was urged   120
Main reason to persuade immediate war,
Did not dissuade me most, and seem to cast

Ominous conjecture on the whole success:
When he who most excels in fact of arms,
In what he counsels and in what excels 125
Mistrustful, grounds his courage on despair
And utter dissolution, as the scope
Of all his aim, after some dire revenge.
First, what revenge? the tow'rs of Heav'n are filled
With armed watch, that render all access 130
Impregnable; oft on the bordering deep
Encamp their legions, or with obscure wing
Scout far and wide into the realm of night,
Scorning surprise. Or could we break our way
By force, and at our heels all Hell should rise 135
With blackest insurrection, to confound
Heav'n's purest light, yet our great enemy
All incorruptible would on his throne
Sit unpolluted, and th' ethereal mould
Incapable of stain would soon expel 140
Her mischief, and purge off the baser fire
Victorious. Thus replused, our final hope
Is flat despair: we must exasperate
Th' almighty victor to spend all his rage,
And that must end us, that must be our cure, 145
To be no more; sad cure; for who would lose,
Though full of pain, this intellectual being,
Those thoughts that wander through eternity,
To perish rather, swallowed up and lost
In the wide womb of uncreated night, 150
Devoid of sense and motion? and who knows,
Let this be good, whether our angry foe
Can give it, or will ever?[5] how he can
Is doubtful; that he never will is sure.
Will he, so wise, let loose at once his ire, 155
Belike through impotence, or unaware,

[5]The sentence means, "Who knows whether God is either able or willing
to destroy angels, even if we would prefer to be destroyed."

To give his enemies their wish, and end
Them in his anger, whom his anger saves
To punish endless? wherefore cease we then?
Say they who counsel war, we are decreed,   160
Reserved and destined to eternal woe;
Whatever doing, what can we suffer more,
What can we suffer worse? is this then worst,
Thus sitting, thus consulting, thus in arms?
What when we fled amain, pursued and strook°   struck 165
With Heav'n's afflicting thunder, and besought
The deep to shelter us? this Hell then seemed
A refuge from those wounds: or when we lay
Chained on the burning lake? that sure was worse.
What if the breath that kindled those grim fires   170
Awaked should blow them into sevenfold rage
And plunge us in the flames? or from above
Should intermitted vengeance arm again
His red right hand to plague us? what if all
Her stores were op'ned, and this firmament   175
Of Hell should spout her cataracts of fire,
Impendent horrors, threat'ning hideous fall
One day upon our heads; while we perhaps
Designing or exhorting glorious war,
Caught in a fiery tempest shall be hurled   180
Each on his rock transfixed, the sport and prey
Of racking whirlwinds, or for ever sunk
Under yon boiling ocean, wrapt in chains;
There to converse with everlasting groans,
Unrespited, unpitied, unreprieved,   185
Ages of hopeless ends; this would be worse.
War therefore, open or concealed, alike
My voice dissuades; for what can force or guile
With him, or who deceive his mind, whose eye
Views all things at one view? he from Heav'n's highth   190
All these our motions vain, sees and derides;
Not more almighty to resist our might

Than wise to frustrate all our plots and wiles.
Shall we then live thus vile, the race of Heav'n
Thus trampled, thus expelled to suffer here   195
Chains and these torments? better these than worse
By my advice; since fate inevitable
Subdues us, and omnipotent decree,
The victor's will. To suffer, as to do,
Our strength is equal, nor the law unjust   200
That so ordains: this was at first resolved,
If we were wise, against so great a foe
Contending, and so doubtful what might fall.
I laugh, when those who at the spear are bold
And vent'rous, if that fail them, shrink and fear   205
What yet they know must follow, to endure
Exile, or ignominy, or bonds, or pain,
The sentence of their conqueror: This is now
Our doom; which if we can sustain and bear,
Our supreme foe in time may much remit   210
His anger, and perhaps thus far removed
Not mind us not offending, satisfied
With what is punished; whence these raging fires
Will slack'n, if his breath stir not their flames.
Our purer essence then will overcome   215
Their noxious vapor, or enured not feel,
Or changed at length, and to the place conformed
In temper and in nature, will receive
Familiar the fierce heat, and void of pain;
This horror will grow mild, this darkness light,   220
Besides what hope the never-ending flight
Of future days may bring, what chance, what change
Worth waiting, since our present lot appears
For happy though but ill, for ill not worst,
If we procure not to ourselves more woe."   225
    Thus Belial with words clothed in reason's garb
Counselled ignoble ease, and peaceful sloth,
Not peace: and after him thus Mammon spake.

"Either to disenthrone the King of Heav'n
We war, if war be best, or to regain   230
Our own right lost: him to unthrone we then
May hope, when everlasting Fate shall yield
To fickle Chance, and Chaos judge the strife:
The former vain to hope argues as vain
The latter: for what place can be for us   235
Within Heav'n's bound, unless Heav'n's Lord supreme
We overpower? Suppose he should relent
And publish grace to all, on promise made
Of new subjection; with what eyes could we
Stand in his presence humble, and receive   240
Strict laws imposed, to celebrate his throne
With warbled hymns, and to his Godhead sing
Forced halleluiahs; while he lordly sits
Our envied sov'reign, and his altar breathes
Ambrosial odors and ambrosial flowers,   245
Our servile offerings. This must be our task
In Heav'n, this our delight; how wearisome
Eternity so spent in worship paid
To whom we hate. Let us not then pursue
By force impossible, by leave obtained   250
Unácceptable, though in Heav'n, our state
Of splendid vassalage, but rather seek
Our own good from ourselves, and from our own
Live to ourselves, though in this vast recess,
Free, and to none accountable, preferring   255
Hard liberty before the easy yoke
Of servile pomp. Our greatness will appear
Then most conspicuous, when great things of small,
Useful of hurtful, prosperous of adverse
We can create, and in what place soe'er   260
Thrive under evil, and work ease out of pain
Through labor and endurance. This deep world
Of darkness do we dread? How oft amidst
Thick clouds and dark doth Heav'n, all-ruling sire

Choose to reside, his glory unobscured,   265
And with the majesty of darkness round
Covers his throne; from whence deep thunders roar
Must'ring their rage, and Heav'n resembles Hell?
As he our darkness, cannot we his light
Imitate when we please? This desert soil   270
Wants not her hidden luster, gems and gold;
Nor want we skill or art, from whence to raise
Magnificence; and what can Heav'n show more?
Our torments also may in length of time
Become our elements, these piercing fires   275
As soft as now severe, our temper changed
Into their temper; which must needs remove
The sensible° of pain. All things invite   sense
To peaceful counsels, and the settled state
Of order, how in safety best we may   280
Compose our present evils, with regard
Of what we are and where, dismissing quite
All thoughts of war; ye have what I advise."
    He scarce had finished, when such murmur filled
Th' assembly, as when hollow rocks retain   285
The sound of blust'ring winds, which all night long
Had roused the sea, now with hoarse cadence lull
Sea-faring men o'erwatched, whose bark by chance
Or pinnace anchors in a craggy bay
After the tempest: Such applause was heard   290
As Mammon ended, and his sentence pleased,
Advising peace: for such another field°   battle
They dreaded worse than Hell: so much the fear
Of thunder and the sword of Michaël
Wrought still within them; and no less desire   295
To found this nether empire, which might rise
By policy, and long process of time,
In emulation opposite to Heav'n.
Which when Beëlzebub perceived, than whom,
Satan except, none higher sat, with grave   300

Aspect he rose, and in his rising seemed
A pillar of state; deep on his front engraven
Deliberation sat and public care;
And princely counsel in his face yet shone,
Majestic though in ruin: sage he stood   305
With Atlantean shoulders fit to bear
The weight of mightiest monarchies; his look
Drew audience and attention still as night
Or summer's noon-tide air, while thus he spake.
   "Thrones and imperial powers, off-spring of Heav'n,   310
Ethereal virtues; or these titles now
Must we renounce, and changing style be called
Princes of Hell? for so the popular vote
Inclines, here to continue, and build up here
A growing empire; doubtless; while we dream,   315
And know not that the King of Heav'n hath doomed
This place our dungeon, not our safe retreat
Beyond his potent arm, to live exempt
From Heav'n's high jurisdiction, in new league
Banded against his throne, but to remain   320
In strictest bondage, though thus far removed,
Under th' inevitable curb, reserved
His captive multitude: For he, be sure,
In highth or depth, still first and last will reign
Sole king, and of his kingdom lose no part   325
By our revolt, but over Hell extend
His empire, and with iron sceptre rule
Us here, as with his golden those in Heav'n,
What° sit we then projecting peace and war?   why
War hath determined° us, and foiled with loss   doomed 330
Irreparable; terms of peace yet none
Vouchsafed or sought; for what peace will be giv'n
To us enslaved, but custody severe,
And stripes, and arbitrary punishment
Inflicted? and what peace can we return,   335
But to our power hostility and hate,

Untamed reluctance, and revenge though slow,
Yet ever plotting how the conqueror least
May reap his conquest, and may least rejoice
In doing what we most in suffering feel?   340
Nor will occasion want, nor shall we need
With dangerous expedition to invade
Heav'n, whose high walls fear no assault or siege,
Or ambush from the deep. What if we find
Some easier enterprise? There is a place   345
(If ancient and prophetic fame in Heav'n
Err not) another world, the happy seat
Of some new race called Man, about this time
To be created like to us, though less
In power and excellence, but favored more   350
Of him who rules above; so was his will
Pronounced among the gods, and by an oath,
That shook Heav'n's whole circumference, confirmed.
Thither let us bend all our thoughts, to learn
What creatures there inhabit, of what mould,   355
Or substance, how endured, and what their power,
And where their weakness, how attempted best,
By force or subtlety: Though Heav'n be shut,
And Heav'n's high arbitrator sit secure
In his own strength, this place may lie exposed   360
The utmost border of his kingdom, left
To their defense who hold it: here perhaps
Some advantageous act may be achieved
By sudden onset, either with Hell fire
To waste his whole creation, or possess   365
All as our own, and drive as we were driven,
The puny habitants, or if not drive,
Seduce them to our party, that their God
May prove their foe, and with repenting hand
Abolish his own works. This would surpass   370
Common revenge, and interrupt his joy
In our confusion, and our joy upraise

In his disturbance; when his darling sons
Hurled headlong to partake with us, shall curse
Their frail original, and faded bliss,   375
Faded so soon. Advise if this be worth
Attempting, or to sit in darkness here
Hatching vain empires." Thus Beëlzebub
Pleaded his devilish counsel, first devised
By Satan, and in part proposed: for whence,   380
But from the author of all ill could spring
So deep a malice, to confound the race
Of mankind in one root, and earth with Hell
To mingle and involve, done all to spite
The great creator? But their spite still serves   385
His glory to augment. The bold design
Pleased highly those infernal states, and joy
Sparkled in all their eyes; with full assent
They vote: whereat his speech he thus renews.
   "Well have ye judged, well ended long debate,   390
Synod of gods, and like to what ye are,
Great things resolved, which from the lowest deep
Will once more lift us up, in spite of Fate,
Nearer our ancient seat; perhaps in view
Of those bright confines, whence with neighboring arms   395
And opportune excursion we may chance
Re-enter Heav'n; or else in some mild zone
Dwell not unvisited of Heav'n's fair light
Secure, and at the bright'ning orient beam
Purge off this gloom; the soft delicious air,   400
To heal the scar of these corrosive fires
Shall breathe her balm. But first whom shall we send
In search of this new world, whom shall we find
Sufficient? who shall tempt with wand'ring feet
The dark unbottomed infinite abyss   405
And through the palpable obscure find out
His uncouth way, or spread his aery flight
Upborne with indefatigable wings

Over the vast abrupt,[6] ere he arrive
The happy isle; what strength, what art can then   410
Suffice, or what evasion bear him safe
Through the strict senteries and stations thick
Of angels watching round? Here he had need
All circumspection, and we now no less
Choice in our suffrage; for on whom we send,   415
The weight of all and our last hope relies."
     This said, he sat; and expectation held
His look suspense, awaiting who appeared
To second, or oppose, or undertake
The perilous attempt; but all sat mute,   420
Pondering the danger with deep thoughts; and each
In other's count'nance read his own dismay
Astonished: none among the choice and prime
Of those Heav'n-warring champions could be found
So hardy as to proffer or accept   425
Alone the dreadful voyage; till at last
Satan, whom now transcendent glory raised
Above his fellows, with monarchal pride
Conscious of highest worth, unmoved thus spake.
     "O progeny of Heav'n, empyreal thrones,   430
With reason hath deep silence and demur
Seized us, though undismayed: long is the way
And hard, that out of Hell leads up to light;
Our prison strong, this huge convex of fire,
Outrageous to devour, immures us round   435
Ninefold, and gates of burning adamant
Barred over us prohibit all egress.
These past, if any pass, the void profound
Of unessential night[7] receives him next
Wide gaping, and with utter loss of being   440
Threatens him, plunged in that abortive gulf.

     [6]*abrupt:* the section of Chaos which separates Earth and Hell, a chasm
or ocean
     [7]*unessential night:* night which lacks body or essence

If thence he scape into whatever world,
Or unknown region, what remains him less
Than unknown dangers and as hard escape.
But I should ill become this throne, O peers,   445
And this imperial sov'reignty, adorned
With splendor, armed with power, if aught proposed
And judged of public moment, in the shape
Of difficulty or danger could deter
Me from attempting. Wherefore do I assume   450
These royalties, and not refuse to reign,
Refusing to accept as great a share
Of hazard as of honor, due alike
To him who reigns, and so much to him due
Of hazard more, as he above the rest   455
High honored sits? Go therefore mighty powers,
Terror of Heav'n, though fallen; intend° at home,   consider
While here shall be our home, what best may ease
The present misery, and render Hell
More tolerable; if there be cure or charm   460
To respite or deceive, or slack the pain
Of this ill mansion: intermit no watch
Against a wakeful foe, while I abroad
Through all the coasts of dark destruction seek
Deliverance for us all: this enterprise   465
None shall partake with me." Thus saying rose
The monarch, and prevented all reply,
Prudent, lest from his resolution raised°   encouraged
Others among the chief might offer now
(Certain to be refused) what erst they feared;   470
And so refused might in opinion stand
His rivals, winning cheap the high repute
Which he through hazard huge must earn. But they
Dreaded not more th' adventure than his voice
Forbidding; and at once with him they rose;   475
Their rising all at once was as the sound
Of thunder heard remote. Towards him they bend

With awful reverence prone; and as a god
Extol him equal to the highest in Heav'n:
Nor failed they to express how much they praised,   480
That for the general safety he despised
His own: for neither do the spirits dammed
Lose all their virtue; lest bad men should boast
Their specious deeds on earth, which glory excites
Or close ambition varnished o'er with zeal.   485
Thus they their doubtful consultations dark
Ended rejoicing in their matchless chief:
As when from mountain tops the dusky clouds
Ascending, while the north wind sleeps, o'erspread
Heav'n's cheerful face, the low'ring element   490
Scowls o'er the dark'n'd landscape snow, or show'r,
If chance the radiant sun with farewell sweet
Extend his ev'ning beam, the fields revive,
The birds their notes renew, and bleating herds
Attest their joy, that hill and valley rings.   495
O shame to men! Devil with devil damned
Firm concord holds, men only disagree
Of creatures rational, though under hope
Of heavenly grace; and god proclaiming peace,
Yet live in hatred, enmity, and strife   500
Among themselves, and levy cruel wars,
Wasting the earth, each other to destroy:
As if (which might induce us to accord)
Man had not hellish foes anow besides,
That day and night for his destruction wait.   505
   The Stygian Council thus dissolved: and forth
In order came the grand infernal peers:
Midst came their mighty paramount,° and seemed   chief
Alone th' antagonist of Heav'n, nor less
Than Hell's dread emperor with pomp supreme,   510
And God-like imitated state; him round
A globe of fiery seraphim[8] inclosed

[8]*seraphim:* the highest order of angels

With bright emblazonry, and horrent° arms.   bristling
Then of their session ended they bid cry
With trumpet's regal sound the great result: 515
Toward the four winds four speedy cherubim[9]
Put to their mouths the sounding alchymy
By herald's voice explained:° the hollow abyss   proclaimed
Heard far and wide, and all the host of Hell
With deaf'ning shout, returned them loud acclaim.   520
Thence more at ease their minds and somewhat raised
By false presumptuous hope, the ranged powers
Disband, and wand'ring, each his several way
Pursues, as inclination or sad choice
Leads him perplexed, where he may likeliest find   525
Truce to his restless thoughts, and entertain
The irksome hours, till this great chief return.
Part on the plain, or in the air sublime
Upon the wing, or in swift race contend,
As at th' Olympian games or Pythian fields;[10]   530
Part curb their fiery steeds, or shun the goal
With rapid wheels, or fronted brígads form.
As when to warn proud cities war appears
Waged in the troubled sky, and armies rush
To battle in the clouds, before each van   535
Prick forth the aery knights, and couch their spears
Till thickest legions close; with feats of arms
From either end of Heav'n the welkin burns.
Others with vast Typhœan[11] rage more fell
Rend up both rocks and hills, and ride the air   540
In whirlwind; Hell scarce holds the wild uproar.
As when Alcides from Oechalia crowned

[9]*cherubim:* the second order of angels, associated particularly with knowledge

[10]Here Milton suggests a combination of the funeral games described in the *Iliad* and the Olympian and Pythian games of ancient Greece, which included contests in song and oratory.

[11]*Typhoean:* Like Typhon, the largest monster ever born, who so frightened the gods when he rushed toward Olympus that they fled to Egypt. When Zeus fought him, Typhon threw whole mountains at Zeus.

With conquest, felt th' envenomed robe, and tore
Through pain up by the roots Thessalian pines,
And Lichas from the top of Oeta threw   545
Into th' Euboic sea.[12] Others more mild,
Retreated in a silent valley, sing
With notes angelical to many a harp
Their own heroic deeds and hapless fall
By doom of battle; and complain that Fate   550
Free virtue should enthrall to force or Chance.
Their song was partial,[13] but the harmony
(What could it less when spirits immortal sing?)
Suspended Hell, and took with ravishment
The thronging audience. In discourse more sweet   555
(For eloquence the soul, song charms the sense,)
Others apart sat on a hill retired,
In thoughts more elevate, and reasoned high
Of Providence, Foreknowledge, Will, and Fate,
Fixed Fate, Free will, Foreknowledge absolute,   560
And found no end, in wand'ring mazes lost.
Of good and evil much they argued then,
Of happiness and final misery,
Passion and apathy, and glory and shame,
Vain wisdom all, and false philosophie: 565
Yet with a pleasing sorcery could charm
Pain for a while or anguish, and excite
Fallacious hope, or arm th' obdured° breast   hardened
With stubborn patience as with triple steel.
Another part in squadrons and gross bands,   570
On bold adventure to discover wide
That dismal world, if any clime perhaps
Might yield them easier habitation, bend
Four ways their flying march, along the banks
Of four infernal rivers they disgorge   575

---

[12]*Alcides . . . sea:* Alcides, or Hercules, received a poisoned shirt from the
King of Oechalia, whom he had conquered. After donning the shirt, Hercules'
anguish was so great that he flung his companion Lichas into the sea.
    [13]*partial:* sung in parts

Into the burning lake their baleful streams;
Abhorred Styx the flood of deadly hate,
Sad Acheron of sorrow, black and deep;
Cocytus nam'd of lamentation loud
Heard on the rueful stream; fierce Phlegeton   580
Whose waves of torrent fire inflame with rage.
Far off from these a slow and silent stream,
Lethe the river of oblivion rolls
Her wat'ry labyrinth, whereof who drinks,
Forthwith his former state and being forgets,   585
Forgets both joy and grief, pleasure and pain.
Beyond this flood a frozen continent
Lies dark and wild, beat with perpetual storms
Of whirlwind and dire hail, which on firm land
Thaws not, but gathers heap, and ruin seems   590
Of ancient pile; all else deep snow and ice,
A gulf profound as that Serbonian[14] bog
Betwixt Damiata and Mount Casius old,
Where armies whole have sunk: the parching air
Burns frore,° and cold performs th' effect of fire.   frosty 595
Thither by harpy-footed furies[15] haled,
At certain revolutions all the damned
Are brought: and feel by turns the bitter change
Of fierce extremes, extremes by change more fierce,
From beds of raging fire to starve in ice   600
Their soft ethereal warmth, and there to pine
Immovable, infixed, and frozen round,
Periods of time, thence hurried back to fire,
They ferry over this Lethean sound
Both to and fro, their sorrow to augment,   605
And wish and struggle, as they pass, to reach
The tempting stream, with one small drop to lose
In sweet forgetfulness all pain and woe,
All in one moment, and so near the brink;

[14]*Serbonian:* Lake Serbonis was sometimes mistaken for solid ground because it could be covered with sand.
[15]*furies:* three hags who, in classical mythology, pursued the damned

But Fate withstands, and to oppose th' attempt   610
Medusa[16] with Gorgonian terror guards
The ford, and if itself the water flies
All taste of living wight,° as once it fled   person
The lip of Tantalus.[17] Thus roving on
In confused march forlorn, th' advent'rous bands   615
With shudd'ring horror pale, and eyes aghast
Viewed first their lamentable lot, and found
No rest: through many a dark and dreary vale
They passed, and many a region dolorous,
O'er many a frozen, many a fiery alp,   620
Rocks, caves, lakes, fens, bogs, dens, and shades of death,
A universe of death, which God by curse
Created evil, for evil only good,
Where all life dies, death lives, and Nature breeds,
Perverse, all monstrous, all prodigious things,   625
Abominable, inutterable, and worse
Than fables yet have feigned, or fear conceived,
Gorgons[18] and Hydras, and Chimeras dire.
   Meanwhile the adversary of God and man,
Satan with thoughts inflamed of highest design,   630
Puts on swift wings, and towards the gates of Hell
Explores his solitary flight; sometimes
He scours the right hand coast, sometimes the left,
Now shaves with level wing the deep, then soars
Up to the fiery concave tow'ring high.   635
As when far off at sea a fleet described
Hangs in the clouds, by equinoctial winds
Close sailing from Bengala, or the Isles
Of Ternate and Tidore, whence merchants bring
Their spicy drugs: they on the trading flood   640
Through the wide Ethiopian° to the cape   Indian Ocean

---

[16]*Medusa:* in classical mythology, a hag so ugly that anyone who gazed on
her turned to stone
   [17]*Tantalus:* a man in mythology, doomed to pay for his crimes by standing
in water which always flowed away from him when he tried to drink
   [18]*Gorgons, and Hydras, and Chimeras:* mythical monsters

Ply stemming nightly toward the pole. So seemed
Far off the flying fiend: at last appear
Hell bounds high reaching to the horrid roof,   645
And thrice threefold the gates, three folds were brass,
Three iron, three of adamantine rock,
Impenetrable, impaled with circling fire,
Yet unconsumed. Before the gates there sat
On either side a formidable shape;   650
The one seemed woman to the waist, and fair,
But ended foul in many a scaly fold
Voluminous and vast, a serpent armed
With mortal sting: about her middle round
A cry of hell hounds never ceasing barked   655
With wide Cerberean mouths full loud, and rung
A hideous peal: yet, when they list, would creep,
If aught disturbed their noise, into her womb,
And kennel there, yet there still barked and howled
Within unseen. Far less abhorred than these   660
Vexed Scylla[19] bathing in the sea that parts
Calabria from the hoarse Trinacrian shore:
Nor uglier follow the night-hag, when called
In secret, riding through the air she comes
Lured with the smell of infant blood, to dance   665
With Lapland[20] witches, while the laboring moon
Eclipses at their charms. The other shape,
If shape it might be called that shape had none
Distinguishable in member, joint, or limb,
Or substance might be called that shadow seemed,
For each seemed either; black it stood as night,   670
Fierce as ten furies, terrible as Hell,
And shook a dreadful dart; what seemed his head
The likeness of a kingly crown had on.
Satan was now at hand, and from his seat

[19]*Scylla:* According to Ovid, Scylla was turned into a monster who harbored
wild dogs in her womb.
[20]*Lapland:* long considered the home and meeting-place of witches

The monster moving onward came as fast,   675
With horrid strides; Hell trembled as he strode.
Th' undaunted fiend what this might be admired,
Admired, not feared; God and his Son except,
Created thing naught valued he nor shunned;
And with disdainful look thus first began.   680
    "Whence and what are thou, execrable shape,
That dar'st, though grim and terrible, advance
Thy miscreated front athwart my way
To yonder gates? through them I mean to pass,
That be assured, without leave asked of thee: 685
Retire, or taste thy folly, and learn by proof,
Hell-born, not to contend with spirits of Heav'n."
    To whom the goblin° full of wrath replied: fiend
"Art thou that traitor angel, art thou he,
Who first broke peace in Heav'n and faith, till then   690
Unbrok'n, and in proud rebellious arms
Drew after him the third part of Heav'n's sons
Conjured° against the Highest, for which both thou   united
And they outcast from God, are here condemned
To waste eternal days in woe and pain?   695
And reck'n'st thou thyself with spirits of Heav'n,
Hell-doomed, and breath'st defiance here and scorn,
Where I reign king, and to enrage thee more,
Thy king and lord? Back to thy punishment,
False fugitive, and to thy speed add wings,   700
Lest with a whip of scorpions I pursue
Thy ling'ring, or with one stroke of this dart
Strange horror seize thee, and pangs unfelt before."
    So spake the grisly terror, and in shape,
So speaking and so threat'ning, grew tenfold   705
More dreadful and deform: on th' other side
Incensed with indignation Satan stood
Unterrified, and like a comet burned,
That fires the length of Ophiucus[21] huge

---

[21]*Ophiuchus:* a large constellation of the northern hemisphere

In th' Artic sky, and from his horrid hair   710
Shakes pestilence and war. Each at the head
Levelled his deadly aim; their fatal hands
No second stroke intend, and such a frown
Each cast at th' other, as when two black clouds
With Heav'n's artillery fraught, come rattling on   715
Over the Caspian,° then stand front to front   Caspian Sea
Hov'ring a space, till winds the signal blow
To join their dark encounter in mid air:
So frowned the mighty combatants, that Hell
Grew darker at their frown, so matched they stood;   720
For never but once more was either like
To meet so great a foe: and now great deeds
Had been achieved, whereof all Hell had rung,
Had not the snaky sorceress that sat
Fast by Hell gate, and kept the fatal key,   725
Ris'n, and with hideous outcry rushed between.
    "O father, what intends thy hand," she cried,
"Against thy only son? What fury O son,
Possesses thee to bend that mortal dart
Against thy father's head? and know'st for whom;   730
For him who sits above and laughs the while
At thee ordained his drudge, to execute
Whate'er his wrath, which he calls justice, bids,
His wrath which one day will destroy ye both."
    She spake, and at her words the hellish pest   735
Forbore, then these to her Satan returned:
    "So strange thy outcry, and thy words so strange
Thou interposest, that my sudden hand
Prevented spares to tell thee yet by deeds
What it intends; till first I know of thee,   740
What thing thou art, thus double-formed, and why
In this infernal vale first met thou call'st
Me father, and that phantasm call'st my son?
I know thee not, nor ever saw till now
Sight more detestable than him and thee."   745
    T' whom thus the portress of Hell gate replied:

"Hast thou forgot me then, and do I seem
Now in thine eye so foul, once deemed so fair
In Heav'n, when at th' assembly, and in sight
Of all the seraphim with thee combined   750
In bold conspiracy against Heav'n's king,
All on a sudden miserable pain
Surprised thee, dim thine eyes, and dizzy swum
In darkness, while thy head flames thick and fast
Threw forth, till on the left side op'ning wide,   755
Likest to thee in shape and count'nance bright,
Then shining heav'nly fair, a goddess armed
Out of thy head I sprung: amazement seized
All th' host of Heav'n; back they recoiled afraid
At first, and called me Sin and for a sign   760
Portentous held me; but familiar grown,
I pleased, and with attractive graces won
The most averse, thee chiefly, who full oft
Thyself in me thy perfect image viewing
Becam'st enamored, and such joy thou took'st   765
With me in secret, that my womb conceived
A growing burden. Meanwhile war arose,
And fields were fought in Heav'n: wherein remained
(For what could else) to our almighty foe
Clear victory, to our part loss and rout   770
Through all the empyrean: down they fell
Driv'n headlong from the pitch of Heaven, down
Into this deep, and in the general fall
I also; at which time this powerful key
Into my hand was giv'n, with charge to keep   775
These gates for ever shut, which none can pass
Without my op'ning. Pensive here I sat
Alone, but long I sat not, till my womb
Pregnant by thee, and now excessive grown
Prodigious motion felt and rueful throes.   780
At last this odious offspring whom thou seest
Thine own begotten, breaking violent way
Tore through my entrails, that with fear and pain

Distorted, all my nether shape thus grew
Transformed: but he my inbred enemy   785
Forth issued, brandishing his fatal dart
Made to destroy: I fled, and cried out Death;
Hell trembled at the hideous name, and sighed
From all her caves, and back resounded Death.
I fled, but he pursued (though more, it seems,   790
Inflamed with lust than rage) and swifter far,
Me overtook his mother all dismayed,
And in embraces forcible and foul
Engend'ring with me, of that rape begot
These yelling monsters that with ceaseless cry   795
Surround me, as thou saw'st, hourly conceived
And hourly born, with sorrow infinite
To me, for when they list into, the womb
That bred them they return, and howl and gnaw
My bowels, their repast; then bursting forth   800
Afresh with conscious terrors vex me round,
That rest or intermission none I find.
Before mine eyes in opposition sits
Grim Death my son and foe, who sets them on,
And me his parent would full soon devour   805
For want of other prey, but that he knows
His end with mine involved; and knows that I
Should prove a bitter morsel, and his bane,
Whenever that shall be; so fate pronounced.
But thou O father, I forewarn thee, shun   810
His deadly arrow; neither vainly hope
To be invulnerable in those bright arms,
Though tempered heav'nly, for that mortal dint,
Save he who reigns above, none can resist."
    She finished, and the subtle fiend his lore   815
Soon learned, now milder, and thus answered smooth.
"Dear daughter, since thou claim'st me for thy sire,
And my fair son here shows't me, the dear pledge
Of dalliance had with thee in Heav'n, and joys
Then sweet, now sad to mention, through dire change   820

Befall'n us unforeseen, unthought of, know
I come no enemy, but to set free
From out this dark and dismal house of pain,
Both him and thee, and all the heav'nly host
Of spirits that in our just pretenses armed   825
Fell with us from on high: from them I go
This uncouth errand sole, and one for all
Myself expose, with lonely steps to tread
Th' unfounded deep, and through the void immense
To search with wand'ring quest a place foretold   830
Should be, and, by concurring signs, ere now
Created vast and round, a place of bliss
In the purlieus of Heav'n, and therein placed
A race of upstart creatures, to supply
Perhaps our vacant room, though more removed,   835
Lest Heav'n surcharged with potent multitude
Might hap to move new broils: be this or aught
Than this more secret now designed, I haste
To know, and this once known, shall soon return
And bring ye to the place where thou and Death   840
Shall dwell at ease, and up and down unseen
Wing silently the buxom air, imbalmed
With odors; there ye shall be fed and filled
Immeasurably, all things shall be your prey."
    He ceased, for both seemed highly pleased, and Death   845
Grinned horrible a ghastly smile, to hear
His famine should be filled, and blest his maw
Destined to that good hour: no less rejoiced
His mother bad, and thus bespake her sire.
    "The key of this infernal pit by due,   850
And by command of Heav'n's all-powerful king
I keep, by him forbidden to unlock
These adamantine gates; against all force
Death ready stands to interpose his dart,
Fearless to be o'ermatched by living might.   855
But what owe I to his commands above

Who hates me, and hath hither thrust me down
Into this gloom of Tartarus profound,
To sit in hateful office here confined,
Inhabitant of Heav'n, and heav'nly-born,   860
Here in perpetual agony and pain,
With terrors and with clamors compassed round
Of mine own brood, that on my bowels feed:
Thou art my father, thou my author, thou
My being gav'st me; whom shall I obey   865
But thee, whom follow? thou wilt bring me soon
To that new world of light and bliss, among
The gods who live at ease, where I shall reign
At thy right hand voluptuous, as beseems
Thy daughter and thy darling, without end."   870
   Thus saying, from her side the fatal key,
Sad instrument of all our woe, she took;
And towards the gate rolling her bestial train,
Forthwith the huge portcullis° high up drew,   fortified grate
Which but herself not all the Stygian powers   875
Could once have moved; then in the key-hole turns
Th' intricate wards, and every bolt and bar
Of massy iron or solid rock with ease
Unfast'ns: on a sudden op'n fly
With impetuous recoil and jarring sound   880
Th' infernal doors, and on their hinges grate
Harsh thunder, that the lowest bottom shook
Of Erebus. She op'ned, but to shut
Excelled her power; the gates wide op'n stood,
That with extended wings a bannered host   885
Under spread ensigns marching might pass through
With horse and chariots ranked in loose array;
So wide they stood, and like a furnace mouth
Cast forth redounding° smoke and ruddy flame.   billowing
Before their eyes in sudden view appear   890
The secrets of the hoary deep, a dark
Illimitable ocean without bound,

Without dimension, where length, breadth, and highth,
And time and place are lost; where eldest Night
And Chaos, ancestors of Nature, hold   895
Eternal anarchy, amidst the noise
Of endless wars, and by confusion stand.
For hot, cold, moist, and dry, four champions fierce
Strive here for mast'ry, and to battle bring
Their embryon atoms; they around the flag   900
Of each his faction, in their several clans,
Light-armed or heavy, sharp, smooth, swift or slow,
Swarm populous, unnumbered as the sands
Of Barca or Cyrene's[22] torrid soil,
Levied to side with warring winds, and poise   905
Their lighter wings. To whom these most adhere,
He rules a moment; Chaos umpire sits,
And by decision more imbroils the fray
By which he reigns: next him high arbiter
Chance governs all. Into this wild abyss,   910
The womb of nature and perhaps her grave,
Of neither sea, nor shore, nor air, nor fire,
But all these in their pregnant causes mixed
Confus'dly, and which thus must ever fight,
Unless th' almightly maker them ordain   915
His dark materials to create more worlds,
Into this wild abyss the wary fiend
Stood on the brink of Hell and looked a while,
Pondering his voyage: for no narrow frith°   bay
He had to cross. Nor was his ear less pealed   920
With noises loud and ruinous (to compare
Great things with small) than when Bellona[23] storms,
With all her battering engines bent to raze
Some capital city; or less than if this frame
Of Heav'n were falling, and these elements   925
In mutiny had from her axle torn

[22]*Barca or Cyrene:* cities in north Africa
[23]*Bellona:* Roman goddess of war

The steadfast earth. At last his sail-broad vans°   wings
He spreads for flight, and in the surging smoke
Uplifted spurns the ground, thence many a league
As in a cloudy chair ascending rides   930
Audacious, but that seat soon failing, meets
A vast vacuity: all unawares
Flutt'ring his pennons vain plumb down he drops
Ten thousand fadom° deep, and to this hour   fathoms
Down had been falling, had not by ill chance   935
The strong rebuff of some tumultuous cloud
Instinct with fire and nitre hurried him
As many miles aloft: that fury stayed
Quenched in a boggy Syrtis,[24] neither sea,
Nor good dry land, nigh foundered on he fares, 940
Treading the crude consistence, half on foot,
Half flying; behoves him now both oar and sail.
As when a gryfon° through the wilderness winged monster
With winged course o'er hill or moory dale,
Pursues the Arimaspian,[25] who by stealth   945
Had from his wakeful custody purloined
The guarded gold: So eagerly the fiend
O'er bog or steep, through strait, rough, dense, or rare,
With head, hands, wings, or feet pursues his way,
And swims or sinks, or wades, or creeps, or flies: 950
At length a universal hubbub wild
Of stunning sounds and voices all confused
Borne through the hollow dark assaults his ear
With loudest vehemence: thither he plies,
Undaunted to meet there whatever power   955
Or spirit of the nethermost abyss
Might in that noise reside, of whom to ask
Which way the nearest coast of darkness lies
Bordering on light; when straight behold the throne

---

[24]*Syrtis:* quicksands off the African coast
[25]*Arimaspian:* one of a one-eyed people of Scythia, who supposedly fought constantly with griffins for the griffins' gold

Of Choas, and his dark pavilion spread   960
Wide on the wasteful deep; with him enthroned
Sat sable-vested Night, eldest of things,
The consort of his reign; and by them stood
Orcus and Ades,[26] and the dreaded name
Of Demogorgon; Rumor next and Chance,   965
And Tumult and Confusion all imbroiled,
And Discord with a thousand various mouths.
    T' whom Satan turning boldly, thus: "Ye powers
And spirits of this nethermost abyss,
Chaos and ancient Night, I come no spy,   970
With purpose to explore or to disturb
The secrets of your realm, but by constraint
Wand'ring this darksome desert, as my way
Lies through your spacious empire up to light,
Alone, and without guide, half lost, I seek   975
What readiest path leads where your gloomy bounds
Confine with Heav'n; or if some other place
From your dominion won, th' ethereal king
Possesses lately, thither to arrive
I travel this profound, direct my course;   980
Directed, no mean recompence it brings
To your behoof, if I that region lost,
All usurpation thence expelled, reduce
To her original darkness and your sway
(Which is my present journey) and once more   985
Erect the standard there of ancient Night;
Yours be th' advantage all, mine the revenge."
    Thus Satan; and him thus the anarch old
With falt'ring speech and visage incomposed
Answered. "I know thee, stranger, who thou art,   990
That mighty leading angel, who of late
Made head against Heav'n's king, though overthrown.
I saw and heard, for such a numerous host
Fled not in silence through the frighted deep

[26]*Orcus and Ades:* names for Demogorgon's region in the underworld

With ruin upon ruin, rout on rout, 995
Confusion worse confounded; and Heav'n gates
Poured out by millions her victorious bands
Pursuing. I upon my frontiers here
Keep residence; if all I can will serve,
That little which is left so to defend, 1000
Encroached on still through our intestine broils.
Weak'ning the sceptre of old Night: first Hell
Your dungeon stretching far and wide beneath;
Now lately Heaven and earth, another world
Hung o'er my realm, linked in a golden chain 1005
To that side Heav'n from whence your legions fell:
If that way be your walk, you have not far;
So much the nearer danger; go and speed;
Havoc and spoil and ruin are my gain."
   He ceased; and Satan stayed not to reply, 1010
But glad that now his sea should find a shore,
With fresh alacrity and force renewed
Springs upward like a pyramid of fire
Into the wild expanse, and through the shock
Of fighting elements, on all sides round 1015
Environed wins his way; harder beset
And more endangered, than when Argo[27] passed
Through Bosporus betwixt the justling rocks:[28]
Or when Ulysses on the larboard shunned
Charybdis, and by th' other whirlpool steered.[29] 1020
So he with difficulty and labor hard
Moved on, with difficulty and labor he;
But he once past, soon after when man fell,
Strange alteration! Sin and Death amain
Following his track, such was the will of Heav'n, 1025
Paved after him a broad and beat'n way

[27]*Argo:* the ship of Jason, who sailed in search of the golden fleece
[28]*the justling rocks:* the Symplegades, boulders which moved and crushed boats attempting to sail between them
[29]*Scylla and Charybdis:* a rock and a whirlpool, representing two equal dangers Ulysses steered between on his way home from Troy. Milton may have thought of both as whirlpools.

Over the dark abyss, whose boiling gulf
Tamely endured a bridge of wondrous length
From Hell continued reaching th' utmost orb[30]
Of this frail world; by which the spirits perverse   1030
With easy intercourse pass to and fro
To tempt or punish mortals, except whom
God and good angels guard by special grace.
But now at last the sacred influence
Of light appears, and from the walls of Heav'n   1035
Shoots far into the bosom of dim night
A glimmering dawn; here Nature first begins
Her fardest° verge, and Chaos to retire   fartherest
As from her outmost works a brok'n foe
With tumult less and with less hostile din,   1040
That Satan with less toil, and now with ease
Wafts on the calmer wave by dubious light
And like a weather-beaten vessel holds°   heads for
Gladly the port, though shrouds and tackle torn;
Or in the emptier waste, resembling air,   1045
Weighs his spread wings, at leisure to behold
Far off th' empyreal Heav'n, extended wide
In circuit, undetermined square or round,
With opal tow'rs and battlements adorned
Of living sapphire, once his native seat;   1050
And fast by hanging in a golden chain
This pendant world, in bigness as a star
Of smallest magnitude close by the moon.
Thither full fraught with mischievous revenge,
Accursed, and in a cursed hour he hies.   1055

[30]*Orb:* the outermost of the ten concentric spheres surrounding the earth

1. Why does Milton emphasize the lavishness of Satan's throne,
   and the importance of Satan's rank in Hell? What does "bad
   eminence" mean in line 6?

2. Milton struggles throughout *Paradise Lost* with the problem of free will. Examine lines 18-21. How does Milton deal with free will as opposed to predestination here? Later, the fallen angels debate such questions while Satan goes in search of Earth (lines 559-569). Why would such questions be particularly thorny ones for anybody trying to justify the ways of God to man? Why would such a debate particularly concern fallen angels?
3. What is Satan's mood as Book II begins? How does he prove that no strife can occur in Hell (see lines 30-40)? Does his logic seem sound? In this speech, what goal does he set for his company? What two means of attaining his goal seem possible?
4. The speeches of Moloch, Beliah, Mammon, and Beëlzebub represent particular ways of looking at the world, or at life. Summarize each argument in your own words. Do any of these approaches to life seem familiar or contemporary to you? Milton apparently felt that these speakers represented particular types of Englishmen. What kind of person is each speaker? How is each course of action appropriate to the speaker who suggests it?
5. As a public official in Cromwell's government, Milton undoubtedly learned a great deal about politics and the way in which people can be manipulated for political ends. Some of this knowledge becomes evident in *Paradise Lost*. What makes Beëlzebub a particularly effective politician (see lines 299-310)? Why does his speech seem a happy compromise after the three which preceded his? What do we find out about the politics of Hell in lines 378-389? What, in lines 466-485, proves that Satan is a shrewd politician?
6. Review the obstacles to Satan's search for Earth as they are listed in lines 432-444. Why is it appropriate that Satan alone should go in search of Earth?
7. Do you think Satan has any admirable characteristics in Books One and Two? Is Satan less admirable at the end of Book Two than he was at the end of Book One? Why or why not? What are the virtues Milton concedes that imps of Hell possess?
8. What does God appear to be like in lines 730-734 of Book Two? In the whole of Book Two? Is there any reason to believe this view of God is distorted? What might distort it?
9. When Satan approaches the Gates of Hell, the narrative becomes more obviously allegorical. That is, abstract words are personified and made to behave as actors in the story. Thus Sin and Death become active players in the drama. What is Sin's parentage? Why is it allegorically appropriate? Do you know the Greek myth from which Milton took his idea about the birth of Sin? If

202 ⁊❧ *The Puritan Poet: John Milton*

not, look it up under *Athena*. What do you learn about Milton's attitude toward women when he makes Sin a female?

10. Who were the parents of Death? Why is this detail allegorically appropriate? What is there about Death's parentage that increases one's sense of evil, horror, and revulsion? What traits characterize Death? Explain how each trait works in the allegory.

11. Satan, Sin, and Death are a triumvirate of horrors. To what does Milton compare them by grouping them in a unit of three? How is the comparison reinforced? What purpose does it serve?

12. Why does Chaos come to the aid of Satan? Why is this encounter between Satan and Chaos so integral to the allegory?

13. Compare Beëlzebub's plan for the future with Satan's promises to Sin, Death, and Chaos. Do you find any discrepancies? How does Satan's approach to Sin and Death fit into the allegory? How does this approach reveal Satan's personal characteristics?

14. Describe Milton's universe as he pictures it in *Paradise Lost*. Where are Heaven and Hell in relation to Earth? What is between Earth, Heaven, and Hell? What image in the closing lines suggests the relationship between Earth and Heaven? What are the connotations and implications of this image?

THE AGE OF REASON AND COMMON SENSE

The Glorious Revolution of 1688, which made William and Mary joint sovereigns of England, was a peaceful change of government that ended years of civil strife. Because most Englishmen were exhausted by political and religious warfare, they welcomed a settlement that promised, at long last, some stability and restraint in public life. The century which followed, from 1688 to the French Revolution of 1789, was predominantly an age which emphasized reason and common sense, dignity and decorum. These characteristics of eighteenth-century culture were based on two assumptions: rules govern all aspects of life, including literature; the reasonable and natural thing to do is to follow these rules.

Because the literary rules were derived from the classics of ancient Greece and Rome, this period is sometimes called the Neoclassic period. In their respect for the classics, eighteenth-century writers were continuing a tradition that went back to the Renaissance. In actuality, they made classical rules serve the social, economic, and political interests peculiar to their own time and produced a literature markedly different from any other. Their reactions against the turmoil of the seventeenth century made "enthusiasm" for religion seem suspect and any strong emotional display unseemly. Their task was to restore order and sanity to a confused and disordered England.

Writers found especially eager readers among those who were gaining wealth and influence in commerce and government. New sources of income in North America and India were helping to make England the most powerful nation in the world. To play the role in society and politics expected of them, the newly rich needed to acquire as quickly as possible the cultural background and the elegant speech and manners of an older aristocracy. Newspapers and magazines were established to offer helpful advice on "correct" conduct. Admiration of proper form found expression in all the arts — the orderly music of Handel, the symmetrical buildings of Sir Christopher Wren, the dignified portraiture of Sir Joshua Reynolds, the balanced furniture of Chippendale, and the trim formal gardens of Georgian houses. For the ruling class, the cultivation of this neoclassical style made life distinctive, elegant, and refined.

Political issues as well as the social graces concerned writers of the period. Men had to devise and master new methods of government now that Parliament rather than the monarchy was dominant. Writers interested themselves in the contests for power waged by the new political parties. Through the Whig party, noblemen and rich businessmen promoted their interests. The Tory party represented a more conservative group made up largely of landowners and Anglican clergy. When George I, a fifty-four-year-old German who spoke no English, came to the throne, he "reigned but did not rule," leaving Parliament under the Whigs to add further to its powers. Until the end of the century, when a new democratic movement began stirring, literature generally reflected the interests of the wealthy ruling families within the parliamentary system.

Other forces helped to create an intellectual climate favorable to the development of an "age of prose and reason" in literature. For many men, the fashionable creed of Deism swept away religious anxieties by making God the "originator of natural law." The universe was an orderly, logical arrangement in which man, by exercising good sense, could find his proper place. "To follow reason," it was said, "was to follow God." The discovery of "natural laws" by scientists gave additional support to a balanced, rational view of life. From these theories practical men were busy inventing the basic machinery for the Industrial Revolution, but the full effects of that upheaval would not be felt until the end of the century.

The result was a literature described as "middle-aged" rather than youthful, cautious rather than exuberant. The classics served as models, providing both the literary forms and the literary standards of restraint, balance, order, and clarity. To this was added a concern for moral improvement, but advocated with politeness rather than passion. The best poetry of the period tended to be satirical, pointing out the discrepancy between man's capacity and his attainment. By witty ridicule, satire encouraged the reader to believe that he could avoid making a fool of himself if he complied with the rules of reason. Eighteenth-century literature was both a criticism of mankind and a plea for common sense.

JOHN DRYDEN was the most influential of the literary leaders who gradually formulated the new philosophy. A scholar of the classics, he applied Greek and Latin standards to his own work, and suggested that such standards should also apply to the works of others. His translations of Homer, Virgil, and other classical poets did much to familiarize English readers with the literature of Greece and Rome.

Dryden was a master of all the literary forms of his day and rose to become the most influential writer of his time in the fields of poetry, drama, and criticism. It was Dryden who popularized the closed heroic couplet—two rhymed iambic pentameter lines that express a complete thought—which was to prevail as the most "proper" poetic form for nearly one hundred years in England. An accomplished satirist, he devastated his enemies in verse; and his clear, crisp essays and prefaces, which served as models for later writers, had a marked influence on English prose style.

ALEXANDER POPE'S favorite targets of satire were the dull and pretentious writers of his day and the minor foibles of society. His verse, neatly fashioned of closed heroic couplets, was the envy of Jonathan Swift, who groaned that Pope "can in one couplet fix/More sense than I can do in six." Pope's "swift play and flash of mind" produced poetry of "grace, judgment and wit." Many of his epigrams—"A little learning is a dangerous thing," "To err is human, to forgive divine," "For fools rush in where angels fear to tread"—have become household expressions.

As a boy, Pope set himself the goal of becoming the "one great poet that was correct." In fulfilling this goal, he demonstrated in both his critical and creative works the classical rules of balance, rationality, and restraint. He contributed directly to the classical revival by his translations of Homer's *Iliad* and *Odyssey,* as well as by his *Imitations of Horace.* In accordance with the standards of his time, which he did much to establish, Pope's poetry was eminently correct.

With penetrating ideas and trenchant wit, Pope seemed to lack nothing except, perhaps, the intensity that comes from inspiration. But in his age, revealing deep feeling was considered equivalent to exposing one's poor taste. Therefore, Pope's verse illustrates the problems of genius in a fairly restricted society. Of necessity, he vented his most profound feelings through satire, often with a vehemence and intensity going far beyond the moderation and reason he advocated. In doing so, however, he created some of the cleverest verse in English literature.

John Dryden

Some of Dryden's best poetry is satirical, for the period in which he lived was more interested in reason and craftsmanship in literature than in imagination. His finest lyrics, however, are serious and convey a true emotion, though expressed in neatly rhymed iambic pentameter couplets. The poem "Alexander's Feast" contains, in the words of Thomas Gray, "thoughts that breathe, and words that burn." This ode was written for St. Cecilia's Day which honored the patron saint of music. The poem reveals Dryden's ability to write in a form other than the heroic couplet. "Alexander's Feast" was written to be set to music, and like his "Song for St. Cecilia's Day" (1687), it deals with the power of music to sway human feelings.

ALEXANDER'S FEAST; OR, THE POWER OF MUSIC

A SONG IN HONOR OF ST. CECILIA'S DAY, 1697

'Twas at the royal feast, for Persia won
    By Philip's warlike son:°   Alexander
    Aloft in awful° state   awesome
    The godlike hero sate°   sat

On his imperial throne;   5
His valiant peers[1] were placed around;
Their brows with roses and with myrtles[2]
      bound:
(So should desert in arms be crowned.)
The lovely Thais,[3] by his side,
Sate like a blooming Eastern bride,   10
In flower of youth and beauty's pride.
      Happy, happy, happy pair!
        None but the brave,
        None but the brave,
        None but the brave deserves the
          fair.   15

CHORUS

Happy, happy, happy pair!
  None but the brave,
  None but the brave,
None but the brave deserves the fair.

Timotheus,[4] placed on high   20
  Amid the tuneful quire,°   choir
  With flying fingers touched the lyre:
The trembling notes ascend the sky,
  And heavenly joys inspire.
The song began from Jove,   25
Who left his blissful seats above,
(Such is the power of mighty love).
A dragon's fiery form belied the god:
Sublime on radiant spires he rode,
When he to fair Olympia[5] pressed;   30

[1]*peers:* those of equal rank and ability
[2]*roses . . . myrtles:* The rose is an emblem of beauty, the myrtle of love.
[3]*Thais:* a Greek courtesan
[4]*Timotheus:* Alexander's favorite musician
[5]*Olympia:* Alexander's mother

And while he sought her snowy breast,
Then round her slender waist he curled,
And stamped an image of himself, a sovereign
    of the world.
The listening crowd admire the lofty sound,
"A present deity," they shout around;   35
"A present deity," the vaulted roofs re-
    bound:
        With ravished ears
        The monarch hears,
        Assumes the god,
        Affects to nod,   40
    And seems to shake the spheres.

CHORUS

        With ravished ears
        The monarch hears,
        Assumes the god,
        Affects to nod,   45
    And seems to shake the spheres.

The praise of Bacchus[6] then the sweet musi-
    cian sung,
    Of Bacchus ever fair, and ever young.
      The jolly god in triumph comes;
      Sound the trumpets, beat the drums;   50
        Flushed with a purple grace
        He shows his honest face:
Now give the hautboys° breath; he comes,   oboes
    he comes.
      Bacchus, ever fair and young,
        Drinking joys did first ordain;   55
      Bacchus' blessings are a treasure,

[6]*Bacchus:* the god of wine and revelry

Drinking is the soldier's pleasure;
 Rich the treasure,
 Sweet the pleasure,
Sweet is pleasure after pain.   60

CHORUS

Bacchus' blessings are a treasure,
Drinking is the soldier's pleasure;
 Rich the treasure,
 Sweet the pleasure,
Sweet is pleasure after pain.   65

Soothed with the sound the king grew vain;
 Fought all his battles o'er again;
And thrice he routed all his foes, and thrice
 he slew the slain.
 The master° saw the madness rise,   musician
 His glowing cheeks, his ardent eyes;   70
 And while he heaven and earth defied,
 Changed his hand, and checked his pride.
  He chose a mournful Muse,
  Soft pity to infuse;
 He sung Darius[7] great and good,   75
  By too severe a fate,
 Fallen, fallen, fallen, fallen,
  Fallen from his high estate,
 And weltering in his blood;
 Deserted at his utmost need   80
 By those his former bounty fed;
 On the bare earth exposed he lies,
 With not a friend to close his eyes.

[7]*Darius:* conquered by Alexander

With downcast looks the joyless victor sate,
   Revolving in his altered soul   85
     The various turns of chance below;
   And, now and then, a sigh he stole,
   And tears began to flow.

CHORUS

  Revolving in his altered soul
    The various turns of chance below;   90
  And, now and then, a sigh he stole,
    And tears began to flow.

The mighty master smiled to see
That love was in the next degree;
'Twas but a kindred sound to move,   95
For pity melts the mind to love.
  Softly sweet, in Lydian[8] measures,
  Soon he soothed his soul to pleasures.
"War," he sung, "is toil and trouble;
Honor but an empty bubble;   100
  Never ending, still beginning,
Fighting still, and still destroying:
  If the world be worth thy winning,
Think, O think it worth enjoying:
  Lovely Thais sits beside thee,   105
  Take the good the gods provide thee."

The many rend the skies with loud applause;
So Love was crowned, but Music won the
    cause.
  The prince, unable to conceal his pain,

---

[8]*Lydian:* a gentle, sensuous mode of music

Gazed on the fair   110
Who caused his care,
And sighed and looked, sighed and looked,
Sighed and looked, and sighed again;
At length, with love and wine at once op-
   pressed,
The vanquished victor sunk upon her breast.   115

CHORUS

The prince, unable to conceal his pain,
Gazed on the fair
Who caused his care,
And sighed and looked, sighed and looked,
Sighed and looked, and sighed again;   120
At length, with love and wine at once op-
   pressed,
The vanquished victor sunk upon her breast.

Now strike the golden lyre again;
A louder yet, and yet a louder strain.
Break his bands of sleep asunder,   125
And rouse him, like a rattling peal of
   thunder.
Hark, hark, the horrid sound
Has raised up his head;

As awaked from the dead,
And, amazed, he stares around.   130
"Revenge, revenge!" Timotheus cries;
"See the Furies arise;
See the snakes that they rear,
How they hiss in their hair,
And the sparkles that flash from their
   eyes?   135

Behold a ghastly band,
Each a torch in his hand!
Those are Grecian ghosts, that in battle were
slain,
And unburied remain
Inglorious on the plain: 140
Give the vengeance due
To the valiant crew.
Behold how they toss their torches on high,
How they point to the Persian abodes,
And glittering temples of their hostile gods!"   145
The princes applaud with a furious joy;
And the king seized a flambeau with zeal to
destroy;
Thais led the way,
To light him to his prey,
And, like another Helen, fired another Troy.   150

CHORUS

And the king seized a flambeau with zeal to
destroy;
Thais led the way,
To light him to his prey,
And, like another Helen, fired another Troy.

Thus long ago,   155
Ere heaving bellows learned to blow,
While organs yet were mute,
Timotheus, to his breathing flute
And sounding lyre,
Could swell the soul to rage, or kindle soft
desire.   160
At last divine Cecilia came,
Inventress of the vocal frame;
The sweet enthusiast, from her sacred store,

Enlarged the former narrow bounds,
And added length to solemn sounds,
With Nature's mother wit, and arts unknown
    before.
    Let old Timotheus yield the prize,
        Or both divide the crown:
    He raised a mortal to the skies;
        She drew an angel down.

165

170

GRAND CHORUS

At last divine Cecilia came,
Inventress of the vocal frame;
The sweet enthusiast, from her sacred store
    Enlarged the former narrow bounds,
    And added length to solemn sounds,
With Nature's mother wit, and arts unknown
    before.
    Let old Timotheus yield the prize,
        Or both divide the crown:
    He raised a mortal to the skies;
        She drew an angel down.

175

180

1. Saint Cecilia is the patron saint of music. Do you think this ode is an appropriate one with which to celebrate St. Cecilia's Day (November 22)? Why or why not? What aspects of the poem's form particularly suggest music?
2. In stanza 1, Dryden creates a scene which suggests that Alexander's feast fulfills every desire. What is the satisfying scene composed of? How has Dryden communicated that Alexander possesses wealth, power, prestige, and love? What suggests that Alexander deserves what he has? What had Alexander accomplished? If you do not know, look up Alexander the Great in the library.

3. The feast seems to please the guests as well as Alexander. Why are the peers of Alexander allowed to wear crowns of roses and myrtle? What is symbolized by wearing the wreaths?
4. In stanza 2, Timotheus's song begins. What does he first sing about in lines 25-34? What extravagant compliment does he pay Alexander? Why is the compliment appropriate for the occasion? What effect does the flattering song have on the crowd? On Alexander?
5. What subjects does Timotheus dwell on as his song continues? In the stanza beginning line 66, we find out the full extent of Timotheus's powers. What do we learn about Alexander?
6. Why is Alexander joyless by line 84? What philosophy does Timotheus weave into his song in lines 99-106? Do you think the outlook expressed here is valid, or was it simply manufactured for the occasion?
7. What happens to Alexander in lines 110-115? What is Timotheus's response? Under what circumstances does the feast break up?
8. In the last stanza, after we have witnessed the extraordinary power exerted by Timotheus, the musician, we find he must share his earned honors with another. Who exerts as much power as Timotheus? What is the difference between the two?

Alexander Pope

A master of the closed heroic couplet, Pope knew how to use it with consummate skill. His readers were especially intrigued by his clever alliteration and the subtle ways in which he quickened or slowed the rhythm of a line by his choice of words, without departing from iambic pentameter. He also produced little surprises of contrasting and parallel structure, of juxtaposition and paradox. The whole poetic experience, however, was kept within the bounds of reason. This was a discipline that Pope demanded of himself and one that his readers greatly admired.

FROM AN ESSAY ON MAN

An Essay on Man consists of four epistles which express in poetic form some of Pope's philosophical ideas. This excerpt from Epistle I is concerned with "the nature and state of man, with respect to the universe."

Presumptuous man! the reason wouldst thou find,
Why formed so weak, so little, and so blind!
First, if thou canst, the harder reason guess,
Why formed no weaker, blinder, and no less!

Ask of thy mother earth, why oaks are made   5
Taller or stronger than the weeds they shade?
Or ask of yonder argent° fields above,   silver
Why Jove's¹ satellites are less than Jove?
   Of systems possible, if 'tis confessed°   acknowledged
That wisdom infinite must form the best,   10
Where all must full or not coherent be,
And all that rises, rise in due degree;
Then, in the scale of reas'ning life, 'tis plain
There must be, somewhere, such a rank as man;
And all the question (wrangle e'er so long)   15
Is only this, if God has placed him wrong?
   Respecting man, whatever wrong we call,
May, must be right, as relative to all.
In human works, though labored on with pain,
A thousand movements scarce one purpose gain;   20
In God's, one single can its end produce;
Yet serves to second too some other use.
So man, who here seems principal° alone,   first in rank
Perhaps acts second to some sphere unknown,
Touches some wheel, or verges to some goal;   25
'Tis but a part we see, and not a whole.
   When the proud steed shall know why man restrains
His fiery course, or drives him o'er the plains;
When the dull ox, why now he breaks the clod,
Is now a victim, and now Egypt's god: 30
Then shall man's pride and dulness comprehend
His actions', passions', being's, use and end;
Why doing, suff'ring, checked, impelled; and why
This hour a slave, the next a deity.
   Then say not man's imperfect, Heav'n in fault;   35
Say rather, man's as perfect as he ought;
His knowledge measured to his state and place,
His time a moment, and a point his space.

¹*Jove:* ruler of the Roman gods

If to be perfect in a certain sphere,
What matter, soon or late, or here or there?   40
The blessed today is as completely so,
As who began a thousand years ago.

. . . .

   What if the foot, ordained the dust to tread,
Or hand to toil, aspired to be the head?
What if the head, the eye, or ear repined   45
To serve mere engines to the ruling mind?
Just as absurd for any part to claim
To be another, in this gen'ral frame:
Just as absurd, to mourn the tasks or pains
The great directing Mind of All ordains.   50
   All are but parts of one stupendous whole,
Whose body, Nature is, and God the soul;
That, changed through all, and yet in all the same,
Great in the earth, as in th' ethereal frame,
Warms in the sun, refreshes in the breeze,   55
Glows in the stars, and blossoms in the trees,
Lives through all life, extends through all extent,
Spreads undivided, operates unspent,
Breathes in our soul, informs our mortal part,
As full, as perfect, in a hair as heart;   60
As full, as perfect, in vile man that mourns,
As the rapt Seraph that adores and burns;
To him no high, no low, no great, no small;
He fills, he bounds, connects, and equals all!
   Cease then, nor Order imperfection name: 65
Our proper bliss depends on what we blame.
Know thy own point: This kind, this due degree
Of blindness, weakness, Heav'n bestows on thee.
Submit—In this, or any other sphere,
Secure to be as blessed as thou canst bear;   70
Safe in the hand of one disposing Pow'r,
Or in the natal, or the mortal hour.

All Nature is but Art, unknown to thee;
All chance, direction, which thou canst not see;
All discord, harmony, not understood;   75
All partial evil, universal good:
And spite of pride, in erring reason's spite,
One truth is clear, "Whatever IS, is RIGHT."

1. What question has man dared to ask that leads Pope to call him "presumptuous"? What harder and more important reason does Pope say man should try to discover? From whom should man seek explanations? In your opinion, what is implied by lines 5-8?
2. Lines 9-16 clearly reflect eighteenth-century enthusiasm for "natural law," suggested here by the "system" in which man has a place. What kind of system is it? By what line of reasoning does Pope arrive at "all the questions" (lines 15 and 16)?
3. In lines 19-26, what distinction is drawn between the works of man and of God? How do you interpret lines 23-25?
4. What must man understand before he can comprehend himself and his "use and end"? How do the metaphors in lines 27-30 make the nature of this understanding clear? What "assumptions" and "judgment of life" does Pope express in lines 35-42? Tell why you think they will, or will not, reassure any "presumptuous man" who finds "heaven in fault" for his imperfections?
5. If man could see the whole rather than the part, what would he understand about his place and rank in "the divine scheme of things"? Why would he accept the fact that he is "as perfect as he ought to be"?
6. Point out examples which you think illustrate Pope's "consummate skill" in using the couplet to make a telling comment, to draw comparisons or contrasts, and to maintain the rhythm and rhyme without the effect becoming stilted and monotonous.
7. In this selection, Pope discusses man's relationship to the universe. But, judging from the last lines, what attitude would you expect Pope to have toward society? What would he probably think of social ambition? of one who wished to change or improve the social order?

THE RAPE OF THE LOCK

Epic poetry, because of its importance to the classical tradition, was held in high esteem by Pope and his contemporaries. Yet he did not hesitate to use it as a vehicle for satire, as in the popular "heroicomical" poem *The Rape of the Lock*. Pope's friend Caryll suggested the idea of celebrating a petty scandal, the theft by Lord Petre of a lock of hair from the head of Miss Arabella Fermor. Pope complied by making Miss Fermor the heroine Belinda in a mock epic that treats this trivial subject in a grand style filled with grace and humor.

CANTO I

What dire offense from am'rous causes springs,
What mighty contests rise from trivial things,
I sing—This verse to Caryll, Muse! is due;
This, ev'n Belinda may vouchsafe to view:
Slight is the subject, but not so the praise,   5
If she inspire, and he approve my lays.
   Say what strange motive, goddess! could compel
A well-bred lord t' assault a gentle belle?
Oh, say what stranger cause, yet unexplored,
Could make a gentle belle reject a lord?   10
In tasks so bold, can little men engage,
And in soft bosoms dwells such mighty rage?
   Sol[1] through white curtains shot a tim'rous ray,
And oped those eyes that must eclipse the day;
Now lap-dogs give themselves the rousing shake,   15
And sleepless lovers, just at twelve, awake:
Thrice rung the bell, the slipper knocked the ground,
And the pressed watch returned a silver sound.
Belinda still her downy pillow pressed,
Her guardian sylph[2] prolonged the balmy rest.   20
'Twas he had summoned to her silent bed
The morning dream that hovered o'er her head

[1]*Sol:* Roman sun god
[2]*sylph:* In this mock epic, the sylphs and nymphs take the place of classical gods and goddesses, who continually intervened in human affairs.

A youth more glitt'ring than a birth-night beau,
(That ev'n in slumber caused her check to glow),
Seemed to her ear his winning lips to lay,   25
And thus in whispers said, or seemed to say.
   Fairest of mortals, thou distinguished care
Of thousand bright inhabitants of air!
If e'er one vision touched thy infant thought,
Of all the nurse and all the priest have taught,   30
Of airy elves by moonlight shadows seen,
The silver token, and the circled green,
Or virgins visited by angel powers,
With golden crowns and wreaths of heav'nly flow'rs,
Hear and believe! thy own importance know,   35
Nor bound thy narrow views to things below.
Some secret truths from learned pride concealed,
To maids alone and children are revealed:
What though no credit doubting wits may give?
The fair and innocent shall still believe.   40
Know then, unnumbered spirits round thee fly,
The light militia of the lower sky;
These, though unseen, are ever on the wing,
Hang o'er the box, and hover round the Ring.[3]
Think what an equipage° thou hast in air,   company of attendants 45
And view with scorn two pages and a chair.
As now your own, our beings were of old,
And once enclosed in woman's beauteous mold;
Thence, by a soft transition, we repair
From earthly vehicles to these of air.   50
Think not, when woman's transient breath is fled,
That all her vanities at once are dead:
Succeeding vanities she still regards,
And though she plays no more, o'erlooks the cards.
Her joy in gilded chariots, when alive,   55
And love of ombre,° after death survive.   fashionable card game
For when the fair in all their pride expire,

   [3]*box . . . Ring:* theater box and circular promenade

To their first elements[4] their souls retire:
The sprites of fiery termagants° in flame   shrews
Mount up, and take a salamander's name.   60
Soft yielding minds to water glide away,
And sip with nymphs, their elemental tea.
The graver prude sinks downward to a gnome,
In search of mischief still on earth to roam.
The light coquettes° in sylphs aloft repair,   flirts 65
And sport and flutter in the fields of air.
    Know further yet; whoever fair and chaste
Rejects mankind, is by some sylph embraced:
For spirits, freed from mortal laws, with ease
Assume what sexes and what shapes they please.   70
What guards the purity of melting maids,
In courtly balls, and midnight masquerades,
Safe from the treach'rous friend, the daring spark,°   beau
The glance by day, the whisper in the dark;
When kind occasion prompts their warm desires,   75
When music softens, and when dancing fires?
'Tis but their sylph, the wise celestials know,
Though honor is the word with men below.
Some nymphs there are, too conscious of their face,
For life predestined to the gnomes' embrace.   80
These swell their prospects and exalt their pride,
When offers are disdained, and love denied.
Then gay ideas crowd the vacant brain;
While peers, and dukes, and all their sweeping train,
And garters,[5] stars, and coronets appear,   85
And in soft sounds "Your Grace" salutes their ear.
'Tis these that early taint the female soul,
Instruct the eyes of young coquettes to roll,
Teach infant-cheeks a bidden blush to know,
And little hearts to flutter at a beau.   90
    Oft when the world imagine women stray,

[4]*first elements:* the four classical elements: fire, water, earth, and air
[5]*garters:* badges of the knightly Order of the Garter

The sylphs through mystic mazes guide their way,
Through all the giddy circle they pursue,
And old impertinence expel by new.
What tender maid but must a victim fall   95
To one man's treat, but for another's ball?
When Florio speaks, what virgin could withstand,
If gentle Damon did not squeeze her hand?
With varying vanities, from every part,
They shift the moving toyshop of their heart;   100
Where wigs with wigs, with sword-knots
    sword-knots strive,
Beaux banish beaux, and coaches coaches drive.
This erring mortals levity may call,
Oh, blind to truth! the sylphs contrive it all.
    Of these am I, who thy protection claim,   105
A watchful sprite, and Ariel is my name.
Late, as I ranged the crystal wilds of air,
In the clear mirror of thy ruling star
I saw, alas! some dread event impend,
Ere to the main this morning sun descend.   110
But Heav'n reveals not what, or how, or where:
Warned by thy sylph, O pious maid beware!
This to disclose is all thy guardian can.
Beware of all, but most beware of man!
    He said; when Shock,[6] who thought she slept too long,   115
Leaped up, and waked his mistress with his tongue.
'Twas then, Belinda! if report say true,   love-letter
Thy eyes first opened on a billet-doux;°
Wounds, charms, and ardors were no sooner read,   120
But all the vision vanished from thy head.
    And now, unveiled, the toilet° stands displayed,   dressing
                                                               table
Each silver vase in mystic order laid.
First, robed in white, the nymph[7] intent adores,
With head uncovered, the cosmetic pow'rs.

[6]*Shock:* Belinda's lap-dog
[7]*the nymph:* Belinda

A heav'nly image in the glass appears,   125
To that she bends, to that her eyes she rears;
Th' inferior priestess,[8] at her altar's side,
Trembling, begins the sacred rites of pride.
Unnumbered treasures ope at once, and here
The various off'rings of the world appear;   130
From each she nicely culls° with curious toil,   chooses
And decks the goddess with the glitt'ring spoils.
This casket India's glowing gems unlocks,
And all Arabia breathes from yonder box.
The tortoise here and elephant unite,   135
Transformed to combs, the speckled and the white.
Here files of pins extend their shining rows,
Puffs, powders, patches, bibles, billets-doux.
Now awful beauty puts on all its arms;
The fair each moment rises in her charms,   140
Repairs her smiles, awakens ev'ry grace,
And calls forth all the wonders of her face;
Sees by degrees a purer blush arise,
And keener lightnings quicken in her eyes.
The busy sylphs surround their darling care;   145
These set the head, and those divide the hair,
Some fold the sleeve, whilst others plait the gown;
And Betty's praised for labors not her own.

[8]*priestess:* Belinda's maid Betty

1. The action of the narrative begins with the whispered message of the youth in the "morning dream." From the preceding lines (1-26), what do you learn — sometimes indirectly — about the time and place of the action, the kind of people involved in the "dire offense," the lady's reaction, and the part played by her guardian sylph?
2. What is Belinda urged to "hear and believe" (lines 27-40)? What picture are you given in lines 41-66 of the "unnumbered spirits" and of their origin? Describe the different kinds of spirits mentioned and the kinds of women they represent.

3. What services do the sylphs perform that men called "honor" (lines 67-78)? Yet some nymphs "taint the female soul." What are they like and what effect do they have on their "prospects" (lines 79-90)? What do the sylphs contrive that erring mortals call "levity" (lines 91-104)?

4. As Belinda's guardian, what advice is Ariel trying to convey through his description of the sylphs and nymphs and through his comments about them? What serious warning does he give Belinda at the end of his speech?

5. When Belinda awakens why does the "vision" vanish from her head? Why does Pope describe her succeeding actions as "sacred rites of pride"? What connection, if any, do you see between this phrase and Ariel's description of the nymphs? Why are the words *goddess* and *priestess* especially appropriate? How do you interpret the last line of this first canto of *The Rape of the Lock?*

6. The mock epic, a rare form of satire, ridicules by presenting a trivial subject in the grandiose style of the true epic. Point out the conventions of epic poetry that you recognize in the first twelve lines. In the lines that follow, what details make clear that this poem is a mock epic rather than a true epic?

7. In this canto, what do you think Pope is satirizing? Which passages, incidents, or lines can you find that indicate satiric intent? State in your own words the theme of *The Rape of the Lock.*

8. From the last twenty lines or so, select two or more couplets which you think illustrate Pope's mastery of this verse pattern. Comment on the rhythm and rhyme, the choice and sound of the words, and the figures of speech.

THE REACTION AGAINST
REASON

The "old world" of the eighteenth century, which Dr. Samuel Johnson admired so much and considered permanent, was based on long-accepted gradations of rank and class privileges. Political, economic, and social power was almost entirely in the hands of the aristocracy (the landed gentry) and of those upper-class merchants and financiers whose wealth and influence made them "socially acceptable." England had good reason to feel complacent and optimistic, for she was enjoying a period of prosperity and comparative quiet at home and of empire-building abroad. In Parliament, Tories and Whigs (the major parties) were in constant battle over particular issues, but neither party favored any change which would upset the economic status quo or threaten the gracious living which characterized the aristocratic cosmopolitan society of London, the center of eighteenth-century life. Thus the reform bills passed by Parliament were devoted to eliminating only the most flagrant abuses of political and economic power. The basic problems received little, if any, attention.

Society played an increasingly important role in dictating the standards not only of manners and dress but also of culture and "taste." It provided patrons for aspiring artists and writers — including those of middle-class origin — and gave money and support to the care of the destitute and diseased and to the improvement of prisons and asylums for the insane. Society's chief concern, however, was to foster in England an era of enlightenment and to enjoy "the best of all possible worlds," even if the masses were deprived of adequate food and decent shelter, and women and children were exploited in factories and mines unfit for human occupation. Great country houses and the drawing rooms of London mansions were the scene of a very different way of life. Here elegant society enjoyed a constant round of parties and elaborate entertainments. Here aristocrats and successful merchants alike took pride in conversing with wit, common sense, and critical intelligence on matters of national and cultural interest.

Yet rebellion was inevitable. Beneath the "aristocratic surface of eighteenth-century manners," there was a new spirit stirring which was to manifest itself in every aspect of English life and thought. Men struck out boldly for the free, the natural, and the democratic.

The causes of this "striking out" were a series of "revolutions," some limited to England, others involving the entire western world. One appeared as the Methodism of John Wesley, a movement which emphasized passion and intuition rather than logic or rational thought. Because Methodism emphasized the worth of the individual believer and the validity of his personal conscience, and because it appealed so strongly to the lower classes, it became a force in shaping democratic thought.

A second and complementary revolution was inspired by the ideas championed by the Earl of Shaftesbury in England and Jean-Jacques Rousseau in France. Man, they contended, is at heart essentially good, and is happiest and best in a state of nature, free from the institutions and the artificial restraints of organized society. His God is a beneficent force that works in and through man and nature. This force is most nearly approached and most clearly perceived, not through reason but through contemplation of, and communion with, nature. Therein lies man's hope for attaining perfection in this world.

Neither of these revolutions had as far-reaching and as catastrophic an effect as the so-called Industrial Revolution which, for a time and for those in power, seemed an unqualified blessing. Yet so rapid was its development during the last half of the eighteenth century that it changed the entire pattern of English life. For centuries England had been a predominantly agricultural nation. Now, as a result of more and more mechanical inventions and the application of steam power to manufacturing and then to transportation, she was soon to become the chief industrial nation of the world.

The individual craftsman and his hand labor—the old "cottage economy"—could not compete with the machine and, as a result, he was forced to leave village and countryside and exist as best he could in the factory slums of the abnormally growing cities. The small farmer was the victim of a parallel revolution in agriculture. The open fields, which had been owned and farmed in common by villagers since Saxon times, were enclosed. Thus agricultural workers were forced off the land and into crowded city slums, where they necessarily worked as unskilled labor. Before the Industrial Revolution had run its course, the "old world" of gracious living which had characterized eighteenth-century London had vanished.

Outside the shores of England, two other revolutions were in the making which were to have a dramatic effect in shaping not only the political and economic future of the nation but also the intellectual and emotional attitudes of its people. The first was the American Revolution which, though condemned by most Englishmen, exemplified for many the right of all men to "life, liberty, and the pursuit of happiness." Within a month after the inauguration of President Washington, in 1789, the Bastille in Paris was seized and the French Revolution was launched in violence and bloodshed. This was followed by the Declaration of the Rights of Man, whose watchwords were *liberty, equality*, and *fraternity*. Although this revolution began as a protest against an outworn social order, its effect was in every way revolutionary. Every European country was shaken; every European countryman found his world changed by this event.

In England, too, the French Revolution aroused conflicting emotions. It was hated and feared by those who saw it as a threat to traditional and revered political and social systems.

It was enthusiastically praised by those who envisioned a world of peace and justice. No wonder the last decades of the eighteenth century reflected old forces in conflict with new; reason with idealistic fervor; authority of church, state, and society with equality, liberty, and fraternity; common-sense compromise with drastic change; industry and city life with communion between man and nature; intellectualism with spiritual and artistic feeling; man in the abstract with man the individual.

The Age of Reason was over—despite Dr. Johnson's efforts to prolong it—and the Romantic age was coming into being. The art of writing had sufficiently escaped the emphasis on reason and sense to allow expression in poetry which, though still restrained and somewhat didactic, was not entirely bound by neoclassical rules and models. In many ways, late eighteenth-century poetry was as transitional as the period in which it was written, but it represented a new intensity of feeling, a greater freedom in choice of subject matter and form, and a genuine concern with the individual and with personal experience. It clearly revealed an awakening of the imagination, the central force of the Romantic prose and poetry of the next century. This awakening was perhaps the last and finest gift of the eighteenth century, and the three poets most responsible for it were Gray, Burns, and Blake.

THOMAS GRAY was the most distinguished member of the "graveyard school," a small group of mid-eighteenth-century poets who wrote long, rather gloomy poems about life, death, immortality, and the departing glories of English rural life. Although considered one of the forerunners of nineteenth-century Romanticism, he shared most of the attitudes of his Neoclassical contemporaries. A classicist by training, he meticulously observed traditional rules of phrasing and poetic form. He was concerned more with man in the abstract than with man the individual, and he valued reason and common sense above fancy and imagination. Most important, he regarded poetry as a useful adornment to life.

Gray's poems are not conspicuous for their originality, either of ideas or of sentiments. The poet's task, as he saw it, was to ennoble and immortalize ideas and sentiments, particularly those common to all men. He agreed with Pope that poetry should consist of "what oft was thought but ne'er so well expressed." The highest praise Dr. Johnson could accord "Elegy Written in a Country Churchyard," Gray's finest and best-known work, was that it "abounds with sentiments to which every bosom returns an echo."

Gray is considered a "transition poet" — or a "pre-Romantic" — because of his love of nature, his nostalgia for the humble, rural life, his respect for the common man, and his tendency to melancholy. In his "Elegy" he pictured country people and country scenes in an idyllic light and made the bold suggestion that the difference between the humble and the powerful was only accidental. Although he could produce light, even playful verse, he was most successful — and apparently most comfortable — when treating subjects which required the subdued tones and plaintive sounds of twilight and melancholy.

ROBERT BURNS, a Scottish peasant, produced poetry which is strikingly different from anything else the eighteenth century has to offer. To an age that demanded rationality, he brought feeling and song. For nearly a hundred years, England had produced few impassioned lyrics of high musical quality. During his brief life, Burns wrote or rewrote between three hundred and four hundred songs, in addition to a great variety of poems in which he expressed his personal joys and sorrows and also his delight in every "earth-born creature and fellow mortal."

Burns's poems and songs, though they embody many moods, are always a superb mingling of emotion and poetic technique. Some are about nature and Burns's feeling for the small, everyday things about him. Others express the intense joys and pain of love the poet experienced. Still others are descriptions and sometimes sharp criticisms of Scottish life, which he knew fully and intimately — the landed gentry with their snobbishness and pretensions; the simple cottagers with their homely pleasures and passionate faith in God. But whatever the theme, Burns's poems reveal a lyrical joy in life and a compassion for people, which sprang from his democratic respect for the common man.

WILLIAM BLAKE'S wife once remarked, "I have very little

of Mr. Blake's company. He is always in Paradise." As a religious mystic, he was preoccupied with perceiving eternal realities beyond the visible, time-bound world. As a literary genius he was concerned with that "one Power" which alone makes a poet: "Imagination, the Divine Vision." Unschooled and out of step with his scientific, rationalistic age, Blake could see meanings—hints of divine truth—in the meanest object or in the most trivial occurrence.

Blake's lyrics glow with an inner light. His vivid images impress themselves on the memory, and his colors startle with their brilliance. As fine a painter and graphic artist as he was a poet, he had a pictorial habit of mind. In fact, he denied that there was any significant difference between painting and poetry. Both were acts of prayer.

Songs of Innocence and *Songs of Experience*, Blake's two most important collections of verse, are companion volumes "showing," he explained, "the two contrary states of the human experience." Innocence, to Blake, meant joy, spontaneity, and obliviousness to the principle of evil. Experience, he believed, destroys this "state of soul" because it leads to an awareness of evil and ugliness. The *Songs of Experience* are, therefore, often bitter, often satirical. Much to Blake's credit, however, they are almost always beautiful. He did not intend to suggest that "innocence" is a higher state than "experience." Rather, he wanted to make clear that one must pass through both states if he is to arrive at a "higher innocence" based on knowledge rather than on ignorance.

In his attempt to express the child's sense of wonder, Blake often used language which is deceptively simple. Actually, his highly imaginative and symbolic use of language makes him the most original and difficult of the three major pre-Romantic poets.

Thomas Gray

As a Neoclassicist, Gray believed that poetry should have propriety of sentiment, harmony of tone, and perfection of form. He frequently achieved a turn of phrase and a verbal compactness worthy of Alexander Pope, whom he greatly admired but did not slavishly imitate. In his "Elegy" he abandons Pope's heroic couplet which, though ideal for stinging satire, is ill-suited to the sentiment of the "graveyard poets." Gray rhymes alternate lines, thus securing more continuity in the four-line stanza. More important, his elegy deals powerfully with the inescapable problem of death.

ELEGY WRITTEN IN A
COUNTRY CHURCHYARD

The curfew tolls the knell of parting day,
   The lowing herd winds slowly o'er the lea,
The plowman homeward plods his weary way,
   And leaves the world to darkness and to me.

Now fades the glimm'ring landscape on the sight,   5
   And all the air a solemn stillness holds,
Save where the beetle wheels his droning flight,
   And drowsy tinklings lull the distant folds;

Save that from yonder ivy-mantled tow'r
   The moping owl does to the moon complain   10
Of such, as wand'ring near her secret bow'r,
   Molest her ancient solitary reign.

Beneath those rugged elms, that yew-tree's shade,
   Where heaves the turf in many a mold'ring heap,
Each in his narrow cell forever laid,   15
   The rude° forefathers of the hamlet sleep.   rugged

The breezy call of incense-breathing Morn,
   The swallow twitt'ring from the straw-built shed,
The cock's shrill clarion, or the echoing horn,
   No more shall rouse them from their lowly bed.   20

For them no more the blazing hearth shall burn,
   Or busy housewife ply her evening care;
No children run to lisp their sire's return,
   Or climb his knees the envied kiss to share.

Oft did the harvest to their sickle yield,   25
   Their furrow oft the stubborn glebe° has broke;   soil
How jocund did they drive their team afield!
   How bowed the woods beneath their sturdy stroke!

Let not Ambition mock their useful toil,
   Their homely joys, and destiny obscure;   30
Nor Grandeur hear with a disdainful smile,
   The short and simple annals of the poor.

The boast of heraldry, the pomp of pow'r,
   And all that beauty, all that wealth e'er gave,
Awaits alike the inevitable hour: 35
   The paths of glory lead but to the grave.

Nor you, ye proud, impute to these the fault,
  If Mem'ry o'er their tomb no trophies raise,
Where through the long-drawn aisle and
    fretted° vault   carved
    The pealing anthem swells the note of praise.   40

Can storied urn or animated bust
  Back to its mansion call the fleeting breath?
Can Honor's voice provoke the silent dust,
  Or Flatt'ry soothe the dull cold ear of Death?

Perhaps in this neglected spot is laid   45
  Some heart once pregnant with celestial fire;
Hands that the rod of empire might have swayed,
  Or waked to ecstasy the living lyre.

But Knowledge to their eyes her ample page
  Rich with the spoils of time did ne'er unroll;   50
Chill Penury repressed their noble rage,
  And froze the genial current of the soul.

Full many a gem of purest ray serene,
  The dark unfathomed caves of ocean bear;
Full many a flower is born to blush unseen,   55
  And waste its sweetness on the desert air.

Some village Hampden,[1] that with dauntless breast
  The little tyrant of his fields withstood;
Some mute inglorious Milton here may rest,
  Some Cromwell guiltless of his country's blood.   60

Th' applause of listening senates to command,
  The threats of pain and ruin to despise,
To scatter plenty o'er a smiling land,
  And read their hist'ry in a nation's eyes,

[1]*Hampden:* John Hampden, who resisted an unjust tax proposed by King
Charles I

Their lot forbade; nor circumscribed alone   65
    Their growing virtues, but their crimes confined;
Forbade to wade through slaughter to a throne,
    And shut the gates of mercy on mankind,

The struggling pangs of conscious truth to hide,
    To quench the blushes of ingenuous shame,   70
Or heap the shrine of Luxury and Pride
    With incense killed at the Muse's flame.

Far from the madding crowd's ignoble strife,
    Their sober wishes never learned to stray;
Along the cool sequestered vale of life   75
    They kept the noiseless tenor of their way.

Yet ev'n these bones from insult to protect
    Some frail memorial still erected nigh,
With uncouth° rimes and shapeless sculpture   awkward
    decked,
    Implores the passing tribute of a sigh.   80

Their name, their years, spelt by th' unlettered Muse,
    The place of fame and elegy supply;
And many a holy text around she strews,
    That teach the rustic moralist to die.

For who, to dumb Forgetfulness a prey,   85
    This pleasing anxious being e'er resigned,
Left the warm precincts of the cheerful day,
    Nor cast one longing ling'ring look behind?

On some fond breast the parting soul relies,
    Some pious drops the closing eye requires;   90
Ev'n from the tomb the voice of Nature cries,
    Ev'n in our ashes live their wonted fires.

For thee, who mindful of th' unhonored dead
  Dost in these lines their artless tale relate;
If chance, by lonely Contemplation led,   95
  Some kindred spirit shall inquire thy fate,

Haply some hoary-headed swain may say,
  "Oft have we seen him at the peep of dawn
Brushing with hasty steps the dews away
  To meet the sun upon the upland lawn.   100

"There at the foot of yonder nodding beech
  That wreathes its old fantastic roots so high,
His listless length at noontide would he stretch,
  And pore upon the brook that babbles by.

"Hard by yon wood, now smiling as in scorn,   105
  Mutt'ring his wayward fancies he would rove,
Now drooping, woeful wan, like one forlorn,
  Or crazed with care, or crossed in hopeless love.

"One morn I missed him on the customed hill,
  Along the heath and near his fav'rite tree;   110
Another came; nor yet beside the rill,
  Nor up the lawn, nor at the wood was he;

"The next with dirges due in sad array
  Slow through the church-way path we saw him borne.
Approach and read (for thou canst read) the lay,   115
  Graved on the stone beneath yon aged thorn."°
                                              hawthorn tree

THE EPITAPH

Here rests his head upon the lap of Earth
  A Youth to Fortune and to Fame unknown.
Fair Science frowned not on his humble birth,
  And Melancholy marked him for her own.   120

Large was his bounty, and his soul sincere,
 Heav'n did a recompense as largely send;
He gave to Mis'ry all he had, a tear,
 He gained from Heav'n ('twas all he wished) a friend.

No farther seek his merits to disclose,   125
 Or draw his frailties from their dread abode,
(There they alike in trembling hope repose),
 The bosom of his Father and his God.

1. Customarily, an elegy is a poem of lament and praise for a specific
   person whom the poet has loved or admired. In this elegy, Gray
   is writing about those "rude forefathers" as little honored in life
   as in death. At what time and place does Gray experience the
   thoughts and emotions conveyed in the poem? What mood does
   he create through his description of the scene?
2. What is Gray's attitude toward those who are "born to blush unseen"? Why is it pointless for Ambition to "mock their useful
   toil" and Grandeur to hear their tale "with a disdainful smile"?
   What reasons does he suggest for the fate and neglect of those
   who "kept the noiseless tenor of their way"?
3. Who do you think Gray means by *thee* in line 93? What truth and
   prediction about life is expressed in the lines spoken by the
   "hoary-headed swain"? From these lines and others, what conclusion do you draw about Gray's attitude toward death?
4. An epitaph is an inscription on a tomb. Would you say that Gray
   is writing his own epitaph or one for all young men of humble
   birth who never know Fame and Fortune? Explain.
5. Though a Romantic at heart, Gray's chief concern was to achieve
   harmony of tone and perfection of form. Point out evidence of his
   success in the rhythm, rhyme, and sounds of his "Elegy."

ODE ON THE DEATH OF A FAVORITE CAT

DROWNED IN A TUB OF GOLDFISHES

'Twas on a lofty vase's side,
Where China's gayest art had dyed
 The azure flowers, that blow;

Demurest of the tabby kind,
The pensive Selima reclined,
    Gazed on the lake below.   5

Her conscious tail her joy declared;
The fair round face, the snowy beard,
    The velvet of her paws,
Her coat, that with the tortoise vies,   10
Her ears of jet, and emerald eyes,
    She saw; and purred applause.

Still had she gazed; but 'midst the tide
Two angel forms were seen to glide,
    The genii of the stream: 15
Their scaly armor's Tyrian hue[1]
Through richest purple to the view
    Betrayed a golden gleam.

The hapless nymph with wonder saw:
A whisker first and then a claw,   20
    With many an ardent wish,
She stretched in vain to reach the prize.
What female heart can gold despise?
    What cat's averse to fish?

Presumptuous maid! with looks intent   25
Again she stretched, again she bent,
    Nor knew the gulf between.
(Malignant Fate sat by, and smiled)
The slipp'ry verge her feet beguiled,
    She tumbled headlong in.   30

---

[1]*Tyrian hue:* purple, made from certain mollusks by the people of Tyre

Eight times emerging from the flood
She mewed to ev'ry watry god,
   Some speedy aid to send.
No dolphin[2] came, no nereid[3] stirred:
Nor cruel Tom, nor Susan heard.   35
   A fav'rite has no friend!

From hence, ye beauties, undeceived,
Know, one false step is ne'er retrieved,
   And be with caution bold.
Not all that tempts your wand'ring eyes   40
And heedless hearts, is lawful prize;
   Nor all, that glisters, gold.

[2]*dolphin:* According to legend, when Arion, a Greek musician, was thrown
overboard, he was rescued on the back of a dolphin.
[3]*nereid:* in Greek mythology, one of the daughters of the sea god Nereus

1. How does the "pensive Selima" make the discovery that leads to
   her sad fate? What causes her to purr applause? Why does Gray
   refer to her as "presumptuous maid"? What is ironic about his
   statement in line 36?
2. What moral is expressed in the last stanza? In the phrase "ye
   beauties," is Gray referring merely to cats or to all female hearts
   who cannot "gold despise"? How do you interpret the warnings
   in this stanza?
3. Two characteristics of the ode are lofty feeling and dignified
   style. Do you find evidence of these in the poem? In your opinion,
   are the feeling and style suited to the subject matter? Or do you
   think they add to the poem's humor? Explain.
4. Always the expert craftsman, Gray took great pains even with his
   light, witty verse. Point out the pattern of the metrical lines in
   each stanza. What effect do the shorter lines create?

Robert Burns

Scottish scenery and dialect, local color, and old legends and songs —all of these Burns used with great skill, as did lesser poets whose works he admired and sometimes imitated. What distinguishes his poetry from theirs is its fresh versification and its impassioned lyricism. In their spontaneous, musical quality, Burns's poems may be compared with the best of the old ballads and Elizabethan songs.

To a Mouse

ON TURNING HER UP IN HER NEST, WITH THE PLOW, NOVEMBER, 1785

Wee, sleekit,° cowrin', tim'rous beastie,   sleek
O, what a panic's in thy breastie!
Thou need na start awa sae hasty
     Wi' bickering brattle!°   noisy scamper
I wad be laith° to rin an' chase thee,   loath   5
     Wi' murdering pattle!°   paddle

I'm truly sorry man's dominion
Has broken Nature's social union,
An' justifies that ill opinion

Which makes thee startle   10
At me, thy poor, earth-born companion
　　An' fellow mortal!

I doubt na, whyles, but thou may thieve;
What then? poor beastie, thou maun° live!　must
A daimen icker in a thrave¹   15
　　'S a sma' request;
I'll get a blessin' wi' the lave,°　　leavings
　　An' never miss't!

Thy wee-bit housie, too, in ruin!
Its silly wa's° the win's are strewin'!　feeble walls 20
An' naething, now, to big° a new ane,°　build; one
　　O' foggage° green!　　　　grass
An' bleak December's win's ensuin',
　　Baith snell° an' keen!　　biting

Thou saw the fields laid bare an' waste,   25
An' weary winter comin' fast,
An' cozie here, beneath the blast,
　　Thou thought to dwell,
Till crash! the cruel coulter° past　plow blade
　　Out thro' thy cell.   30

That wee bit heap o' leaves an' stibble,°　stubble
Has cost thee monie a weary nibble!
Now thou's turned out, for a' thy trouble,
　　But house or hald,°　　possession
To thole° the winter's sleety dribble,　endure 35
　　An' cranreuch° cauld!　　frost

¹*A daimen . . . thrave:* an occasional ear out of a pile of sheaves

But Mousie, thou art no thy lane,°   not alone
In proving foresight may be vain:
The best-laid schemes o' mice an' men
         Gang aft agley,°   often go awry   40
An' lea'e us nought but grief an' pain,
         For promised joy!

Still thou art blest, compared wi' me!
The present only toucheth thee;
But och! I backward cast my e'e,   45
         On prospects drear!
An' forward, though I canna see,
         I guess an' fear!

1. What is the speaker's attitude toward the mouse? How does the mouse behave toward the man?
2. What does "Nature's social union" (line 8) mean? What has disrupted that union? To what level does the speaker's regard raise the mouse in stanza 2?
3. Why does the speaker overlook the petty thievery of the mouse? What has he just accidentally done to the mouse?
4. What moral does the speaker formulate as a result of his accidental encounter with the mouse?
5. Why does the speaker feel the mouse is more fortunate than he?

A RED, RED ROSE

O, my luve is like a red, red rose,
     That's newly sprung in June.
O, my luve is like the melodie,
     That's sweetly played in tune.

As fair art thou, my bonie lass,   5
     So deep in luve am I,
And I will luve thee still, my dear,
     Till a' the seas gang dry.

Till a' the seas gang dry, my dear,
  And the rocks melt wi' the sun!   10
And I will luve thee still, my dear,
  While the sands o' life shall run.

hour glass — time

And fare thee weel, my only luve,
  And fare thee weel a while!
And I will come again, my luve,   15
  Though it were ten thousand mile!

1. Two outstanding qualities of this poem are its simplicity and spontaneity. Support this statement by pointing out specific lines. Try to show how this poem would appear less spontaneous if it were less carefully constructed.
2. Is the speaker in this poem young or old? Consider carefully the language clues, particularly the frequent use of hyperbole. Is hyperbole in keeping with the character of the speaker? Is he sincere? What does the music of the poem tell you about his sincerity?
3. Note the similes the speaker uses to describe his love. What do they imply of her characteristics?

HIGHLAND MARY

Ye banks and braes° and streams around   hillsides
  The castle o' Montgomery,
Green be your woods, and fair your flowers,
  Your waters never drumlie!°   muddy
There summer first unfald her robes,   5
  And there the langest tarry!
For there I took the last farweel
  O' my sweet Highland Mary!

How sweetly bloomed the gay green birk,°   birch
  How rich the hawthorn's blossom,   10
As underneath their fragrant shade
  I clasped her to my bosom!

> The golden hours on angel wings
>   Flew o'er me and my dearie:
> For dear to me as light and life   15
>   Was my sweet Highland Mary.
>
>
> Wi' monie a vow and locked embrace
>   Our parting was fu' tender;
> And, pledging aft to meet again,
>   We tore oursels asunder.   20
> But I, fell death's untimely frost,
>   That nipped my flower sae early!
> Now green's the sod, and cauld's the clay,
>   That wraps my Highland Mary!
>
>
> O, pale, pale now, those rosy lips   25
>   I aft hae kissed sae fondly;
> And closed for ay, the sparkling glance
>   That dwalt on me sae kindly;
> And moldering now in silent dust
>   That heart that lo'ed me dearly!   30
> But still within my bosom's core
>   Shall live my Highland Mary.

1. What emotions are conveyed in the poem? How important are Burns's references to nature in conveying these emotions? Explain.
2. Why do you think Burns devoted stanzas 1 and 2 to picturing the beauty of the scene where he "took the last fareweel"? What lines in stanzas 3 and 4 are more sad and dramatic by contrast?
3. Tell why you do, or do not, consider the extended image in lines 21 and 22 effective. Which words and phrases represent the poetic diction admired in the eighteenth century? In your opinion, do they succeed in expressing the poet's emotions? Discuss.
4. Of this poem, Burns wrote, "The foregoing song pleases myself; I think it is in my happiest manner. . . ." while he probably meant

best by *happiest,* what do you think of Burns's assessment of his work? What, about the style of this poem do you think would please him?

JOHN ANDERSON MY JO

John Anderson my jo,° John,   sweetheart
  When we were first acquent,
Your locks were like the raven,
  Your bonnie brow was brent;°   smooth
But now your brow is beld,° John,   bald 5
  Your locks are like the snaw,°   snow
But blessings on your frosty pow,°   head
  John Anderson my jo!

John Anderson my jo, John,
  We clamb the hill thegither,   10
And monie a cantie° day, John,   happy
  We've had wi' ane anither;
Now we maun° totter down, John,   must
  And hand in hand we'll go,
And sleep thegither at the foot,   15
  John Anderson my jo!

1. What do you think prompted the speaker in the poem to pay this tribute to John Anderson? What has been the relationship between them over the years? With what emotions does she view these years and the imminent "sleep thegither"?
2. Much of the meaning, as well as the emotion of the poem, is expressed figuratively. Identify the poetic devices used in stanza 1 and tell why they are effective. What do the words *hill* and *sleep* symbolize in stanza 2?

3. Burns was rarely guilty of sentimentality — that is, an affected or superficial emotion. In your opinion, does he achieve his purpose without sentimentality in this poem? Explain.
4. How "musical" can a poem be which has a somewhat somber theme? Point out those poetic qualities — rhythm, rhyme, alliteration, and the like — which account for the "music" of this poem.
5. Substitute modern English words for the dialect, and read one or two stanzas aloud. Does the music of the poem gain or lose by this substitution? Explain.

To a Louse

ON SEEING ONE ON A LADY'S BONNET AT CHURCH

Ha! whare ye gaun, ye crowlin' ferlie?°   crawling wonder
Your impudence protects you sairly;°   greatly
I canna say but ye strunt° rarely   strut
    Owre gauze and lace,
Tho' faith! I fear ye dine but sparely   5
    On sic a place.

Ye ugly, creepin', blastit wonner,
Detested, shunned by saunt an' sinner,
How daur ye set your fit° upon her —   feet
    Sae fine a lady!   10
Gae somewhere else and seek your dinner
    On some poor body.

Swith! in some beggar's hauffet squattle:[1]
There ye may creep and sprawl and sprattle,°   struggle
Wi' ither kindred, jumping cattle,
    In shoals and nations;
Whare horn nor bane° ne'er daur unsettle   bone-comb
    Your thick plantations.

[1] *Swith . . . squattle:* Quick, sprawl in some beggar's head.

Now haud° you there! ye're out o' sight,   stay
Below the fatt'rils,° snug an' tight;   ribbon ends 20
Na, faith ye yet! ye'll no be right
        Till ye've got on it—
The vera tapmost, tow'ring height
        O' Miss's bonnet.

My sooth! right bauld ye set your nose out,   25
As plump an' grey as onie grozet;° any gooseberry
O for some rank, mercurial rozet,°   rosin
        Or fell° red smeddum,° deadly; powder
I'd gie ye sic a hearty dose o't,
        Wad dress your droddum.[2]   30

I wad na been suprised to spy
You on an auld wife's flainen toy;° flannel cap
Or aiblins some bit duddie boy,[3]
        On 's wyliecoat;° flannel vest
But Miss's fine Lunardi!° fye! bonnet 35
        How daur ye do't?

O Jenny, dinna toss your head,
An' set your beauties a' abread!° abroad
Ye little ken what cursèd speed
        The blastie's makin'!   40
Thae winks an' finger-ends, I dread,
        Are notice takin'!

O wad some Power the giftie gie us
To see oursels as ithers see us!
It wad frae monie a blunder free us,   45
        An' foolish notion;
What airs in dress an' gait wad lea'e us,
        An' ev'n devotion!

[2]*Wad . . . droddum:* Would put an end to you
[3]*Or . . . boy:* Or perhaps on some little ragged boy

1. Why is the incident described in this poem especially amusing? Is it what happens, the descriptive details, the poet's comments and attitude, the language, or a combination of all these that makes the poem "work"? Find examples in the poem to support your answers.
2. In your opinion, is the tone of this poem playful, gently satirical, bitterly satirical? What words and phrases suggest the tone?
3. What actions by the louse make it appear increasingly impudent? Which of Jenny's actions make her appear ridiculous? From the poet's reactions to the scene, what impression do you gain of his personality and his view of life?
4. Lines 43 and 44 are still frequently quoted. Why? Do you think the purpose of the last stanza is to teach a lesson? Or is Burns making an ironic comment about the values which some people consider important? Explain.
5. Explain the meaning and the relevance of the opening lines of the last stanza, and of the last line. In your opinion, is the last stanza solemn or ironic? Explain.
6. Note the unusual rhyme scheme in stanza 3. This is typical of the tail-rhyme stanza, which Burns borrowed from Scottish popular songs. (See page 511.) In some stanzas the rhyme appears to be faulty to the eye, but it might not to the ear. The sound of the rhymed word would, of course, depend on the Scottish pronunciation. Discuss the sounds of those words which *look* unfamiliar. When they are end words, try to find a clue to their pronunciation in the words with which they are supposed to rhyme.

Is There for Honest Poverty

Is there for° honest poverty   *because of*
    That° hings his head, an' a' that?   *one who*
The coward slave, we pass him by—
    We dare be poor for a' that!
For a' that, an' a' that,   5
    Our toils obscure, an' a' that,
The rank is but the guinea's stamp;
    The man's the gowd° for a' that.   *gold*

What though on hamely fare we dine,
    Wear hoddin° grey, an' a' that?   woolen 10
Gie fools their silks, and knaves their wine—
    A man's a man for a' that.
For a' that, an' a' that,
    Their tinsel show, an' a' that,
The honest man, though e'er sae poor,   15
    Is king o' men for a' that.

Ye see yon birkie° ca'd "a lord,"   young chap
    Wha struts, an' stares, an' a' that?
Though hundreds worship at his word,
    He's but a cuif° for a' that.   ninny 20
For a' that, an' a' that,
    His ribband, star, an' a' that,
The man o' independent mind,
    He looks an' laughs at a' that.

A prince can mak a belted knight,   25
    A marquis, duke, an' a' that!
But an honest man's aboon° his might—   above
    Guid faith, he mauna fa'° that!   can't improve on
For a' that, an' a' that,
    Their dignities,° an' a' that,   honors 30
The pith o' sense an' pride o' worth
    Are higher rank than a' that.

Then let us pray that come it may
    (As come it will for a' that)
That sense and worth o'er a' the earth   35
    Shall bear the gree° an' a' that!   win the victory
For a' that, an' a' that,
    It's comin' yet for a' that,
That man to man the world o'er
    Shall brithers be for a' that.   40

1. What does Burns mean by "a man's a man for a' that"? Describe the two groups of men he contrasts. In what important ways are they different? What is Burns's attitude toward each group? Which words and phrases convey it?
2. For what does Burns urge us to pray (lines 33-36)? Considering the "revolutions" which were taking place or developing at the time he wrote this poem (see pages 226-229), do you think he was being overly optimistic in the closing lines? When he uses the word *brithers*, what kind of brotherhood do you think he envisions? How far do you think we have come since Burns's time in creating the kind of world in which he believed?
3. As in the old ballads which Burns loved and often used as poetic models, certain phrases are repeated many times. Discuss the effect of this repetition on the sound of the poem, the ideas expressed, and the over-all tone. What is unusual about the rhyme?
4. Burns wrote to a friend about this poem, "A great critic on songs says that Love and Wine are the exclusive themes for song writing. The following is on neither subject, and consequently is no song. . . ." Do you agree with the critic's definition of *song*? Why would Burns agree, since he wrote this poem to be set to music? What do you think he means by *song*?

William Blake

Blake was one of those rarities — a natural artist, a poet who sings because he must. He wrote as spontaneously as he breathed, shunning all those ornamentations and displays of learning resorted to by more conventional poets. Nature, the streets of London, and his own fantastic imagination were the sources of his imagery. The Holy Bible and the life of the common people provided him with symbols of richness and depth. Blake achieved the brilliant simplicity of his poems by stripping thought to its most basic form.

FROM Songs of Innocence

INTRODUCTION

Piping down the valleys wild,
Piping songs of pleasant glee,
On a cloud I saw a child,
And he laughing said to me:

"Pipe a song about a Lamb!"   5
So I piped with merry cheer.
"Piper, pipe that song again."
So I piped: he wept to hear.

"Drop thy pipe, thy happy pipe;
Sing thy songs of happy cheer."   10
So I sung the same again,
While he wept with joy to hear.

"Piper, sit thee down and write
In a book, that all may read."
So he vanished from my sight,   15
And I plucked a hollow reed,

And I made a rural pen,
And I stained the water clear,
And I wrote my happy songs
Every child may joy to hear.   20

1. What emotions are conveyed in this opening poem of *Songs of Innocence?* What does the Lamb mean to the child? What leads him to ask for a song about the lamb? What does it symbolize for the poet? Why would his songs be happy and full of cheer? Can you suggest any reason why the child weeps when the poet pipes the song? Do you think he is deeply moved or is he saddened?
2. Note that nowhere in this poem is anything mentioned which is not sweet and pure—the very nature of innocence. Why does Blake describe his songs as those which "every child may joy to hear"? Is he using the word *child* literally, or is he using it symbolically to stand for the children of God? Discuss.
3. Blake might have used the word *Poems* in the title rather than *Songs*. Why is the latter more descriptive of the total effect?

The Lamb

Little Lamb, who made thee?
Dost thou know who made thee?
Gave thee life, and bid thee feed,
By the stream and o'er the mead;

Gave thee clothing of delight,   5
Softest clothing, woolly, bright;
Gave thee such a tender voice,
Making all the vales rejoice?
Little Lamb, who made thee?
Dost thou know who made thee?   10

Little Lamb, I'll tell thee,
Little Lamb, I'll tell thee:
He is callèd by thy name,
For he calls himself a Lamb.
He is meek, and he is mild;   15
He became a little child.
I a child, and thou a lamb,
We are callèd by his name.
   Little Lamb, God bless thee!
   Little Lamb, God bless thee!   20

1. What picture of the Lamb is conveyed in stanza 1? What words would you choose to describe the feelings of the poet as he pictures this small creature?
2. In stanza 2, what answer does the poet give to the questions asked in stanza 1? What likeness is brought out between the Lamb and his maker? How does this likeness extend to the poet himself?
3. From what you know about Blake's religious beliefs (see page 231), what do you think he means in line 18? In lines 19 and 20, is he referring specifically to the little Lamb itself or to what it symbolizes? Explain.
4. As in many of Blake's poems, the meaning is inseparable from the simplicity and the beauty of the language and the melodious sound. Point out lines and phrases which you consider particularly effective.

HOLY THURSDAY

'Twas on a Holy Thursday, their innocent faces clean,
The children walking two and two, in red and blue and green,
Grey-headed beadles° walked before, with   parish officers
    wands as white as snow,
Till into the high dome of Paul's¹ they like Thames'
    waters flow.

O what a multitude they seemed, these flowers of
    London town!   5
Seated in companies they sit with radiance all their own.
The hum of multitudes was there, but multitudes of lambs,
Thousands of little boys and girls raising their innocent hands.

Now like a mighty wind they raise to heaven the voice of song,
Or like harmonious thunderings the seats of heaven among. 10
Beneath them sit the agèd men, wise guardians of the poor;
Then cherish pity, lest you drive an angel from your door.

  ¹*Paul's:* St. Paul's, a cathedral in London

1. In this poem, the beauty of innocence is pictured in the children's visit to St. Paul's on Holy Thursday. What similes and metaphors convey impressions of sight and sound? How do you explain the reference in line 7 to the children as lambs?
2. The tone of the poem changes in the last line. To whom is this line directed? How do you interpret it?
3. Point out the many ways in which this poem reveals the graphic artist as well as the poet.

FROM Songs of Experience

THE TYGER

Tyger! Tyger! burning bright,
In the forests of the night;
What immortal hand or eye
Could frame° thy fearful symmetry?   shape

In what distant deeps or skies   5
Burnt the fire of thine eyes?
On what wings dare he aspire?
What the hand dare seize the fire?

And what shoulder, and what art,
Could twist the sinews of thy heart?   10
And when thy heart began to beat,
What dread hand? and what dread feet?

What the hammer? what the chain?
In what furnace was thy brain?
What the anvil? what dread grasp   15
Dare its deadly terrors clasp?

When the stars threw down their spears,
And watered heaven with their tears,
Did he smile his work to see?
Did he who made the Lamb make thee?ʼ   20

Tyger! Tyger! burning bright,
In the forests of the night;
What immortal hand or eye
Dare frame thy fearful symmetry?

1. What impression of the tiger and his maker do you gain from lines 1-16? In what lines does Blake suggest the possibility of some unknown, supernatural force?
2. Some critics interpret the tiger as Blake's symbol for the fierce forces in the soul, and the "forests of the night" as "ignorance, repression, and superstition." Is Blake picturing here the opposite of God's love and care, and of the innocence symbolized by the Lamb? Discuss.
3. What is the primary question Blake asks in this poem? Why, in your opinion, does he not answer his own question, as he did in "The Lamb"? To whom does *he* refer in lines 19 and 20? What reason can you see for not capitalizing the *h*, as is customary when the reference is to God?
4. Explain the profound difference in meaning between lines 3 and 4 and lines 23 and 24. What do these lines reveal about Blake's concept of God?
5. Some critics have interpreted the imagery in lines 17 and 18 as suggesting that hoped-for time when men will lay down their arms and, with compassion for the suffering of their fellow men, will strive for peace. Can this interpretation be supported by evidence in the poem? If you accept it, point out what you think is the significance of the Creator's smile and the mention of the Lamb in the concluding lines of the stanza.
6. Which images in the poem impress themselves on the memory? What is unusual about the structure of the lines in stanzas 2, 3, and 4? Describe the effect achieved by these lines.

HOLY THURSDAY

Is this a holy thing to see
In a rich and fruitful land,
Babes reduced to misery,
Fed with cold and usurous° hand?   greedy

Is that trembling cry a song?   5
Can it be a song of joy?
And so many children poor?
It is a land of poverty!

And their sun does never shine,
And their fields are bleak and bare,   10
And their ways are filled with thorns:
It is eternal winter there.

For where'er the sun does shine,
And where'er the rain does fall,
Babe can never hunger there,   15
Nor poverty the mind appal.

1. Before you discuss this poem, reread the "Holy Thursday" which Blake wrote earlier for his first volume, *Songs of Innocence*. In the London of his day he could have viewed both scenes on the same day as he walked through the streets. What contrasts between the children and their song do you find most startling?
2. Line 8 seems to be a contradiction of lines 1 and 2. How do you interpret line 8?
3. Note that each line of stanza 3 is an image chosen to dramatize the kind of existence that is the fate of these "children poor." Discuss the meaning conveyed by each image, especially "eternal winter" in line 12.
4. Blake believed that "in the fatherhood of God" all — rich and poor — have equal rights and privileges. In your opinion, does the last stanza express that belief in figurative language? Support your opinion.
5. Does the word *there* in line 12 and line 15 refer to the same place or to different places? Is the second *there* a different land or city, an ideal world of plenty, or the heaven after death? Base your answer on your interpretation of the entire poem and on what you know about Blake.

THE CLOD AND THE PEBBLE

"Love seeketh not itself to please,
Nor for itself hath any care,
But for another gives its ease,
And builds a Heaven in Hell's despair."

So sung a little Clod of Clay,   5
Trodden with the cattle's feet,
But a Pebble of the brook
Warbled out these meters meet:

"Love seeketh only self to please,
To bind another to its delight,   10
Joys in another's loss of ease,
And builds a Hell in Heaven's despite."

1. Contrast the view of love held by the Clod with that held by the
   Pebble. In what ways do these views reveal an entirely different
   attitude toward life? Why is the Clod of Clay an appropriate symbol for one view, and the Pebble for the other view?
2. Is the love which the Pebble describes really love? If not, what
   word would you use to describe it? Do you find the Clod's description of love entirely satisfactory? Give reasons for your answers.
3. What effect is created by the structural similarity of the first and
   third stanzas? Compare the last lines of these two stanzas and
   point out their similarities and differences.

THE CHIMNEY-SWEEPER

A little black thing among the snow,
Crying "weep! weep!" in notes of woe!
"Where are thy father and mother, say?" —
"They are both gone up to the church to pray.

"Because I was happy upon the heath,   5
And smiled among the winter's snow,
They clothed me in the clothes of death,
And taught me to sing the notes of woe.

"And because I am happy and dance and sing,
They think they have done me no injury,   10
And are gone to praise God and his priest and king,
Who make up a heaven of our misery."

1. Chimney-sweepers were small children who earned their living
   by climbing down into chimneys in order to remove the soot.
   Their job was so dangerous that many were killed or injured per-
   forming it. They solicited work by crying "sweep, sweep" in the
   streets. What reason can you see for Blake's changing their traditional cry to "weep, weep"? In so doing, does he suggest anything
   about the age of the child?
2. Who is the likely speaker in line 3? In the chimney-sweeper's
   reply, do you think he is speaking about his *real* parents? Or are
   the words *father* and *mother* intended to represent all people who
   directly, or indirectly, determine the fate of children? Give reasons to support your opinion.
3. How do you interpret the last two lines of the poem? How does
   the child's simple explanation dramatize the bitter irony of a
   situation that was all too common in Blake's day? Is the attitude
   reflected in this poem consistent with Blake's religious and humanitarian beliefs?
4. This poem is built on contrasts which heighten its emotional appeal and bring out its theme. Point out these contrasts and why
   they are effective. What general truth or observation on life is the
   theme of the poem?

THE ROMANTIC POETS

That historical stage commonly referred to as the Romantic period occurred during the first thirty years of the nineteenth century. Literally speaking, it was "born" in 1798 with the publication of a small volume of poems by William Wordsworth and Samuel Taylor Coleridge called *Lyrical Ballads*. At the time, this volume was considered — even by some eminent critics — as foolish and unimportant, but it gave to English poetry a new direction and freedom. It revived the imaginative spirit which had given rise to such abundant, varied, and intense literary expression during the English Renaissance. This spirit almost completely dominated English literary thought and expression for three decades and was the creative force which brought into being some of the most sensitive and profound poetry written in the English language.

The words *romantic* and *romanticism* have special meanings when used as literary terms. They indicate a particular way of perceiving and interpreting the universe by employing the faculties of imagination and intuition. The faculty of reason is not ignored, but it is subordinate to the other two, as the "head" is to the "heart."

The Romantics felt the need to find a more satisfactory explanation of the visible world and man's place in it than that provided by the scientists and philosophers of their day. They believed that imagination was the divine spark, the part of God in every man which provided the insight and perception that enabled him to approach truth. In fact, they felt that to view life without imagination was to limit seriously one's perception, even of the things in one's immediate surroundings. Their concern was not with the obvious, but with some hidden truth or beauty in reality. Thus, the literature of the Romantic period is permeated with a new sense of wonder.

Part of this wonder is reflected in a love of Nature and in man's involvement with his natural surroundings. A fascination with the past, particularly ancient and medieval times, is also evident in the prose and poetry of this period.

The Romantics placed great value on the individual. They cherished the freedom to think and act according to their own beliefs, and to express with emotional intensity their personal feelings of pleasure and pain, of restlessness, dissatisfaction, and anger. They asserted a belief in the freedom of all men, and particularly a belief in the natural dignity of the common man. To express these values, the poets revived the lyric, the ballad, and the sonnet as valid forms in which to express themselves.

These events and attitudes seemed the very antithesis of the so-called Neoclassical movement, which dominated the greater part of the eighteenth century. Pope and his admirers considered unbridled imagination of little significance or importance, although they admired the apt use of images and figurative language to "picture" the visible world. They saw the poet's role as that of an interpreter rather than a creator. His purpose was to display with all possible charm and truth the familiar appearance of life rather than to explore its mysteries. Above all, since Neoclassical poets thought they had discovered the "perfect" form of poetic expression—the couplet—they felt the use or creation of other forms was unnecessary and revealed a lack of "taste."

In the *Lyrical Ballads* of 1798, both Wordsworth and Coleridge discarded the Neoclassical conventions which had dictated English literature for nearly a century and a half. Wordsworth's method was to scrutinize common things intensely. His purpose was to help his reader to perceive the beauty in the familiar world around him. Coleridge attempted exactly the opposite, for he dealt primarily with the supernatural. But as Wordsworth stated in his preface to the second edition of the *Lyrical Ballads*, both of them were striving to express themselves in direct and living language—Wordsworth, in the language of common speech, and Coleridge, in the language of old ballads and romances.

Wordsworth and Coleridge enjoyed a rare and mutually beneficial relationship. Together with Wordsworth's sister Dorothy, they spent many hours sharing thoughts and feelings about life, nature, and poetry. Intellectually and spiritually atuned, they understood and responded sensitively to one another's periods of inspiration and despair. Yet they were very different kinds of people. Wordsworth was tough-minded, energetic, and outspoken—often even bellicose; Coleridge was painfully sensitive, gentle, and always ready to consider both sides of any question.

Yet the poetry of these two men seems to contradict, rather than confirm, the impressions conveyed by their personalities and their reactions to the political turmoil of their day. Wordsworth appears the gentle, contemplative observer, keenly sensitive to the world of nature. Coleridge appears the man of action, creating worlds of his own or appealing to the senses and emotions rather than to the mind.

WILLIAM WORDSWORTH'S philosophy was shaped largely by his love for the beauty and the humble people of the Lake District in northwestern England, where he passed his youth and where he returned to live the last fifty years of his life. He believed that men can be truly happy and virtuous only if they are in contact with nature and responsive to her "teaching." In an age of rapid urbanization, he championed the rustic life because "in that condition the essential passions of the heart find a better soil in which they can attain their maturity, are less under restraint, and speak a plainer and more emphatic language." Life in towns, he believed, corrupts and deadens the finer instincts of man. He himself found it difficult to communicate with most men; yet there was no reticence or lack of emotion in his relationships with his wife, his sister, and the few close friends who shared his love of nature.

Wordsworth insisted on the importance to poetry of intense emotion "recollected in tranquillity." Art of any stature, he wrote, can be created only "by a man who, being possessed of more than usual organic sensibility, has also thought long and deeply. For our continued influxes of feeling are modified and directed by our thoughts, which are indeed the representatives of all our past feelings."

Scorning the pose affected by many poets of the seventeenth and eighteenth centuries, he maintained that the poet is simply "a man speaking to men." Nevertheless, he was convinced that "the act of creation in the highest sense involves a special insight into the nature of things." The poet must, therefore, never forget that the purpose of art is to communicate, not to a few but to all sorts and conditions of men. At the same time, he must never allow the spirit of communion with others to subdue his own individuality.

❦SAMUEL TAYLOR COLERIDGE shared Wordsworth's belief that nature is a teacher of moral truths, but he did not agree that poetry must glorify the rustic way of life. Coleridge doubted that uneducated rustics were inspired and elevated by their contact with nature, for he noted that rural life was often crude and rural people were often hardhearted. He doubted, too, that poetic diction could or should be based on the "language really used by men." In a famous refutation of some of Wordsworth's poetic theories, he claimed that there *was* no common language of the lower classes, and that poems "might not be so managed in the language of ordinary life as to produce the pleasurable interest which it is the peculiar business of poetry to impart." Therefore, he always adapted his language to the particular poetic task at hand, using in a literary ballad, for example, the kind of language traditionally associated with the ballad form.

Coleridge possessed almost unlimited intellectual energy. A man of wide interests and encyclopedic learning, he was continually inspired by ideas for new scholarly and artistic projects—most of which he failed to carry to their conclusion. A brilliant talker, he introduced new methods of literary criticism and energized the minds of leading essayists and lesser poets. In his time, he exercised far more influence than Wordsworth. In our time, he shares with Wordsworth the credit for having opened the door to one of the greatest periods of poetic creation in the history of literature.

The late Romantic poets—Byron, Shelley, and Keats— seemed to the Englishmen of their day assertive nonconformists. When Napoleon was defeated at Waterloo, they were barely beyond adolescence. They had heard and read about the idealism that motivated the French Revolution, but they had suffered little, if any, from the terror and upheaval which followed it. Neither had they experienced the disillusionment and resurgence of patriotism of the early Romantic poets, Wordsworth and Coleridge. Although England had emerged the victor in the Napoleonic Wars, it had suffered as much as the nation it vanquished. The age-old British tradition of civil liberties was in grave danger. The expanded wartime economy was threatened by severe financial and agricultural crises. Guardians of the status quo became increasingly determined to suppress any evidence of dissent or resistance which might lead to revolutionary activity. The late Romantic poets— especially Byron and Shelley—would not be suppressed. They insisted on justice for all men and, for themselves, almost unlimited freedom of thought and expression.

All three poets both shared characteristics with and differed from their distinguished predecessors, Wordsworth and Coleridge. Along with Wordsworth, they loved natural beauty. Nevertheless, they did not regard nature primarily as a teacher of moral truths. To Byron, mountains, oceans, and forests were magnificent spectacles. To Shelley, all the natural world was informed and unified by a universal, *amoral* force. To Keats, nature's sights, sounds, and smells were a constant sensual delight. They shared Coleridge's fascination with the remote in time and place. Byron was attracted by the pageantry and splendor of bygone ages and by the mysteriousness of distant places. (Before he was ten, he had read every book on the Orient that he could find.) Shelley viewed history as a dark record of man's inhumanity to man, with occasional glimpses of heroic self-sacrifice to kindle hope. Keats was entranced by the beauty of ancient Greece and Rome and the flamboyance of the Middle Ages.

Still, though Byron, Shelley, and Keats are traditionally treated as a group, the differences among them are greater than the similarities. Each was a unique individual — Byron in his aristocratic hatred of tyranny, Shelley in his democratic idealism, and Keats in his reliance on the senses. Each looked into himself for the particular experiences on which to base his poetry.

GEORGE GORDON, LORD BYRON inspired legends even among his own contemporaries, who were intrigued by his various and daring exploits, his intense commitment to freedom, and the mystery with which he surrounded himself. Goethe, the great German Romantic poet, called him a "fiery mass of living valor hurling itself on life." Other readers and fellow writers identified him with his most famous literary creation — the "Byronic hero," who first appeared in *Childe Harold's Pilgrimage:*

> "That man of loneliness and mystery,
> Scarce seen to smile, and seldom heard to sigh."

With the publication of the first two cantos of *Childe Harold's Pilgrimage* in 1812, Byron became the most celebrated poet in Europe and England. Scandal, however, turned the British public against him, and, bitter, he left England, never to return.

Byron differed from his fellow Romantics in two important ways. First, though fascinated with the wonders of nature, he felt no urge to look beyond them for ulterior meanings. Second, he was far more concerned with poetic conventions and correctness of form than any of his distinguished contemporaries. He often expressed great admiration for the Neoclassical poets — especially for Pope, whom he called "the most perfect" of English poets. "The good old and now neglected heroic couplet" he found "the best adapted measure to our language." If he rarely achieved the polish and verbal economy that characterize Pope's couplets, it was partly because he lacked his master's patience. "I can never recast anything," he said. "I am like the tiger; if I miss the first spring, I go grumbling back to my jungle."

PERCY BYSSHE SHELLEY was always the dedicated revolutionary. A firm believer in the perfectibility of man, he envisioned an ideal world liberated and transformed by love and the spirit of freedom. In the manner of many idealists, he recognized and denounced evils more readily than he devised plans for correcting them. Nevertheless, he was always willing to engage his poetic talents in the struggle against injustice and oppression. "Poets," he wrote, "are the unacknowledged legislators of the world."

An idealist in philosophy as well as in social and political matters, Shelley was deeply influenced by Plato's concept of an absolute, eternal spirit of Beauty that is revealed only occasionally and imperfectly in man and nature. Partly because of the inconstancy of this "spirit," Shelley's exaltation often gave way to melancholy. As he became increasingly aware that life is as often tragic as it is joyful, he learned to come to terms with the darker emotions. "The pleasure that is in sorrow," he wrote, "is sweeter than the pleasure of pleasure itself. And hence the saying, 'It is better to go to the house of mourning than to the house of mirth.'"

JOHN KEATS remarked in a letter, "I am certain of nothing but the holiness of the Heart's affections and the truth of the Imagination. What the imagination seizes as Beauty must be Truth. . . . I have never yet been able to perceive how anything can be known for truth by consecutive reasoning." Keats shared Shelley's belief that only the pursuit of beauty—whether in nature or in art—can give real meaning to human life. This beauty was not, however, the "intellectual beauty" of Shelley, but a more sensuous variety. Keats longed for "a life of sensations rather than of thought" and claimed that one must participate in nature in order to understand it. "If a sparrow comes before my window," he said, "I take part in its existence and pick about the gravel."

Despite his belief that "beauty is truth, truth beauty," Keats was not blind to the ugliness in the world. He knew "the boredom, and the horror" as well as the glory, and he feared the suppression of the spirit of man, weighed down by a life without beauty or joy.

William Wordsworth

Wordsworth's major contribution to poetry was his demonstration that verse could communicate effectively the wonder of everyday experience in direct, unadorned language. But Wordsworth was not satisfied merely to record his sensory impressions; he believed that every "fact" suggests a greater truth. "There is scarcely one of my poems," he wrote to a friend, "which does not aim to direct the attention to some moral sentiment, or to some general principle, or law of thought. . . ." To express some of these more philosophic reflections, he revised the sonnet form, which had been neglected by the Neoclassicists; and also, as in "Tintern Abbey," he used a more elevated language, often with quiet and deep musical effects.

LINES WRITTEN IN EARLY SPRING

I heard a thousand blended notes,
While in a grove I sate° reclined,   sat
In that sweet mood when pleasant thoughts
Bring sad thoughts to the mind.

To her fair works did Nature link   5
The human soul that through me ran;
And much it grieved my heart to think
What man has made of man.

Through primrose tufts, in that green bower,
The periwinkle trailed its wreaths;   10
And 'tis my faith that every flower
Enjoys the air it breathes.

The birds around me hopped and played,
Their thoughts I cannot measure: —
But the least motion which they made,   15
It seemed a thrill of pleasure.

The budding twigs spread out their fan,
To catch the breezy air;
And I must think, do all I can,
That there was pleasure there.   20

If this belief from heaven be sent,
If such be Nature's holy plan,
Have I not reason to lament
What man has made of man?

1. In what way are lines 3 and 4 paradoxical (see Glossary, page 510)? What are the poet's "pleasant thoughts"? What are his "sad thoughts"? Why do the former "bring" the latter? Support your answers with evidence from the poem—especially from stanzas 2 and 6.
2. What are the "thousand" blended notes that Wordsworth heard while sitting in a grove? What do the flowers, the birds, and the "budding twigs" (stanzas 3-5) have in common? What is "this belief" referred to in line 21?
3. What is the poet's conception of "Nature's holy plan"? What does he mean by "what man has made of man"? Indicate the clues in the poem that led to your interpretation of these key phrases.
4. What insight do you think Wordsworth gained into the meaning of life as he recollected "in tranquility" the scene pictured in this poem?

LINES COMPOSED A FEW MILES ABOVE TINTERN ABBEY

ON REVISITING THE BANKS OF THE WYE DURING A TOUR, JULY 13, 1798

Five years have past; five summers, with the length
Of five long winters! and again I hear
These waters, rolling from their mountain-springs
With a soft inland murmur.—Once again
Do I behold these steep and lofty cliffs,   5
That on a wild secluded scene impress
Thoughts of more deep seclusion; and connect
The landscape with the quiet of the sky.
The day is come when I again repose
Here, under this dark sycamore, and view   10
These plots of cottage-ground, these orchard-tufts,
Which at this season, with their unripe fruits,
Are clad in one green hue, and lose themselves
'Mid groves and copses. Once again I see
These hedge rows, hardly hedge rows, little lines   15
Of sportive wood run wild: these pastoral farms,
Green to the very door; and wreaths of smoke
Sent up, in silence, from among the trees!
With some uncertain notice, as might seem
Of vagrant dwellers in the houseless woods,   20
Or of some hermit's cave, where by his fire
The hermit sits alone.
                       These beauteous forms,
Through a long absence, have not been to me
As is a landscape to a blind man's eye:
But oft, in lonely rooms, and 'mid the din   25
Of towns and cities, I have owed to them
In hours of weariness, sensations sweet,

Felt in the blood, and felt along the heart;
And passing even into my purer mind,
With tranquil restoration: — feelings too   30
Of unremembered pleasure: such, perhaps,
As have no slight or trivial influence
On that best portion of a good man's life,
His little, nameless, unremembered acts
Of kindness and of love. Nor less, I trust,   35
To them I may have owed another gift,
Of aspect more sublime; that blessed mood
In which the burthen of the mystery,
In which the heavy and the weary weight
Of all this unintelligible world,   40
Is lightened: — that serene and blessed mood,
In which the affections gently lead us on, —
Until, the breath of this corporeal frame
And even the motion of our human blood
Almost suspended, we are laid asleep   45
In body, and become a living soul:
While with an eye made quiet by the power
Of harmony, and the deep power of joy,
We see into the life of things.
                              If this
Be but a vain belief, yet, oh! how oft—   50
In darkness and amid the many shapes
Of joyless daylight; when the fretful stir
Unprofitable, and the fever of the world,
Have hung upon the beatings of my heart—
How oft, in spirit, have I turned to thee,   55
O sylvan Wye! thou wanderer through the woods,
How often has my spirit turned to thee!
And now, with gleams of half-extinguished thought,
With many recognitions dim and faint,
And somewhat of a sad perplexity,   60
The picture of the mind revives again:
While here I stand, not only with the sense

Of present pleasure, but with pleasing thoughts
That in this moment there is life and food
For future years. And so I dare to hope,   65
Though changed, no doubt, from what I was when first
I came among these hills; when like a roe
I bounded o'er the mountains, by the sides
Of the deep rivers, and the lonely streams,
Wherever nature led: more like a man   70
Flying from something that he dreads than one
Who sought the thing he loved. For nature then
(The coarser pleasures of my boyish days,
And their glad animal movements all gone by)
To me was all in all. — I cannot paint   75
What then I was. The sounding cataract
Haunted me like a passion: the tall rock,
The mountain, and the deep and gloomy wood,
Their colors and their forms, were then to me
An appetite; a feeling and a love,   80
That had no need of a remoter charm,
By thought supplied, nor any interest
Unborrowed from the eye. — That time is past,
And all its aching joys are now no more,
And all its dizzy raptures. Not for this   85
Faint I, nor mourn nor murmur; other gifts
Have followed; for such loss, I would believe,
Abundant recompense. For I have learned
To look on nature, not as in the hour
Of thoughtless youth; but hearing oftentimes   90
The still, sad music of humanity,
Nor harsh nor grating, though of ample power
To chasten and subdue. And I have felt
A presence that disturbs me with the joy
Of elevated thoughts; a sense sublime,   95
Of something far more deeply interfused,
Whose dwelling is the light of setting suns,
And the round ocean and the living air,

And the blue sky, and in the mind of man:
A motion and a spirit, that impels   100
All thinking things, all objects of all thought,
And rolls through all things. Therefore am I still
A lover of the meadows and the woods,
And mountains; and of all that we behold
From this green earth; of all the mighty world   105
Of eye, and ear,—both what they half create,
And what perceive; well pleased to recognize
In nature and the language of the sense
The anchor of my purest thoughts, the nurse,
The guide, the guardian of my heart, and soul   110
Of all my moral being.
                              Nor perchance,
If I were not thus taught, should I the more
Suffer my genial spirits to decay:
For thou art with me here upon the banks
Of this fair river; thou my dearest friend,[1]   115
My dear, dear friend; and in thy voice I catch
The language of my former heart, and read
My former pleasures in the shooting lights
Of thy wild eyes. Oh! yet a little while
May I behold in thee what I was once,   120
My dear, dear sister! and this prayer I make,
Knowing that Nature never did betray
The heart that loved her; 'tis her privilege,
Through all the years of this our life, to lead
From joy to joy: for she can so inform   125
The mind that is within us, so impress
With quietness and beauty, and so feed
With lofty thoughts, that neither evil tongues,
Rash judgments, nor the sneers of selfish men,
Nor greetings where no kindness is, nor all   130
The dreary intercourse of daily life,

[1]*dearest friend:* his sister, Dorothy Wordsworth

Shall e'er prevail against us, or disturb
Our cheerful faith, that all which we behold
Is full of blessings. Therefore let the moon
Shine on thee in thy solitary walk;   135
And let the misty mountain-winds be free
To blow against thee: and, in after years,
When these wild ecstasies shall be matured
Into a sober pleasure; when thy mind
Shall be a mansion for all lovely forms,   140
Thy memory be as a dwelling-place
For all sweet sounds and harmonies; oh! then,
If solitude, or fear, or pain, or grief,
Should be thy portion, with what healing thoughts
Of tender joy wilt thou remember me,   145
And these my exhortations! Nor, perchance—
If I should be where I no more can hear
Thy voice, nor catch from thy wild eyes these gleams
Of past existence—wilt thou then forget
That on the banks of this delightful stream   150
We stood together; and that I, so long
A worshipper of Nature, hither came
Unwearied in that service: rather say
With warmer love—oh! with far deeper zeal
Of holier love. Nor wilt thou then forget,   155
That after many wanderings, many years
Of absence, these steep woods and lofty cliffs,
And this green pastoral landscape, were to me
More dear, both for themselves and for thy sake!

1. On revisiting the banks of the Wye, what "once again" makes a
   deep impression on Wordsworth? Why has the time seemed so
   long since his last visit? Why does he feel that he owes so much
   to "these beauteous forms" (line 22), which he feels as well as
   remembers? What gifts does he mention? Give your interpretation of lines 47-49.

2. In what mood does he again view the scene and recall his earlier responses to it? Give your interpretation of lines 47-49.
3. To what is he referring in lines 91-93? What is this "presence" which disturbs him? Explain in your own words the "oneness" which Wordsworth feels with nature (lines 107-111).
4. Why is it important that Wordsworth's sister Dorothy is present when he revisits the banks of the Wye? What "prayer" does he make for her? From this portion of the poem, what insight do you gain into the character of both and the relationship between them?
5. Chart the rhythm pattern of lines 1-8. Identify the predominant metrical foot and line. Point out lines in which, for the meaning, you need to alter the regular rhythm. Describe the effect. What words would you use to describe the over-all tone of the poem?
6. In your opinion, how important to the total effect of the poem are the rhythm and the sound of the words? Point out examples of effective alliteration and assonance. Comment on the choice of words. If they are not those "really used by men," how would you describe Wordsworth's language?

SHE DWELT AMONG THE
UNTRODDEN WAYS

She dwelt among the untrodden ways
   Beside the springs of Dove,[1]
A maid whom there were none to praise
   And very few to love:

A violet by a mossy stone   5
   Half hidden from the eye!
— Fair as a star, when only one
   Is shining in the sky.

She lived unknown, and few could know
   When Lucy ceased to be;   10
But she is in her grave, and, oh,
   The difference to me!

[1]*Dove:* an English stream

1. Which of the following words would you use to describe the tone of this poem: bitter, mournful, sentimental, tragic? Explain. What words and phrases convey the maid's isolation, the mood of solitude?
2. Several critics have claimed that the implied comparisons in stanza 2 are extraordinarily delicate and beautiful. Do you agree? Support your opinion with specific comments on the effectiveness, appropriateness, and compactness of the comparisons.
3. Despite its simple language, the poem conveys an impression of the poet's intense feeling. Point out examples, especially in the last stanza, which suggest such intensity.
4. This poem is one of Wordsworth's "Lucy poems." Whether an actual Lucy existed is unknown. In either case, what might she have symbolized for Wordsworth?

LONDON, 1802

Milton! thou should'st be living at this hour:
England hath need of thee: she is a fen
Of stagnant waters: altar, sword, and pen,
Fireside, the heroic wealth of hall and bower,
Have forfeited their ancient English dower   5
Of inward happiness. We are selfish men;
Oh! raise us up, return to us again;
And give us manners, virtue, freedom, power.
Thy soul was like a star, and dwelt apart:
Thou hadst a voice whose sound was like the sea: 10
Pure as the naked heavens, majestic, free,
So didst thou travel on life's common way,
In cheerful godliness; and yet thy heart
The lowliest duties on herself did lay.

1. Why does Wordsworth wish that Milton were "living at this hour"? What changes have occurred which have destroyed the nation's "inward happiness"? Relate the conditions which grieved Wordsworth about London in 1802 with the revolutions taking place at that time.
2. Why does he believe that England needs Milton? What could

Milton contribute that would "raise us up"? What impression do you gain of the character of Milton from lines 9-14?

3. Lines 3 and 4 contain five examples of metonymy (see page 509). What specific groups of people are referred to indirectly? Why are the "substituted" words more forceful than the general words customarily used?

4. Which of the sonnet forms does this one more nearly resemble: Italian or Shakespearean? What scene, idea, or incident is presented in the octave? Is the sestet a development of the octave or an application? Does the poet arrive at a conclusion based on the octave? Discuss.

THE WORLD IS TOO MUCH WITH US

The world is too much with us; late and soon,
Getting and spending, we lay waste our powers:
Little we see in Nature that is ours;
We have given our hearts away, a sordid boon!
The sea that bares her bosom to the moon;   5
The winds that will be howling at all hours,
And are up-gathered now like sleeping flowers;
For this, for every thing, we are out of tune;
It moves us not. — Great God! I'd rather be
A Pagan suckled in a creed outworn;   10
So might I, standing on this pleasant lea,
Have glimpses that would make me less forlorn;
Have sight of Proteus[1] rising from the sea;
Or hear old Triton[2] blow his wreathèd horn.

[1]*Proteus:* sea god in the service of Neptune, god of the sea
[2]*Triton:* sea god who raised or calmed waves by blowing a trumpet made of a conch shell

1. What does the phrase "the world" mean in line 1? What reasons does Wordsworth give for believing that "the world is too much with us"? What has caused man to be "out of tune" with Nature?

To what have we "given our hearts away"? Why does he describe this giving as "a sordid boon"?

2. What aspects of Nature are suggested in lines 5-7? Do these lines adequately convey the forces and beauties of the natural world? Explain. To what does *It* refer in line 9? How do you interpret that brief statement?

3. Why would the visions described in lines 13 and 14 have made the poet "less forlorn"? Why would he have preferred to be a "Pagan suckled in a creed outworn"? (If necessary, look up information about ancient Greek life and mythology before attempting to answer these questions.)

4. This poem is often ranked among the greatest English sonnets. Identify the sonnet form (see page 513). How is the transition from the octave to the sestet effected? Point out examples of the compactness of the language and of the poet's choice of words to create an effect of intense forcefulness.

THE SOLITARY REAPER

Behold her, single in the field,
Yon solitary Highland lass!
Reaping and singing by herself;
Stop here, or gently pass!
Alone she cuts and binds the grain,   5
And sings a melancholy strain;
Oh listen! for the vale profound
Is overflowing with the sound.

No nightingale did ever chaunt
More welcome notes to weary bands   10
Of travellers in some shady haunt,
Among Arabian sands:
A voice so thrilling ne'er was heard
In spring time from the cuckoo-bird,
Breaking the silence of the seas   15
Among the farthest Hebrides.[1]

[1]*Hebrides:* two groups of islands off the coast of Scotland

Will no one tell me what she sings?—
Perhaps the plaintive numbers flow
For old, unhappy, far-off things,
And battles long ago: 20
Or is it some more humble lay,
Familiar matter of today?
Some natural sorrow, loss, or pain,
That has been, and may be again?

Whate'er the theme, the Maiden sang   25
As if her song could have no ending;
I saw her singing at her work,
And o'er the sickle bending;—
I listened, motionless and still;
And, as I mounted up the hill,   30
The music in my heart I bore,
Long after it was heard no more.

1. Long after the reaper's song was heard no more, the poet bears it
   in his heart. Why? How does the sound of it impress him, even
   though he cannot hear the words? Of what occasions does it remind him (see stanza 2)?
2. Note the question in line 17. Why doesn't he mind greatly that
   the theme of the song remains a mystery? What do you think was
   the mood of the singer? What words and phrases in the poem
   suggest it?
3. Chart the rhythm and the rhyme of the first stanza, noting the
   combination of different rhythms to create different effects. Discuss these effects and point out others in the remaining stanzas.
   What is the rhyme scheme? Is it consistent throughout each
   stanza? In what lines is there a faulty rhyme? Tell why you do, or
   do not, think this detracts from the beauty of the poem.
4. The title could have been merely "The Reaper." What important
   clue does the word *solitary* give you to the mood of the poem and
   to the poet's attitude toward the subject and toward life?

SHE WAS A PHANTOM OF DELIGHT

She was a phantom of delight
When first she gleamed upon my sight;
A lovely apparition, sent
To be a moment's ornament;
Her eyes as stars of twilight fair;   5
Like twilight's, too, her dusky hair;
But all things else about her drawn
From May-time and the cheerful dawn;
A dancing shape, an image gay,
To haunt, to startle, and waylay.   10

I saw her upon nearer view,
A spirit, yet a woman too!
Her household motions light and free,
And steps of virgin-liberty;
A countenance in which did meet   15
Sweet records, promises as sweet;
A creature not too bright or good
For human nature's daily food;
For transient sorrows, simple wiles,
Praise, blame, love, kisses, tears, and smiles.   20

And now I see with eye serene
The very pulse of the machine;
A being breathing thoughtful breath,
A traveller between life and death;
The reason firm, the temperate will,   25
Endurance, foresight, strength, and skill;
A perfect woman, nobly planned,
To warn, to comfort, and command;
And yet a spirit still, and bright
With something of angelic light.   30

1. Wordsworth had known his wife, Mary Hutchinson, since early childhood. Each stanza in this poem represents one stage in his long attraction and devotion to her. What is she like at each stage and what qualities does he most admire? Why does seeing her with "eye serene" increase his appreciation of her? How does the final couplet serve to unify the entire poem?

2. Note Wordsworth's frequent use of metaphors and similes to convey his impressions of his wife. Show how these comparisons differ from stanza to stanza to suit both the change in the person and the poet's attitude toward her.

3. Here Wordsworth uses the couplet, which the Neoclassical poets of the preceding century considered the "perfect" poetic form. How well suited is it to the subject? Are there any instances in which the poet might have chosen a better word if he had not been limited by the rhyme? What advantages can you see in the couplet form?

Samuel Taylor Coleridge

Coleridge's special genius is best revealed in his masterpieces, "Kubla Khan" and "The Rime of the Ancient Mariner." In "Kubla Khan," with its wonderful music and Oriental images, he displays his fascination for the remote and the obscure. In "The Rime of the Ancient Mariner," Coleridge reveals through vivid and exact language his remarkable ability to blend the supernatural and the familar in order to evoke wonder and terror. Although Coleridge wrote a comparatively small body of poetry, these two poems, together with his "Christabel," place him among the major poets in English literature.

KUBLA KHAN

OR, A VISION IN A DREAM

In Xanadu did Kubla Khan[1]
A stately pleasure-dome decree:
Where Alph, the sacred river, ran
Through caverns measureless to man
    Down to a sunless sea.   5
So twice five miles of fertile ground

[1] *Kubla Khan:* founder of the Mongol dynasty in China in the thirteenth century

With walls and towers were girdled round:
And there were gardens bright with sinuous rills,
Where blossomed many an incense-bearing tree;
And here were forests ancient as the hills,   10
Enfolding sunny spots of greenery.

But oh! that deep romantic chasm which slanted
Down the green hill athwart a cedarn cover!
A savage place! as holy and enchanted
As e'er beneath a waning moon was haunted   15
By woman wailing for her demon-lover!
And from this chasm, with ceaseless turmoil seething,
As if this earth in fast thick pants were breathing,
A mighty fountain momently was forced;
Amid whose swift half-intermitted burst   20
Huge fragments vaulted like rebounding hail,
Or chaffy grain beneath the thresher's flail:
And 'mid these dancing rocks at once and ever
It flung up momently the sacred river.
Five miles meandering with a mazy motion   25
Through wood and dale the sacred river ran,
Then reached the caverns measureless to man,
And sank in tumult to a lifeless ocean:
And 'mid this tumult Kubla heard from far
Ancestral voices prophesying war!   30

    The shadow of the dome of pleasure
    Floated midway on the waves;
    Where was heard the mingled measure
    From the fountain and the caves.
It was a miracle of rare device,   35
A sunny pleasure-dome with caves of ice!

    A damsel with a dulcimer
    In a vision once I saw:
    It was an Abyssinian maid,

And on her dulcimer she played,   40
Singing of Mount Abora.
Could I revive within me
Her symphony and song,
To such a deep delight 'twould win me,
That with music loud and long,   45
I would build that dome in air,
That sunny dome! those caves of ice!
And all who heard should see them there,
And all should cry, Beware! Beware!
His flashing eyes, his floating hair!   50
Weave a circle round him thrice,
And close your eyes with holy dread,
For he on honey-dew hath fed,
And drunk the milk of Paradise.

1. Coleridge claimed that this poem came to him while he slept, and that he wrote it down exactly as he remembered it when he awoke. Whether this is actually so or not, the power of the poem lies in its exotic, dreamlike images and compelling music. Point out specific words and phrases that create a sense of mystery and romantic strangeness.
2. Explain how the sound reinforces the meaning in line 25. What musical device does Coleridge use here? Point out other lines which effectively mingle sound and meaning.
3. Coleridge stated that his purpose in poetry was to create a "willing suspension of disbelief" in the reader and to make the supernatural believable. Reread the first stanza of this poem. Clearly, the description of the scene has a remote, dreamlike quality. But how does Coleridge make this description immediate and convincing? Point out details in the poem which support your answer.
4. The poem shifts tone and rhythm at certain points. Where do these shifts occur? What effect do they achieve?
5. Give examples of similes and metaphors which add to the mood of the poem.

THE RIME OF THE ANCIENT MARINER

ARGUMENT

How a Ship, having first sailed to the Equator, was driven by
Storms to the cold Country toward the South Pole; how the Ancient Mariner cruelly and in contempt of the laws of hospitality
killed a Sea-bird and how he was followed by many and strange
Judgments: and in what manner he came back to his own Country.

PART 1

An ancient
Mariner meeteth
three Gallants
bidden to a wed-
ding-feast and
detaineth one.

It is an ancient Mariner,
And he stoppeth one of three.
"By thy long gray beard and glittering eye,
Now wherefore stopp'st thou me?

"The Bridegroom's doors are opened wide,   5
And I am next of kin;
The guests are met, the feast is set:
May'st hear the merry din."

He holds him with his skinny hand,
"There was a ship," quoth he.   10
"Hold off! unhand me, gray-beard loon!"
Eftsoons° his hand dropped he.   quickly

He holds him with his glittering eye—
The Wedding-Guest stood still,

The Wedding-
Guest is spell-
bound by the eye
of the old sea-
faring man, and
constrained to
hear his tale.

And listens like a three years' child: 15
The Mariner hath his will.

The Wedding-Guest sat on a stone:
He cannot choose but hear;
And thus spake on that ancient man,
The bright-eyed Mariner.   20

"The ship was cheered, the harbor cleared,
Merrily did we drop
Below the kirk,° below the hill,   church
Below the lighthouse top.

The Mariner tells
how the ship
sailed southward
with a good
wind and fair
weather, till it
reached the
Line.[1]

"The Sun came up upon the left,   25
Out of the sea came he!
And he shone bright, and on the right
Went down into the sea.

"Higher and higher every day,
Till over the mast at noon—"   30
The Wedding-Guest here beat his breast,
For he heard the loud bassoon.

The Wedding-
Guest heareth
the bridal music;
but the Mariner
continueth his
tale.

The bride hath paced into the hall,
Red as a rose is she;
Nodding their heads before her goes   35
The merry minstrelsy.

The Wedding-Guest he beat his breast,
Yet he cannot choose but hear;
And thus spake on that ancient man,
The bright-eyed Mariner.   40

The ship driven
by a storm
toward the South
Pole.

"And now the Storm-blast came, and he
Was tyrannous and strong:
He struck with his o'ertaking wings,
And chased us south along.

"With sloping masts and dipping prow,   45
As who pursued with yell and blow
Still treads the shadow of his foe,

---

[1]*Line:* the equator

And forward bends his head,
The ship drove fast, loud roared the blast,
And southward aye we fled.   50

"And now there came both mist and snow,
And it grew wondrous cold:
And ice, mast-high, came floating by,
As green as emerald.   54

The land of ice
and of fearful
sounds where
no living thing
was to be seen.

"And through the drifts° the snowy clifts° mist;
Did send a dismal sheen: icebergs
Nor shapes of men nor beasts we ken°—   see
The ice was all between.

"The ice was here, the ice was there,
The ice was all around: 60
It cracked and growled, and roared
   and howled,
Like noises in a swound!°   dream

Till a great sea-
bird, called the
Albatross, came
through the
snow-fog, and
was received
with great joy
and hospitality.

"At length did cross an Albatross,
Thorough° the fog it came;   through
As if it had been a Christian soul,   65
We hailed it in God's name.

"It ate the food it ne'er had eat,°   eaten
And round and round it flew.
The ice did split with a thunder fit;
The helmsman steered us through!   70

And lo! the
Albatross
proveth a bird
of good omen,
and followeth
the ship as it
returned north-
ward through
fog and float-
ing ice.

"And a good south wind sprung up behind;
The Albatross did follow,
And every day, for food or play,
Came to the mariners' hollo!

"In mist or cloud, on mast or shroud,°   rope 75
It perched for vespers° nine;   evenings
Whiles all the night, through fog-smoke white,
Glimmered the white moon shine."

The ancient
Mariner in-
hospitably
killeth the pious
bird of good
omen.

"God save thee, ancient Mariner!
From the fiends, that plague thee thus!—   80
Why look'st thou so?"—"With my crossbow
I shot the Albatross.

PART 2

"The Sun now rose upon the right:
Out of the sea came he,
Still hid in mist, and on the left   85
Went down into the sea.

"And the good south wind still blew behind,
But no sweet bird did follow,
Nor any day for food or play
Came to the mariners' hollo!   90

His shipmates
cry out against
the ancient
Mariner, for kill-
ing the bird of
good luck.

"And I had done a hellish thing,
And it would work 'em woe:
For all averred, I had killed the bird
That made the breeze to blow.
Ah wretch! said they, the bird to slay,   95
That made the breeze to blow!

But when the
fog cleared off,
they justify the
same, and thus
make themselves
accomplices in
the crime.

"Nor dim nor red, like God's own head,
The glorious Sun uprist:
Then all averred, I had killed the bird
That brought the fog and mist.   100
'Twas right, said they, such birds to slay,
That bring the fog and mist.

The fair breeze continues; the ship enters the Pacific Ocean, and sails northward, even till it reaches the Line.

"The fair breeze blew, the white foam flew,
The furrow° followed free;   wake
We were the first that ever burst   105
Into that silent sea.

The ship hath been suddenly becalmed

"Down dropped the breeze, the sails dropped down,
'Twas sad as sad could be;
And we did speak only to break
The silence of the sea!   110

"All in a hot and copper sky,
The bloody Sun, at noon,
Right up above the mast did stand,
No bigger than the Moon.

"Day after day, day after day,   115
We stuck, nor breath nor motion;
As idle as a painted ship
Upon a painted ocean.

And the Albatross begins to be avenged.

"Water, water, every where,
And all the boards did shrink;   120
Water, water, every where,
Nor any drop to drink.

"The very deep did rot: O Christ!
That ever this should be!
Yea, slimy things did crawl with legs   125
Upon the slimy sea.

A Sprit had followed them; one of the invisible inhabitants of this planet, neither departed

"About, about, in reel and rout
The death-fires danced at night;
The water, like a witch's oils,
Burnt green and blue and white.   130

souls nor angels. . . . They are very numerous, and there is no climate or element without one or more.

"And some in dreams assurèd were
Of the Spirit that plagued us so;
Nine fathom deep he had followed us
From the land of mist and snow.

The shipmates, in their sore distress, would fain throw the whole guilt on the ancient Mariner; in sign whereof they hang the dead sea-bird round his neck.

"And every tongue, through utter drought,   135
Was withered at the root;
We could not speak, no more than if
We had been choked with soot.

"Ah! well-a-day! what evil looks
Had I from old and young!   140
Instead of the cross, the Albatross
About my neck was hung.

PART 3

The ancient Mariner beholdeth a sign in the element afar off.

"There passed a weary time. Each throat
Was parched, and glazed each eye.
A weary time! a weary time!   145
How glazed each weary eye,
When looking westward, I beheld
A something in the sky.

"At first it seemed a little speck,
And then it seemed a mist;   150
It moved and moved, and took at last
A certain shape, I wist.°   knew

"A speck, a mist, a shape, I wist!
And still it neared and neared:
As if it dodged a water-sprite,   155
It plunged and tacked and veered.

At its nearer
approach, it
seemeth him to
be a ship; and at
a dear ransom
he freeth his
speech from the
bonds of thirst.

"With throats unslaked, with black lips baked,
We could nor laugh nor wail;
Through utter drought all dumb we stood!
I bit my arm, I sucked the blood,   160
And cried, A sail! A sail!

"With throats unslaked, with black lips baked,
Agape they heard me call:
A flash of joy; Gramercy! they for joy did grin,
And all at once their breath drew in,   165
As they were drinking all.

And horror
follows. For can
it be a ship that
comes onward
without wind
or tide?

"See! see! (I cried) she tacks no more!
Hither to work us weal;
Without a breeze, without a tide,
She steadies with upright keel!   170

"The western wave was all aflame.
The day was well-nigh done!
Almost upon the western wave
Rested the broad bright Sun;
When that strange shape drove suddenly   175
Betwixt us and the Sun.

It seemeth him
but the skeleton
of a ship.

"And straight the Sun was flecked with bars,
(Heaven's Mother send us grace!)
As if through a dungeon-gate he peered
With broad and burning face.   180

"Alas! (thought I, and my heart beat loud)
How fast she nears and nears!
Are those her sails that glance in the Sun,
Like restless gossameres?

And its ribs are seen as bars on the face of the setting Sun. The Specter-Woman and her Death-mate, and no other on board the skeleton ship.

"Are those her ribs through which the Sun   185
Did peer, as through a gate?
And is that Woman all her crew?
Is that a Death? and are there two?
Is Death that woman's mate?

Like vessel, like crew!

"Her lips were red, her looks were free,° wild
Her locks were yellow as gold: 191
Her skin was white as leprosy,
The Nightmare Life-in-Death was she,
Who thicks man's blood with cold.

Death and Life-in-Death have diced for the ship's crew, and she (the latter) winneth the ancient Mariner.

"The naked hulk alongside came,   195
And the twain were casting dice;
'The game is done! I've won! I've won!'
Quoth she, and whistles thrice.

No twilight within the courts of the Sun.

"The Sun's rim dips; the stars rush out:
At one stride comes the dark;   200
With far-heard whisper, o'er the sea,
Off shot the specter-bark.

"We listened and looked sideways up!
At the rising of the Moon,
Fear at my heart, as at a cup,
My life blood seemed to sip!   205
The stars were dim, and thick the night,
The steersman's face by his lamp gleamed
    white;
From the sails the dew did drip—
Till clomb above the eastern bar
The hornèd Moon, with one bright star   210
Within the nether tip.

One after
another,

"One after one, by the star-dogged Moon,
Too quick for groan or sigh,
Each turned his face with a ghastly pang,
And cursed me with his eye.   215

His shipmates
drop down
dead.

"Four times fifty living men,
(And I heard nor sigh nor groan)
With heavy thump, a lifeless lump,
They dropped down one by one.

But Life-in-
Death begins
her work on the
ancient Mariner.

"The souls did from their bodies fly—   220
They fled to bliss or woe!
And every soul, it passed me by,
Like the whizz of my crossbow!"

PART 4

The Wedding-
Guest feareth
that a Spirit is
talking to him;

"I fear thee, ancient Mariner!
I fear thy skinny hand!   225
And thou art long, and lank, and brown,
As is the ribbed sea-sand.

But the ancient
Mariner assureth
him of his bodily
life, and pro-
ceedeth to relate
his horrible
penance.

"I fear thee and thy glittering eye,
And thy skinny hand, so brown."—
"Fear not, fear not, thou Wedding-Guest!   230
This body dropped not down.

"Alone, alone, all, all alone,
Alone on a wide, wide sea!
And never a saint took pity on
My soul in agony.   235

He despiseth the
creatures of the
calm,

"The many men, so beautiful!
And they all dead did lie:
And a thousand thousand slimy things
Lived on; and so did I.

And envieth that
they should live,
and so many
lie dead.

"I looked upon the rotting sea,   240
And drew my eyes away;
I looked upon the rotting deck,
And there the dead men lay.

"I looked to heaven, and tried to pray;
But or° ever a prayer had gushed,   *before* 245
A wicked whisper came, and made
My heart as dry as dust.

"I closed my lids, and kept them close,
And the balls like pulses beat;
For the sky and the sea, and the sea and the sky
Lay like a load on my weary eye,   251
And the dead were at my feet.

But the curse
liveth for him in
the eye of the
dead men.

"The cold sweat melted from their limbs,
Nor rot nor reek did they:
The look with which they looked on me   255
Had never passed away.

In his lonliness
and fixedness
he yearneth
towards the
journeying
Moon, and the
stars that still
sojourn, yet still
move onward;

"An orphan's curse would drag to hell
A spirit from on high;
But oh! more horrible than that
Is a curse in a dead man's eye!   260
Seven days, seven nights, I saw that curse,
And yet I could not die.

"The moving Moon went up the sky,
And nowhere did abide:
Softly she was going up,   265
And a star or two beside —

"Her beams bemocked the sultry main,
Like April hoar-frost spread;
But where the ship's huge shadow lay,
The charmèd water burnt alway   270
A still and awful red.

"Beyond the shadow of the ship,
I watched the water-snakes:
They moved in tracks of shining white,
And when they reared, the elfish light   275
Fell off in hoary flakes.

"Within the shadow of the ship
I watched their rich attire:
Blue, glossy green, and velvet black,
They coiled and swam; and every track   280
Was a flash of golden fire.

"Oh happy living things! no tongue
Their beauty might declare:
A spring of love gushed from my heart,
And I blessed them unaware;   285
Sure my kind saint took pity on me,
And I blessed them unaware.

"The selfsame moment I could pray;
And from my neck so free
The Albatross fell off, and sank   290
Like lead into the sea.

PART 5

"O sleep! it is a gentle thing,
Beloved from pole to pole!
To Mary Queen the praise be given!
She sent the gentle sleep from Heaven,   295
That slid into my soul.

By grace of the
holy Mother, the
Ancient Mariner
is refreshed with
rain.

"The silly° buckets on the deck,   empty
That had so long remained,
I dreamt that they were filled with dew;
And when I awoke, it rained.   300

"My lips were wet, my throat was cold,
My garments all were dank;
Sure I had drunken in my dreams,
And still my body drank.

"I moved, and could not feel my limbs: 305
I was so light—almost
I thought that I had died in sleep,
And was a blessèd ghost.

He heareth
sounds and
seeth strange
sights and
commotions in
the sky and the
element.

"And soon I heard a roaring wind:
It did not come anear;   310
But with its sound it shook the sails,
That were so thin and sere.°   dry

"The upper air burst into life!
And a hundred fire-flags sheen,°   lighting
To and fro they were hurried about!   315
And to and fro, and in and out,
The wan stars danced between.

"And the coming wind did roar more loud,
And the sails did sigh like sedge;°   tall rushes
And the rain poured down from one black cloud;
The Moon was at its edge.   321

"The thick black cloud was cleft, and still
The Moon was at its side:
Like waters shot from some high crag,
The lightning fell with never a jag,   325
A river steep and wide.

"The loud wind never reached the ship,
Yet now the ship moved on!
Beneath the lightning and the Moon
The dead men gave a groan.   330

"They groaned, they stirred, they all uprose,
Nor spake, nor moved their eyes;
It had been strange, even in a dream,
To have seen those dead men rise.

"The helmsman steered, the ship moved on; 335
Yet never a breeze up blew;
The mariners all 'gan work the ropes,
Where they were wont to do;
They raised their limbs like lifeless tools—
We were a ghastly crew.   340

"The body of my brother's son
Stood by me, knee to knee:
The body and I pulled at one rope,
But he said nought to me."

The bodies of the ship's crew are inspirited, and the ship moves on:

But not by the
souls of the
men, nor by
demons of earth
or middle air,
but by a blessed
troop of angelic
spirits, sent
down by the
invocation of
the guardian
saint.

"I fear thee, ancient Mariner!"   345
"Be calm, thou Wedding-Guest!
'Twas not those souls that fled in pain,
Which to their corses° came again,   corpses
But a troop of spirits blest:

"For when it dawned—they dropped their arms,
And clustered round the mast;   351
Sweet sounds rose slowly through their mouths,
And from their bodies passed.

"Around, around, flew each sweet sound,
Then darted to the Sun;   355
Slowly the sounds came back again,
Now mixed, now one by one.

"Sometimes a-dropping from the sky
I heard the skylark sing;
Sometimes all little birds that are,   360
How they seemed to fill the sea and air
With their sweet jargoning!°   confused
                                    sounds

"And now 'twas like all instruments,
Now like a lonely flute;
And now it is an angel's song,   365
That makes the heavens be mute.

"It ceased; yet still the sails made on
A pleasant noise till noon,
A noise like of a hidden brook
In the leafy month of June,   370
That to the sleeping woods all night
Singeth a quiet tune.

"Till noon we quietly sailed on,
Yet never a breeze did breathe:
Slowly and smoothly went the ship, 375
Moved onward from beneath.

The lonesome
Spirit from the
South-Pole
carries on the
ship as far as
the Line, in
obedience to the
angelic troop,
but still
requireth
vengeance.

"Under the keel nine fathom deep,
From the land of mist and snow,
The Spirit slid: and it was he
That made the ship to go. 380
The sails at noon left off their tune,
And the ship stood still also.

"The Sun, right up above the mast,
Had fixed her to the ocean:
But in a minute she 'gan stir, 385
With a short uneasy motion—
Backwards and forwards half her length
With a short uneasy motion.

"Then like a pawing horse let go,
She made a sudden bound: 390
It flung the blood into my head,
And I fell down in a swound.

The Polar
Spirit's fellow
demons, the in-
visible habitants
of the element,
take part in his
wrong; and two
of them relate,
one to the other,
that penance
long and heavy
for the ancient
Mariner hath
been accorded
to the Polar
Spirit, who

"How long in that same fit I lay,
I have not to declare;
But ere my living life returned, 395
I heard, and in my soul discerned,
Two voices in the air.

"'Is it he?' quoth one, 'Is this the man?
By him who died on cross,
With his cruel bow he laid full low 400
The harmless Albatross.

returneth
southward.

"'The spirit who bideth by himself
In the land of mist and snow,
He loved the bird that loved the man
Who shot him with his bow.'   405

"The other was a softer voice,
As soft as honey-dew:
Quoth he, 'The man hath penance done,
And penance more will do.'

PART 6

First Voice

"But tell me, tell me! speak again,   410
Thy soft response renewing—
What makes that ship drive on so fast?
What is the ocean doing?'

Second Voice

"'Still as a slave before his lord,
The ocean hath no blast;   415
His great bright eye most silently
Up to the Moon is cast—

"'If he may know which way to go;
For she guides him smooth or grim.
See, brother, see! how graciously   420
She looketh down on him.'

First Voice

The Mariner
hath been cast

"'But why drives on that ship so fast,
Without or wave or wind?'

Second Voice

into a trance;
for the angelic
power causeth
the vessel to
drive northward
faster than hu-
man life could
endure.

"'The air is cut away before,
And closes from behind.   425

"'Fly, brother, fly! more high, more high!
Or we shall be belated:
For slow and slow that ship will go,
When the Mariner's trance is abated.'

The supernat-
ural motion is
retarded; the
Mariner awakes,
and his penance
begins anew.

"I woke, and we were sailing on   430
As in a gentle weather:
'Twas night, calm night, the Moon was high;
The dead men stood together.

"All stood together on the deck,
For a charnel-dungeon° fitter: burial
                                             vault   435
All fixed on me their stony eyes,
That in the Moon did glitter.

"The pang, the curse, with which they died,
Had never passed away:
I could not draw my eyes from theirs,   440
Nor turn them up to pray.

The curse is fi-
nally expiated.

"And now this spell was snapped: once more
I viewed the ocean green,
And looked far forth, yet little saw
Of what had else been seen—   445

"Like one, that on a lonesome road
Doth walk in fear and dread,
And having once turned round, walks on,

And turns no more his head;
Because he knows, a frightful fiend   450
Doth close behind him tread.

"But soon there breathed a wind on me,
Nor sound nor motion made:
Its path was not upon the sea,
In ripple or in shade.   455

"It raised my hair, it fanned my cheek
Like a meadow-gale of spring—
It mingled strangely with my fears,
Yet it felt like a welcoming.

"Swiftly, swiftly flew the ship,   460
Yet she sailed softly too:
Sweetly, sweetly blew the breeze—
On me alone it blew.

And the ancient
Mariner behold-
eth his native
country.

"Oh! dream of joy! is this indeed
The lighthouse top I see?   465
Is this the hill? Is this the kirk?
Is this mine own countree?

"We drifted o'er the harbor-bar,
And I with sobs did pray—
O let me be awake, my God!   470
Or let me sleep alway.

"The harbor-bay was clear as glass,
So smoothly it was strewn!°   spread evenly
And on the bay the moonlight lay,
And the shadow of the Moon.   475

"The rock shone bright, the kirk no less,
That stands above the rock:
The moonlight steeped in silentness
The steady weathercock.

The angelic
spirits leave the
dead bodies,
"And the bay was white with silent light,   480
Till rising from the same,
Full many shapes, that shadows were,
In crimson colors came.

"A little distance from the prow
Those crimson shadows were: 485
I turned my eyes upon the deck—
Oh, Christ! what saw I there!

And appear in
their own forms
of light.
"Each corse° lay flat, lifeless and flat,   corpse
And, by the holy rood!°   cross
A man all light, a seraph°-man,   angel
On every corse there stood.   491

"This seraph-band, each waved his hand:
It was a heavenly sight!
They stood as signals to the land,
Each one a lovely light;   495

"This seraph-band, each waved his hand,
No voice did they impart—
No voice; but oh! the silence sank
Like music on my heart.

"But I soon I heard the dash of oars,   500
I heard the Pilot's cheer;
My head was turned perforce away,
And I saw a boat appear.

"The Pilot and the Pilot's boy,
I heard them coming fast: 505
Dear Lord in Heaven! it was a joy
The dead men could not blast.

"I saw a third—I heard his voice:
It is the Hermit good!
He singeth loud his godly hymns   510
That he makes in the wood.
He'll shrieve° my soul, he'll wash away   absolve
The Albatross's blood.   from sin

PART 7

The Hermit of   "This Hermit good lives in that wood
the wood   Which slopes down to the sea.   515
How loudly his sweet voice he rears!
He loves to talk with mariners
That come from a far countree.

"He kneels at morn, and noon, and eve—
He hath a cushion plump: 520
It is the moss that wholly hides
The rotted old oak-stump.

"The skiff boat neared: I heard them talk,
'Why, this is strange, I trow!°   think
Where are those lights so many and fair,   525
That signal made but now?

Approacheth   "'Strange, by my faith!' the Hermit said—
the ship with   'And they answered not our cheer!°   call
wonder.   The planks look warped! and see those sails,
How thin they are and sere!   530

I never saw aught like to them,
Unless perchance it were

"'Brown skeletons of leaves that lag
My forest-brook along;
When the ivy-tod° is heavy with snow,   bush
And the owlet whoops to the wolf below,   536
That eats the she-wolf's young.'

"'Dear Lord! it hath a fiendish look'—
(The Pilot made reply)
'I am afeared'—'Push on, push on!'   540
Said the Hermit cheerily.

"The boat came closer to the ship,
But I nor spake nor stirred;
The boat came close beneath the ship,
And straight° a sound was heard.   immediately

The ship suddenly sinketh.

Under the water it rumbled on,   546
Still louder and more dread:
It reached the ship, it split the bay;
The ship went down like lead.

The ancient Mariner is saved in the Pilot's boat.

"Stunned by that loud and dreadful sound,   550
Which sky and ocean smote,
Like one that hath been seven days drowned
My body lay afloat;
But swift as dreams, myself I found
Within the Pilot's boat.   555

"Upon the whirl, where sank the ship,
The boat spun round and round;
And all was still, save that the hill
Was telling of the sound.

"I moved my lips—the Pilot shrieked   560
And fell down in a fit;
The holy Hermit raised his eyes,
And prayed where he did sit.

"I took the oars: the Pilot's boy,
Who now doth crazy go,   565
Laughed loud and long, and all the while
His eyes went to and fro.
'Ha! ha!' quoth he, 'full plain I see,
The Devil knows how to row.'

"And now, all in my own countree,   570
I stood on the firm land!
The Hermit stepped forth from the boat,
And scarcely he could stand.

The ancient
Mariner earn-
estly entreateth
the Hermit to
shrieve him; and
the penance of
life falls on him.

"'O shrieve me, shrieve me, holy man!'
The Hermit crossed his brow.   575
'Say quick,' quoth he, 'I bid thee say—
What manner of man art thou?'

"Forthwith this frame of mine was wrenched
With a woeful agony,
Which forced me to begin my tale;   580
And then it left me free.

And ever and
anon throughout
his future life
an agony con-
straineth him to
travel from land
to land

"Since then, at an uncertain hour,
That agony returns:
And till my ghastly tale is told,
This heart within me burns.   585

"I pass, like night, from land to land;
I have strange power of speech;
That moment that his face I see

I know the man that must hear me:
To him my tale I teach.   590

"What loud uproar bursts from that door!
The wedding-guests are there:
But in the garden-bower the bride
· And bride-maids singing are:
And hark the little vesper bell,   595
Which biddeth me to prayer!

"O Wedding-Guest! this soul hath been
Alone on a wide, wide sea:
So lonely 'twas, that God himself
Scarce seemèd there to be.   600

"O sweeter than the marriage-feast,
'Tis sweeter far to me,
To walk together to the kirk
With a goodly company!—

"To walk together to the kirk,   605
And all together pray,
While each to his great Father bends,
Old men, and babes, and loving friends,
And youths and maidens gay!

"Farewell, farwell! but this I tell   610
To thee, thou Wedding-Guest!

And to teach, by   He prayeth well, who loveth well
his own example,   Both man and bird and beast.
love and rever-
ence to all things
that God made
and loveth.   "He prayeth best, who lovest best
All things both great and small;   615
For the dear God who loveth us,
He made and loveth all."

The Mariner, whose eye is bright,
Whose beard with age is hoar,
Is gone: and now the Wedding-Guest   620
Turned from the bridegroom's door.

He went like one that hath been stunned,
And is of sense forlorn:
A sadder and a wiser man,
He rose the morrow morn.   625

1. Events in this poem do move in a mysterious way, but Wordsworth's criticism to the contrary, there is a cause-effect relationship between actions and results, between crime and
   punishment. Summarize the "plot" in detail, pointing out this
   relationship as it involves not only the ancient Mariner but the
   entire crew.
2. Coleridge does not reveal the motive for killing the albatross,
   but the act was a crime. Was it against nature, God, the sanctified
   relations between guest and host—one or all? Discuss.
3. Why is the Mariner alternately blamed and praised for killing
   the albatross? Judging by the events involving the albatross, and
   by the reactions of both the ancient Mariner and the other mariners toward the bird, what do you think the albatross symbolizes?
   Perhaps you think it has no symbolic meaning. In either case,
   give reasons to support your opinion.
4. To what sufferings are the mariners subjected? Why is the hallu-
   cination of the "specter bark" such a tragic irony? How do you
   interpret the Mariner's name for the Woman (line 193)? What
   reason can you see for the ancient Mariner's not dropping down
   with the others?
5. What tortures is the Mariner forced to endure alone? Why do you
   think he considered the "curse in a dead man's eye" more horrible than that of an orphan? In what ways does nature mock his
   desperate plight?
6. A single action on the Mariner's part marks the beginning of the
   spell's breaking. What is this action? How do you explain the
   results?
7. Which incidents, impressions, and emotions in Part 5 do you
   think are real? Which are dreamed or imagined? Are all portrayed
   so convincingly that the reader cannot distinguish between
   them? Cite specific lines and passages to support your answers.

8. What is the purpose of the dialogue between the two voices (lines 398-429)? What information does it provide the reader?

9. When the Mariner wakes from his trance, what new ordeal does he face? What clues can you find in this poem to explain how "the spell was snapped"? Why does he utter the prayer in lines 470 and 471?

10. What supernatural sight does the Mariner see when he turns his eyes to the deck (line 486)? What emotions does he feel? What hopes does he see fulfilled by the arrival of the skiff boat from the shore? Why does the Pilot want to turn back? Who restrains him?

11. The account given of the sinking of the ship and the rescue of the Mariner is as fantastic as any of the preceding events. Through the use of what details does Coleridge make it seem consistent with the entire account and equally believable?

12. Why must the Mariner continue to retell his "ghastly tale"? Where and to whom does he tell it? What does he find even sweeter than "the marriage feast"?

13. What message does he leave with the wedding guest? What reason do you have for thinking that the effect was what the Mariner intended? Tell why you do, or do not, think that Coleridge demonstrated in this poem his belief in imagination as a vehicle of truth? Do you think the moral of the poem is too emphatic? Coleridge did. Discuss.

14. Point out some of the images which made the deepest impression on you, and discuss their emotional impact. Do you find any interesting effects gained from juxtaposing images of very different kinds? Can you discover instances in which an image of great beauty is placed beside an image which evokes horror? Why would such images be mixed together?

George Gordon, Lord Byron

Byron's approach to the art of poetry was as individualistic and paradoxical as his approach to the art of living. In his love of form, he showed an affinity with the eighteenth-century Neoclassicists, rather than with the early Romantics. Yet in his spontaneity, in the assertion of personal emotions, and in his hatred of tyranny, he was a true Romantic. His poetry is energetic and heroic rather than sensitive or prophetic; his images are concrete rather than suggestive. He had no elaborate theories about beauty. Instead he chose to recreate historical events, personalities, and distant places through the imagination. Unlike Wordsworth, who saw Nature as a quiet, kind, and calming force, Byron reveled in wild and turbulent Nature, which he identified with his own rebellious personality.

SHE WALKS IN BEAUTY

She walks in beauty, like the night
    Of cloudless climes and starry skies;
And all that's best of dark and bright
    Meet in her aspect and her eyes:
Thus mellowed to that tender light   5
    Which heaven to gaudy day denies.

One shade the more, one ray the less,
    Had half impaired the nameless grace
Which waves in every raven tress,
    Or softly lightens o'er her face;   10
Where thoughts serenely sweet express
    How pure, how dear their dwelling-place.

And on that cheek, and o'er that brow,
    So soft, so calm, yet eloquent,
The smiles that win, the tints that glow,   15
    But tell of days in goodness spent,
A mind at peace with all below,
    A heart whose love is innocent!

1. The subject of this poem is Lady Wilmot Horton, Byron's cousin by marriage. When he first met her she was wearing a black gown with silver spangles. Which of her qualities — physical as well as spiritual — does he praise most highly? Why is her beauty greater than that of "gaudy day" and her cheek and brow "eloquent"?
2. In speaking of Byron, Keats wrote, "There is this great difference between us. He describes what he sees — I describe what I imagine. Mine is the hardest task. You see the difference." Which lines in this poem show the inspiration of imagination? Which are principally descriptive? What is your interpretation — figurative rather than literal — of the title, "She Walks in Beauty"?

THE DESTRUCTION OF SENNACHERIB

The Assyrian[1] came down like the wolf on the fold,
And his cohorts were gleaming in purple and gold;
And the sheen of their spears was like stars on the sea,
When the blue wave rolls nightly on deep Galilee.

[1]*Assyrian:* King Sennacherib, who invaded Palestine in the 7th century B.C.

Like the leaves of the forest when Summer is green,   5
That host with their banners at sunset were seen:
Like the leaves of the forest when Autumn hath blown,
That host on the morrow lay withered and strown.

For the Angel of Death spread his wings on the blast,
And breathed in the face of the foe as he passed;   10
And the eyes of the sleepers waxed deadly and chill,
And their hearts but once heaved — and forever grew still!

And there lay the steed with his nostril all wide,
But through it there rolled not the breath of his pride;
And the foam of his gasping lay white on the turf,   15
And cold as the spray of the rock-beating surf.

And there lay the rider distorted and pale,
With the dew on his brow, and the rust on his mail:
And the tents were all silent — the banners alone —
The lances unlifted — the trumpet unblown.   20

And the widows of Ashur are loud in their wail,
And the idols are broke in the temple of Baal;
And the might of the Gentile, unsmote by the sword,
Hath melted like snow in the glance of the Lord!

1. How were Sennacherib and "his cohorts" destroyed? (If you are
   unfamiliar with the Biblical account, read it in II Kings 19:35.)
   Would the poem have been more moving and dramatic if Byron
   had pictured the conflict rather than describing the results?
2. Who were "the widows of Ashur"? Why were the idols in the
   temple of Baal broken? Who was "the Gentile"? (If necessary,
   find information about ancient Assyrian civilization before you
   attempt to answer these questions.)
3. The tone of the poem changes dramatically in stanza 2. Show how
   the parallel similes in that stanza provide the transition from one

tone to the other. Point out other similes in the poem and show
how they help to picture the over-all scene.

4. Byron's technique in lines 11-20 resembles the "panning" technique of the motion-picture cameraman. In both cases, a scene
is conveyed and an atmosphere evoked through an accumulation
of images or "vignettes." What emotion is evoked by each of the
images in these nine lines? What words would you use to describe
the over-all, "cumulative" effect of these lines?

5. Identify the predominant rhythm of the poem. Why is it especially
appropriate to the subject matter and tone? Do you think that the
repeated use of *and* does, or does not, give the poem a sense of
dramatic intensity and forward movement? Discuss.

THE PRISONER OF CHILLON

1

My hair is gray, but not with years,
    Nor grew it white
    In a single night,
As men's have grown from sudden fears:
My limbs are bowed, though not with toil,   5
    But rusted with a vile repose,
For they have been a dungeon's spoil,
    And mine has been the fate of those
To whom the goodly earth and air
Are banned, and barred—forbidden fare;   10
But this was for my father's faith,
I suffered chains and courted death;
That father perished at the stake
For tenets° he would not forsake;   principles
And for the same his lineal race   15
In darkness found a dwelling-place.
We were seven—who now are one,
    Six in youth, and one in age,
Finished as they had begun,

Proud of Persecution's rage;   20
One in fire, and two in field,°   battle
Their belief with blood have sealed,
Dying as their father died,
For the God their foes denied;
Three were in a dungeon cast,   25
Of whom this wreck is left the last.

2

There are seven pillars of Gothic mold
In Chillon's dungeons deep and old,
There are seven columns, massy and gray,
Dim with a dull imprisoned ray,   30
A sunbeam which hath lost its way,
And through the crevice and the cleft
Of the thick wall is fallen and left;
Creeping o'er the floor so damp,
Like a marsh's meteor lamp: 35
And in each pillar there is a ring,
      And in each ring there is a chain;
That iron is a cankering thing,
      For in these limbs its teeth remain,
With marks that will not wear away,   40
Till I have done with this new day,
Which now is painful to these eyes,
Which have not seen the sun so rise
For years—I cannot count them o'er,
I lost their long and heavy score   45
When my last brother drooped and died,
And I lay living by his side.

3

They chained us each to a column stone,
And we were three—yet, each alone;
We could not move a single pace,   50

We could not see each other's face,
But with the pale and livid light
That made us strangers in our sight:
And thus together, yet apart,
Fettered in hand, but joined in heart,   55
'Twas still some solace, in the dearth
Of the pure elements of earth,
To hearken to each other's speech,
And each turn comforter to each
With some new hope or legend old,   60
Or song heroically bold;
But even these at length grew cold.
Our voices took a dreary tone,
An echo of the dungeon stone,
    A grating sound—not full and free   65
    As they of yore were wont to be:
    It might be fancy, but to me
They never sounded like our own.

4

I was the eldest of the three,
    And to uphold and cheer the rest   70
    I ought to do—and did my best;
And each did well in his degree.
    The youngest, whom my father loved,
Because our mother's brow was given
To him, with eyes as blue as heaven—   75
    For him my soul was sorely moved:
And truly might it be distressed
To see such bird in such a nest;
For he was beautiful as day
    (When day was beautiful to me   80
    As to young eagles, being free)—
    A polar day, which will not see
A sunset till its summer's gone,

Its sleepless summer of long light,
The snow-clad offspring of the sun: 85
    And thus he was as pure and bright,
And in his natural spirit gay,
With tears for naught but others' ills,
And then they flowed like mountain rills,
Unless he could assuage° the woe   relieve
Which he abhorred to view below.   91

5

The other was as pure of mind,
But formed to combat with his kind;
Strong in his frame, and of a mood
Which 'gainst the world in war had stood,   95
And perished in the foremost rank
    With joy — but not in chains to pine:
His spirit withered with their clank,
    I saw it silently decline —
    And so perchance in sooth did mine: 100
But yet I forced it on to cheer
Those relics of a home so dear.
He was a hunter of the hills,
    Had followed there the deer and wolf;
    To him this dungeon was a gulf,   105
And fettered feet the worst of ills.

6

    Lake Leman° lies by Chillon's walls: Lake Geneva
A thousand feet in depth below
Its massy waters meet and flow;
Thus much the fathom-line was sent   110
From Chillon's snow-white battlement
    Which round about the wave enthralls:°   captivates

A double dungeon wall and wave
Have made—and like a living grave,
Below the surface of the lake   115
The dark vault lies wherein we lay:
We heard it ripple night and day;
    Sounding o'er our heads it knocked;
And I have felt the winter's spray
Wash through the bars when winds were high   120
And wanton° in the happy sky;   *unruly*
    And then the very rock hath rocked,
    And I have felt it shake, unshocked,
Because I could have smiled to see
The death that would have set me free.   125

7

I said my nearer brother pined,
I said his mighty heart declined,
He loathed and put away his food;
It was not that 'twas coarse and rude,
For we were used to hunter's fare,   130
And for the like had little care:
The milk drawn from the mountain goat
Was changed for water from the moat,
Our bread was such as captives' tears
Have moistened many a thousand years,   135
Since man first pent his fellow men
Like brutes within an iron den;
But what were these to us or him?
These wasted not his heart or limb;
My brother's soul was of that mold   140
Which in a palace had grown cold,
Had his free breathing been denied
The range of the steep mountain's side.
But why delay the truth?—he died.
I saw, and could not hold his head,   145

Nor reach his dying hand — nor dead —
Thought hard I strove, but strove in vain,
To rend and gnash my bonds in twain.
He died — and they unlocked his chain,
And scooped for him a shallow grave   150
Even from the cold earth of our cave.
I begged them, as a boon,° to lay   favor
His corse° in dust whereon the day   corpse
Might shine — it was a foolish thought,
But then within my brain it wrought,   155
That even in death his freeborn breast
In such a dungeon could not rest.
I might have spared my idle prayer;
They coldly laughed — and laid him there:
The flat and turfless earth above   160
The being we so much did love;
His empty chain above it leant,
Such murder's fitting monument!

8

But he, the favorite and the flower,
Most cherished since his natal° hour,   birth 165
His mother's image in fair face,
The infant love of all his race,
His martyred father's dearest thought,
My latest care, for whom I sought
To hoard my life, that his might be   170
Less wretched now, and one day free;
He, too, who yet had held untired
A spirit natural or inspired —
He, too, was struck, and day by day
Was withered on the stalk away.   175
Oh, God! it is a fearful thing
To see the human soul take wing
In any shape, in any mood: —

I've seen it rushing forth in blood,
I've seen it on the breaking ocean   180
Strive with a swoll'n convulsive motion,
I've seen the sick and ghastly bed
Of Sin delirious with its dread:
But these were horrors—this was woe
Unmixed with such—but sure and slow: 185
He faded, and so calm and meek,
So softly worn, so sweetly weak,
So tearless, yet so tender—kind,
And grieved for those he left behind;
With all the while a cheek whose bloom   190
Was as a mockery of the tomb,
Whose tints as gently sunk away
As a departing rainbow's ray;
An eye of most transparent light,
That almost made the dungeon bright;   195
And not a word of murmur, not
A groan o'er his untimely lot—
A little talk of better days,
A little hope my own to raise,
For I was sunk in silence—lost   200
In this last loss, of all the most;
And then the sighs he would suppress
Of fainting nature's feebleness,
More slowly drawn, grew less and less:
I listened, but I could not hear—   205
I called, for I was wild with fear;
I knew 'twas hopeless, but my dread
Would not be thus admonishèd.°   advised
I called, and thought I heard a sound—
I burst my chain with one strong bound,   210
And rushed to him—I found him not,
I only stirred in this black spot,
I only lived, *I* only drew
The accursèd breath of dungeon-dew;

The last—the sole—the dearest link   215
Between me and the eternal brink,
Which bound me to my failing race,
Was broken in this fatal place.
One on the earth, and one beneath—
My brothers—both had ceased to breathe: 220
I took that hand which lay so still,
Alas! my own was full as chill;
I had not strength to stir, or strive,
But felt that I was still alive—
A frantic feeling, when we know   225
That what we love shall ne'er be so.
    I know not why
    I could not die,
I had no earthly hope—but faith,
And that forbade a selfish death.   230

9

What next befell me then and there
    I know not well—I never knew;
First came the loss of light, and air,
    And then of darkness too:
I had no thought, no feeling—none—   235
Among the stones I stood a stone,
And was, scarce conscious what I wist,°   knew
As shrubless crags within the mist;
For all was blank, and bleak, and gray;
It was not night, it was not day,   240
It was not even the dungeon-light,
So hateful to my heavy sight,
But vacancy absorbing space,
And fixedness—without a place;
There were no stars, no earth, no time,   245
No check, no change, no good, no crime—
But silence, and a stirless breath

Which neither was of life nor death;
A sea of stagnant idleness,
Blind, boundless, mute, and motionless!   250

10

A light broke in upon my brain —
    It was the carol of a bird;
It ceased, and then it came again,
    The sweetest song ear ever heard,
And mine was thankful till my eyes   255
Ran over with the glad surprise,
And they that moment could not see
I was the mate of misery;
But then by dull degrees came back
My senses to their wonted° track;   accustomed 260
I saw the dungeon walls and floor
Close slowly round me as before;
I saw the glimmer of the sun
Creeping as it before had done,
But through the crevice where it came   265
That bird was perched, as fond and tame,
    And tamer than upon the tree;
A lovely bird, with azure wings,
And song that said a thousand things,
    And seemed to say them all for me!   270
I never saw its like before,
I ne'er shall see its likeness more:
It seemed like me to want a mate,
But was not half so desolate,
And it was come to love me when   275
None lived to love me so again,
And cheering from my dungeon's brink,
Had brought me back to feel and think.
I know not if it late were free,
    Or broke its cage to perch on mine,   280

But knowing well captivity,
    Sweet bird! I could not wish for thine!
Or if it were, in wingèd guise,
A visitant from Paradise;
For—Heaven forgive that thought! the while   285
Which made me both to weep and smile—
I sometimes deemed that it might be
My brother's soul come down to me;
But then at last away it flew,
And then 'twas mortal—well I knew,   290
For he would never thus have flown,
And left me twice so doubly lone,—
Lone—as the corse within its shroud,
Lone—as a solitary cloud,
    A single cloud on a sunny day,   295
While all the rest of heaven is clear,
A frown upon the atmosphere
That hath no business to appear
    When skies are blue and earth is gay.

11

A kind of change came in my fate,   300
My keepers grew compassionate;
I know not what had made them so,
They were inured° to sights of woe,   hardened
But so it was—my broken chain
With links unfastened did remain,   305
And it was liberty to stride
Along my cell from side to side,
And up and down, and then athwart,°   across
And tread it over every part;
And round the pillars one by one,   310
Returning where my walk begun,
Avoiding only, as I trod,
My brothers' graves without a sod;

For if I thought with heedless tread
My step profaned their lowly bed,   315
My breath came gaspingly and thick,
And my crushed heart fell blind and sick.

12

I made a footing in the wall,
    It was not therefrom to escape,
For I had buried one and all   320
    Who loved me in a human shape;
And the whole earth would henceforth be
A wider prison unto me:
No child, no sire, no kin had I,
No partner in my misery;   325
I thought of this, and I was glad,
For thought of them had° made me mad;   would have
But I was curious to ascend
To my barred windows, and to bend
Once more, upon the mountains high,   330
The quiet of a loving eye.

13

I saw them—and they were the same,
They were not changed like me in frame;
I saw their thousand years of snow
On high—their wide long lake below,   335
And the blue Rhone¹ in fullest flow;
I heard the torrents leap and gush
O'er channeled rock and broken bush;
I saw the white-walled distant town,
And whiter sails go skimming down.   340
And then there was a little isle,
Which in my very face did smile,

¹*Rhone:* river in southeastern France

The only one in view;
A small green isle, it seemed no more,
Scarce broader than my dungeon floor,   345
But in it there were three tall trees,
And o'er it blew the mountain breeze,
And by it there were waters flowing,
And on it there were young flowers growing,
    Of gentle breath and hue.   350
The fish swam by the castle wall,
And they seemed joyous each and all;
The eagle rode the rising blast,
Methought he never flew so fast
As then to me he seemed to fly;   355
And then new tears came in my eye,
And I felt troubled — and would fain°   would have
                     preferred
I had not left my recent chain.
And when I did descend again,
The darkness of my dim abode   360
Fell on me as a heavy load;
It was as is a new-dug grave,
Closing o'er one we sought to save —
And yet my glance, too much oppressed,
Had almost need of such a rest.   365

14

It might be months, or years, or days —
    I kept no count, I took no note,
I had no hope my eyes to raise,
    And clear them of their dreary mote;°   dust particle
At last men came to set me free,   370
    I asked not why, and recked° not where,   cared
It was at length the same to me,
Fettered or fetterless to be,
    I learned to love despair.
And thus when they appeared at last,   375

And all my bonds aside were cast,
These heavy walls to me had grown
A hermitage—and all my own!
And half I felt as they were come
To tear me from a second home.   380
With spiders I had friendship made,
And watched them in their sullen trade,
Had seen the mice by moonlight play,
And why should I feel less than they?
We were all immates of one place,   385
And I, the monarch of each race,
Had power to kill—yet, strange to tell!
In quiet we had learned to dwell;
My very chains and I grew friends,
So much a long communion tends   390
To make us what we are—even I
Regained my freedom with a sigh.

1. Who is the speaker in the poem? From stanzas 1 and 2 what do
   you learn about the reason for his imprisonment, the fate of his
   family, and the dungeon in which he alone remains?
2. As the speaker recounts his tragic tale, what does he reveal about
   himself as a person? How does he feel toward each of his imprisoned brothers? How is each different from the other and
   from him?
3. Why are the accounts of the brothers' deaths so moving? Discuss
   the dramatic effect of the details chosen by the poet to picture
   each death—and the speaker's reaction to it—and of the poetic
   language and form in which these details are presented. Which
   lines or passages do you consider especially dramatic or moving?
   How do you interpret lines 223-230?
4. With what images and comparisons does Byron convey the speaker's state of mind and spirit after the death of his last brother?
   What "light" arouses him (lines 251 and 252)? Describe how he
   responds and the reasons why. Note that he feels sorrow as well
   as joy.
5. How does the speaker make use of the greater freedom unexpectedly given him? Do you think he really would have rejected

freedom if it had been offered to him (see lines 318-331)? Why does the "small green isle" make such a deep impression on him? What might it (and the three trees) and the eagle symbolize? How do you explain the speaker's reaction expressed in lines 356-365?

6. What is the all-pervading mood of the final stanza? Discuss the details which the speaker mentions, his observations and comments about life and himself, his choice of words with strong emotional appeal — all of which contribute to the creation of the mood.

7. A prisoner's release is generally the climax of all preceding events — the point of highest interest and dramatic intensity. Is it the climax of the story told in this poem? If not, does the climax occur earlier? Are there a series of "high points" but no climax? Perhaps the effect of the last stanza depends on the anticlimactic effect of the release and the understatement of it and the speaker's reactions. Give reasons to support your answers to the above questions.

8. Byron was no more a conformist in form and technique than in choice of subject matter. Point out variations in stanza length, metrical line, and rhyme and rhythm which create a particular effect or illustrate Byron's mastery of the poet's craft.

Percy Bysshe Shelley

Shelley's thoughts—and, consequently, his poems—soar above the world of common concerns and concrete fact. To Shelley, truth was an unattainable ideal; beauty was an "intellectual" abstraction; and love, a spirit. He turned again and again to the insubstantial and airy aspects of nature—water, light, clouds, wind, and air—for the imagery of his poetry. When he felt it was necessary, however, he could and did speak out with vigor and indignation, as in "Song to the Men of England." He was also a hard-working, practical-minded craftsman, as his odes amply prove. "Ode to the West Wind" is almost classical in the intricate, symmetrical arrangement of its images and stanzas.

SONG TO THE MEN OF ENGLAND

This poem was inspired by the Manchester Massacre, an attack by British soldiers in 1819 on a crowd assembled to petition Parliament for a redress of grievances regarding taxation.

> Men of England, wherefore plow
> For the lords who lay ye low?
> Wherefore weave with toil and care
> The rich robes your tyrants wear?

Wherefore feed, and clothe, and save,   5
From the cradle to the grave,
Those ungrateful drones who would
Drain your sweat—nay, drink your blood?

Wherefore, bees of England, forge
Many a weapon, chain, and scourge,   10
That these stingless drones may spoil
The forced produce of your toil?

Have ye leisure, comfort, calm,
Shelter, food, love's gentle balm?
Or what is it ye buy so dear   15
With your pain and with your fear?

The seed ye sow, another reaps;
The wealth ye find, another keeps;
The robes ye weave, another wears;
The arms ye forge, another bears.   20

Sow seed—but let no tyrant reap;
Find wealth—let no impostor heap;
Weave robes—let not the idle wear;
Forge arms—in your defense to bear.

Shrink to your cellars, holes, and cells;   25
In halls ye deck another dwells.
Why shake the chains ye wrought? Ye see
The steel ye tempered glance° on ye.   strike

With plow and spade, and hoe and loom,
Trace your grave, and build your tomb,   30
And weave your winding-sheet, till fair
England be your sepulcher.

1. Who are the "men of England" to whom this poem is addressed? From stanzas 1-4 what do you learn about the social and economic life of England at the time of the massacre, the attitude of the privileged class, and the plight of those who demand justice?
2. What values are contrasted in stanzas 1-3 and in stanza 4? What point do you think lines 13-16 bring home to those being addressed? How do you interpret the second question (lines 15 and 16)?
3. What is the purpose of stanza 5? In what ways does the effect of stanza 6 depend on it? What course of action is Shelley urging? Tell why you think that the way he presents his challenge is, or is not, dramatic and persuasive.
4. Do stanzas 7 and 8 reveal a change in mood? Is Shelley suggesting that what he urged in stanza 6 is useless? Is he describing a more feasible way of securing justice? Compare your interpretation of these last two stanzas with the interpretations of your classmates. Why are the last lines so ironic?
5. Note the metaphor in line 7. Point out its meaning and the way it is developed through line 12.
6. What words, phrases, and lines in the poem express Shelley's belief that the ills of the world are the result of centuries of tyranny, greed, violence, and the exploitation of the "common man" — including women and children?

TO NIGHT

Swiftly walk over the western wave,
    Spirit of Night!
Out of the misty eastern cave,
Where, all the long and lone daylight,
Thou wovest dreams of joy and fear,   5
Which make thee terrible and dear,—
    Swift be thy flight!

Wrap thy form in a mantle gray,
    Star-inwrought!
Blind with thine hair the eyes of Day;   10

Kiss her until she be wearied out,
Then wander o'er city, and sea, and land,
Touching all with thine opiate wand—
    Come, long-sought!

When I arose and saw the dawn,   15
    I sighed for thee;
When light rode high, and the dew was gone,
And noon lay heavy on flower and tree,
And the weary Day turned to his rest,
Lingering like an unloved guest,   20
    I sighed for thee.

Thy brother Death came, and cried,
    "Wouldst thou me?"
Thy sweet child Sleep, the filmy-eyed,
Murmured like a noontide bee,   25
"Shall I nestle near thy side?
Wouldst thou me?"—And I replied,
    "No, not thee!"

Death will come when thou art dead,
    Soon, too soon—   30
Sleep will come when thou art fled;
Of neither would I ask the boon
I ask of thee, belovèd Night—
Swift be thine approaching flight,
    Come soon, soon!   35

1. Usually "Night" is eagerly awaited because it brings its "sweet child Sleep." Or "Night" is associated with Death, which can bring an end to suffering or worldly cares. What lines in the poem make clear that the poet sighs for night for a different reason? What is that reason? Note especially lines 4-6 and lines 12 and 13. Why would the coming of "belovèd night" be a "boon"?

2. Since the poem is addressed to Night, the poet would naturally personify it. Does he also personify Day, Death, and Sleep? Which images picture these three, and Night? What would you say is the poet's attitude toward each of them?

3. Few poets gave freer reign to their imaginations than Shelley, or were more versatile in their uses of poetic forms and techniques. What is unusual about the number of lines in each stanza of this poem, and the length and arrangement of the lines? Do the stanzas differ in rhythm? If so, why?

4. Chart the rhyme scheme of stanza 1. Is it the same in the following stanzas? Do you find the occasional use of repetition in place of rhyme less effective? Discuss.

ODE TO THE WEST WIND

Shelley wrote: "This poem was conceived and chiefly written in a wood that skirts the Arno, near Florence, and on a day when that tempestuous wind, whose temperature is at once mild and animating, was collecting the vapors which pour down the autumnal rains. They began, as I foresaw, at sunset with a violent tempest of hail and rain, attended by that magnificent thunder and lightning peculiar to the Cisalpine regions. The phenomenon alluded to at the conclusion of the third stanza is well known to naturalists. The vegetation at the bottom of the sea, of rivers, and of lakes, sympathizes with that of the land in the change of seasons, and is consequently influenced by the winds which announce it."

1

O wild West Wind, thou breath of Autumn's being,
Thou, from whose unseen presence the leaves dead
Are driven, like ghosts from an enchanter fleeing,

Yellow, and black, and pale, and hectic red,
Pestilence-stricken multitudes: O thou,   5
Who chariotest to their dark wintry bed

The wingèd seeds, where they lie cold and low,
Each like a corpse within its grave, until
Thine azure sister of the Spring shall blow

Her clarion o'er the dreaming earth, and fill   10
(Driving sweet buds like flocks to feed in air)
With living hues and odors plain and hill:

Wild Spirit, which art moving everywhere;
Destroyer and preserver; hear, oh, hear!

2

Thou on whose stream, mid the steep sky's commotion,   15
Loose clouds like earth's decaying leaves are shed,
Shook from the tangled boughs of Heaven and Ocean,

Angels of rain and lightning: there are spread
On the blue surface of thine airy surge,
Like the bright hair uplifted from the head   20

Of some fierce Maenad,[1] even from the dim verge
Of the horizon to the zenith's height,
The locks of the approaching storm. Thou dirge

Of the dying year, to which this closing night
Will be the dome of a vast sepulcher,   25
Vaulted with all thy congregated might

Of vapors, from whose solid atmosphere
Black rain, and fire, and hail will burst: oh, hear!

[1]*Maenad:* priestess of Bacchus, the god of wine

3

Thou who didst waken from his summer dreams
The blue Mediterranean, where he lay,   30
Lulled by the coil of his crystalline streams,

Beside a pumice° isle in Baiae's² bay,   volcanic stone
And saw in sleep old palaces and towers
Quivering within the wave's intenser day,

All overgrown with azure moss and flowers   35
So sweet, the sense faints picturing them! Thou
For whose path the Atlantic's level powers

Cleave themselves into chasms, while far below
The sea-blooms and the oozy woods which wear
The sapless foliage of the ocean, know   40

Thy voice, and suddenly grow gray with fear,
And tremble and despoil themselves: oh, hear!

4

If I were a dead leaf thou mightest bear;
If I were a swift cloud to fly with thee;
A wave to pant beneath thy power, and share   45

The impulse of thy strength, only less free
Than thou, O uncontrollable! If even
I were as in my boyhood, and could be

The comrade of thy wanderings over heaven,
As then, when to outstrip thy skyey speed   50
Scarce seemed a vision; I would ne'er have striven

²*Baiae:* a seaside town at the western end of the Bay of Naples

As thus with thee in prayer in my sore need.
Oh, lift me as a wave, a leaf, a cloud!
I fall upon the thorns of life! I bleed!

A heavy weight of hours has chained and bowed   55
One too like thee: tameless, and swift, and proud.

5

Make me thy lyre, even as the forest is:
What if my leaves are falling like its own!
The tumult of thy mighty harmonies

Will take from both a deep, autumnal tone,   60
Sweet though in sadness. Be thou, Spirit fierce,
My spirit! Be thou me, impetuous one!

Drive me dead thoughts over the universe
Like withered leaves to quicken a new birth!
And, by the incantation of this verse,   65

Scatter, as from an unextinguished hearth
Ashes and sparks, my words among mankind!
Be through my lips to unawakened earth

The trumpet of a prophecy! O Wind,
If Winter comes, can Spring be far behind?   70

1. In line 14 the west wind is identified as both "destroyer and preserver." Point out the lines and images in Part 1 which picture the
   wind in this dual role. Is this idea contrary to the laws of nature?
2. What images in Part 2 extend the picture and mood of destruction? Note especially the reference to death. What emotion is
   conveyed in lines 15-28, especially in the final words, "oh hear"?

3. What is being pictured in Part 3? Is the west wind portrayed as destroyer, preserver, both, or neither? Is "oh, hear" repeated (line 42) for its meaning or for its poetic effect? Compare your interpretations with those of other members of the class. Part 3 reveals Shelley's deep interest in the bottom of the sea. What aspect of the poet's nature might this represent in contrast to the west wind which the poet also identifies with himself?

4. What likeness does Shelley draw between himself and the west wind? Why does he consider himself in "sore need" of help? State in your own words the meaning you think he intended to convey in lines 44-52.

5. What requests does Shelley make of the west wind in lines 57-67 of Part 5? Note the image of leaves falling in line 58 and of withered leaves in line 64. What clue to the symbolic meaning do you see in "dead thoughts" (line 63)? Is the same idea expressed in a different image in lines 66 and 67?

6. The last three lines reveal both the essence of Shelley's prayer and his belief in a brighter day — a time when liberty, equality, and fraternity will be realities rather than ideals. What do you think Winter and Spring symbolize? Do you think he feels like a "prophet crying in the wilderness," his message unheard by an "unawakened earth"? From what you know about him and the time in which he lived, what do you think he would have destroyed and what would he have preserved?

7. Each part of this poem is composed of fourteen lines — four three-lines stanzas followed by a couplet (see *terza rima,* page 513). Chart the rhyme scheme of Part 1 to show the interlocking of the four stanzas and the couplet.

8. Which images, similes, and metaphors do you consider particularly effective? Why?

To a Skylark

Hail to thee, blithe Spirit!
Bird thou never wert,
That from Heaven, or near it,
Pourest thy full heart
In profuse strains of unpremeditated art.   5

Higher still and higher
 From the earth thou springest
Like a cloud of fire;
 The blue deep thou wingest,
And singing still dost soar, and soaring ever singest.   10

In the golden lightning
 Of the sunken sun,
O'er which clouds are bright'ning,
 Thou dost float and run;
Like an unbodied joy whose race is just begun.   15

The pale purple even°   evening
 Melts around thy flight;
Like a star of Heaven,
 In the broad daylight
Thou art unseen, but yet I hear thy shrill delight,   20

Keen as are the arrows
 Of that silver sphere,
Whose intense lamp narrows
 In the white dawn clear
Until we hardly see—we feel that it is there.   25

All the earth and air
 With thy voice is loud,
As, when night is bare,
 From one lonely cloud
The moon rains out her beams, and Heaven is overflowed.

What thou art we know not;   31
 What is most like thee?
From rainbow clouds there flow not
 Drops so bright to see
As from thy presence showers a rain of melody.   35

Like a Poet hidden
   In the light of thought,
Singing hymns unbidden,
   Till the world is wrought
To sympathy with hopes and fears it heeded not: 40

Like a highborn maiden
   In a palace tower,
Soothing her love-laden
   Soul in secret hour
With music sweet as love, which overflows her bower: 45

Like a glowworm golden
   In a dell of dew,
Scattering unbeholden
   Its aërial hue   49
Among the flowers and grass, which screen it from the view!

Like a rose embowered
   In its own green leaves,
By warm winds deflowered,
   Till the scent it gives   54
Makes faint with too much sweet those heavy wingèd thieves:

Sound of vernal° showers   spring
   On the twinkling grass,
Rain-awakened flowers,
   All that ever was
Joyous, and clear, and fresh, thy music doth surpass: 60

Teach us, Sprite or Bird,
   What sweet thoughts are thine:
I have never heard
   Praise of love or wine
That panted forth a flood of rapture so divine.   65

Chorus Hymeneal,°   marriage song
    Or triumphal chant,
Matched with thine would be all
    But an empty vaunt,°   boast
A thing wherein we feel there is some hidden want.   70

What objects are the fountains
    Of thy happy strain?
What fields, or waves, or mountains?
    What shapes of sky or plain?
What love of thine own kind? what ignorance of pain?   75

With thy clear keen joyance
    Languor cannot be:
Shadow of annoyance
    Never came near thee:
Thou lovest—but ne'er knew love's sad satiety.° excess gratification 80

Waking or asleep,
    Thou of death must deem
Things more true and deep
    Than we mortals dream,
Or how could thy notes flow in such a crystal stream?   85

We look before and after,
    And pine for what is not:
Our sincerest laughter
    With some pain is fraught;
Our sweetest songs are those that tell of saddest thought.   90

Yet if we could scorn
    Hate, and pride, and fear;
If we were things born
    Not to shed a tear,
I know not how thy joy we ever should come near.   95

Better than all measures
    Of delightful sound,
Better than all treasures
    That in books are found,
Thy skill to poet were, thou scorner of the ground!   100

Teach me half the gladness
    That thy brain must know,
Such harmonious madness
    From my lips would flow
The world should listen then—as I am listening now.   105

1. How do "we" differ from the skylark in what we seek and in our expression of joy? Do you think Shelley thought we could ever "come near" the skylark's joy? Why is its skill of such great value to the poet? What unfulfilled hope is expressed in the final line?
2. How do you interpret lines 2 and 31? With what is the bird compared in the four consecutive stanzas, lines 36-55? What do all these comparisons have in common? Discuss the way in which the Poet, maiden, glowworm, and rose are related to the skylark.
3. Why does the poet want to know what inspired the bird to such joyous song? What must it know, or not know, to produce such a "crystal stream" of music? (See lines 61-85.) What contrast between the bird and man is expressed in lines 86-90?
4. In what way is the stanza pattern unusual? What is the predominant rhythm of the first four lines? Identify the metrical feet and line, then point out the way in which the fifth line differs from the others. What term is used to identify such a line?

John Keats

Sensitive to all forms of beauty, Keats loved both art and the glories of nature, both the delicate tracings on an ancient Grecian urn and the varied seascape of the British coast. Unlike Shelley, who saw reality predominantly as abstract and intangible, Keats saw the world as concrete, touchable, and filled with objects that all the senses could enjoy. Perhaps it is his lushness of images, his superb lyricism, and the honesty and directness with which he communicates experience that has frequently made him the most popular of the Romantic poets.

WHEN I HAVE FEARS THAT I MAY CEASE TO BE

When I have fears that I may cease to be
   Before my pen has gleaned° my teeming brain,   picked clean
Before high-pilèd books, in charact'ry,°   letters
   Hold like rich garners° the full-ripened grain;   granaries
When I behold, upon the night's starred face,   5
   Huge cloudy symbols of a high romance,
And think that I may never live to trace

    Their shadows, with the magic hand of chance;
And when I feel, fair creature of an hour!
    That I shall never look upon thee more,   10
Never have relish° in the faery power   pleasure
    Of unreflecting° love! — then on the shore   impulsive
Of the wide world I stand alone, and think
Till love and fame to nothingness do sink.

1. What are the three dreams which Keats fears will not be fulfilled?
   What do they reveal about his ambition, his temperament, and
   his attitude toward the person addressed in the poem?
2. How do you interpret his concluding statement, beginning with
   the phrase "then on the shore" (line 12)? What is the all-pervasive
   mood of the poem? Why are the closing lines especially moving?
   Do they impress you as sad, despairing, disillusioned, fatalistic?
   Choose any word you think describes the effect of these lines
   and tell why.
3. Point out the imagery used to convey the nature of each dream
   and how the poet feels about it. What does he mean by "full-
   ripened grain," "cloudy symbols of a high romance," "shadows,"
   and "the magic hand of chance"?
4. Which of the two sonnet forms does this poem more closely resemble? Show how the development of the central idea and the
   structure are related. State in your own words what you think
   that idea is.

ON FIRST LOOKING INTO
CHAPMAN'S HOMER

Much have I travelled in the realms of gold,
    And many goodly states and kingdoms seen;
    Round many western islands have I been
Which bards in fealty° to Apollo[1] hold.   allegiance
Oft of one wide expanse had I been told   5
    That deep-browed Homer ruled as his demesne;°   domain

[1]*Apollo:* god of poetry and music

Yet did I never breathe its pure serene
Till I heard Chapman speak out loud and bold:
Then felt I like some watcher of the skies
    When a new planet swims into his ken;°   range of sight 10
Or like stout Cortez[2] when with eagle eyes
    He stared at the Pacific—and all his men
Looked at each other with a wild surmise°—   wonder
    Silent, upon a peak in Darien.[3]

1. Until Keats read George Chapman's vivid translation he was not
   aware of the beauty of the great Homeric epics, the *Iliad* and the
   Odyssey. What similes in lines 9-14 convey the deep impression
   which the discovery of Homer's poetry made on him? How are
   they related to each other and to his discovery?
2. Explain why the extended metaphor in lines 1-4 is such an effective description of his previous discoveries in great literature.
   Discuss the figurative meaning of the words and phrases used in
   developing this metaphor.
3. As in the preceding sonnet, Keats used the rhyme scheme of one
   of the two major sonnet forms and the arrangement of thought
   which is characteristic of the other form. What situation or idea
   is expressed in the first eight lines? What observation or conclusion is expressed in the remaining six lines? What is the over-all
   idea and mood of the sonnet?
4. This sonnet, written when Keats was twenty, is considered one
   of his best. Why do you think it continues to win praise?

ODE ON A GRECIAN URN

Thou still unravished bride of quietness,
Thou foster-child of silence and slow time,
Sylvan historian, who canst thus express
    A flowery tale more sweetly than our rime:
What leaf-fringed legend haunts about thy shape   5

---

[2]*Cortez:* Spanish conqueror. Keats undoubtedly was referring to Balboa.
[3]*Darien:* district in the isthmus that joins Central and South America

Of deities or mortals, or of both,
 In Tempe¹ or the dales of Arcady?²
What men or gods are these? What maidens loath?° reluctant
What mad pursuit? What struggle to escape? 9
 What pipes and timbrels?° What wild ecstasy? tambourines

Heard melodies are sweet, but those unheard
 Are sweeter; therefore, ye soft pipes, play on;
Not to the sensual ear, but, more endeared,
 Pipe to the spirit ditties of no tone:
Fair youth, beneath the trees, thou canst not leave 15
 Thy song, nor ever can those trees be bare;
  Bold Lover, never, never canst thou kiss,
Though winning near the goal—yet, do not grieve;
 She cannot fade, though thou hast not thy bliss,
  Forever wilt thou love, and she be fair! 20

Ah, happy, happy boughs! that cannot shed
 Your leaves, nor ever bid the Spring adieu;
And, happy melodist, unwearièd,
 Forever piping songs forever new;
More happy love! more happy, happy love! 25
 Forever warm and still to be enjoyed,
  Forever panting, and forever young;
All breathing human passion far above,
 That leaves a heart high-sorrowful and cloyed,
  A burning forehead, and a parching tongue. 30

Who are these coming to the sacrifice?
 To what green altar, O mysterious priest,
Lead'st thou that heifer lowing at the skies,
 And all her silken flanks with garlands dressed?
What little town by river or sea shore, 35

¹*Tempe:* valley in Greece
²*Arcady:* pastoral district in Greece

Or mountain-built with peaceful citadel,
    Is emptied of this folk, this pious morn?
And, little town, thy streets for evermore
    Will silent be; and not a soul to tell
      Why thou art desolate, can e'er return.   40

O Attic³ shape! Fair attitude! with brede°   embroidery
    Of marble men and maidens overwrought,
With forest branches and the trodden weed;
    Thou, silent form, dost tease us out of thought
As doth eternity: Cold Pastoral!⁴   45
    When old age shall this generation waste,
      Thou shalt remain, in midst of other woe
Than ours, a friend to man, to whom thou say'st,
    "Beauty is truth, truth beauty," — that is all
      Ye know on earth, and all ye need to know.   50

³*Attic:* from Attica in Greece
⁴*Cold Pastoral:* poem in marble

1. No urn has been found that corresponds with the one described here; thus, to some degree, it was an invention of Keats' fancy. Several facts about the urn are fairly clear: it is marble and the figures on it are carved in relief; it pictures two separate scenes, different in temper and spirit; and though they may be complementary, they are not united. Describe the first scene and the mood it evokes. How many characters are involved in this scene and in what way? What is pictured in the second scene? What clue to the mood is provided in the phrase "this pious man"? How do you interpret lines 38-40?
2. The plan of this poem is as classical as the subject. The poem has three parts: an introduction or beginning, a main subject or middle, and a conclusion or end. From the introduction, stanza 1, what do you learn about the impressions which the urn makes on Keats? What does it express "more sweetly than our rime" that excites his curiosity? What questions does it raise in his mind?
3. Stanzas 2-4 present the main subject: the scenes on the urn as the poet saw them with the full force of his imagination. Do you think Keats envied the "fair youth" and the "bold lover"? Why does he

repeat the word *happy* again and again in describing the first
scene? How do you interpret lines 28-30?

4. In stanza 5, the conclusion, what relationship does Keats suggest
between the experience gained from the urn and its "elusive
character and meaning"? To whom is this last stanza addressed?
To whom does *ye* refer (line 50)? Why is "thou" a friend to man?
What is the central idea of the conclusion?

5. Explain how the scenes on the Grecian urn are a study in the
oneness of rest and motion. Another way of expressing rest and
motion is permanence and change. This was a subject with which
Keats was very much concerned. How does the urn — and art
generally — solve the problem of permanence and change?

ODE TO A NIGHTINGALE

My heart aches, and a drowsy numbness pains
   My sense, as though of hemlock I had drunk,
Or emptied some dull opiate to the drains
   One minute past, and Lethe-wards[1] had sunk:
'Tis not through envy of thy happy lot,   5
   But being too happy in thine happiness,—
      That thou, light-wingèd Dryad° of the trees,   nymph
         In some melodious plot
   Of beechen green, and shadows numberless,
      Singest of summer in full-throated ease.   10

O, for a draught of vintage! that hath been
   Cooled a long age in the deep-delvèd earth,
Tasting of Flora[2] and the country green,
   Dance, and Provençal song,[3] and sunburnt mirth!
O for a breaker full of the warm South,   15
   Full of the true, the blushful Hippocrene,[4]
      With beaded bubbles winking at the brim,

[1]*Lethe-wards:* toward Lethe, the river of forgetfulness in Hades
[2]*Flora:* goddess of flowers
[3]*Provençal song:* song of troubadours in Provence, southern France
[4]*Hippocrene:* fountain of the Muses

And purple-stainèd mouth;
That I might drink, and leave the world unseen,
And with thee fade away into the forest dim: 20

Fade far away, dissolve, and quite forget
What thou among the leaves hast never known,
The weariness, the fever, and the fret
Here, where men sit and hear each other groan;
Where palsy shakes a few, sad, last gray hairs,   25
Where youth grows pale, and specter-thin, and dies;
Where but to think is to be full of sorrow
And leaden-eyed despairs,
Where Beauty cannot keep her lustrous eyes,
Or new Love pine at them beyond tomorrow.   30

Away! away! for I will fly to thee,
Not charioted by Bacchus and his pards,[5]
But on the viewless° wings of Poesy,   invisible
Though the dull brain perplexes and retards:
Already with thee! tender is the night,   35
And haply the Queen-Moon is on her throne,
Clustered around by all her starry Fays;°   fairies
But here there is no light,
Save what from heaven is with the breezes blown
Through verdurous glooms and winding mossy ways.   40

I cannot see what flowers are at my feet,
Nor what soft incense hangs upon the boughs,
But, in embalmèd darkness, guess each sweet
Wherewith the seasonable month endows
The grass, the thicket, and the fruit-tree wild;   45
White hawthorn, and the pastoral eglantine;
Fast fading violets covered up in leaves;
And mid-May's eldest child,

---

[5]*pards:* leopards which drew the chariot of Bacchus, god of wine

The coming musk-rose, full of dewy wine,
   The murmurous haunt of flies on summer eves.   50

Darkling I listen; and, for many a time
   I have been half in love with easeful Death,
Called him soft names in many a musèd rime,
   To take into the air my quiet breath;
Now more than ever seems it rich to die,   55
   To cease upon the midnight with no pain,
      While thou art pouring forth thy soul abroad
         In such an ecstasy!
   Still wouldst thou sing, and I have ears in vain—
      To thy high requiem become a sod.   60

Thou wast not born for death, immortal Bird!
   No hungry generations tread thee down;
The voice I hear this passing night was heard
   In ancient days by emperor and clown:
Perhaps the self-same song that found a path   65
   Through the sad heart of Ruth, when, sick for home,
      She stood in tears amid the alien corn;[6]
         The same that oft-times hath
   Charmed magic casements, opening on the foam
      Of perilous seas, in faery lands forlorn.   70

Forlorn! the very word is like a bell
   To toll me back from thee to my sole self!
Adieu! the fancy cannot cheat so well
   As she is famed to do, deceiving elf.
Adieu! adieu! thy plaintive anthem fades   75
   Past the near meadows, over the still stream,
      Up the hill-side; and now 'tis buried deep
         In the next valley-glades:
   Was it a vision, or a waking dream?
      Fled is that music:—Do I wake or sleep?   80

[6]*Through . . . corn:* After the death of her husband, Ruth followed Naomi
to Bethlehem, where she gleaned barley in the fields.

1. When Keats wrote this ode, he knew he had only a short time to live—a fact that heightens its emotional appeal and melancholy beauty. Why does the idea of fading away with the nightingale have such a strong appeal for Keats? How do you explain his decision not to respond to the bird's "high requiem"?

2. This sonnet, like "Ode on a Grecian Urn," has what Aristotle prescribed—a clearly defined beginning, middle, and end. Stanza 1 provides the introduction or beginning. From it, what do you learn about the state of mind and body of the poet and of his reaction to the bird's full-throated song?

3. Stanzas 2-7 represent the middle part—the development of the main subject. What magic potions (stanza 2) might make it possible to "fade away into the forest dim"? What has the bird never known that Keats wants to forget? Point out evidence in stanza 3 of Keat's despair over the "boredom and horror" all around him as well as over his own sad plight.

4. Describe the imaginary world that Keats visits "on the viewless wings of Poets." Point out the sensory impressions in which he finds delight and the effectiveness of the language and the images he uses in communicating them to the reader.

5. How do you interpret stanza 6, which seems to present a paradox? Note, especially, lines 55 and 59 and 60. What meaning does Keats convey through the words *high requiem* and *sad* in line 60? Do the last two lines of this stanza mark a turning point in the idea and mood developed thus far in the poem? What attitude do they imply toward the human lot, whatever its trials?

6. In stanza 7, the poem reaches a high point both in emotional intensity and in poetic expression. What "elusive character and meaning" do you think Keats brings out by referring to the skylark as "immortal Bird" and by stating that it was not "born to die"? What does it represent that cannot be trod down? What does the poet imply is the relationship between the bird's song and a "timeless order of things" to which all beauty belongs? Is the song beyond the grasp of death? Discuss.

7. The end or conclusion is presented in stanza 8. What brings Keats back to reality? How does he feel about his enrapturing experience? What significance do you see in the fading away and final silence of the bird's song and Keats's reference to it as "thy plaintive anthem"? The quality which first attracts him to the song is its joyousness.

8. Neither the world nor the poet's bitter fate differ more at the end of the poem than at the beginning. Yet by attempting to understand the bird's rapture, and to enter into it, a change has taken place within the poet. Do the questions he asks in the final lines

suggest that he is less sure of himself? Is he more aware of the contrast between beauty that endures and beauty that perishes? Is the eternal which endures something which man can glimpse but cannot grasp or escape into? State in your own words the meaning of the poem.

THE EVE OF ST. AGNES

St. Agnes' Eve[1]—Ah, bitter chill it was!
The owl, for all his feathers, was a-cold;
The hare limped trembling through the frozen grass,
And silent was the flock in woolly fold:
Numb were the Beadsman's[2] fingers, while he told   5
His rosary, and while his frosted breath,
Like pious incense from a censer old,
Seemed taking flight for heaven, without a death,
Past the sweet Virgin's picture, while his prayer he saith.

His prayer he saith, this patient, holy man;   10
Then takes his lamp, and riseth from his knees,
And back returneth, meager, barefoot, wan,
Along the chapel aisle by slow degrees:
The sculptured dead, on each side, seem to freeze,
Emprisoned in black, purgatorial rails: 15
Knights, ladies, praying in dumb° orat'ries,   silent
He passeth by; and his weak spirit fails
To think how they may ache in icy hoods and mails.

Northward he turneth through a little door,
And scarce three steps, ere Music's golden tongue   20
Flattered to tears this agèd man and poor;
But no—already had his deathbell rung:

[1]*St. Agnes' Eve:* January 20th, the coldest night of the year
[2]*Beadsman:* man who prays for the soul of another

The joys of all his life were said and sung:
His was harsh penance on St. Agnes' Eve:
Another way he went, and soon among   25
Rough ashes sat he for his soul's reprieve,
And all night kept awake, for sinners' sake to grieve.

That ancient Beadsman heard the prelude soft;
And so it chanced, for many a door was wide,
From hurry to and fro. Soon, up aloft,   30
The silver, snarling trumpets 'gan to chide:
The level chambers, ready with their pride,
Were glowing to receive a thousand guests:
The carvèd angels, ever eager-eyed,
Stared, where upon their heads the cornice rests,   35
With hair blown back, and wings put crosswise on their breasts.

At length burst in the argent° revelry,
With plume, tiara, and all rich array,
Numerous as shadows haunting faerily
The brain, new stuffed, in youth, with triumphs gay   40
Of old romance. These let us wish away,
And turn, sole-thoughted, to one Lady there,
Whose heart had brooded, all that wintry day,
On love, and winged St. Agnes' saintly care,
As she had heard old dames full many times declare.   45

They told her how, upon St. Agnes' Eve,
Young virgins might have visions of delight,
And soft adorings from their loves receive
Upon the honeyed middle of the night,
If ceremonies due they did aright;   50
As, supperless to bed they must retire,
And couch supine their beauties, lily white;
Nor look behind, nor sideways, but require
Of Heaven with upward eyes for all that they desire.

Full of this whim was thoughtful Madeline: 55
The music, yearning like a god in pain,
She scarcely heard: her maiden eyes divine,
Fixed on the floor, saw many a sweeping train
Pass by — she heeded not at all: in vain
Came many a tiptoe, amorous cavalier,   60
And back retired; not cooled by high disdain,
But she saw not: her heart was otherwhere:
She sighed for Agnes' dreams, the sweetest of the year.

She danced along with vague, regardless eyes,
Anxious her lips, her breathing quick and short: 65
The hallowed hour was near at hand: she sighs
Amid the timbrels,° and the thronged resort   tambourines
Of whisperers in anger, or in sport;
'Mid looks of love, definance, hate, and scorn,
Hoodwinked with faery fancy; all amort,°   dead 70
Save to St. Agnes and her lambs unshorn,
And all the bliss to be before to-morrow morn.

So, purposing each moment to retire,
She lingered still. Meantime, across the moors,
Had come young Porphyro, with heart on fire   75
For Madeline. Beside the portal doors,
Buttressed from moonlight, stands he, and implores
All saints to give him sight of Madeline,
But for one moment in the tedious hours,
That he might gaze and worship all unseen;   80
Perchance speak, kneel, touch, kiss — in sooth such things
     have been.

He ventures in: let no buzzed whisper tell:
All eyes be muffled, or a hundred swords
Will storm his heart, Love's fev'rous citadel:
For him, those chambers held barbarian hordes,   85
Hyena foemen, and hot-blooded lords,
Whose very dogs would execrations howl

Against his lineage: not one breast affords
Him any mercy, in that mansion foul,
Save one old beldame,° weak in body and in soul.   woman 90

Ah, happy chance! the aged creature came,
Shuffling along with ivory-headed wand,
To where he stood, hid from the torch's flame,
Behind a broad hall-pillar, far beyond
The sound of merriment and chorus bland: 95
He startled her; but soon she knew his face,
And grasped his fingers in her palsied hand,
Saying, "Mercy, Porphyro! hie thee from this place;
They are all here to-night, the whole blood-thirty race!

"Get hence! get hence! there's dwarfish Hildebrand;   100
He had a fever late, and in the fit
He cursèd thee and thine, both house and land:
Then there's that old Lord Maurice, not a whit
More tame for his gray hairs—Alas me! flit!
Flit like a ghost away."—Ah, Gossip° dear,   godmother 105
We're safe enough; here in this armchair sit,
And tell me how"—"Good saints! not here, not here;
Follow me, child, or else these stones will be thy bier."

He followed through a lowly archèd way,
Brushing the cobwebs with his lofty plume,   110
And as she muttered "Well-a—well-a-day!"
He found him in a little moonlight room,
Pale, latticed, chill, and silent as a tomb.
"Now tell me where is Madeline," said he,
"Oh tell me, Angela, by the holy loom   115
Which none but secret sisterhood may see,
When they St. Agnes' wool are weaving piously."[3]

---

[3]*Which none . . . piously:* Formerly, when the hymn *Agnus Dei* was sung
on St. Agnes' Day, two lambs were sacrificed and their wool woven into cloth
by nuns.

"St. Agnes! Ah! it is St. Agnes' Eve—
Yet men will murder upon holy days:
Thou must hold water in a witch's sieve,   120
And be liege-lord of all the Elves and Fays,
To venture so: it fills me with amaze
To see thee, Porphyro! St. Agnes' Eve!
God's help! my lady fair the conjuror° plays   magician
This very night: good angels her deceive!   125
But let me laugh awhile, I've mickle° time to
    grieve."   much

Feebly she laugheth in the languid moon,
While Porphyro upon her face doth look,
Like puzzled urchin on an agèd crone
Who keepeth closed a wond'rous riddle-book,   130
As spectacled she sits in chimney nook.
But soon his eyes grew brilliant, when she told
His lady's purpose; and he scarce could brook°   keep back
Tears, at the thought of those enchantments cold,
And Madeline asleep in lap of legends old.   135

Sudden a thought came like a full-blown rose,
Flushing his brow, and in his painèd heart
Made purple riot: then doth he propose
A stratagem, that makes the beldame start:
"A cruel man and impious thou art: 140
Sweet lady, let her pray, and sleep, and dream
Alone with her good angels, far apart
From wicked men like thee. Go, go!—I deem
Thou canst not surely be the same that thou didst seem."

"I will not harm her, by all saints I swear,"   145
Quoth Porphyro: "O may I ne'er find grace
When my weak voice shall whisper its last prayer,
If one of her soft ringlets I displace,
Or look with ruffian passion in her face:

Good Angela, believe me by these tears;   150
Or I will, even in a moment's space,
Awake, with horrid shout, my foemen's ears,
And beard them, though they be more fanged than wolves
    and bears."

"Ah! why wilt thou affright a feeble soul?
A poor, weak, palsy-stricken, churchyard thing,   155
Whose passing-bell may ere the midnight toll;
Whose prayers for thee, each morn and evening,
Were never missed." Thus plaining, doth she bring
A gentler speech from burning Porphyro;
So woeful, and of such deep sorrowing,   160
That Angela gives promises she will do
Whatever he shall wish, betide her weal or woe.

Which was, to lead him, in close secrecy,
Even to Madeline's chamber, and there hide
Him in a closet, of such privacy   165
That he might see her beauty unespied,
And win perhaps that night a peerless bride,
While legioned faeries paced the coverlet,
And pale enchantment held her sleepy-eyed.
Never on such a night have lovers met,   170
Since Merlin paid his Demon all the monstrous debt.[4]

"It shall be as thou wishest," said the Dame:
"All cates° and dainties shall be storèd there   delicacies
Quickly on this feast-night: by the tambour°   embroidery
    frame
Her own lute thou wilt see: no time to spare,   175
For I am slow and feeble, and scarce dare
On such a catering trust my dizzy head.

---

[4]*Since . . . debt:* Merlin was imprisoned in a rock by Vivien, to whom he
had taught magic.

Wait here, my child, with patience; kneel in prayer
The while: Ah! thou must needs the lady wed,
Or may I never leave my grave among the dead."   180

So saying, she hobbled off with busy fear.
The lover's endless minutes slowly passed:
The dame returned, and whispered in his ear
To follow her, with agèd eyes aghast
From fright of dim espial. Safe at last,   185
Through many a dusky gallery, they gain
The maiden's chamber, silken, hushed, and chaste;
Where Porphyro took covert, pleased amain°   greatly
His poor guide hurried back with agues in her brain.

Her faltring hand upon the balustrade,   190
Old Angela was feeling for the stair,
When Madeline, St. Anges' charmèd maid,
Rose, like a missioned spirit, unaware:
With silver taper's light, and pious care,
She turned, and down the agèd gossip led   195
To a safe level matting. Now prepare,
Young Porphyro, for gazing on that bed;
She comes, she comes again, like ring-dove
          frayed° and fled.   frightened

Out went the taper as she hurried in;
Its little smoke, in pallid moonshine, died: 200
She closed the door, she panted, all akin
To spirits of the air, and visions wide:
No uttered syllable, or, woe betide!
But to her heart, her heart was voluble,
Paining with eloquence her balmy side;   205
As though a tongueless nightingale should swell
Her throat in vain, and die, heart-stifled, in her dell.

A casement high and triple-arched there was,
All garlanded with carven imag'ries
Of fruits, and flowers, and bunches of knot-grass,   210
And diamonded with panes of quaint device,
Innumerable of stains and splendid dyes,
As are the tiger-moth's deep-damasked wings;
And in the midst, 'mong thousand heraldries,
And twilight saints, and dim emblazonings,   215
A shielded scutcheon blushed with blood of queens and kings.

Full on this casement shone the wintry moon,
And threw warm gules° on Madeline's fair breast,   red
As down she knelt for heaven's grace and boon;
Rose-bloom fell on her hands, together pressed,   220
And on her silver cross soft amethyst,
And on her hair a glory, like a saint:
She seemed a splendid angel, newly dressed,
Save wings, for heaven: — Porphyro grew faint:
She knelt, so pure a thing, so free from mortal taint.   225

Anon his heart revives: her vespers done,
Of all its wreathéd pearls her hair she frees;
Unclasps her warmèd jewels one by one;
Loosens her fragrant bodice; by degrees
Her rich attire creeps rustling to her knees: 230
Half-hidden, like a mermaid in seaweed,
Pensive awhile she dreams awake, and sees,
In fancy, fair St. Agnes in her bed,
But dares not look behind, or all the charm is fled.

Soon, trembling in her soft and chilly nest,   235
In sort of wakeful swoon, perplexed she lay,
Until the poppied warmth of sleep oppressed
Her soothèd limbs, and soul fatigued away;
Flown, like a thought, until the morrow-day;

Blissfully havened both from joy and pain;   240
Clasped like a missal where swart Paynims° pray;   dark
                                                    pagans
Blinded alike from sunshine and from rain,
As though a rose should shut, and be a bud again.

Stol'n to this paradise, and so entranced,
Porphyro gazed upon her empty dress,   245
And listened to her breathing, if it chanced
To wake into a slumberous tenderness;
Which when he heard, that minute did he bless,
And breathed himself: then from the closet crept,
Noiseless as fear in a wide wilderness,   250
And over the hushed carpet, silent, stepped,
And 'tween the curtains peeped, where, lo!—how fast she slept.

Then by the bedside, where the faded moon
Made a dim, silver twilight, soft he set
A table, and, half anguished, threw thereon   255
A cloth of woven crimson, gold and jet:—
O for some drowsy Morphean amulet!°   sleep-inducing charm
The boisterous, midnight, festive clarion,
The kettle-drum, and far-heard clarinet,
Affray his ears, though but in dying tone:—   260
The hall door shuts again, and all the noise is gone.

And still she slept an azure-lidded sleep,
In blanchèd linen, smooth, and lavendered,
While he from forth the closet brought a heap
Of candied apple, quince, and plum, and gourd;   265
With jellies soother than the creamy curd,
And lucent syrups, tinct with cinnamon;
Manna and dates, in argosy° transferred   merchant ship
From Fez;⁵ and spicèd dainties, every one,
From silken Samarcand⁶ to cedared Lebanon.⁷   270

⁵*Fez:* a city in Morocco
⁶*Samarcand:* a city in Turkestan famed for its silks
⁷*Lebanon:* a mountain range in Syria famed for its cedar forests

These delicates he heaped with glowing hand
On golden dishes and in baskets bright
Of wreathèd silver: sumptuous they stand
In the retirèd quiet of the night,
Filling the chilly room with perfume light.—   275
"And now, my love, my seraph fair, awake!
Thou art my heaven, and I thine eremite:° religious hermit
Open thine eyes, for meek St. Agnes' sake,
Or I shall drowse beside thee, so my soul doth ache."

Thus whispering, his warm, unnervèd arm   280
Sank in her pillow. Shaded was her dream
By the dusk curtains:—'twas a midnight charm
Impossible to melt as icèd stream:
The lustrous salvers in the moonlight gleam;
Broad golden fringe upon the carpet lies: 285
It seemed he never, never could redeem
From such a steadfast spell his lady's eyes;
So mused awhile, entoiled in woofèd° phantasies.   woven

Awakening up, he took her hollow lute,—
Tumultuous,—and, in chords that tenderest be,   290
He played an ancient ditty, long since mute,
In Provence called, "La belle dame sans merci,"[8]
Close to her ear touching the melody;—
Wherewith disturbed, she uttered a soft moan:
He ceased—she panted quick—and suddenly   295
Her blue affrayèd eyes wide open shone:
Upon his knees he sank, pale as smooth-sculptured stone.

Her eyes were open, but she still beheld,
Now wide awake, the vision of her sleep:
There was a painful change, that nigh expelled   300
The blisses of her dream so pure and deep,

[8]*La belle . . . merci:* The Beautiful Lady Without Pity, the title of a poem
by Keats.

At which fair Madeline began to weep,
And moan forth witless words with many a sigh;
While still her gaze on Porphyro would keep;
Who knelt, with joinèd hands and piteous eye,   305
Fearing to move or speak, she looked so dreamingly.

"Ah, Porphyro!" said she, "but even now
Thy voice was at sweet tremble in mine ear,
Made tunable with every sweetest vow;
And those sad eyes were spiritual and clear: 310
How changed thou art! how pallid, chill, and drear!
Give me that voice again, my Porphyro,
Those looks immortal, those complainings dear!
Oh leave me not in this eternal woe,
For if thou diest, my Love, I know not where to go."   315

Beyond a mortal man impassioned far
At these voluptuous accents, he arose,
Ethereal, flushed, and like a throbbing star
Seen 'mid the sapphire heaven's deep repose;
Into her dream he melted, as the rose   320
Blendeth its odor with the violet,—
Solution sweet: meantime the frost-wind blows
Like Love's alarum pattering the sharp sleet
Against the window-panes; St. Agnes' moon hath set.

'Tis dark: quick pattereth the flaw-blown° sleet: wind-blown
"This is no dream, my bride, my Madeline!"   326
'Tis dark: the icèd gusts still rave and beat:
"No dream, alas! and woe is mine!
Porphyro will leave me here to fade and pine.—
Cruel! what traitor could thee hither bring?   330
I curse not, for my heart is lost in thine,
Though thou forsakest a deceivèd thing;—
A dove forlorn and lost with sick unprunèd wing."

"My Madeline! sweet dreamer! lovely bride!
Say, may I be for aye thy vassal blest?   335
Thy beauty's shield, heart-shaped and vermeil° dyed?   red
Ah, silver shrine, here will I take my rest
After so many hours of toil and quest,
A famished pilgrim,—saved by miracle.
Though I have found, I will not rob thy nest   340
Saving of thy sweet self; if thou think'st well
To trust, fair Madeline, to no rude infidel.

"Hark 'tis an elfin storm from faery land,
Of haggard seeming, but a boon indeed:
Arise—arise! the morning is at hand;—   345
The bloated wassailers will never heed:—
Let us away, my love, with happy speed;
There are no ears to hear, or eyes to see,—
Drowned all in Rhenish° and the sleepy mead: Rhine wine
Awake! arise! my love, and fearless be,   350
For o'er the southern moors I have a home for thee."

She hurried at his words, beset with fears,
For there were sleeping dragons all around,
At glaring watch, perhaps, with ready spears—
Down the wide stairs a darkling way they found.—   355
In all the house was heard no human sound.
A chain-drooped lamp was flickering by each door;
The arras,° rich with horseman, hawk, and hound,   tapestry
Fluttered in the besieging wind's uproar;
And the long carpets rose along the gusty floor.   360

They glide, like phantoms, into the wide hall;
Like phantoms to the iron porch, they glide;
Where lay the Porter, in uneasy sprawl,
With a huge empty flagon by his side:
The wakeful bloodhound rose, and shook his hide,   365

But his sagacious eye an inmate owns:
By one, and one, the bolts full easy slide:—
The chains lie silent on the footworn stones;—
The key turns, and the door upon its hinges groans.

And they are gone: ay, ages long ago   370
These lovers fled away into the storm.
That night the Baron dreamt of many a woe,
And all his warrior-guests, with shade and form
Of witch, and demon, and large coffin-worm,
Were long be-nightmared. Angela the old   375
Died palsy-twitched, with meager face deform;
The Beadsman, after thousand aves° told,   prayers
For aye unsought-for slept among his ashes cold.

1. The setting for this ancient tale of young love must have been a
   huge castle. What picture of it can you piece together from the
   details given in the opening stanzas and throughout the poem?
   What reason can you see for beginning with the chapel where the
   Beadsman prays by the light of a single lamp? What images in
   stanzas 1 and 2 convey the impressions of bitter cold? Why does
   the Beadsman turn away from "music's golden tongue"?
2. A very different scene and mood is introduced in stanza 4. What
   is taking place "up aloft"? Why is "thoughtful Madeline" indifferent to it? What has she heard the old dames declare? What ceremonies must she do aright if she is to enjoy St. Agnes' dreams?
3. While she lingers at the dance, what scene is taking place beside
   the portal doors? Why does the old beldame urge Porphyro to
   "get hence"? When, safely hidden, he reminds her what night it
   is, why does she laugh and say "good angels her deceive"?
4. What stratagen does he propose that makes Angela call him a cruel
   and impious man? What daring promise does he make that reassures yet frightens her? Finally, what plan of action does she
   outline? Why does he have to wait before carrying it out? Where
   does she finally lead him?
5. In the description of Madeline's chamber and the cermonies
   preceding her retirement and the anticipated St. Agnes' dream,
   Keats gives free rein to his artistry in portraying sights and sounds,

colors and textures, and all the hidden thoughts and emotions of a young girl. Point out the ones you consider most unusual and effective. Note, too, the similes and metaphors and the way in which they heighten the impressions and the over-all mood of the scene.

6. When Porphyro is certain that Madeline is asleep, what preparations does he make to carry out the vision of St. Agnes' Eve? Why does he wish for "some drowsy Morphean amulet"? In this scene, Keats again appeals to all the senses, including taste, touch, and smell. Point out examples.

7. Why does Porphyro fear that all his preparations are in vain? How does he awaken Madeline? Is this in keeping with the old dames' tale? How does Madeline react? How do you interpret stanza 36? What is the effect of lines 323 and 324? How are joy and sorrow, dream and reality, blended in stanzas 37-39?

8. In stanza 40, Keats brings the reader back to reality. Describe the change in mood. What gives this stanza and the following one both dramatic intensity and a sense of urgency? What is the meaning of the image in line 353? Note the simile in lines 361 and 362, and the figurative language in lines 360, 365, and 369.

9. The last stanza, like the denouement of a story, ties up the loose ends, telling the reader that the tale is complete. What else does it achieve in terms of dramatic effect, of recapturing the mood created in the opening stanzas, and of intensifying the excitement of the mysterious and supernatural that pervades the entire poem? Cite specific words and images which achieve these.

THE VICTORIAN POETS

The Victorian Age takes its name from Queen Victoria, who reigned sixty-four years, from 1837 to 1901. Although life in the closing years of her reign was far different from that in the opening years, there were, nevertheless, certain attitudes toward life which continued throughout and bound these years together. One was pride in the growing power of England; another was optimism born of the new science. A third was the Puritan idealism which dominated and directed the thinking in the royal court, as well as in circles made up of the fiercely respectable middle classes. The Victorians advocated decency, gentility, and adherence to social conventions. Thought was often directed toward drawing didactic morals.

At midcentury, England's economy—based on coal, steam, steel, and railroads—surpassed anything known elsewhere in the world. Never had a people been so happy and blessed! Unfortunately, this unrivaled happiness was enjoyed only by the privileged class, which gradually included more and more middle-class financiers and industrialists. Intent upon earning money by any means, they allowed the blight of industrialism to deface the countryside. In their disregard for the beauty of nature, they were no more guilty than some of the aristocrats who augmented their waning fortunes by investing in mines and factories far removed from their elegant country estates.

Wealth inherited and acquired depended upon the exploitation of natural resources and of men, women, and children in booming industries. As Disraeli pointed out, Queen Victoria ruled over two nations—the rich and the poor—"who are as ignorant of each other's habits, thoughts, and feelings, as if they were dwellers in different zones, or inhabitants of different planets; who are formed by a different breeding, are fed by different food, are ordered by different manners, and are not governed by the same laws."

Victorian writers were deeply concerned about the growth of democratic institutions, the friction between workers and employers, the conflict between religion and science, and the state of English culture. Such concern for changing attitudes, values, and beliefs is inevitably reflected in the poetry of the period. Almost always an attitude of moral seriousness, the most characteristic trait of the period, is present. For example, Matthew Arnold, the leading literary critic of the day, judged poetry primarily by the extent to which the writer approached his subject with "high seriousness."

The Romantic movement did not cease when Victoria mounted the throne. Nor were Victorian writers in revolt against it. The spirit of Romanticism continued to influence the innermost consciousness of the leading writers, although the burning flame of the earlier period was reduced to a warm glow of sustained light. Romanticism survived in a crusading humanitarian spirit and lofty idealism.

But whereas the Romantic writers expressed best their feelings, the Victorians excelled at expressing more analytic thought. The conflict between religion and science was of major importance to poets, and they expressed their convictions in stately verse. For Tennyson and Browning, the process of evolution was merely "God's way of doing things." Thus, while affirming a strong faith in God, they were able to speak confidently of scientific progress. Matthew Arnold was beset with doubts, but joined other poets in decrying the emphasis on facts and material things, rather than on faith and spiritual values. This preoccupation with grave issues necessarily affected both the content and tone of the poetry. While experiments in meter were widespread, the poetry is largely careful and controlled, rather than exuberant and spontaneous. Chiefly, it is earnest.

ALFRED, LORD TENNYSON was, perhaps, the most representative, as well as the greatest, poet of the Victorian Age, and upon the death of Wordsworth in 1850, was made Poet Laureate. Even as a youth he gave evidence of being a poet, and he devoted his entire life to perfecting his craft. Two of his long poems, *Maud* and *Idylls of the King*, secured a large audience even in an age that was turning more and more to the novel and to philosophic inquiry into life.

Tennyson followed a middle course in the intellectual and social controversies of the nineteenth century. Without giving up his religious faith, he worked out typically Victorian compromise solutions to problems raised by advancing education, democracy, and science.

He could say with confidence,

> Behold we know not anything;
> I can but trust that good shall fall
> At last—far off—at last, to all.

With the twentieth century and the reaction against Victorianism, Tennyson was accused of shallow thinking. Moreover, some of his verses impressed modern readers as artificially ornate, sentimental, and too "pretty." Ironically, the very qualities most admired during his lifetime, later caused his work to fall from favor. But more recent criticism has revived his literary reputation and placed him among England's major poets. A superb craftsman, he excels at combining romantic themes, sensuous imagery, and lyrical expression of the highest quality.

ROBERT BROWNING is almost as well known for his rescue of the semi-invalid Elizabeth Barrett from her Wimpole Street home as for his poetry. He fell in love first with her poems, and then with her, and their idyllic marriage has become something of a literary legend. Each benefited from the stimulating intellectual companionship which they enjoyed during their residence in Florence, where they became interested in Italian politics and Italian art.

Browning's poetry reveals the Victorian craving for analysis
and moral criticism, a systematic quest for truth. His object,
according to his own statement, was "the study of incidents
which go to compose the development of a soul." To give his
findings poetic expression, he evolved the dramatic monologue, a poetic form which consists of the words of a single
character whose speech reveals the dramatic situation and
the psychology of the speaker. That he created such a variety of characters is evidence of his interest in all aspects of
human nature. Scoundrels fascinated him more than virtuous
people, perhaps because he was so interested in exposing self-
deception. Each monologue contains some moral judgment.
Souls steeped in vice or crime use words which plainly hint
at Browning's attitude toward them. His passionate condem-
nation is equally clear.

Browning's poetry is resolutely optimistic. The spirit of the
song of the little silk-weaver in his drama *Pippa Passes* is
characteristic of his own attitude toward life:

> The year's at the spring
> And day's at the morn;
> Morning's at seven;
> The hill-side's dew-pearled:
> The lark's on the wing;
> The snail's on the thorn;
> God's in his heaven—
> All's right with the world!

In poem after poem, he emphasized God's love and presented
evil and falsehood only as distortions of love and truth. He
cheerfully believed that obstructions produce strength and
that difficulties increase power. Sharing the idealistic Victorian belief that one should strive for human perfectibility,
Browning taught that "a man's reach should exceed his grasp"
and that achievement indicates meager aspirations, not
greatness.

In contrast with Tennyson, who was noted for his musical
verse and clarity of statement, Browning was often rougher
in form and more obscure in meaning. At first he was admired
only by those willing to wrestle with his cryptic statements

and erudite allusions. But today there is little doubt that he consciously departed from conventional themes and that the freshness of his treatment and the boldness of his experiments with various meters resulted in widening the boundaries of his art, thereby affecting future English poetry.

MATTHEW ARNOLD is equally important as a poet and as a literary critic. In his poems, the quiet control of his emotions has its counterpart in his poetic technique. The qualities he valued most were clearness of arrangement and simplicity of style, rather than rich imagery and abundant illustration. Most of Arnold's poetry is concerned with the conflicts and uncertainties of his time. It reflects a pensive melancholy which, though Romantic in origin, is tempered by the sedateness of the Victorian Age.

As Arnold reflected upon the great cultural problems of his day, he lamented that the old established values were being abandoned with the march of progress and that nothing of worth was taking their place. It seemed to him that his generation was "wandering between two worlds, one dead, the other powerless to be born." Writing to his mother, he said: "My poems represent, on the whole, the main movement of mind of the last quarter of a century, and thus they will probably have their day as people become conscious to themselves of what movement of mind is and interested in the literary productions which reflect it." By "main movement of mind" he meant the thoughts of Victorian intellectuals who found themselves adrift from old moorings upon a wide, uncharted sea.

ALGERNON CHARLES SWINBURNE became famous—even notorious—with the publication of his *Poems and Ballads* in 1866. Writing in the tradition of young rebels whose love of liberty and aggressive resistance to authority both fascinate and alarm society, Swinburne denounced authoritative religions and their dogmas, praised pagan civilizations, professed pantheistic leanings, glorified the Middle Ages, and idealized sensuous beauty. The Italian patriot Mazzini became for him the symbol of man's eternal struggle against tyranny. In addition to expressing these essentially Romantic themes, Swinburne revolted against the rule of Puritanism and the subjection of literature to the conservative tone of Victorian social life in the latter half of the nineteenth century.

So completely does Swinburne surrender to the intoxication of language in his poetry that his inspiration very often seems to follow no other guidance. Sometimes sound is so enthralling that it becomes hypnotic, and the reader may suddenly realize that he has been reading along with pleasure without knowing what is being said. At his best, however, as in "When the Hounds of Spring," meaning and music reinforce each other in the work of this most lyrical of Victorian poets.

Alfred, Lord Tennyson

Tennyson was one of the most meticulous English poets. Again and again he revised his work to condense passionate outbursts into compact phrases, and to convey a profound theme in language that is simple and clear, in images that remain fresh and compelling. In many of his poems, he reworked a classical theme, giving it romantic sentiment while using it as a vehicle for a moral message. His narrative poems are filled with interesting characters confronted with grave moral decisions. Thus he sought for, and found, a balance between romanticism and classicism. Whether the poem is a dramatic monologue, a chivalric narrative, or an intense lyric, Tennyson's work continues to astonish because of its technical perfection.

Tears, Idle Tears

Tears, idle tears, I know not what they
    mean,
Tears from the depth of some divine despair
Rise in the heart, and gather to the eyes,
In looking on the happy autumn-fields,
And thinking of the days that are no more.   5

Fresh as the first beam glittering on a sail,
That brings our friends up from the under-
    world,

Sad as the last which reddens over one
That sinks with all we love below the verge;
So sad, so fresh, the days that are no more.   10

Ah, sad and strange as in dark summer
          dawns
The earliest pipe of half-awakened birds
To dying ears, when unto dying eyes
The casement slowly grows a glimmering
          square;
So sad, so strange, the days that are no more.   15

Dear as remembered kisses after death,
And sweet as those by hopeless fancy feigned
On lips that are for others; deep as love,
Deep as first love, and wild with all regret;
O Death in Life, the days that are no more.   20

1. "Tears, Idle Tears" was designed as a song to be sung in Tennyson's long, narrative poem, *The Princess*. What parts seem especially songlike? How is it like a ballad? How is it different from the ballads or folk songs you know? What musical devices do you find in lines 2, 11, and 14?
2. Occasionally, lines are punctuated internally. Do you feel Tennyson worked deliberately to place the breaks in lines 1, 3, 10, and 11? Why or why not?
3. Identify the contrasts around which Tennyson builds each stanza. What does he accomplish by using this structure for his poem?
4. A series of similes is presented in stanzas 2, 3, and 4. What subject do these similes describe? Are all equally appropriate to the subject? Why or why not?

NOW SLEEPS THE CRIMSON PETAL

Now sleeps the crimson petal, now the
    white;
Nor waves the cypress in the palace walk;
Nor winks the gold fin in the porphyry font.
The fire-fly wakens; waken thou with me.

Now droops the milkwhite peacock like a
    ghost,   5
And like a ghost she glimmers on to me.

Now lies the Earth all Danaë to the stars,
And all thy heart lies open unto me.

Now slides the silent meteor on, and leaves
A shining furrow, as thy thoughts in me.   10

Now folds the lily all her sweetness up,
And slips into the bosom of the lake.
So fold thyself, my dearest, thou, and slip
Into my bosom and be lost in me.

1. This melodious song also appears in *The Princess* and is read aloud by a princess watching all night by the bedside of a wounded prince. Explain why the song is particularly appropriate for this dramatic situation.
2. What is the mood of the poem? What devices effectively establish this mood? How does the mood differ from that of "Tears, Idle Tears"?
3. Danaë was a maiden Zeus loved and visited by assuming the form of golden coins which showered upon her. What does the poet suggest about the earth when he compares it to Danaë? What is the relationship between the earth and the stars?

4. The silent meteor in line 9 develops further the star imagery introduced in line 7. What effect does this imagery produce? Into what patterns do the images of the poem fall?

THE LADY OF SHALOTT

PART 1

On either side the river lie
Long fields of barley and of rye,
That clothe the wold° and meet the sky;   plain
And through the field the road runs by
      To many towered Camelot;[1]   5
And up and down the people go,
Gazing where the lilies blow°   bloom
Round an island there below,
      The island of Shalott.

Willows whiten, aspens quiver,   10
Little breezes dusk and shiver
Through the wave that runs for ever
By the island in the river
      Flowing down to Camelot.
Four gray walls, and four gray towers,   15
Overlook a space of flowers,
And the silent isle imbowers
      The Lady of Shalott.

By the margin, willow-veiled,
Slide the heavy barges trailed   20
By slow horses; and unhailed
The shallop° flitteth silken-sailed   light boat
      Skimming down to Camelot:

---

[1]*Camelot:* the legendary English town where King Arthur had his court

But who hath seen her wave her hand?
Or at the casement seen her stand?   25
Or is she known in all the land,
      The Lady of Shalott?

Only reapers, reaping early
In among the bearded barley,
Hear a song that echoes cheerly   30
From the river winding clearly,
      Down to towered Camelot;
And by the moon the reaper weary,
Piling sheaves in uplands airy,
Listening, whispers, "'Tis the fairy   35
      Lady of Shalott."

PART 2

There she weaves by night and day
A magic web with colors gay.
She has heard a whisper say,
A curse is on her if she stay   40
      To look down to Camelot.
She knows not what the curse may be,
And so she weaveth steadily,
And little other care hath she,
      The Lady of Shalott.   45

And moving through a mirror° clear   magic crystal
That hangs before her all the year,
Shadows of the world appear.
There she sees the highway near
      Winding down to Camelot;   50
There the river eddy whirls,
And there the surly village-churls,
And the red cloaks of market girls,
      Pass onward from Shalott.

Sometimes a troop of damsels glad,   55
An abbot on an ambling pad,°   slow horse
Sometimes a curly shepherd-lad,
Or long-haired page in crimson clad,
          Goes by to towered Camelot;
And sometimes through the mirror blue   60
The knights come riding two and two:
She hath no loyal knight and true,
          The Lady of Shalott.

But in her web she still delights
To weave the mirror's magic sights,   65
For often through the silent nights
A funeral, with plumes and lights
          And music, went to Camelot;
Or when the moon was overhead,
Came two young lovers lately wed: 70
"I am half sick of shadows," said
          The Lady of Shalott.

PART 3

A bow-shot from her bower-eaves,
He rode between the barley-sheaves,
The sun came dazzling through the leaves,   75
And flamed upon the brazen greaves°   leg armor
          Of bold Sir Lancelot.
A red-cross[2] knight for ever kneeled
To a lady in his shield,
That sparkled on the yellow field,   80
          Beside remote Shalott.

The gemmy bridle glittered free,
Like to some branch of stars we see
Hung in the golden Galaxy.°   Milky Way

[2]*red-cross:* St. George's cross, the national emblem of England

The bridle bells rang merrily   85
      As he rode down to Camelot;
And from his blazoned baldric° slung   ornamented belt
A mighty silver bugle hung,
And as he rode his armor rung,
      Beside remote Shalott.   90

All in the blue unclouded weather
Thick-jewelled shone the saddle-leather,
The helmet and the helmet-feather
Burned like one burning flame together,
      As he rode down to Camelot;   95
As often through the purple night,
Below the starry clusters bright,
Some bearded meteor, trailing light,
      Moves over still Shalott.

His broad clear brow in sunlight glowed;   100
On burnished hooves his war-horse trode;
From underneath his helmet flowed
His coal-black curls as on he rode,
      As he rode down to Camelot.
From the bank and from the river   105
He flashed into the crystal mirror,
"Tirra lirra," by the river
      Sang Sir Lancelot.

She left the web, she left the loom,
She made three paces through the room,   110
She saw the water-lily bloom,
She saw the helmet and the plume,
      She looked down to Camelot.
Out flew the web and floated wide;
The mirror cracked from side to side;   115
"The curse is come upon me," cried
      The Lady of Shalott.

PART 4

In the stormy east-wind straining,
The pale yellow woods were waning,
The broad stream in his banks complaining,   120
Heavily the low sky raining
      Over towered Camelot;
Down she came and found a boat
Beneath a willow left afloat,
And round about the prow she wrote   125
      The Lady of Shalott.

And down the river's dim expanse
Like some bold seër° in a trance,   prophet
Seeing all his own mischance—
With a glassy countenance   130
      Did she look to Camelot.
And at the closing of the day
She loosed the chain, and down she lay;
The broad stream bore her far away,
      The Lady of Shalott.   135

Lying, robed in snowy white
That loosely flew to left and right—
The leaves upon her falling light—
Through the noises of the night
      She floated down to Camelot;   140
And as the boat-head wound along
The willowy hills and fields among,
They heard her singing her last song,
      The Lady of Shalott.

Heard a carol, mournful, holy,   145
Chanted loudly, chanted lowly,
Till her blood was frozen slowly,

And her eyes were darkened wholly,
    Turned to towered Camelot.
For ere she reached upon the tide   150
The first house by the water-side,
Singing in her song she died,
    The Lady of Shalott.

Under tower and balcony,
By garden-wall and gallery,   155
A gleaming shape she floated by,
Dead-pale between the houses high,
    Silent into Camelot.
Out upon the wharfs they came,
Knight and burgher, lord and dame,   160
And round the prow they read her name,
    The Lady of Shalott.

Who is this? and what is here?
And in the lighted palace near
Died the sound of royal cheer;   165
And they crossed themselves for fear,
    All the knights at Camelot:
But Lancelot mused a little space;
He said, "She has a lovely face;
God in his mercy lend her grace,   170
    The Lady of Shalott."

1. According to Tennyson's own notes, lines 71 and 72 are the key to the symbolic meaning of the poem. What happens to the lady when she moves from the world of illusion into the world of reality? Should she have stayed with her shadows or abandoned them earlier? How do you interpret the curse?
2. Note the division of the poem into four unified parts. What scene is presented in part 1? What is the mood, and which words help

to create it? From this part, what impression do you gain of the Lady of Shalott?

3. Which words in part 2 create an air of mystery? What medieval scenes are presented? Why do the last of these cause the lady to cry out against shadows?

4. From the details in part 3, what impression do you gain of Sir Lancelot? Point out the words which convey the glow of a medieval illumination. What meaning is implied by the metaphor in lines 96-99? How is this related to what happens to the lady? How is the swiftness of the curse emphasized?

5. Describe the change in mood in part 4, and point out the words and phrases which help to create it. What qualities impress you most in Tennyson's portrayal of the lady's journey "down the river's dim expanse"? How did the inhabitants of Camelot react to what they saw? Tell why you do, or do not, find the last stanza a satisfactory ending of the narrative. What dramatic irony is achieved in Lancelot's musing and comment?

6. What effect does the rhythm have on the poem? What is the effect of the constant repetition and rhyming of Camelot and Shalott? In your opinion, do lines 5 and 8 serve as a balladlike refrain, or do they become monotonous and therefore detract from the over-all effect of the poem? Give reasons to support your answer.

7. In what ways is this poem romantic in subject and treatment? What words or lines impressed you most because of their sensuous imagery?

8. Show how both assonance and alliteration play an important part in the melodic effect of the lines.

ULYSSES

It little profits that an idle king,
By this still hearth, among these barren crags,[1]
Matched with an agèd wife, I mete and dole
Unequal laws unto a savage race,
That hoard, and sleep, and feed, and know not me.   5

[1]*barren crags:* the island of Ithaca

I cannot rest from travel; I will drink
Life to the lees.° All times I have enjoyed   dregs
Greatly, have suffered greatly, both with those
That loved me, and alone; on shore, and when
Through scudding drifts° the rainy Hyades[2]   vapory clouds   10
Vexed the dim sea. I am become a name;
For always roaming with a hungry heart
Much have I seen and known—cities of men
And manners, climates, councils, governments,
Myself not least, but honored of them all,—   15
And drunk delight of battle with my peers,
Far on the ringing plains of windy Troy.
I am a part of all that I have met;
Yet all experience is an arch wherethrough
Gleams that untravelled world, whose margin fades   20
Forever and forever when I move.
How dull it is to pause, to make an end,
To rust unburnished, not to shine in use!
As though to breathe were life! Life piled on life
Were all too little, and of one to me   25
Little remains; but every hour is saved
From that eternal silence, something more,
A bringer of new things; and vile it were
For some three suns to store and hoard myself,
And this gray spirit yearning in desire   30
To follow knowledge like a sinking star,
Beyond the utmost bound of human thought.
     This is my son, mine own Telemachus,
To whom I leave the scepter and the isle—
Well-loved of me, discerning to fulfil   35
This labor, by slow prudence to make mild
A rugged people, and through soft degrees
Subdue them to the useful and the good.
Most blameless is he, centered in the sphere
Of common duties, decent not to fail   40
In offices of tenderness, and pay

[2]*Hyades:* constellation associated with rain

Meet adoration to my household gods,
When I am gone. He works his work, I mine.
    There lies the port; the vessel puffs her sail;
There gloom the dark broad seas. My mariners,   45
Souls that have toiled, and wrought, and thought with me—
That ever with a frolic welcome took
The thunder and the sunshine, and opposed
Free hearts, free foreheads—you and I are old;
Old age hath yet his honor and his toil.   50
Death closes all; but something ere the end,
Some work of noble note, may yet be done,
Not unbecoming men that strove with gods.
The lights begin to twinkle from the rocks;
The long day wanes; the slow moon climbs; the deep   55
Moans round with many voices. Come, my friends.
'Tis not too late to seek a newer world.
Push off, and sitting well in order smite
The sounding furrows; for my purpose holds
To sail beyond the sunset, and the baths   60
Of all the western stars, until I die.
It may be that the gulfs will wash us down;
It may be we shall touch the Happy Isles,[3]
And see the great Achilles,[4] whom we knew.
Though much is taken, much abides; and though   65
We are not now that strength which in old days
Moved earth and heaven; that which we are, we are—
One equal temper of heroic hearts,
Made weak by time and fate, but strong in will
To strive, to seek, to find, and not to yield.   70

[3]*Happy Isles:* the place where heroes went after their death
[4]*Achilles:* hero in the Trojan War

1. Why does Ulysses say, "I am become a name"? How do you interpret his statement in lines 6 and 7? What reason would he have for saying that he has seen and known "myself not least"? Explain why he finds being an "idle king" intolerable?
2. What does "I am a part of all that I have met" reveal about the

nature of human experience and, especially, of the way Ulysses lives his life? Express in your own words your interpretation of lines 19-21 and lines 24-32. Tell why you think he is, or is not, speaking figuratively.

3. What is Ulysses' attitude toward Telemachus? What reason do you have for believing that Ulysses does not think his son's "work" as important as his own has been?

4. Why does Ulysses feel such a bond between himself and his mariners? What does he propose that they attempt to do together? Why? In Ulysses' speech to them, do you find any acceptance of the limitations brought about by age? What does he mean by "much abides" and by "that which we are, we are" (lines 65, 67)?

5. The goal of thoughtful living is to learn to know oneself. What evidence do you find in the poem that Ulysses has discovered who he really is? Has this knowledge affected his philosophy and his actions?

6. What is the "message" of the poem? Do you think Ulysses' philosophy is a typically Victorian outlook? Does it have a meaning for people today?

7. Identify the verse form used in this poem. What is the effect of the many run-on lines and the frequent stops within the lines? The poem falls into three sections. What idea is developed in each?

8. Ulysses appears to be a lusty, virile, and sincere person. How do the words which Tennyson used help to convey this impression? Cite examples from the poem.

9. Which words, phrases, or lines impressed you most by their melodious sound and by the pictures they created in your mind? Point out examples of Tennyson's ability to condense passionate outbursts into compact phrases and images that remain fresh and compelling.

FROM In Memoriam

In Memoriam A. H. H. Obiit 1833

On September 15, 1833, Arthur Henry Hallam died suddenly in Vienna at the age of twenty-two. The death triggered a profound emotional breakdown in his close friend, Alfred, Lord

Tennyson. Suddenly, with no preparation for the event, Tennyson was confronted with the fact of death—a fact philosophers and psychologists assert we spend our lives trying to ignore or forget. Because this death seemed totally purposeless, Tennyson found himself asking the most painful and difficult of questions: What is the meaning of human life? Does man have a purpose? Is there a God? If God is completely good, then why does he permit suffering and evil to coexist with him? Over a period of years, Tennyson struggled with these questions, occasionally expressing his despair, his doubts, and his hopes in poems with the same stanzaic pattern. In 1850 these poems, under the title *In Memoriam*, were published as a memorial to Hallam. They earned Tennyson the Poet Laureateship of England. Following are selections from this long poem.

PROLOGUE

Strong Son of God, immortal Love,
    Whom we, that have not seen thy face,
    By faith, and faith alone, embrace,
Believing where we cannot prove;

Thine are these orbs of light and shade;   5
    Thou madest Life in man and brute;
    Thou madest Death; and lo, thy foot
Is on the skull which thou hast made.

Thou wilt not leave us in the dust:
    Thou madest man, he knows not why,   10
    He thinks he was not made to die;
And thou hast made him; thou art just.

Thou seemest human and divine,
    The highest, holiest manhood, thou.
    Our wills are ours, we know not how;   15
Our wills are ours, to make them thine.

Our little systems have their day;
They have their day and cease to be;
    They are but broken lights of thee,
And thou, O Lord, art more than they.   20

We have but faith; we cannot know,
    For knowledge is of things we see;
    And yet we trust it comes from thee,
A beam in darkness; let it grow.

Let knowledge grow from more to more,   25
    But more of reverence in us dwell;
    That mind and soul, according well,
May make one music as before,

But vaster. We are fools and slight;
    We mock thee when we do not fear.   30
    But help thy foolish ones to bear;
Help thy vain worlds to bear thy light.

Forgive what seemed my sin in me,
    What seemed my worth since I began;
    For merit lives from man to man,   35
And not from man, O Lord, to thee.

Forgive my grief for one removed,
    Thy creature, whom I found so fair.
    Itrust he lives in thee, and there
I find him worthier to be loved.   40

Forgive these wild and wandering cries,
    Confusions of a wasted youth;
    Forgive them where they fail in truth,
And in thy wisdom make me wise.

1. *In Memoriam* is a kind of emotional record of Tennyson's life from 1833 to 1849. The Prologue to the lyrics summarizes the conclusions to which Tennyson came after his years of suffering. In stanza 1, what does he imply makes religious belief possible? What attitude toward reason do you find here?
2. In lines 5-16, what view of Christ (the Strong Son of God to whom the words are addressed) emerges? How does Tennyson understand the nature of Christ?
3. What is the poet's attitude toward Christ? Notice particularly lines 16-20. What emotion or attitude does he seek to instill in himself throughout this prologue?
4. In lines 21-29 what attitude does Tennyson express toward knowledge? In the Prologue, does he imply a difference between knowledge and reason? If so, what is that difference?
5. For what sin does the speaker ask forgiveness in line 33? Explain lines 33-36. Why is merit mentioned along with a plea for forgiveness? Show how lines 37-38 are simply a more specific version of lines 33-34.
6. What hope for Hallam does Tennyson end by asserting? What hope for himself?

7

Dark house,[1] by which once more I stand
    Here in the long unlovely street,
    Doors, where my heart was used to beat
So quickly, waiting for a hand,

A hand that can be clasped no more —   5
    Behold me, for I cannot sleep,
    And like a guilty thing I creep
At earliest morning to the door.

He is not here; but far away
    The noise of life begins again,   10
    And ghastly thro' the drizzling rain
On the bald street breaks the blank day.

[1]*house:* Hallam's house in London where he lived as a student

1. What mood dominates this lyric? How does Tennyson's treatment of the images here—the house, the door, the street—help create the mood?
2. What associations does Tennyson evoke or stimulate in lines 8-9? What do these lines tell you about his emotional condition? Why does he compare himself to "a guilty thing"?
3. *Synecdoche* is a figure of speech in which a part of something stands for the whole thing. Where in this lyric do you find an example of synecdoche? Use this example to explain why it is sometimes more effective to refer to a fragment than to the whole object.
4. Often a poet's most powerful effects come from his meticulous choice of words. In poetry, connotations and sounds of words are as important as meaning, and two words with the same meaning can have very different effects on a line of verse. What difference to the poem would it have made if Tennyson had changed each of the following:
    - (a) *dark* to *black* (line 1)
    - (b) *unlovely* to *deserted* or *and ugly* (line 2)
    - (c) *hand that can be clasped* to *voice that can be heard* (line 5)
    - (d) *noise* to *work* (line 10)
    - (e) *drizzling* to *falling* (line 11)
5. The last line is one of the most poetically successful in English poetry. How many different kinds of sound patterns do you find here? What is the rhythm? When scanned, how does the line differ from others in the poem? How do both the sound and the rhythm of the line reinforce and enlarge the meaning of the words?

27

I envy not in any moods
 The captive void of noble rage,
 The linnet born within the cage,
That never knew the summer woods;

I envy not the beast that takes   5
 His license in the field of time,
 Unfettered by the sense of crime,
To whom a conscience never wakes;

Nor, what may count itself as blest,
    The heart that never plighted troth   10
    But stagnates in the weeds of sloth;
Nor any want-begotten rest.

I hold it true, whate'er befall;
    I feel it, when I sorrow most;
    'Tis better to have loved and lost   15
Than never to have loved at all.

1. Why are the captive, linnet, beast, and heart in the same series? What do they have in common? Do they differ in any significant way?
2. What does "weeds of sloth" mean (line 11)? Why *weeds?*
3. Tennyson came to believe so firmly in the truth expressed in lines 15-16 that he repeated the lines later in *In Memoriam.* Do you think this epigram is true? Why or why not?
4. What does the last stanza have to do with the three which preceded it? Why are they parts of the same lyric?

126

Love is and was my lord and king,
    And in his presence I attend
    To hear the tidings of my friend,
Which every hour his couriers bring.

Love is and was my king and lord,   5
    And will be, tho' as yet I keep
    Within his court on earth, and sleep
Encompassed by his faithful guard,

And hear at times a sentinel
    That moves about from place to place,   10
    And whispers to the worlds of space,
In the deep night, that all is well.

1. The same metaphor, or pattern of imagery, runs throughout this poem. How would you describe it? How effective do you find it?
2. What rhetorical device do you find in line 1? What kind of love is Tennyson talking about?
3. What kind of tidings do you think were brought each hour? Who or what are the couriers of love? Who or what is love's faithful guard? the sentinel?
4. These three short stanzas represent three emotional stages Tennyson went through after the death of Hallam. How would you describe each stage? How do they differ?

Robert Browning

Robert Browning's poetry abounds in a spirit of joy and courage that is unusual in either the work of his comtemporaries or those poets of the age which followed. His marching songs reflect a gay optimism; his lyrics express a cheerful and energetic view of life. However, many consider Browning's dramatic monologues his most important contribution to English literature. They show his preoccupation with the psychological motives which his characters reveal through their own words. Like Shakespeare, Browning centered his interest in humanity. "Nothing else is worth study," he said. To express the states of mind of his many characters, Browning developed an independent style with unusual rhythms, grotesque rhymes, and abrupt, broken phrasing. The use of harsh, colloquial idiom, together with his keen insight into the minds of his characters, has made Browning one of the most popular of the Victorian poets in the twentieth century.

HOME-THOUGHTS, FROM ABROAD[1]

Oh, to be in England
Now that April's there,
And whoever wakes in England
Sees, some morning, unaware,

[1]*Abroad:* Browning was visiting Italy.

That the lowest boughs and the brushwood sheaf   5
Round the elm-tree bole° are in tiny leaf,   trunk
While the chaffinch sings on the orchard bough
In England—now!

And after April, when May follows,
And the whitethroat builds, and all the swallows!   10
Hark, where my blossomed pear-tree in the hedge
Leans to the field and scatters on the clover
Blossoms and dewdrops—at the bent spray's edge—
That's the wise thrush; he sings each song twice over,
Lest you should think he never could recapture   15
The first fine careless rapture!
And though the fields look rough with hoary dew,
All will be gay when noontide wakes anew
The buttercups, the little children's dower
—Far brighter than this gaudy melon-flower!   20

1. Why does Browning want to be in England "now"? What impression of England emerges? What significance would this poem have for people who are not native Englishmen? How do you interpret the comparison implied in the last line?
2. What words or lines impressed you most by their sounds and by the pictures they create in your mind? What sensory connotation does even the name England assume?
3. This poem illustrates Browning's independent style. In stanza 1, how do the first four lines differ from the last four? Is the predominant metrical foot iambic or trochaic? What is the effect of changing to dactylic in lines 5-7 and of the short, broken eighth line?
4. The lines in stanza 2 are even more varied in rhythm. Read them aloud, letting the sense of each line determine where the accent falls. How many kinds of metrical feet can you identify? How does the rhythm of this poem contribute to the mood?

PROSPICE[1]

Fear death? — to feel the fog in my throat,
    The mist in my face,
When the snows begin, and the blasts denote
    I am nearing the place,
The power of the night, the press of the storm,   5
    The post of the foe;
Where he stands, the Arch Fear[2] in a visible form,
    Yet the strong man must go:
For the journey is done and the summit attained,
    And the barriers fall,   10
Though a battle's to fight ere the guerdon° be gained,   reward
    The reward of it all.
I was ever a fighter, so — one fight more,
    The best and the last!
I would hate that death bandaged my eyes, and forbore,   15
    And bade me creep past.
No! let me taste the whole of it, fare like my peers,
    The heroes of old,
Bear the brunt, in a minute pay glad life's arrears
    Of pain, darkness and cold.   20
For sudden the worst turns the best to the brave,
    The black minute's at end,
And the elements' rage, the fiend-voices that rave,
    Shall dwindle, shall blend,
Shall change, shall become first a peace out of pain,   25
    Then a light, then thy breast,
O thou soul of my soul! I shall clasp thee again,
    And with God be the rest!

[1]*Prospice:* look forward (Latin)
[2]*Arch Fear:* Death

1. What is the central metaphor of the poem? What details develop this metaphor? What words support this metaphor or are in harmony with it?
2. How does the speaker choose to meet death? Why? In your opinion, is this poem too personal to have universal significance? Why, or why not?
3. Explain lines 21 and 22. Does the tone of the poem change after that point, or does it not? What reward is looked for after death?
4. Is the speaker's mood sentimental, frightened, joyous, defiant, adventurous, or devout? Be able to defend your answer.
5. In this poem, as in every good poem, structure and meaning are closely related. The first sentence of twelve lines is followed by two sentences, both having eight lines. Each sentence sets forth a definite idea. State these three successive ideas in your own words.

MY LAST DUCHESS

In this dramatic monologue, the Duke of Ferrara, a nobleman of Renaissance Italy, is showing a portrait of his last wife to a representative of the count whose daughter he is planning to marry.

That's my last Duchess painted on the wall,
Looking as if she were alive. I call
That piece a wonder, now; Frà Pandolf's[1] hands
Worked busily a day, and there she stands.
Will't please you sit and look at her? I said   5
"Frà Pandolf" by design, for never read
Strangers like you that pictured countenance,
The depth and passion of its earnest glance,
But to myself they turned (since none puts by
The curtain I have drawn for you, but I)   10
And seemed as they would ask me, if they durst,
How such a glance came there; so, not the first

---

[1]*Frà Pandolf:* the imaginary artist who painted the portrait

Are you to turn and ask thus. Sir, 'twas not
Her husband's presence only, called that spot
Of joy into the Duchess' cheek: perhaps   15
Frà Pandolf chanced to say, "Her mantle laps
Over my lady's wrist too much," or "Paint
Must never hope to reproduce the faint
Half-flush that dies along her throat." Such stuff
Was courtesy, she thought, and cause enough   20
For calling up that spot of joy. She had
A heart—how shall I say?—too soon made glad,
Too easily impressed; she like whate'er
She looked on, and her looks went everywhere.
Sir, 'twas all one! My favor at her breast,   25
The dropping of the daylight in the west,
The bough of cherries some officious fool
Broke in the orchard for her, the white mule
She rode with round the terrace—all and each
Would draw from her alike the approving speech,   30
Or blush, at least. She thanked men,—good! but thanked
Somehow—I know not how—as if she ranked
My gift of a nine-hundred-years-old name
With anybody's gift. Who'd stoop to blame
This sort of trifling? Even had you skill   35
In speech—(which I have not)—to make your will
Quite clear to such an one, and say, "Just this
Or that in you disgusts me; here you miss,
Or there exceed the mark"—and if she let
Herself be lessoned so, nor plainly set   40
Her wits to yours, forsooth, and made excuse,
—E'en then would be some stooping; and I choose
Never to stoop. Oh sir, she smiled, no doubt,
Whene'er I passed her; but who passed without
Much the same smile? This grew; I gave commands;   45
Then all smiles stopped together. There she stands
As if alive. Will't please you rise? We'll meet

The company below, then. I repeat,
The Count your master's known munificence°   generosity
Is ample warrant that no just pretense   50
Of mine for dowry will be disallowed;
Though his fair daughter's self, as I avowed
At starting, is my object. Nay, we'll go
Together down, sir. Notice Neptune,² though,
Taming a sea-horse, thought a rarity,   55
Which Claus of Innsbruck³ cast in bronze for me!

²*Neptune:* god of the sea
³*Claus of Innsbruck:* an imaginary sculptor

1. In a dramatic monologue the words of a single character are as
   revealing of his own nature as of the dramatic situation, which is
   the subject of the poem. State your impression of the Duke's
   character. In which of his remarks is his true nature most clearly
   revealed? Is the impression he gives of himself the one he intends? Explain.
2. How significant is it that the Duke begins and ends his monologue with references to art? Comment upon his artistic sensibility and his human relationships. How are the stories about his
   former wife related to his expectations in his next marriage? What
   is his purpose in telling these stories? What do you think are his
   real reasons for wanting to marry again?
3. What impression of the Duchess' character do you think the Duke
   intends to convey? Is your impression the same as his? If not, how
   does it differ? How do the ways in which she annoyed him further illuminate his character? Cite examples.
4. What do you think the Duke means in lines 43-46? From the
   words he chooses and the rhythm of his speech, what new insight
   into his character do you gain? What is the difference between
   the lines in which he speaks about his former wife and the lines
   in which he discusses art?
5. This poem is often considered the best example of a dramatic
   monologue. Point out the qualities which impress you and justify
   the praise given this poem. When you read it, are you aware that
   lines rhyme? Why is the rhyme less apparent than in most poems
   written in couplets?

THE BISHOP ORDERS HIS TOMB
AT SAINT PRAXED'S CHURCH

John Ruskin said of this dramatic monologue, "I know of no other piece of modern English, prose or poetry, in which there is so much told, as in these lines, of the Renaissance spirit—its worldliness, inconsistency, pride, hypocrisy, ignorance of itself, love of art, of luxury, and of good Latin."

Vanity, saith the preacher, vanity!
Draw round my bed: is Anselm keeping back?
Nephews[1]—sons mine . . . ah God, I know not! Well—
She, men would have to be your mother once,
Old Gandolf[2] envied me, so fair she was!   5
What's done is done, and she is dead beside,
Dead long ago, and I am Bishop since,
And as she died so must we die ourselves,
And thence ye may perceive the world's a dream.
Life, how and what is it? As here I lie   10
In this state-chamber, dying by degrees,
Hours and long hours in the dead night, I ask
"Do I live, am I dead?" Peace, peace seems all.
Saint Praxed's ever was the church for peace;
And so, about this tomb of mine. I fought   15
With tooth and nail to save my niche, ye know:
—Old Gandolf cozened° me, despite my care;   cheated
Shrewd was that snatch from out the corner South
He graced his carrion with, God curse the same!
Yet still my niche is not so cramped but thence   20
One sees the pulpit o' the epistle-side,[3]
And somewhat of the choir, those silent seats,
And up into the aery dome where live

[1]*Nephews:* a pious fiction since they were his illegitimate children
[2]*Gandolf:* the Bishop's hated predecessor and rival in love
[3]*epistle-side:* right side of the altar

The angels, and a sunbeam's sure to lurk:
And I shall fill my slab of basalt° there,   dark marble   25
And 'neath my tabernacle° take my rest,   canopy
With those nine columns round me, two and two,
The odd one at my feet where Anselm stands:
Peach-blossom marble all, the rare, the ripe
As fresh-poured red wine of a mighty pulse.   30
— Old Gandolf with his paltry onion-stone,°   streaked marble
Put me where I may look at him! True peach,
Rosy and flawless: how I earned the prize!
Draw close: that conflagration of my church
— What then? So much was saved if aught were missed!   35
My sons, ye would not be my death? Go dig
The white-grape vineyard where the oil-press stood,
Drop water gently till the surface sink,
And if ye find . . . Ah God, I know not, I! . . .
Bedded in store of rotten fig-leaves soft,   40
And corded up in a tight olive-frail,°   basket
Some lump, ah God, of *lapis lazuli,*°   semiprecious stone
Big as a Jew's head cut off at the nape,
Blue as a vein o'er the Madonna's breast . . .
Sons, all have I bequeathed you, villas, all,   45
That brave Frascati[4] villa with its bath,
So, let the blue lump poise between my knees,
Like God the Father's glove on both his hands
Ye worship in the Jesu Church[5] so gay,
For Gandolf shall not chose but see and burst!   50
Swift as a weaver's shuttle fleet our years:
Man goeth to the grave, and where is he?
Did I say basalt for my slab, sons? Black—
'Twas ever antique-black I meant! How else
Shall ye contrast my frieze to come beneath?   55
The bas-relief in bronze ye promised me,
Those Pans and Nymphs ye wot° of, and perchance   know

[4]*Frascati:* a fashionable district near Rome
[5]*Jesu Church:* the Church of the Jesuits in Rome

Some tripod,[6] thyrsus,[7] with a vase or so,
The Saviour at his sermon on the mount,
Saint Praxed in a glory, and one Pan   60
Ready to twitch the Nymph's last garment off,
And Moses with the tables[8] . . . but I know
Ye mark me not! What do they whisper thee,
Child of my bowels, Anselm? Ah, ye hope
To revel down my villas while I gasp   65
Bricked o'er with beggar's mouldy travertine°   marble
Which Gandolf from his tomb-top chuckles at!
Nay, boys, ye love me—all of jasper,° then!   quartz
'Tis jasper ye stand pledged to, lest I grieve
My bath must needs be left behind, alas!   70
One block, pure green as a pistachio-nut,
There's plenty jasper somewhere in the world—
And have I not Saint Praxed's ear to pray
Horses for ye, and brown Greek manuscripts,
And mistresses with great smooth marbly limbs?   75
—That's if ye carve my epitaph aright,
Choice Latin, picked phrase, Tully's every word,
No gaudy ware like Gandolf's second line—
Tully, my masters? Ulpian serves his need![9]
And then how I shall lie through centuries,   80
And hear the blessed mutter of the mass,
And see God made and eaten all day long,
And feel the steady candle-flame, and taste
Good strong thick stupefying incense-smoke!
For as I lie here, hours of the dead night,   85
Dying in state and by such slow degrees,
I fold my arms as if they clasped a crook,°   bishop's staff

[6]*tripod:* the priestess of Apollo at Delphi sat on a tripod
[7]*thyrsus:* staff surmounted by leaves with grapes or berries carried by
worshipers of Dionysus
[8]*The bas-relief . . . the tables:* the mingling of Christian and pagan symbolism; characteristic of the Renaissance, intended to show the Bishop's
lack of respect for sacred things
[9]*Choice Latin . . . his need!* Tully is Cicero, whom the Bishop takes as
setting the standard. He regards Ulpian inferior.

And stretch by feet forth straight as stone can point,
And let the bedclothes, for a mortcloth,° drop   shroud
Into great laps and folds of sculptor's-work: 90
And as yon tapers dwindle, and strange thoughts
Grow, with a certain humming in my ears,
About the life before I lived this life,
And this life too, popes, cardinals and priests,
Saint Praxed at his sermon on the mount,[10]   95
Your tall pale mother with her talking eyes,
And new-found agate urns as fresh as day,
And marble's language, Latin pure, discreet,
—Aha, *elucescebat*[11] quoth our friend?
No Tully, said I, Ulpian at the best!   100
Evil and brief hath been my pilgrimage.
All *lapis*, all sons! Else I give the Pope
My villas! Will ye ever eat my heart?
Ever your eyes were as a lizard's quick,
They glitter like your mother's for my soul,   105
Or ye would heighten my impoverished frieze,
Piece out its starved design, and fill my vase
With grapes, and add a vizor and a term,°   bust
And to the tripod ye would tie a lynx
That in his struggle throws the thyrsus down,   110
To comfort me on my entablature
Whereon I am to lie till I must ask
"Do I live, am I dead?" There, leave me, there!
For ye have stabbed me with ingratitude
To death—ye wish it—God, ye wish it! Stone—   115
Gritstone,° a-crumble! Clammy squares which sweat   sand-stone
As if the corpse they keep were oozing through—
And no more *lapis* to delight the world!
Well, go! I bless ye. Fewer tapers there,

[10]*Saint Praxed . . . mount:* Saint Praxed (Prassede) was a female saint of first-century Rome. This is one of several indications that the Bishop's mind is wandering.
[11]*elucescebat:* it became manifest. The Bishop prefers the pure classical form, *elucebat*.

But in a row: and, going, turn your backs   120
—Ay, like departing altar-ministrants,
And leave me in my church, the church for peace,
That I may watch at leisure if he leers—
Old Gandolf—at me, from his onion-stone,
As still he envied me, so fair she was!   125

1. What kind of person is the bishop? From what he reveals about
   himself, would you say he is a learned man? Is he artistically
   sensitive? Point out the dominant traits of his character, good and
   bad. In what does he take delight?
2. The bishop gives several reasons for hating Old Gandolf. What
   are they? How does he propose to get even with Gandolf?
3. Describe the tomb the bishop insists on having. What causes
   him to choose certain materials? Why does he change his mind
   several times? What is interesting about the bronze bas-relief
   he would like? Do you think Browning is being satirical, or is
   he giving an accurate description of Renaissance art? What does
   the bishop want to have done with the *lapis lazuli?* What does he
   reveal about himself by the directions he gives for obtaining it?
4. From the way the bishop speaks to his "sons," do you think he
   trusts them? What will they gain if they carry out his wishes?
   What will be the consequences if they disobey?
5. From the rewards promised the "sons," what impression do you
   gain of them? What is their attitude toward the bishop? Can you
   see any reason for the bishop to tell them of his faults?
6. What is the bishop's attitude toward death? How does Browning
   indicate that the bishop's mind wanders? During the "hours of
   the dead night," what does he imagine? What strange thoughts
   haunt him? Are they consistent with the kind of person he reveals himself to be throughout the poem? Explain.
7. A deathbed scene in itself has dramatic possibilities. The one
   pictured in this monologue involves a bishop whose immorality
   is matched only by his love of the beautiful. The setting, fifteenth-
   century Italy, provides Browning with a wealth of pictorial details. Most of the poem is devoted to the bishop's instructions regarding his tomb. Tell why you think that Browning was, or was
   not, more concerned with it than with portraying the character
   of the bishop.

Elizabeth Barrett Browning

More widely read as a poet than her husband when they were married, Elizabeth Barrett Browning is best known today for her sonnet sequence, *Sonnets from the Portuguese*, and her strong social protest poems, such as "The Cry of the Children." In *Sonnets from the Portuguese* — so called because Robert Browning playfully referred to her as his "little Portuguese" — Mrs. Browning expresses her love for her husband.

How Do I Love Thee?

How do I love thee? Let me count the ways.
I love thee to the depth and breadth and height
My soul can reach, when feeling out of sight
For the ends of Being and Ideal Grace.
I love thee to the level of everyday's   5
Most quiet need, by sun and candlelight.
I love thee freely, as men strive for Right;
I love thee purely, as they turn from Praise.
I love thee with the passion put to use
In my old griefs, and with my childhood's faith.   10

I love thee with a love I seemed to lose
With my lost saints,—I love thee with the breath,
Smiles, tears, of all my life!—and, if God choose,
I shall but love thee better after death.

1. This is the most famous of all the *Sonnets from the Portuguese.* What qualities make it a classic expression of love of woman for man?
2. Discuss the "ways." Do the individual expressions of love encompass the whole of life? Discuss the imagery which develops each way.
3. The resonance of this poem is created by the use of open vowels. How do the sounds in "depth, and breadth and height" echo the meaning? How does the simplicity of diction help the poem to achieve the depth of feeling that it has?
4. This poem utilizes one of the most effective rhetorical devices: repetition. Point out examples of repetition of phrases and syntax. Do you feel the poem would be more effective at any point with less repetition?

IF THOU MUST LOVE ME,
LET IT BE FOR NAUGHT

If thou must love me, let it be for naught
Except for love's sake only. Do not say
"I love her for her smile—her look—her way
Of speaking gently—for a trick of thought
That falls in well with mine, and certes° brought   in truth 5
A sense of pleasant ease on such a day"—
For these things in themselves, Belovèd, may
Be changed, or change for thee—and love, so wrought,
May be unwrought so. Neither love me for
Thine own dear pity's wiping my cheeks dry: 10

A creature might forget to weep, who bore
Thy comfort long, and lose thy love thereby!
But love me for love's sake, that evermore
Thou mayst love on, through love's eternity.

1. Why does the poet request that she be loved only for love's sake? Why would any other reasons for love be unsatisfactory? What examples does she cite?
2. What does the poet imply about human frailty when she says that things in themselves "may be changed, or change for thee"? How do you interpret lines 11 and 12?
3. What is the effect of the many run-on lines? Compare the rhyme scheme with that of the preceding sonnet. How does the scheme resemble that of the Petrarchan or Italian sonnet? Is this resemblance also reflected in the way the idea or theme is developed? Explain. What is the idea or theme?
4. How many times is the word *love* used in one sense or another? As a rule, so much repetition becomes monotonous. Tell why you think it does not become so in this sonnet.

Matthew Arnold

Matthew Arnold wrote most of his poetry early in his career before he turned to prose to become one of the most influential critics of literature and life. His poetry, unlike Robert Browning's, expresses doubt and disillusion, a melancholy questioning of the Victorian Age, and an unremitting sense of isolation. Arnold saw poetry as a "criticism of life," and so his verse is serious, clear in thought, and meditative. Despite the underlying sadness and pessimism, however, his poetry has beauty, power, and technical skill.

SELF-DEPENDENCE

Weary of myself, and sick of asking
What I am, and what I ought to be,
At this vessel's prow I stand, which bears me
Forwards, forwards, o'er the starlit sea.

And a look of passionate desire   5
O'er the sea and to the stars I send:
"Ye who from my childhood up have calmed me,
Calm me, ah, compose me to the end!

"Ah, once more," I cried, "ye stars, ye waters,
On my heart your mighty charm renew;   10
Still, still let me, as I gaze upon you,
Feel my soul becoming vast like you!"

From the intense, clear, star-sown vault of heaven,
Over the lit sea's unquiet way,
In the rustling night-air came the answer: 15
"Wouldst thou *be* as these are? *Live* as they.

"Unaffrighted by the silence round them,
Undistracted by the sights they see,
These demand not that the things without° them   outside
Yield them love, amusement, sympathy.   20

"And with joy the stars perform their shining,
And the sea its long moon-silvered roll;
For self-poised they live, nor pine with noting
All the fever of some differing soul.

"Bounded by themselves, and unregardful   25
In what state God's other works may be,
In their own tasks all their powers pouring,
These attain the mighty life you see."

O air-born voice! long since, severely clear,
A cry like thine in mine own heart I hear: 30
"Resolve to be thyself; and know that he
Who finds himself loses his misery!"

1. What request does the poet make of the stars and the sea? From
   what does he seek release? What effect does he hope their "mighty
   charm" will have on him?
2. Line 16 is explained by stanzas 5-8. In what spirit do the stars

shine and the sea roll? Why are they able to "attain the mighty life" the poet envies? What "lesson" can he learn from them? How do these stanzas suggest one may achieve calm?

3. Explain the last two lines. What beneficent effect can result from gaining self-dependence?

4. Explain the full significance of line 17. Why might silence be frightening and hinder self-dependence? What do lines 19 and 20 say about one's ability to find love, amusement, or sympathy without making a contribution oneself?

5. What is the mood of the poet at the beginning of the poem? What is his mood in the last stanza? What do you think Arnold's purpose might have been in writing this poem?

To Marguerite

Yes! in the sea of life enisled,
With echoing straits between us thrown,
Dotting the shoreless watery wild,
We mortal millions live *alone*.
The islands feel the enclasping flow,   5
And then their endless bounds they know.

But when the moon their hollows lights,
And they are swept by balms of spring,
And in their glens, on starry nights,
The nightingales divinely sing;   10
And lovely notes, from shore to shore,
Across the sounds and channels pour—

Oh! then a longing like despair
Is to their farthest caverns sent;
For surely once, they feel, we were   15
Parts of a single continent!
Now round us spreads the watery plain—
Oh, might our marges meet again!

Who ordered, that their longing's fire
Should be, as soon as kindled, cooled?   20
Who renders vain their deep desire?
A god, a god their severance ruled!
And bade betwixt their shores to be
The unplumbed, salt, estranging sea.

1. Paraphrase in your own words the first four lines. What does the sea represent? To what does Arnold compare men? What do the straits symbolize? What statement about life does Arnold make in his first sentence?
2. What do the "bounds" of the islands represent (line 6)? Why does the "enclasping flow" make the islands figuratively and literally aware of their bounds? Why are the bounds endless?
3. Arnold's poems often include several moods, as this poem does. Describe the mood of each stanza. Where does the mood change? What purpose is served by each change of mood? What is the mood at the end of the poem? Do these changes of mood prevent the poem from seeming unified? If not, what unites it?
4. What desire is expressed in the third stanza? How does the imagery help communicate this desire?
5. What does Arnold mean in stanza 4 by "a god"? Why didn't he capitalize *god*? What kind of god did he imagine?
6. Why do you think Arnold entitled his poem as he did? What might the nightingales represent in the second stanza? What is he trying to tell Marguerite through this poem?

THE BURIED LIFE

Light flows our war of mocking words, and yet,
Behold, with tears mine eyes are wet!
I feel a nameless sadness o'er me roll.
Yes, yes, we know that we can jest,
We know, we know that we can smile!   5

But there's a something in this breast,
To which thy light words bring no rest,
And thy gay smiles no anodyne.°   relief from pain
Give me thy hand, and hush awhile,
And turn those limpid eyes on mine,   10
And let me read there, love! thy inmost soul.
Alas! is even love too weak
To unlock the heart, and let it speak?
Are even lovers powerless to reveal
To one another what indeed they feel?   15
I knew the mass of men concealed
Their thoughts, for fear that if revealed
They would by other men be met
With blank indifference, or with blame reproved;
I knew they lived and moved   20
Tricked in disguises, alien to the rest
Of men, and alien to themselves—and yet
The same heart beats in every human breast!

But we, my love!—doth a like spell benumb
Our hearts, our voices?—must we too be dumb?   25
Ah! well for us, if even we,
Even for a moment, can get free
Our heart, and have our lips unchained;
For that which seals them hath been deep-ordained!
Fate, which foresaw   30
How frivolous a baby man would be—
By what distractions he would be possessed,
How he would pour himself in every strife,
And well-nigh change his own identity—
That it might keep from his capricious play   35
His genuine self, and force him to obey
Even in his own despite his being's law,
Bade through the deep recesses of our breast
The unregarded river of our life

Pursue with indiscernible flow its way;   40
And that we should not see
The buried stream, and seem to be
Eddying at large in blind uncertainty,
Though driving on with it eternally.

But often, in the world's most crowded streets,   45
But often, in the din of strife,
There rises an unspeakable desire
After the knowledge of our buried life;
A thirst to spend our fire and restless force
In tracking out our true, original course;   50
A longing to inquire
Into the mystery of this heart that beats
So wild, so deep in us—to know
Whence our lives come and where they go.
And many a man in his own breast then delves,   55
But deep enough, alas! none ever mines.
And we have been on many thousand lines,
And we have shown, on each, spirit and power;
But hardly have we, for one little hour,
Been on our own line, have we been ourselves—   60
Hardly had skill to utter one of all
The nameless feelings that course through our breast,
But they course on for ever unexpressed.
And long we try in vain to speak and act
Our hidden self, and what we say and do   65
Is eloquent, is well—but 'tis not true!
And then we will no more be racked
With inward striving, and demand
Of all the thousand nothings of the hour
Their stupefying power;   70
Ah yes, and they benumb us at our call!
Yet still, from time to time, vague and forlorn,
From the soul's subterranean depth upborne
As from an infinitely distant land,

Come airs, and floating echoes, and convey   75
A melancholy into all our day.

Only—but this is rare—
When a beloved hand is laid in ours,
When, jaded with the rush and glare
Of the interminable hours,   80
Our eyes can in another's eyes read clear,
When our world-deafened ear
Is by the tones of a loved voice caressed—
A bolt is shot back somewhere in our breast,
And a lost pulse of feeling stirs again;   85
The eye sinks inward, and the heart lies plain,
And what we mean, we say, and what we would, we know.
A man becomes aware of his life's flow,
And hears its winding murmur; and he sees
The meadows where it glides, the sun, the breeze.   90

And there arrives a lull in the hot race
Wherein he doth for ever chase
That flying and elusive shadow, rest.
An air of coolness plays upon his face,
And an unwonted calm pervades his breast.   95
And then he thinks he knows
The hills where his life rose,
And the sea where it goes.

1. In the third line of "The Buried Life," Arnold states that he feels "a nameless sadness." He spends the rest of the poem trying to trace the source of that feeling. What causes the sadness?
2. In your own words, explain Arnold's analysis of the human predicament. What dilemma is acknowledged in lines 12-23? What relationship do members of society have with each other? What are the purposes and limitations of speech? To what extent does man's will control his activities? What does Arnold mean by "true, original course" in line 50?

3. What hope does the speaker express in lines 24-29? At what point in the poem does he return to this hope?
4. To what does the title of this poem refer? What image in lines 30-44 represents the title's meaning? What contrast does Arnold suggest in these lines?
5. Discuss the water images of this poem, and how Arnold develops, combines, and uses them. What analogy or figure of speech in the last line of the poem makes the river image of line 39 especially appropriate?
6. This poem is not one which explores a single, strong feeling. Rather, the poem is dynamic and moves and changes as the speaker's mind moves from thought to thought. Can you see the specific stages in which the poet argues with himself, or tries to get at his problem from different directions? How many such divisions are in the poem? Where are they? Does the poet ever discover a permanently reliable resolution to his conflicts?

DOVER BEACH

The sea is calm tonight,
The tide is full, the moon lies fair
Upon the straits;—on the French coast the light
Gleams and is gone; the cliffs of England stand,
Glimmering and vast, out in the tranquil bay.   5
Come to the window, sweet is the night-air!
Only, from the long line of spray
Where the sea meets the moon-blanched land,
Listen! you hear the grating roar
Of pebbles which the waves draw back, and fling,   10
At their return, up the high strand,
Begin, and cease, and then again begin,
With tremulous cadence slow, and bring
The eternal note of sadness in.

Sophocles[1] long ago   15
Heard it on the Aegean,[2] and it brought
Into his mind the turbid° ebb and flow   clouded
Of human misery;we
Find also in the sound a thought,
Hearing it by this distant northern sea.   20

The Sea of Faith
Was once, too, at the full, and round earth's shore
Lay like the folds of a bright girdle furled.
But now I only hear
Its melancholy, long, withdrawing roar,   25
Retreating, to the breath
Of the night-wind, down the vast edges drear
And naked shingles° of the world.   pebbled shores

Ah, love, let us be true
To one another! for the world, which seems   30
To lie before us like a land of dreams,
So various, so beautiful, so new,
Hath really neither joy, nor love, nor light,
Nor certitude, nor peace, nor help for pain;
And we are here as on a darkling plain   35
Swept with confused alarms of struggle and flight,
Where ignorant armies clash by night.

[1]*Sophocles:* a Greek writer of tragedies in the fifth century B.C.
[2]*Aegean:* the sea between Greece and Asia Minor

1. Why does the poet seek reassurance in a love that is true? How is the real word unlike "the land of dreams" which seems "to lie before us"? What do "ignorant armies" and "night" symbolize?
2. What does the scene portrayed in lines 1-6 reveal about the mood of the poet? How does the mood change beginning with the word *Only* in line 7?
3. To what does *it* refer in line 16? What did *it* bring to the mind of

Sophocles? What comparison does the poet draw between "we"
and Sophocles?

4. In stanza 3, Arnold moves from the real sea to the metaphorical
"Sea of Faith." Point out the ways in which he develops the metaphor to express his thought and attitude. Note the force of the
images and of such words as *withdrawing* and *retreating*. What is
the mood of this stanza?

5. Each of the first three stanzas has been concerned with the sea,
literally or figuratively. In stanza 4 the focus is entirely on the
land, specifically on the "darkling plain." How do you interpret
the two similes, "like a land of dreams" and "as on a darkling
plain"? What meaning and emotion do you think Arnold intended them to convey? Describe the mood of this stanza.

6. How does this poem illustrate Arnold's stoical acceptance of life?
Does it reveal a desire to withdraw from the world, a need for
active participation, or some of both? Explain.

7. The sound of the lines, as well as the choice and arrangement of
the words, is especially appropriate to the thought or impressions
conveyed. Which lines suggest moving water? What is the effect
of the two series introduced by *so* and *nor* in lines 32-34?

8. Study the meter, rhythm, and rhyme of this poem. How many
kinds of irregularity do you find? Would the poem be more effective if Arnold had followed set patterns? Explain.

Algernon Charles Swinburne

Swinburne's poetry does not lack ideas, but it is sometimes hard to find the idea in the rush of melodious words. The heavy alliteration and swaying rhythms enhance the sensuousness of his verse. While his frank interest in hitherto forbidden subjects made Swinburne the *enfant terrible* of Victorian poetry, he was perhaps the one most sensitive to intricate sound patterns of the later Victorian poets.

WHEN THE HOUNDS OF SPRING

Atalanta in Calydon is a drama in the classical Greek form based on the ancient legend of the Calydonian boar hunt. Swinburne said he hoped "to do something original in English which might in some degree reproduce for English readers the likeness of a Greek tragedy with something of its true poetic life and charm." This is the most famous of the many musical lyrics from Swinburne's drama.

When the hounds of spring are on winter's traces,
    The mother of months[1] in meadow or plain
Fills the shadows and windy places
    With lisp of leaves and ripple of rain;

[1]*mother of months:* Artemis (Diana), goddess of the moon and of the hunt

And the brown bright nightingale amorous   5
Is half assuaged° for Itylus,[2]   appeased
For the Thracian ships and the foreign faces,
    The tongueless vigil, and all the pain.

Come with bows bent and with emptying of quivers,
    Maiden most perfect, lady of light,   10
With a noise of winds and many rivers,
    With a clamor of waters, and with might;
Bind on thy sandals, O thou most fleet,
Over the splendor and speed of thy feet;
For the faint east quickens, the wan west shivers,   15
    Round the feet of the day and the feet of the night.

Where shall we find her, how shall we sing to her,
    Fold our hands round her knees, and cling?
Oh, that man's heart were as fire and could spring to her,
    Fire, or the strength of the streams that spring!   20
For the stars and the winds are unto her
As raiment,° as songs of the harp-player;   clothing
For the risen stars and the˘ fallen cling to her,
    And the southwest-wind and the west-wind sing.

For winter's rains and ruins are over,   25
    And all the season of snows and sins;
The days dividing lover and lover,
    The light that loses, the night that wins;
And time remembered is grief forgotten,
And frosts are slain and flowers begotten,   30
And in green underwood and cover
    Blossom by blossom the spring begins.

---

[2]*Itylus:* son of Procne and Tereus, king of Thrace. Tiring of his wife, Tereus cut out her tongue to insure her silence. Then, pretending she was dead,
he married her sister Philomela. In revenge, the sister killed Tereus' son
Itylus. When Tereus sought the women to punish them, the gods turned him
into a hawk, Procne into a swallow, and Philomela into a nightingale. The
nightingale is traditionally associated with romantic love.

The full streams feed on flower of rushes,
    Ripe grasses trammel° a traveling foot,   hamper
The faint fresh flame of the young year flushes   35
    From leaf to flower and flower to fruit;
And fruit and leaf are as gold and fire,
And the oat° is heard above the lyre,   shepherd's pipe
And the hoofèd heel of a satyr³ crushes
    The chestnut-husk at the chestnut-root.   40

And Pan⁴ by noon and Bacchus⁵ by night,
    Fleeter of foot than the fleet-foot kid,
Follows with dancing and fills with delight
    The Maenad and the Bassarid;⁶
And soft as lips that laugh and hide   45
The laughing leaves of the trees divide,
And screen from seeing and leave in sight
    The god pursuing, the maiden hid.

The ivy falls with the Bacchanal's hair
    Over her eyebrows hiding her eyes;   50
The wild vine slipping down leaves bare
    Her bright breast shortening into sighs;
The wild vine slips with the weight of its leaves,
But the berried ivy catches and cleaves
To the limbs that glitter, the feet that scare   55
    The wolf that follows, the fawn that flies.

³*satyr:* demigod, half man and half goat
⁴*Pan:* god of woods and fields
⁵*Bacchus:* god of wine
⁶*The Maenad and the Bassarid:* female devotees of Bacchus

1. In Greek mythology, the gods were identified with nearly every aspect of life, including the changes in the seasons. When it was time for spring, Artemis, goddess of the moon and the hunt, would send her hounds to drive winter away. This myth captured Swinburne's imagination because it conveyed the restless movement

and aggression supposedly energized by the coming of spring. How does Swinburne convey these feelings in the first two stanzas? What sensory details in stanza 1 suggest the coming of spring?

2. To whom is stanza 2 addressed? What details of dress and movement make clear her identity? What connection do you see between her role as goddess of the moon and the images in lines 15 and 16 and in lines 21-24?

3. What scene is described in lines 25-28? Comment on the meaning of lines 29 and 30. What images in lines 33-40 picture the lush beauty of spring?

4. The last two stanzas portray the celebration associated with the season, at which Pan and Bacchus led the revelry. What images in these stanzas capture the pagan nature of the celebration?

5. Do you see any resemblance between the first and last lines of this poem? What impression do the last three lines leave with the reader?

6. What is the predominant rhythm? What effects are gained through rhythm?

7. Discuss the effect created by the insistent alliteration. Do you consider the alliteration to be an ornament or an integral part of the poem? What other musical devices do you find besides alliteration? Do you agree with Tennyson that Swinburne was "a reed through which all things blow into music"?

BRIDGING THE CENTURIES

Modern English poetry had its beginning in the last decades of the nineteenth century when the creative impulse which had inspired such great poetry during the Romantic period was no longer an energizing force. Some of the late Victorian poets withdrew into a dream world of their own fashioning; others, like Browning, recognized the discrepancy between the real world and the ideal but found salvation in faith founded on personal, spiritual experience. All were skilled craftsmen, and their poetry was highly poetic, often in an exquisite and decorative way. It delighted the cultured readers of the day, but much of it lacked both originality and vigor.

What England needed was poets who had the strength and courage to cut themselves free from Victorian conventions and techniques, to concern themselves with the divided aims of a confused and artistically indifferent world, and to find a stronger language in which to convey man's capacity for experience and his unique response to it.

Four poets met this need: Thomas Hardy, A. E. Housman, William Butler Yeats, and Gerard Manley Hopkins. Working boldly and independently of one another, each developed his own themes and expressed them in poetry that was highly individualistic. In certain respects, however, they were alike.

All sought some sustaining equivalent for the old ideas of the great Victorian time, which had gradually disintegrated. All rejected the decadent aestheticism of "art for art's sake." Instead, they chose to record experience sharply and exactly, capturing as best they could the particular quality of a scene or the vitality of an experience or emotion.

In his own way, each of these poets was an innovator—Hopkins the most daring of them all. As a group, they indicated and influenced the direction that the poetry of the next century was to take. Hardy, Housman, and Yeats made skillful and original use of established poetic forms and techniques. When these did not serve their purpose, they created their own. All four poets helped to forge a new poetic language, often creating effects of remarkable intensity and beauty and giving new meaning to subjects which many of their Victorian predecessors—and contemporaries—would have considered unpoetic.

GERARD MANLEY HOPKINS, the most modern poet writing in the last decades of the nineteenth century, died before Hardy and Housman had published their first volumes of verse. Hopkins' poems, however, did not reach the public until 1918, when his friend Robert Bridges, the Poet Laureate, published them in a single volume. Since then, they have been a major force in shaping modern poetry.

Writing verse was never easy for Hopkins; rather, it was a continually changing struggle with new material. Hopkins was a delighted observer of natural beauty who chose to become an ascetic Jesuit. The tension between his inclinations and his will is the source of the deeply personal poetry he wrote.

To express such heightened feelings, Hopkins went far beyond the experimentation of the nineteenth century or any preceding century, particularly in the handling of rhythm and language. He made use, for example, of poetic techniques he discovered in medieval and Anglo-Saxon poetry, such as alliteration, word combinations like the old kennings, and what he called "sprung rhythm": four or five stressed syllables to a line, with an indefinite number of unstressed syllables. He also made use of internal rhyme and assonance, and metaphor piled upon metaphor.

"Poetical language," Hopkins wrote in a letter to Bridges,

"should be the current language heightened, to any degree heightened and unlike itself, but not . . . an obsolete one." There is no poetry of religious enthusiasm in the English language which has more daring and skill than the poetry of Hopkins.

THOMAS HARDY was an established, though somewhat controversial, novelist before he turned to the writing of poetry as a literary career. During the last thirty years of his life, he produced seven volumes of poetry and the stupendous "epic drama" *The Dynasts.* In his poems, as in his novels, the true genius of Hardy is revealed when his subject is the Wessex country and its people, which were his very breath and blood. Here, too, he conveyed the impression that human life is controlled by an aimless and impersonal Destiny before which men are pitiably helpless. Yet the world Hardy pictured is one in which beauty is possible, too, though it exists in the midst of chaos and pain.

Hardy's style, at its best, is cold and exact, rather than graceful. Partly, his style may result from his being well along in life when he began writing poetry. Partly he seemed bitter because man must learn to endure life, only to be rewarded with death. There were moments, however, in which he found and expressed the delights of being alive and of finding earthly beauty. Then the meter of the lines has the melodious flow of a song.

A. E. HOUSMAN bears little resemblance to Hardy in style or philosophy. When *A Shropshire Lad* was published in 1896, it was enormously influential because of its clean, spare, understated lines. Housman saw the world as a place in which human beings struggled with cruel fate, met death on a scaffold, or died fighting in causeless, futile wars. It is little wonder, therefore, that "the prevailing wind that blows through Housman's verse is a chilly one; irony, skepticism, and resignation are the climates it brings. Yet he is a fine poet with his neatly ruled margins and his terse epigrammatic style. His poems always carry tension and power; while the last two lines of each are usually reserved for an irony which comes like a spray of cold water."[1] Because Housman was completely

[1]Lawrence Durrell, *A Key to Modern British Poetry* (Norman, Oklahoma: University of Oklahoma Press, 1952), p. 111.

without hope, he cultivated in himself a stoic serenity. It is this emotion, melodiously phrased, which his poetry conveys.

WILLIAM BUTLER YEATS produced his finest poetry during the last twenty years of his life—poetry in which the primary quality was a wisdom that came from his sense of nobility and his sense of reverence. T. S. Eliot considered him the greatest poet of the modern world—"certainly the greatest in this language, and as far as I am able to judge, in any language."

Yeats's early poetry has its own special beauty, but it is lush, romantic, and thoroughly a product of nineteenth century influences. Then in 1896, Yeats met the Irish playwright, Lady Gregory; this meeting probably provided the turning point in his life. He became actively involved in the Abbey Theater and, even more so, in the Irish literary movement. During this middle period in his life, he developed an enduring interest in Irish legends, fairy tales, and the supernatural. His brief involvement in politics during Ireland's struggle for independence was somewhat disillusioning, but it helped him to judge life more realistically and made him realize where his real strength lay. His early poems had moved English and Irish readers alike with their wild tenderness. His late poems were just as passionate and imaginative, but they had greater force. In place of his former gentleness was now a pointed and frank irony. The romantic lyricism was replaced by a masculine truthfulness. His imagination was now rooted in the common facts of the world, and was disciplined by a more analytic assessment of life's possibilities.

In his last years, Yeats read modern poets and eagerly attempted to understand what they were trying to express. He then managed, with almost unparalleled success, to incorporate into his poetry what he had learned through his years of experimentation and thought. Beneath the apparent simplicity of statement of his last poems resides a rich complexity of suggestions, as well as an intensity of feeling. Perhaps no poet more successfully combines appeals to both head and heart. Great poetry, Yeats insisted, needed great subjects, but its true function was "to evoke joy and minister to the emotions."

Gerard Manley Hopkins

Gerard Manley Hopkins' metrics and vocabulary were not mere invention. He chose and perfected them because in no other way could he best say what he had to say. Like Shakespeare, he forced language into his own mold, making words do service as new parts of speech, and ruthlessly omitting "unnecessary" words, usually definite and indefinite articles and relative pronouns. Hopkins himself was aware that his poetry made unusual demands on the reader and offered this advice: "take breath and read it with the ears, as I always wish to be read, and my verse becomes all right."

SPRING

Nothing is so beautiful as spring—
    When weeds, in wheels, shoot long and lovely and lush;
    Thrush's eggs look little low heavens, and thrush
Through the echoing timber does so rinse and wring
The ear, it strikes like lightnings to hear him sing;   5
    The glassy peartree leaves and blooms, they brush
    The descending blue; that blue is all in a rush
With richness; the racing lambs too have fair their fling.
    What is all this juice and all this joy?

A strain of the earth's sweet being in the beginning   10
In Eden garden. — Have, get, before it cloy,°   weary
   Before it cloud, Christ, lord, and sour with sinning,
Innocent mind and Mayday in girl and boy,
   Most, O maid's child, thy choice and worthy the winning.

1. The word *joy* (line 9) is the key to the mood and purpose of this sonnet. Point out the sense impressions conveyed in the images, similes, and the personification (lines 4 and 5) in the octave (stanza 1). Which do you find especially effective? Explain why.
2. The sestet (stanza 2) answers the question asked in line 9. How do you interpret the figurative meaning of "all this juice"? What idea is brought out in the reference to "Eden garden" (lines 10 and 11)? What is "worthy the winning"? Is the winning possible to everyone? Note especially the references to "innocent mind," and "Mayday" (May is the Virgin Mary's month). How do you explain the urgency implied in "Have, get" (namely, share in the joy) in line 11?
3. Hopkins believed that God works through man and that man must work through God. How does this knowledge explain the invocation, "Christ, lord" in line 12? How is the invocation expressed in a different way in the final line? To whom does the word *thy* in the same line refer?
4. What theme do you think Hopkins intended to bring out in this sonnet? Point out how the theme is developed in the octave and sestet.
5. Which characteristics of Hopkins' very original handling of rhythm and language are evident in this poem? Point out examples.

GOD'S GRANDEUR

   The world is charged with the grandeur of God.
     It will flame out, like shining from shook foil;[1]
     It gathers to a greatness, like the ooze of oil

[1]*shook foil:* Hopkins wrote, "I mean foil in its sense of leaf or tinsel. . . . Shaken goldfoil gives off broad glares like sheet lightning. . . ."

Crushed.² Why do men then now not reck° his rod? ^take heed of

Generations have trod, have trod, have trod;   5

  And all is seared with trade; bleared, smeared with toil;

  And wears man's smudge and shares man's smell: the soil

Is bare now, nor can foot feel, being shod.

And for all this, nature is never spent;

  There lives the dearest freshness deep down things;   10

And though the last lights off the black West went

  Oh, morning, at the brown brink eastward, springs —

Because the Holy Ghost over the bent

  World broods with warm breast and with ah! bright wings.

²*oil crushed:* Under the great pressures of the earth, natural oil sometimes oozes upward toward the surface ground. Or, the lines may refer to olive oil crushed in an olive press.

1. What picture of the world is created in the first sentence, ending with the word *crushed* (line 4)? What do the similes in this sentence contribute to that picture? How are they related to the word *charged* in line 1?
2. What reason did Hopkins have for asking the question in line 4? What did he mean? What contrast is brought out in lines 5-8? How do you interpret the closing statement of the octave, "the soil is bare now, nor can foot feel, being shod"?
3. What "problem" or idea did Hopkins develop in stanza 1 (the octave)? What word or words describe the over-all mood?
4. State in your own words the conclusion you think that Hopkins intended to bring out in the sestet (stanza 2). How do you interpret the opening phrase of the sestet, "And for all this"? Why is nature "never spent"? What lines provide the explanation?
5. Lines 10-12 require a careful reading because of their grammatical structure and their compression. State in your own words your interpretation of them. Do you think Hopkins intended "the last lights off the black West" and "at the brown brink eastward" (lines 11-12) to have figurative or symbolic meanings? If so, what are they?
6. What image is created in lines 13 and 14? What is the effect of "ah!" before "bright wings"? How does this exclamation change or intensify the idea expressed in the image?

7. Identify the sonnet form by the rhyme scheme. Is the rhythm pattern the customary iambic pentameter or must you read the sonnet with the ears," letting the meaning and emphasis of each line determine the accent? Give evidence for your opinion by reading any group of rhymed lines.
8. This poem is less experimental in language and rhythm than many of Hopkins' poems. Point out evidences of those poetic techniques for which he is famous. What is unusual about lines 5-7? Select several lines which you consider especially effective and tell why.

PIED BEAUTY

Glory be to God for dappled things—
  For skies of couple-color as a brinded cow;
    For rose-moles all in stipple upon trout that swim;
Fresh-firecoal chestnut-falls; finches' wings;
    Landscape plotted and pieced—fold, fallow, and plow;   5
    And áll trádes, their gear and tackle and trim.

All things counter, original, spare, strange;
  Whatever is fickle, freckled (who knows how?)
    With swift, slow; sweet, sour; adazzle, dim;
He fathers-forth° whose beauty is past change: begets 10
               Praise him.

1. Both the first and last lines make clear that this is a poem of praise to God for the ever-changing delights of nature. What does He fathers-forth? Note the contrast brought out in line 10 between His beauty and the beauty of nature described earlier. What is meant by "past change"? How does beauty which is past change contrast with beauties previously mentioned? Why does the poem end with this emphasis on such a contrast?

2. This poem is a perfect example of Hopkins' close observation of, and excitement about, the natural world, in its most detailed and particularized forms." What are the "dappled things" in lines 2 and 3? Note the color images in line 4: the bursting of the green chestnut husk which exposes the red-brown nut, and the browns and yellows of the finches' wings. What is unusual about the grammatical structure of line 4?
3. Describe the variations in the landscape suggested in line 5. Why do the words *plotted* and *pieced* suggest a patchwork? (The word *fold* as used here refers to a pasture area, usually for sheep.) What colors are suggested by it and by the words *fallow* and *plow?*
4. What trades are suggested in line 6? Why does Hopkins mention trades in the same stanza with beauties of nature?
5. In lines 7-9, Hopkins seems to suggest things that are either unique or opposite. You may need to consult a dictionary to interpret these lines. Then discuss the meaning of the title and the appropriateness of the title.
6. Do you think Hopkins is suggesting that all these things are *signs* of God's power of invention? By their beauty, do they "praise him"? Is the final line addressed to them or to all men? Discuss.
7. Point out examples of alliteration and assonance.
8. What is the rhyme scheme? How does it link the two stanzas together? What is unusual about stanza 2 in length and rhyme?
9. Instead of trying to determine the rhythm by scanning it, read it aloud "with the ears," allowing four or five accented words or syllables to the line. (Note the two words marked for accent.) Hopkins intended his poetry to have the sound of speech and not the regular rhythm patterns of traditional verse. Do you think he was successful in achieving this goal? What effect does the rhythm have on the poem?

I WAKE AND FEEL THE FELL OF DARK

I wake and feel the fell of dark, not day.
What hours, O what black hours we have spent
This night! what sights you, heart, saw; ways you went!
And more must, in yet longer light's delay.

With witness° I speak this. But where I say   evidence 5
Hours I mean years, mean life. And my lament
Is cries countless, cries like dead letters sent
To dearest him that lives alas! away.

I am gall, I am heartburn. God's most deep decree
Bitter would have me taste: my taste was me;   10
Bones built in me, flesh filled, blood brimmed the curse.
Selfyeast of spirit a dull dough sours. I see
The lost are like this, and their scourge to be
As I am mine, their sweating selves; but worse.

1. A poet aims to use words so rich and evocative that they can suggest several things at one time. No poet excels Hopkins in finding such rich phrases. How many different possibilities for example, can you find in the first line? One meaning of *fell* is *skin* or *pelt*. If this interpretation is accepted, what image of dark does the line create? How would waking and feeling the pelt of some animal affect you at night?

   Fell is also a noun meaning the act of cutting down a tree. Or *fell* can mean all the timber cut down in a season. If you choose either of these meanings, what does the line tell you about Hopkins' attitude toward night? Do you see other possible interpretations of the word and the line?

2. Who are the *we* of line 2? What exactly are *we* experiencing in the poem?

3. In the second quatrain, Hopkins expands *night* so that it becomes a metaphor for *all of life*. What statement about his life do these lines make?

4. Once you know that Hopkins was a priest, whom may you assume he means by "dearest him"? What does he mean by cries? Why is the comparison of cries to dead letters particularly effective here? Where were the letters sent?

5. After Adam disobeyed God and ate the fruit of the tree of knowledge, God cursed him: "Because thou has done this, thou art cursed above all cattle, and above every beast of the field. . . . In the sweat of thy face shalt thou eat bread, till thou return unto the ground." (Genesis 3:14, 19).

   When Hopkins says "my taste was me" he seems to refer to this curse, and perhaps to the taste of sweat. How does he elaborate his sense of being totally cursed in line 11?

6. Line 12 refers to a method of baking. To conserve yeast, one adds a bit of risen dough to unlevened dough, in which it acts as a yeast. Bread baked from such dough has a slightly sour taste. Hopkins uses the dough as a symbol for himself. What is he saying about his spiritual condition in line 13?

7. To whom does Hopkins compare himself in the last three lines? Why is he in better condition than they?

8. Read this poem aloud and listen to the music of the lines. Is it smooth or rough? serene or agitated? Do you think this is, or is not, an appropriate music for the poet's theme?

Thomas Hardy

No poet since Wordsworth had a more intimate knowledge of the English countryside than Thomas Hardy or a deeper feeling of compassion for all suffering things, "tongued or dumb." He loved Nature but, unlike Wordsworth, was not consoled by her, nor did he ever experience her "holy calm." If he was exceedingly unhappy, as many have claimed, he still considered his "obstinate questionings in the exploration of reality" as "the first step towards the soul's betterment and the body's also." It is these continual "obstinate questionings" which have won for Hardy a place among the modern poets, even though he lived the first sixty years of his life in the nineteenth century.

SHELLEY'S SKYLARK

Hardy wrote this poem in March, 1887, in the neighborhood of Leghorn, Italy, where Shelley had earlier written his ode "To a Skylark."

> Somewhere afield here something lies
> In Earth's oblivious eyeless trust
> That moved a poet to prophecies —
> A pinch of unseen, unguarded dust:

The dust of the lark that Shelley heard,   5
And made immortal through times to be;—
Though it only lived like another bird,
And knew not its immortality:

Lived its meek life; then, one day, fell—
A little ball of feather and bone;   10
And how it perished, when piped farewell,
And where it wastes, are alike unknown.

Maybe it rests in the loam I view,
Maybe it throbs in a myrtle's green,
Maybe it sleeps in the coming hue   15
Of a grape on the slopes of yon inland scene.

Go find it, faeries, go and find
That tiny pinch of priceless dust,
And bring a casket silver-lined,
And framed of gold that gems encrust;   20

And we will lay it safe therein,
And consecrate it to endless time;
For it inspired a bard to win
Ecstatic heights in thought and rhyme.

1. Why does Hardy search for the "dust of the lark"? How has this bird been "made immortal"? Can you find any evidence in the poem for the statement in lines 7 and 8? Is there a contradiction here? If so, what is it?
2. In stanza 2, Hardy uses both *immortal* and *immortality*. Does he intend to convey a similar or quite different meaning? Prove your answer by stating in your own words the ideas expressed in this stanza.
3. In stanzas 3 and 4, what does Hardy share with you? What do these lines reveal about his attitude toward the bird and toward its likely end?

4. What reason can you see for Hardy's calling on the faeries to help him? How and why does he think this small bird should be consecrated "to endless time"?
5. Hardy's poetry, as well as his prose, reflects his keen and almost mystical sense of all things in nature — including man — being inextricably linked together. What evidence of this "sense" can you find in this poem?

THE DARKLING THRUSH

I leant upon a coppice° gate   thicket
    When Frost was spectre-gray,
And Winter's dregs made desolate
    The weakening eye of day.
The tangled bine-stems° scored the sky   woodbine 5
    Like strings of broken lyres,
And all mankind that haunted nigh
    Had sought their household fires.

The land's sharp features seemed to be
    The Century's corpse[1] outleant,   10
His crypt° the cloudy canopy,   grave
    The wind his death-lament.
The ancient pulse° of germ and birth   seed
    Was shrunken hard and dry,
And every spirit upon earth   15
    Seemed fervorless° as I.   dejected

At once a voice arose among
    The bleak twigs overhead
In a full-hearted evensong
    Of joy illimited;°   unrestrained 20

[1]*Century's corpse:* the dead body of the nineteenth century. Hardy wrote this poem in 1900.

An aged thrush, frail, gaunt, and small,
  In blast-beruffled plume,
Had chosen thus to fling his soul
  Upon the growing gloom.

So little cause for carolings   25
  Of such ecstatic sound
Was written on terrestrial° things   earthly
  Afar or nigh around,
That I could think there trembled through
  His happy good-night air   30
Some blessed Hope, whereof he knew
  And I was unaware.

1. Why is the poet deeply grateful to the aged thrush for its "full-
   hearted" evensong? How is the impression it made on him in-
   tensified by his own mood and his surroundings?
2. What is the nature of the scene viewed from the coppice gate?
   What words and images help you picture the scene and share the
   poet's reaction to it?
3. Point out one personal and one general comparison in stanza 2
   and discuss what attitude they reveal toward life at that time and
   place.
4. What details does the author notice about the thrush? What is
   suggested by the phrase "blast-beruffled plume," in line 22? How
   do lines 21 and 22 relate to the desolate scene portrayed in
   stanza 1?
5. Hardy uses a number of words in the poem in an unusual way; for
   example, *darkling* in the title and *spectre-gray* in line 2. What do
   these words mean? Find other examples and discuss the effect
   they have on the meaning and the mood of the poem.
6. This poem is a good example of the double-quatrain stanza pattern. Chart the rhyme scheme and the rhythm pattern. Identify
   the predominant metrical foot. Where the poet has varied the
   rhythm, try to explain the reason for this variation.

In Time of
"The Breaking of Nations"[1]

Only a man harrowing° clods   plowing
  In a slow silent walk
With an old horse that stumbles and nods
  Half asleep as they stalk.

Only thin smoke without flame   5
  From the heaps of couch-grass;
Yet this will go onward the same
  Though Dynasties pass.

Yonder a maid and her wight°   man
  Come whispering by: 10
War's annals will fade into night
  Ere their story die.

[1]*"The Breaking of Nations"*: The phrase comes from Jeremiah 51:20; it refers here to World War I. Hardy wrote this poem in 1915.

1. What meaning does Hardy illustrate through the scene described in stanza 1? What is the mood of this stanza? What words create this mood?
2. How do lines 5 and 6 extend the idea implied in stanza 1? How do you explain the use of *only* as the first word in stanzas 1 and 2? To what does *this* refer in line 7? What is the relationship between lines 7 and 8 and the preceding lines?
3. Note the end punctuation (line 10) which indicates a link between the first two lines of stanza 3 and the last two. What are "war's annals" referred to in line 11? Is the word *night* used literally or figuratively? How do you interpret that line and the final one?
4. By means of several related images, a poet may suggest the theme of a poem—the particular truth or observation about life or people that he wants to bring out. What theme is expressed in this poem?
5. Note the regular rhyme scheme. Try to chart the rhythm pattern of at least the first stanza. Is it fairly regular or not? Discuss the

most interesting variations, such as the spondiac feet in line 2 and
the dactylic feet in lines 1, 5, and 9, and the effect of variations on
the total poem.

THE MAN HE KILLED

"Had he and I but met
By some old ancient inn,
We should have sat us down to wet°   drink
Right many a nipperkin!°   half pint of ale

"But ranged as infantry,   5
And staring face to face,
I shot at him as he at me,
And killed him in his place.

"I shot him dead because —
Because he was my foe,   10
Just so: my foe of course he was;
That's clear enough; although

"He thought he'd 'list,° perhaps,   enlist
Off-hand like — just as I —
Was out of work — had sold his traps° —belongings 15
No other reason why.

"Yes; quaint and curious war is!
You shoot a fellow down
You'd treat if met where any bar is,
Or help to half-a-crown."   20

1. Who do you think is the speaker in the poem? To what question
can he find no justifiable answer?

2. In what ways are he and his "foe" alike? What is so ironical about the situation they could not escape?
3. What truth do you think Hardy intended this poem to bring out? State this theme in your own words.
4. What meaning do you think was intended by line 17? The tone of the poem is as casual as everyday conversation. What is the mood?
5. Why is the quatrain an appropriate stanza form for this poem? Does the regularity of the rhythm and rhyme detract from the dramatic effect of the poem? Discuss.

A. E. Housman

A. E. Housman's poems have the clean, graceful lines of the Latin lyrics he spent his life studying. Often, in fact, he surpassed his models in creating telling effects with the simplest words, images, and meters. He presented his vignettes of death and loss in short, controlled stanzas which are frequently detached and wry in tone. The simplicity of his style throws into relief the bare contrast between the promise of youth and its continual betrayal. Housman charmed his readers, despite his pessimism, by his magic feeling for imagery and rhythm, his careful manipulation of rhyme, and his choice of the right concrete detail. In the most conventional poetic forms, he could achieve effects that delight with their unexpectedness.

REVEILLE

Wake: the silver dusk returning
    Up the beach of darkness brims,
And the ship of sunrise burning
    Strands upon the eastern rims.

Wake: the vaulted shadow shatters,   5
    Trampled to the floor it spanned,
And the tent of night in tatters
    Straws the sky-pavilioned land.

Up, lad, up, 'tis late for lying:
    Hear the drums of morning play;   10
Hark, the empty highways crying
    "Who'll beyond the hills away?"

Towns and countries woo together,
    Forelands beacon, belfries call;
Never lad that trod on leather   15
    Lived to feast his heart with all.

Up, lad: thews° that lie and cumber°   muscles;
                                          burden
    Sunlit pallets never thrive;
Morns abed and daylight slumber
    Were not meant for man alive.   20

Clay lies still, but blood's a rover;
    Breath's a ware that will not keep.
Up, lad: when the journey's over
    There'll be time enough to sleep.

1. What does the word *reveille* mean? Where in the poem does the
   poet use single words to emphasize this meaning?
2. This poem has been praised for its beautiful imagery. Point out
   the images in stanza 1. Why are they unusual? What is the "vaulted shadow" in line 5? What meaning is conveyed in each line of
   stanza 2?
3. What is the meaning of lines 10, 14, and 16? What picture of the
   morning, and of the poet's feelings about it, are conveyed in the
   first four stanzas?

4. In stanzas 5 and 6, why does the poet urge the "lad" to wake and enjoy the early morning? Discuss the meaning conveyed by the three metaphors in lines 21 and 22. Are the words *journey* and *sleep* to be interpreted literally or figuratively? What is their figurative meaning? What comment on life do these last two lines express?
5. In what ways do you think the rhythm and rhyme scheme contribute to the mood of the poem? Is the mood one of urgency, excitement, exhilaration, impatience? Find evidence in the poem to support your opinion.
6. What is the theme of "Reveille"? From what you know of Housman, what would have been his response to "reveille"?

TO AN ATHLETE DYING YOUNG

The time you won your town the race
We chaired you through the market-place;
Man and boy stood cheering by,
And home we brought you shoulder-high.

To-day, the road all runners come,   5
Shoulder-high we bring you home,
And set you at your threshold down,
Townsman of a stiller town.

Smart lad, to slip betimes° away   early
From fields where glory does not stay   10
And early though the laurel grows
It withers quicker than the rose.

Eyes the shady night has shut
Cannot see the record cut,°   broken
And silence sounds no worse than cheers   15
After earth has stopped the ears:

Now you will not swell the rout°   mob
Of lads that wore their honors out,
Runners whom renown outran
And the name died before the man.   20

So set, before its echoes fade,
The fleet foot on the sill of shade,°   death
And hold to the low lintel° up   doorway
The still-defended challenge-cup.

And round that early-laurelled° head   honored 25
Will flock to gaze the strengthless dead,
And find unwithered on its curls
The garland briefer than a girl's.

1. What is the meaning of "chaired" in line 2? Notice how the image
   is continued in stanza 2. What two events are contrasted here?
   Explain "townsman of a stiller town."
2. In line 9, is the speaker in the poem addressing the "smart lad"
   or speaking about him? Why is the lad "smart"? What opinion of
   earthly honors is expressed in lines 10-12 and 17-20? Tell why you
   do, or do not, hold the same view.
3. What meaning does the image of line 13 convey? Note the metaphor in line 14. What comparison is implied? Is the tone of lines
   15 and 16 sad or bitter? Give reasons for your answer,
4. In stanza 6, is the speaker still addressing the lad? State in your
   own words the speaker's message. How do you interpret line 24
   and the last stanza?
5. The title clearly suggests that the purpose of the poem is to express the speaker's thoughts and feelings about an athlete's untimely death. In your opinion, did the writer also have other
   purposes? What other implications do you find in the poem?
6. What rhythm pattern predominates in this poem? What rhythmic
   variations in stanzas 1 and 2 are required to emphasize the meaning and to give the words their natural stress? Identify other variations of metrical feet throughout the poem and explain their effect
   on the meaning and mood.
7. The rhymed couplet sometimes gives a poem a "sing-song" quality. Try to explain why, if you allow the meaning to guide you in
   the reading, you are not aware of this quality.

BE STILL, MY SOUL, BE STILL

Be still, my soul, be still: the arms you bear are brittle,
    Earth and high heaven are fixt of old and founded strong.
Think rather,—call to thought, if now you grieve a little,
    The days when we had rest, O soul, for they were long.

Men loved unkindness then, but lightless in the quarry   5
    I slept and saw not; tears fell down, I did not mourn;
Sweat ran and blood sprang out and I was never sorry:
    Then it was well with me, in days ere I was born.

Now, and I muse for why and never find the reason,
    I pace the earth, and drink the air, and feel the sun.   10
Be still, be still, my soul; it is but for a season:
    Let us endure an hour and see injustice done.

Ay, look: high heaven and earth ail from the prime
    foundation;
    All thoughts to rive° the heart are here, and all   rend
    are vain:
Horror and scorn and hate and fear and indignation—   15
    Oh why did I awake? When shall I sleep again?

1. What do you think the poet means by the opening two lines of
   this poem? When have the poet and his soul rested? Why does he
   say the days were long?
2. What were those days like "ere I was born" (line 8)? How does
   he react to them? Explain the figure of speech, "lightless in the
   quarry" (line 5), which he apparently means to account for his
   reactions.
3. What is it that the poet muses about but can "never find the reason"? Line 10 would suggest that his life is fairly tolerable, yet
   he concludes, "Let us endure an hour and see injustice done."
   Why?
4. Note that he returns, in stanza 4, to the idea expressed in line 2.
   What do you think he implys in this stanza? How do you interpret

his closing questions in which the words *awake* and *sleep* are used in a figurative rather than a literal sense?

5. Is the mood of the poem one of complete hopelessness? What theme, if any, is suggested? How is this poem similar to, or different from, other Housman poems you have read? Base your opinions on your interpretation of the poet's words.

6. What is the predominant metrical line? Discuss the effect on the pace, tone, and mood of the poem. Point out instances in which Housman varies the usual iambic rhythm by using a different metrical foot, a pause or caesura, or a combination of these. Describe what he achieves in each instance.

OH STAY AT HOME, MY LAD, AND PLOUGH

Oh stay at home, my lad, and plough
  The land and not the sea,
And leave the soldiers at their drill,
And all about the idle hill
  Shepherd your sheep with me.   5

Oh stay with company and mirth
  And daylight and the air;
Too full already is the grave
Of fellows that were good and brave
  And died because they were.   10

1. Why do you think Housman wrote this poem? Is it addressed to a particular lad or to all lads?

2. What is implied concerning the futility of warfare and bravery in battle? Point out words and images which convey the poet's attitude.

3. How does the ironic last line affect the poem?

William Butler Yeats

William Butler Yeats called himself one of the "last Romantics," and in form and subject his poems resemble those of such distinguished predecessors as Wordsworth and Keats. Yet in mood and treatment, they are boldly modern, rich in symbolism and paradoxes, and written in a style in which simple but suggestive words convey extraordinarily complex implications. Because of his unique ability to imply several sophisticated ideas with a few familiar words, Yeats is now considered by many critics the greatest poet of the twentieth century.

THE SONG OF WANDERING AENGUS

I went out to the hazel wood,
Because a fire was in my head,
And cut and peeled a hazel wand,
And hooked a berry to a thread;
And when white moths were on the wing,   5
And moth-like stars were flickering out,
I dropped the berry in a stream
And caught a little silver trout.

When I had laid it on the floor
I.went to blow the fire aflame,   10
But something rustled on the floor,
And some one called me by my name:
It had become a glimmering girl
With apple blossom in her hair
Who called me by my name and ran   15
And faded through the brightening air.

Though I am old with wandering
Through hollow lands and hilly lands,
I will find out where she has gone,
And kiss her lips and take her hands;   20
And walk among long dappled grass,
And pluck till time and times are done
The silver apples of the moon,
The golden apples of the sun.

1. Although Yeat's poetry takes on more and more meaning as one
   learns what the poet himself felt about his images, or what legends
   he obliquely mentioned, still his poems stand alone, as good
   poems must. Without any knowledge of Aengus, what can you
   conclude this poem is about? What does the phrase "a fire was in
   my head" suggest? What kind of man might experience such a
   sensation?
2. The girl represents some desirable quality or thing. What, specifically, do you think she symbolizes? What kind of man would
   pursue such an elusive ideal for his whole life? Do you think
   Aengus could represent some aspect of Yeats? If so, which aspect?
3. At what time of day does stanza 1 occur? Why is the time appropriate to the poem as a whole?
4. Throughout this poem, Yeats associates the objects he describes
   with lightness or whiteness. What particular things does he describe in this way? What do the silver and golden apples represent? Are the apples related to the apple blossom mentioned in
   line 15? What effects does Yeats achieve by repeated reference
   to white or light things?

5. Aengus is the "master of Love," a hero of Irish folklore who carried a hazel rod. Also legendary are women of Sidhe who, disguised as fish, enchanted living men. What purpose is served when these two legends are combined? What does the combination suggest?

6. Because of the superb musical quality of his verse, Yeats has been called one of the major lyric poets of all time. Point out lines in this poem that you feel particularly support this statement.

A COAT

I made my song a coat
Covered with embroideries
Out of old mythologies
From heel to throat;
But the fools caught it,   5
Wore it in the world's eyes
As though they'd wrought it.
Song, let them take it,
For there's more enterprise
In walking naked.   10

1. Does line 1 mean "I made a coat *for* my song" or "I made a coat *from* my song"? How is the poem different if you read the first line in one way rather than the other? Are there any other ways to read line 1? Which reading do you prefer? Why?

2. Yeats was ridiculed more than once for believing in a compound of mysticism, obscure philosophy, folklore, and legend, beliefs which he wove into his poetry. If this poem is read as an answer to such ridicule, what does the poem mean?

3. What type of men would Yeats consider fools? In terms of the poem, how had fools so offended him?

4. When Yeats ends his poem stating "there's more enterprise/In walking naked," what does *enterprise* mean? What attitude do the lines reveal toward the restrictions of society? Toward the body?

THE WILD SWANS AT COOLE[1]

The trees are in their autumn beauty,
The woodland paths are dry,
Under the October twilight the water
Mirrors a still sky;
Upon the brimming water among the stones   5
Are nine-and-fifty swans.

The nineteenth autumn has come upon me
Since I first made my count;
I saw, before I had well finished,
All suddenly mount   10
And scatter wheeling in great broken rings
Upon their clamorous wings.

I have looked upon those brilliant creatures,
And now my heart is sore.
All's changed since I, hearing at twilight,   15
The first time on this shore,
The bell-beat of their wings above my head,
Trod with a lighter tread.

Unwearied still, lover by lover,
They paddle in the cold   20
Companionable streams or climb the air;
Their hearts have not grown old;
Passion or conquest, wander where they will,
Attend upon° them still.   accompany

[1]*Coole* (Coo-li): estate of Lady Gregory, the Irish playwright who interested
Yeats in the Irish literary movement

But now drift on the still water,   25
Mysterious, beautiful;
Among what rushes will they build,
By what lake's edge or pool
Delight men's eyes when I awake some day
To find they have flown away?   30

1. Because of Yeats's mystical nature, many of the real objects he wrote about and his simple observations have a deeper meaning. What season and time of day are pictured in stanza 1? What is the mood of this scene? Why is the season appropriate for the thoughts in the poem?

2. How long has it been since the speaker in the poem first counted the swans? What happens before he has "well finished" his count? What is unusual about the image in line 12?

3. How do you interpret the word *brilliant* in line 13? Why is the speaker's heart sore? Is the change he refers to in the birds and their flight, in himself, or in both? Explain.

4. In stanza 4, the speaker reveals why he admires the "brilliant creatures" who come to Coole. What do lines 19 and 22 bring out? How do you interpret lines 23 and 24? On the basis of the total meaning of the poem, tell why you do, or do not, think he is somewhat envious of them.

5. In stanza 5, the speaker ceases his musing and comes back to the present. What words recapture both the impression and the mood? What is the literal meaning conveyed in the closing question (lines 27-30)? What is the symbolic meaning? The word *awake* is especially significant. What connection can you see between the symbolic meaning of *autumn* and *twilight* (stanza 1) and of *still* in lines 4 and 25?

6. Interpreted literally, this poem describes an experience that, at two different times, made a deep impression on Yeats. What deeper or symbolic meaning might he have intended the poem to convey?

7. What word, or words, would you use to describe the mood of the poem and of the speaker? Point out the variations in the metrical lines and feet that help to create this mood and make the rhythm suit the thought.

AN IRISH AIRMAN FORESEES HIS DEATH

I know that I shall meet my fate
Somewhere among the clouds above;
Those that I fight I do not hate,
Those that I guard I do not love;
My country is Kiltartan Cross,   5
My countrymen Kiltartan's poor,
No likely end could bring them loss
Or leave them happier than before.
Nor law, nor duty bade me fight,
Nor public men, nor cheering crowds,   10
A lonely impulse of delight
Drove to this tumult in the clouds;
I balanced all, brought all to mind,
The years to come seemed waste of breath,
A waste of breath the years behind   15
In balance with this life, this death.

1. When the title and first two lines of a poem give away what is going to happen, do you see any point in continuing the poem? Defend your answer.
2. What usual reasons for going to war does the speaker say were *not* responsible for his going to meet his fate? How do you interpret his comments about his countrymen (lines 5-8) and his statement in line 4?
3. What do you think the speaker means by a "lonely impulse of delight" (line 11)? How is this related to what is implied in line 16? Give your interpretation of the last four lines.
4. This is a highly personal poem, revealing the speaker's innermost thoughts and feelings. Discuss the changes of mood, where they occur, and what words and phrases help to create them. Do you think that there is also an over-all mood? If so, what is it?
5. In several lines, the poet departs from the predominant iambic rhythm. Point out these lines. Discuss the effect of each variation in metrical feet.

EASTER 1916

With the outbreak of World War I, the promise of Home Rule
for Ireland was delayed. This was much resented by the Sinn
Fein, the political group promoting the Irish Free State. Resent-
ment smoldered until Easter 1916 when, expectant of German
aid, less than two thousand Irish patriots attempted to seize Dublin by force. The aid never arrived—the British Navy had cut off
the German support—and the Easter Rebellion not only failed but
led to the imprisonment or execution of its leaders and to the
military occupation of Ireland. Yeats deplored the needless sacrifice of lives, but he recognized that the Rebellion had "transformed a nation of mean-spirited clowns into something glorious."
After nearly six years of civil war, the Irish Free State was founded
in 1922, and Yeats became one of its first senators.

I have met them at close of day
Coming with vivid faces
From counter or desk among grey
Eighteenth-century houses.
I have passed with a nod of the head   5
Or polite meaningless words,
Or have lingered awhile and said
Polite meaningless words,
And thought before I had done
Of a mocking tale or a gibe   10
To please a companion
Around the fire at the club,
Being certain that they and I
But lived where motley is worn:
All changed, changed utterly: 15
A terrible beauty is born.

That woman's days were spent
In ignorant good-will,
Her nights in argument
Until her voice grew shrill.   20

What voice more sweet than hers
When, young and beautiful,
She rode to harriers?°   hounds
This man had kept a school
And rode our wingèd horse;   25
This other his helper and friend
Was coming into his force;
He might have won fame in the end,
So sensitive his nature seemed,
So daring and sweet his thought.   30
This other man I had dreamed
A drunken, vainglorious lout.
He had done most bitter wrong
To some who are near my heart,
Yet I number him in the song;   35
He, too, has resigned his part
In the casual comedy;
He, too, has been changed in his turn,
Transformed utterly:
A terrible beauty is born.   40

Hearts with one purpose alone
Through summer and winter seem
Enchanted to a stone
To trouble the living stream.
The horse that comes from the road,   45
The rider, the birds that range
From cloud to tumbling cloud,
Minute by minute they change;
A shadow of cloud on the stream
Changes minute by minute;   50
A horse-hoof slides on the brim,
And a horse plashes within it;
The long-legged moor-hens dive,

And hens to moor-cocks call;
Minute by minute they live: 55
The stone's in the midst of all.

Too long a sacrifice
Can make a stone of the heart.
O when may it suffice?
That is Heaven's part, our part   60
To murmur name upon name,
As a mother names her child
When sleep at last has come
On limbs that had run wild.
What is it but nightfall?   65
No, no, not night but death;
Was it needless death after all?
For England may keep faith
For all that is done and said.
We know their dream; enough   70
To know they dreamed and are dead;
And what if excess of love
Bewildered them till they died?
I write it out in a verse—
MacDonagh and MacBride   75
And Connolly and Pearse
Now and in time to be,
Wherever green is worn,
Are changed, changed utterly:
A terrible beauty is born.   80

1. One of the first "changes" pictured in the poem is that among the
people whom Yeats knew and who had risked everything in the
Rebellion. What subtle clues are you given to the nature of this
change? How do you interpret lines 13 and 14? The dictionary
meaning of *motley* is "cloth of mixed colors." It also means "a

garment of various colors worn by a jester." Yeats may also have been referring to the English troops, popularly known as the Black and Tans, which were sent in after the Easter Rebellion to suppress the guerrilla warfare in 1918 and which terrorized the country.

2. In stanza 2 is a tribute to some of the leaders of the Rebellion. "That woman" (line 17) is the imprisoned Countess Marciewicz, "this man" (line 24) is Patrich Pearse, who commanded the Easter Rebellion and was executed. What contrast is made in lines 17-23? What figurative meaning is intended in line 25? Why is the other man numbered in Yeats's song? What irony is expressed in the words "casual comedy"?

3. Note, in line 43, the metaphor "stone" to describe the "one purpose" of those dedicated to the Rebellion. What does Yeats mean by the statement in lines 41-44 and the final statement in line 56? Discuss the purpose and the figurative meaning of lines 45-55.

4. In the last stanza Yeats reflects on this historic event. What is he suggesting in lines 57 and 58? (Note the extension of the "stone" metaphor.) What answer does he give to his own questions in lines 59, 65, and 67? What ray of hope is suggested in lines 68 and 69?

5. What do "we know," and what is "enough to know"? Note the repetition at the end of the poem, almost the exact lines which appear at the end of stanza 1. Try to express in your own words why Yeats believes that all has "changed utterly." How do you interpret the haunting line "A terrible beauty is born"? Does it always have the same meaning? Or does it have a slightly different meaning each time it appears in the poem? Discuss.

6. Pictures and mementos of the men named in lines 75 and 76 are preserved in a Dublin museum. The Irish now look upon the Easter Rebellion as Americans do upon the uprising at Lexington and Concord. What is implied by "wherever green is worn"?

7. This is one of the greatest of Yeats's later poems, in which he makes greater and more effective use of words as symbols. Point out the words in this poem which you think symbolize a thought, emotion, or concept. Discuss the symbolic meaning you think Yeats intends them to convey.

8. This poem has both rhyme and rhythm, though neither is strictly regular. Tell why you think they are effective. Comment, too, on the language. The subject of this poem is highly dramatic, and the feelings expressed in it are deeply felt. Would a more learned and traditionally poetic treatment have been more appropriate? Tell why or why not.

SAILING TO BYZANTIUM

1

That is no country for old men. The young
In one another's arms, birds in the trees
—Those dying generations—at their song,
The salmon-falls, the mackerel-crowded seas,
Fish, flesh, or fowl, commend all summer long   5
Whatever is begotten, born, and dies.
Caught in that sensual music all neglect
Monuments of unageing intellect.

2

An aged man is but a paltry thing,
A tattered coat upon a stick, unless   10
Soul clap its hands and sing, and louder sing
For every tatter in its mortal dress,
Nor is there singing school but studying
Monuments of its own magnificence;
And therefore I have sailed the seas and come   15
To the holy city of Byzantium.

3

O sages standing in God's holy fire
As in the gold mosaic of a wall,
Come from the holy fire, perne in a gyre,[1]
And be the singing-masters of my soul.   20
Consume my heart away; sick with desire
And fastened to a dying animal
It knows not what it is; and gather me
Into the artifice of eternity.

[1]*perne in a gyre:* move in a circular or spiral motion

4

Once out of nature I shall never take   25
My bodily form from any natural thing,
But such a form as Grecian goldsmiths make
Of hammered gold and gold enamelling
To keep a drowsy Emperor awake;
Or set upon a golden bough to sing   30
To lords and ladies of Byzantium
Of what is past, or passing, or to come.

1. For convenience, assume that "that country" referred to in line 1 is twentieth century Ireland. Why does the poet feel out of place there? What impression of contemporary life is conveyed by the images in stanza 1? Why does Yeats call the young, and the singing birds, "dying generations"? What two ideas are conveyed by this phrase? What set of opposites is established in lines 7 and 8?
2. In the second stanza, Yeats explains why he wants to live in Byzantium. What does the word *Byzantium* suggest to you? Yeats associated the city with mosaics, gold and silver work, illuminated manuscripts, and other highly intricate and beautiful art forms. But the fact that Byzantium's great period of art occurred over a thousand years ago increased the city's symbolic appeal for the poet. Why? Why would Yeats state at the end of stanza 2 that he had already *come* to Byzantium?
3. Uusually the word *artifice* has negative connotations because it suggests something created through art rather than nature. Yeats, however, apparently does not use the word negatively. Why does the poet wish in stanza 3 to be gathered "into the artifice of eternity"? Why is eternity associated with artifice, not nature? How does stanza 4 further develop this view of artifice?
4. What does the poet state in stanza 2 can save an old man from being only a paltry thing?
5. What would the singing school in stanza 2 symbolize? In stanza 3, whom does the poet ask to be his singing masters? What kind of song does he wish to learn? What is the relationship between the singing school of stanza 2, the singing masters of stanza 3 and the golden bird who sings in stanza 4?
6. What contrast does the whole poem develop between the bird mentioned in line 2 and the bird of stanza 4? How does the subject matter of the two birds' songs differ?

THE COMING OF WISDOM WITH TIME

Though leaves are many, the root is one;
Through all the lying days of my youth
I swayed my leaves and flowers in the sun;
Now I may wither into the truth.

POLITICS

"In our time the destiny of man presents its meaning in political terms."—THOMAS MANN

How can I, that girl standing there,
My attention fix
On Roman or on Russian
Or on Spanish politics?
Yet here's a travelled man that knows   5
What he talks about,
And there's a politician
That has read and thought,
And maybe what they say is true
Of war and war's alarms,   10
But O that I were young again
And held her in my arms!

1. What is the central metaphor in "The Coming of Wisdom with Time"?
2. What statement about life do you feel the poet is making through his metaphor?
3. What does he mean by "the truth"?
4. Describe the speaker in "Politics." Where is he?
5. Do you think the poem makes any judgments about what is important? What statement about politics does the poem make?
6. Can you justify the distortion of normal syntax in the first four lines in "Politics"?

THE MODERNS

For almost a century after the defeat of Napoleon at Waterloo, England had enjoyed freedom from major wars. By 1914, however, Europe was divided into two great armed camps: the first, a Triple Alliance composed of Italy, Austria-Hungary, and the German Empire; the second, a Triple Entente consisting of Russia, France, and Great Britain. The "armaments race" was well on its way, and the setting for war was complete. On July 28, the fuse was lighted when Serbian nationalists assassinated the heir to the Austrian throne. For some time Austria had sought an opportunity to crush nationalistic aspiration in the Balkans; thus it immediately declared war on Serbia. By August 4, all the powers were in a state of war, and the German army was marching across neutral Belgium to attack France. In protest against this violation of Belgian neutrality — which England, Prussia, and the other major European nations had signed treaties to protect — England then entered the war. At first Italy remained neutral; later she joined the Triple Entente, maintaining that Germany and Austria had been the aggressors.

World War I soon developed into the bloodiest struggle the world had ever seen, a war of attrition that stretched six hundred miles from the English Channel almost to Switzerland. Millions of soldiers faced one another from deep, rat-infested trenches. Except in the air, the individual soldier counted for little. Indeed, there was little romance to this war. Opposing lines of soldiers hurled at each other all the terrible weapons that the ingenuity of man had invented: hand gre- nades, rifle and machine-gun bullets, trench-mortar shells, shrapnel, and poison gases. Occasionally, following an artil- lery barrage, a company of soldiers would dash across no- man's-land to attack the enemy in hand-to-hand bayonet combat or to capture prisoners for questioning. Hundreds of thousands of soldiers were sacrificed in what seemed to the survivors a futile attempt to accomplish something without worth or meaning. As a result, many soldiers became disillu- sioned; many carried on the battle only because there seemed little else they could do.

After more than four years of bloodshed, the war was finally over, but the price had been heavy. England had lost eight per cent of her national wealth and was no longer first in inter- national banking and trade. Her war debt was so great that no one knew how she could ever pay it. Her greatest loss, how- ever, was in human lives—almost an entire generation of young men.

When World War I came to an end, England was beset with many problems for which the past provided no answers. Thousands of able-bodied men and women found themselves without jobs and forced to live on government dole. Thou- sands depended on bread lines to keep body and soul to- gether. The form of government in England remained the same, but on the continent three dictators seized control: Stalin in the U.S.S.R., Hitler in Germany, and Mussolini in Italy. All signs pointed toward another war, which disarma- ment agreements, peace pacts, and the League of Nations seemed powerless to prevent.

There were other causes for uncertainty and unrest, partic- ularly among young writers. The discoveries by Freud and Jung of the effect of the subconscious and the studies of hu- man behavior by Watson seemed to indicate that man was the product of his heredity and environment. How, then, could he determine his own character, much less his own destiny? In which of the opposing philosophies—conservatism or materialism — might he find not merely something to believe in but an article of faith? The spirit of the time was one of doubt and questioning. Economics, governmental systems, religion, society, science — all were subjected to close scrutiny. So were the tested ideas and techniques of past writers and the symbols through which they communicated their thoughts, emotions, and impressions. These symbols, drawn from Judeo-Christian religions or from Greek and Roman literature and mythology, belonged to the past. If they were no longer valid, then modern writers must discover new symbols. They must also find new techniques suited to the expression of new ideas for a new audience.

While using these new forms, poets have articulated the vast confusion and uncertainty of the twentieth century — an uncertainty born of wars and rumors of wars, of crumbling traditions and beliefs, of doubt about even the most universally accepted values. Naturally, each good poet has spoken in his own, individual way; and it is still difficult to make generalizations about the period as a whole. But each poet has confronted the larger questions of the century as honestly as he could, and each has made his own contribution to English poetry.

DAME EDITH SITWELL perhaps attracted as much attention by her colorful personality as by her vivid poetry. Both reveal her love of the unique, the mysterious, the remote. A figure who often appeared in public in medieval costumes, Miss Sitwell found early in life that she must work to avoid being eclipsed by her poet brothers, Sir Osbert and Sacheverell. The imagery in her unusual verse is composed of exotic animals, plants, jewels, and musical instruments. She often uses brilliant colors to make a comparison more vivid. The tone is sometimes worldly-wise or cynical, but the poems, nevertheless, communicate a great affirmation of living things.

A poet who is equally important for his studies of mythology, his critical essays, and his translations of the classics, ROBERT GRAVES uniquely fills the role of the "man of letters in the modern world." He is a world traveler who has studied many important literatures and who makes his permanent home on the island of Majorca, off the coast of Spain. But he says of his poetry, "somehow these poems have never adopted a foreign accent or coloring; they remain true to the Anglo-Irish poetic tradition into which I was born." Graves combines traditional forms and contemporary themes.

WYSTAN HUGH AUDEN is perhaps the best known of the post-World War I group and the most original. He has experimented with almost every type of rhythm and form from lyrics set to jazz-time and from exceptionally well-controlled sonnets to free verse.

In nearly everything he has written, Auden's major concern has been with "the human element." His landscapes are merely a background for human beings, whom he has surveyed in every human emotion from aspiration to misery. He has often been critical of the political and social causes for man's thwarted existence. Yet he has always believed that man, instinctively desiring to lead "the Good Life," is frustrated, partly by his selfish rebellion against necessity and partly by his innate sinfulness. Man has been endowed with free will so that he can choose, but he must ask some power greater than himself for the strength or the conscience to achieve what he chooses.

STEPHEN SPENDER has described himself as "an autobiographer restlessly searching for forms in which to express the stages of my development." Unlike some biographers, he is always honest, and in those poems where emotion and reflection merge—where the outer world is touched by the light of the inner—his poetry has both intensity and beauty. He found in modern industrialism and its machines a rich source of subject matter and vivid imagery.

DYLAN THOMAS, a Welshman, reveled in the romanticism which Auden and Spender shunned. He was too young in the 1930's to be in the modern movement during its early and somewhat revolutionary period, but he soon found a place near them with *Eighteen Poems,* published when he was just twenty. Though his themes and techniques are not startlingly varied, as are Auden's, yet his poems are undoubtedly the works of a genius, intoxicated with language and sound.

His early poems, which contain some of his best work, reveal his preoccupation with the theme that man starts to die from the moment he is born. Thomas saw death as a force unifying all living things.

JOHN BETJEMAN has been stigmatized as the great favorite of the "mass middle-brow public." There is little doubt that many people find him the most (if not the only) readable contemporary poet. We certainly cannot assume because of this that he is "superior" to other poets who are less accessible to the general public. Yet, it would be "literary snobbism" of the worst kind to ignore or belittle the reasons for Betjeman's appeal. Quite clearly, he is expressing ideas, evoking emotions, manipulating symbols that have value to many people, and is doing it in a way that they find persuasive and rewarding. The fact that many of his poems are written in meters usually associated with comic or "light" verse does not invalidate his great verbal skill and his poetic insight into aspects of human experience. The casual and idiomatic tone of "Devonshire Street W. 1" enhances rather than diminishes its poignant reminder of human mortality.

Frequently, modern poets have developed a "persona," or mask, through which to address the reader. The wry and self-deprecating persona in PHILIP LARKIN'S poetry is intelligent enough to assess ruthlessly his own limitations and possibilities. Larkin expresses in his poetry neither kinship with Nature nor sensuous enjoyment of it — though he wistfully appreciates such pleasure from a distance. His philosophy seems to have passed beyond despair to an ironical acceptance of things as they are. In mood, his verse is somewhat reminiscent of Matthew Arnold's. A careful technician, Larkin devises intricate patterns within conventional forms, without ever allowing his rhythm or rhymc to draw attention to itself.

Dame Edith Sitwell

Like the poetry of Swinburne or Dylan Thomas, Edith Sitwell's verse often presents lovely sounds more effectively than logical thoughts. Her poems are discursive and loosely structured, but full of such musical devices as assonance, consonance, and especially, alliteration. Within the free verse form, she employs startling surrealistic images which combine dissimilar objects representing unfamiliar animals and things—lynxes and lyres, tigers, emeralds, sphinxes and sapphires. Despite the difficulty of much of her poetry, power has been seen in it, as well as a criticism of the disorder and ugliness of civilization after World War I.

Heart and Mind

Said the Lion to the Lioness—"When you are amber dust—
No more a raging fire like the heat of the Sun
(No liking but all lust)—
Remember still the flowering of the amber blood and bone,
The rippling of bright muscles like a sea,
Remember the rose-prickles of bright paws,   5

Though we shall mate no more
Till the fire of that sun the heart and the moon-cold bone
  are one."

Said the Skeleton lying upon the sands of Time—   9
"The great gold planet that is the mourning heat of the Sun
Is greater than all gold, more powerful
Than the tawny body of a Lion that fire consumes
Like all that grows or leaps . . . so is the heart
More powerful than all dust. Once I was Hercules
Or Samson, strong as the pillars of the seas: 15
But the flames of the heart consumed me, and the mind
Is but a foolish wind."

Said the Sun to the Moon—"When you are but a lonely
  white crone,
And I, a dead King in my golden armour somewhere in a
  dark wood,
Remember only this of our hopeless love: 20
That never till Time is done
Will the fire of the heart and the fire of the mind be one."

1. The three stanzas of this poem seem to make three different statements about heart and mind. What are they? Does the poet allow
   one of the statements to seem truer than the other two?
2. A contrast between sun and moon is found in stanzas 1 and 3. Is
   such a contrast implied in stanza 2? If not, how is stanza 2 related
   to the rest of the poem?
3. When does the lion hope the lioness will remember what he asks
   her?
4. What does line 8 mean? How will the two manage to mate when
   this condition occurs?
5. Color is used in this poem with great effectiveness. What colors
   dominate? With what are these colors associated? Point out shades
   of the same color mentioned in the first stanza.

SOLO FOR EAR-TRUMPET

The carriage brushes through the bright
Leaves (violent jets from life to light).
Strong polished speed is plunging, heaves
Between the showers of bright hot leaves.
The window-glasses glaze our faces   5
And jar them to the very bases,—
But they could never put a polish
Upon my manners, or abolish
My most distinct disinclination
For calling on a rich relation!   10
In her house,—bulwark built between
The life man lives and visions seen,—
The sunlight hiccups white as chalk,
Grown drunk with emptiness of talk,
And silence hisses like a snake,   15
Invertebrate and rattling ache. . . .

Till suddenly, Eternity
Drowns all the houses like a sea,
And down the street the Trump of Doom
Blares,—barely shaking this drawing-room,   20
Where raw-edged shadows sting forlorn
As dank dark nettles. Down the horn
Of her ear-trumpet I convey
The news that: "It is Judgment Day!"
"Speak louder; I don't catch, my dear!"   25
I roared: *"It is the Trump we hear!"*
"The *What?*"—"The TRUMP!" . . .
"I shall complain—
Those boy-scouts practicing again!"

1. What contrast in mood do you find in the first stanza? At what point does the tone change? What purpose is accomplished by this contrast?
2. What do the images of lines 13 through 16 communicate about the speaker's attitude toward her aunt?
3. What does the second stanza say about the aunt's perceptions? values? outlook? character?
4. What metaphors and similes in this poem particularly increase its effectiveness? Which convey a vivid sensory impression?
5. What details contribute to the humor in this poem?

Robert Graves

Robert Graves uses conventional rhythms, forms, and rhymes in his poetry while still attaining a uniquely personal expression. He often re-examines commonplace things in order to make a comment on the everyday scene. His didactic poems present the bit of common sense or wisdom to be gleaned from the ordinary.

WARNING TO CHILDREN

Children, if you dare to think
Of the greatness, rareness, muchness,
Fewness of this precious only
Endless world in which you say
You live, you think of things like this: 5
Blocks of slate enclosing dappled
Red and green, enclosing tawny
Yellow nets, enclosing white
And black acres of dominoes,
Where a neat brown paper parcel 10
Tempts you to untie the string.
In the parcel a small island,

On the island a large tree,
On the tree a husky fruit.
Strip the husk and pare the rind off: 15
In the kernel you will see
Blocks of slate enclosed by dappled
Red and green, enclosed by tawny
Yellow nets, enclosed by white
And black acres of dominoes,   20
Where the same brown paper parcel—
Children, leave the string alone!
For who dares undo the parcel
Finds himself at once inside it,
On the island, in the fruit,   25
Blocks of slate about his head,
Finds himself enclosed by dappled
Green and red, enclosed by yellow
Tawny nets, enclosed by black
And white acres of dominoes,   30
With the same brown paper parcel
Still untied upon his knee.
And, if he then should dare to think
Of the fewness, muchness, rareness,
Greatness of this endless only   35
Precious world in which he says
He lives—he then unties the string.

1. What impression of the world and of human life does this poem
   convey? How can you assume that the poet views human experience?
2. Parts of this poem suggest the box-within-a-box-within-a-box
   prank you may have played yourself when giving a present. Why
   does the idea of finding, endlessly, a smaller kernel within each
   shell have such fascination?
3. Why did the poet make this poem a piece of advice to children?
   What would the poem have been like if children hadn't been
   mentioned?

4. Graves constantly juxtaposes opposites such as *muchness* and *fewness* in this poem. Why?
5. What activity could "untying the string" represent? Why does Graves warn children against untying the string? Do you think his warning is genuine?

TRAVELLER'S CURSE AFTER MISDIRECTION

(FROM THE WELSH)

May they stumble, stage by stage
On an endless pilgrimage,
Dawn and dusk, mile after mile,
At each and every step, a stile;
At each and every step withal
May they catch their feet and fall;
At each and every fall they take
May a bone within them break;
And may the bone that breaks within
Not be, for variation's sake,
Now rib, now thigh, now arm, now shin,
But always, without fail, THE NECK.

1. Of course, this poem is not to be taken too seriously. Why do curses more often amuse than horrify us?
2. How does the *length* of the curse affect the poem? Would a more concise curse have been stronger, or does the poem accelerate steadily toward the final phrase? What is the difference in the psychological effects of long and of short curses?

W. H. Auden

No other modern poet has done more than W. H. Auden to demonstrate the resources of poetry. That Auden is a master of mood, language, and form is evident even in the poetry of his social-criticism period. His great gift is economy: each poem is a series of concrete details which produce sensations and associations in the reader's mind which the reader is left to interpret for himself. Auden's best poetry springs from his comprehension of suffering, joy, love, and pity; to anger and disgust has been added the compassion of one who feels he shares in the world's guilt.

In Memory of W. B. Yeats

(d. Jan. 1939)

1

He disappeared in the dead of winter:
The brooks were frozen, the airports almost deserted,
And snow disfigured the public statues;
The mercury sank in the mouth of the dying day.

O all the instruments agree   5
The day of his death was a dark cold day.

Far from his illness
The wolves ran on through the evergreen forest,
The peasant river was untempted by the fashionable
    quays;°   docks
By mourning tongues   10
The death of the poet was kept from his poems.

But for him it was his last afternoon as himself,
An afternoon of nurses and rumours;
The provinces of his body revolted,
The squares of his mind were empty,   15
Silence invaded the suburbs,
The current of his feeling failed: he became his admirers.

Now he is scattered among a hundred cities
And wholly given over to unfamiliar affections;
To find his happiness in another kind of wood   20
And be punished under a foreign code of conscience.
The words of a dead man
Are modified in the guts of the living.

But in the importance and noise of tomorrow
When the brokers are roaring like beasts on the floor of
    the Bourse,°   stock exchange 25
And the poor have the sufferings to which they are
    fairly accustomed,
And each in the cell of himself is almost convinced of
    his freedom;
A few thousand will think of this day
As one thinks of a day when one did something slightly
    unusual.

O all the instruments agree   30
The day of his death was a dark cold day.

2

You were silly like us: your gift survived it all;
The parish of rich women,[1] physical decay,
Yourself; mad Ireland hurt you into poetry.
Now Ireland has her madness and her weather still,   35
For poetry makes nothing happen: it survives
In the valley of its saying where executives
Would never want to tamper; it flows south
From ranches of isolation and the busy griefs,
Raw towns that we believe and die in; it survives,   40
A way of happening, a mouth.

3

Earth, receive an honoured guest;
William Yeats is laid to rest:
Let the Irish vessel lie
Emptied of its poetry.   45

Time that is intolerant
Of the brave and innocent,
And indifferent in a week
To a beautiful physique,

Worships language and forgives   50
Everyone by whom it lives;
Pardons cowardice, conceit,
Lays its honours at their feet.

[1]*parish of rich women:* Yeats had several wealthy patrons; Lady Gregory was especially hospitable to him at her estate called Coole (see page 442).

Time that with this strange excuse
Pardoned Kipling[2] and his views,   55
And will pardon Paul Claudel,[3]
Pardons him for writing well.

In the nightmare of the dark
All the dogs of Europe bark,
And the living nations wait,   60
Each sequestered in its hate;

Intellectual disgrace
Stares from every human face,
And the seas of pity lie
Locked and frozen in each eye.   65

Follow, poet, follow right
To the bottom of the night,
With your unconstraining voice
Still persuade us to rejoice;

With the farming of a verse   70
Make a vineyard of the curse,
Sing of human unsuccess
In a rapture of distress;

In the deserts of the heart
Let the healing fountain start,   75
In the prison of his days
Teach the free man how to praise.

[2]*Kipling:* Rudyard Kipling (1865-1936) was at the turn of the century a
leading apologist for British imperialism.
[3]*Paul Claudel:* (1868-1955), a French Roman Catholic poet who was ar-
dently anti-Protestant

1. How does Auden use the season in which Yeats died to create the proper mood for an elegy? What is the literal and the metaphorical meaning of line 4?
2. In lines 7-11, the natural scenes mentioned seem completely different from those in the first six lines. What is the purpose of this contrast? What is the connection between lines 7-9 and 10-11?
3. What does Auden imply when he personifies the poems in line 11? How is this implication reinforced in lines 18-23?
4. To what is Yeats metaphorically compared in lines 14-17? What implications are conveyed by this comparison? What is the relationship between the phrase *he became his admirers* and the second and fourth verse paragraphs?
5. What is the meaning of lines 18-21? Does "The Song of Wandering Aengus" (see page 439) shed any light on line 20? Is it possible to understand Auden's line without referring to the Yeat's poem?
6. To what extent do lines 22-23 explain the preceding four lines? How could Yeats "be punished under a foreign code of conscience"? Why does Auden deliberately choose so "unpoetic" a word as *guts* for line 23?
7. What attitude toward the future and toward human life do lines 24-27 convey? What do the brokers and the poor have in common?
8. Explain why Yeats's admirers will think of the day he died as "one thinks of a day when one did something unusual" (line 29). What did the admirers do on that day?
9. Why might Auden repeat lines 5 and 6 in lines 30 and 31? What different meaning does *instruments* acquire in the second pair of lines?
10. What images and references in part 2 tie lines 32-41 to part 1? What is the function of part 2? What does Auden mean when he says that "poetry makes nothing happen" but is rather "a way of happening"? What is the difference? Why does the phrase *a way of happening* take as an appositive or explanatory synonym, *a mouth*?
11. Reread Yeats's poems and then explain why Auden mentions Yeats's physical decay (line 33). Why does he call Ireland *mad*?
12. What is the poetic effect of having shorter lines in each part of the poem?
13. What relationship between earth and the poet is suggested in line 42? What does Auden mean when he compares Yeats to an "Irish vessel"?

14. Why, according to Auden, does the poet receive honor when brave, innocent, and beautiful people do not? Do you feel this generalization is accurate? What does *strange excuse* mean in line 54?
15. How is line 58 related to part 2? How does the remainder of part 3 explain line 58?
16. What do lines 59-77 suggest are the functions of the poet?
17. What specific images recur at several points in the poem? What conclusions about man's life does the poem express?
18. To what curse does Auden refer in line 71? How might a poet make a vineyard of this curse? What kind of life does *vineyard* suggest? What is the effect of the paradoxes with which this poem concludes?

LOOK, STRANGER

Look, stranger, at this island now
The leaping light for your delight discovers,
Stand stable here
And silent be,
That through the channels of the ear   5
May wander like a river
The swaying sound of the sea.

Here at the small field's ending pause
Where the chalk° wall falls to the foam,   soft white stone
   and its tall ledges
Oppose the pluck   10
And knock of the tide,
And the shingle° scrambles after the sucking surf, gravel
And the gull lodges
A moment on its sheer side.
Far off like floating seeds the ships   15
Diverge on urgent voluntary errands;

And the full view
Indeed may enter
And move in memory as now these clouds do,
That pass the harbor mirror   20
And all the summer through the water saunter.

1. This poem gives the reader one of those rare glimpses of Auden directing his acutely perceptive eye on nature rather than on man. The highly lyrical quality is also rare, though he is such a skilled craftsman that he fits mood, language, and form to whatever subject he chooses. What purpose do you think he had in writing this poem? Are the speaker and the stranger standing on "this island" or are they observing an island some distance from shore? How do you interpret line 3? Why does the speaker urge the stranger to be silent?

2. What impressions are created by the images in stanza 2? Why are the verbs especially effective?

3. Stanza 3 is composed of two similes. In the first, what added meaning is conveyed by the word *seeds* and the phrase "urgent voluntary errands"? In the second, what comparison does the poet make to the movement of the clouds? What impressions are created in the mind by the images in lines 19 and 20?

4. Point out the ways in which the three stanzas are alike and different in length of line, occasional rhyme, and rhythm pattern. Why would the effect have been spoiled if lines 3 and 4 in each stanza had been combined into a single line? Can you see any reason for the long lines in stanza 2?

5. Poets sometimes invert the word order of a line for the sake of the rhyme. What reason can you see for the inverted order of lines 2 and 20? What is lost when this order is changed to the usual order?

6. In a number of lines, Auden achieves a surprisingly melodious effect through the use of alliteration and consonance. Point out examples which you consider especially effective.

Stephen Spender

Like his fellow poets, Stephen Spender has taken his symbols from industrial society and made metaphors out of the details of the modern scene. At the same time, he has drawn many of his images from nature. In several of his best and most popular poems he has revealed his special gift for describing and annotating experiences. Many of his poems are intensely personal—a view of man and of the world observed with the inward, rather than the outward, eye. Because he hated the war-makers, who stood to profit financially, he saw the hideous struggle and sacrifice of life as meaningless. He shares Shelley's belief that "Hell is a city much like London."

WITHOUT THAT ONCE CLEAR AIM

Without that once clear aim, the path of flight
To follow for a lifetime through white air,
This century chokes me under roots of night.
I suffer like history in Dark Ages, where
Truth lies in dungeons, too deep for whisper.   5
We hear of towers long broken off from sight
And tortures and wars, smoky and dark with rumor,
But on Mind's buried thought there falls no light.

Watch me who walk through coiling streets where rain
And fog choke every sigh; round corners of day,
Road-drills explore new areas of pain,
Nor trees reach leaf-lit branches down to play.
The city climbs in horror to my brain,
The writings are my only wings away.

1. Why does the speaker in the poem feel choked by "this century"?
   To what might he be referring in lines 1 and 2? What do you think
   Spender intended that "roots of night" should symbolize? How
   is this idea extended in the comparison made in lines 4-8? How
   do you interpret "Mind's buried thought"? State in your own
   words the proposition or argument developed in these first eight
   lines—the octave.
2. In the sestet, the poet moves from the general to the specific and
   from the past to the present. What impression of the city is conveyed in lines 9-12? Which words and phrases best reveal the
   over-all mood of the scene? Would you describe the mood of the
   poet as one of pity, or of fatigue and despair resulting from the
   ravages of one war, the approach of another, and a depression?
   Does the statement in line 13 reveal a similar or different mood?
   Explain.
3. Line 14 picks up the image in line 1, "the path of flight." Without
   such a path, what is the speaker's only alternative? Do you think
   he considers it a satisfactory or a futile substitute? Explain.
4. What influences of traditional romantic poetry are evident in the
   references made in the poem and in the poetic language? In your
   opinion is the poem less effective because of these influences or
   more so? Explain.

ULTIMA RATIO REGUM

The guns spell money's ultimate reason
In letters of lead on the Spring hillside.
But the boy lying dead under the olive trees

Was too young and too silly
To have been notable to their important eye.   5
He was a better target for a kiss.

When he lived, tall factory hooters never summoned him.
Nor did restaurant plate-glass doors revolve to wave him in.
His name never appeared in the papers.
The world maintained its traditional wall   10
Round the dead with their gold sunk deep as a well,
Whilst his life, intangible as a Stock Exchange rumor,
      drifted outside.

O too lightly he threw down his cap
One day when the breeze threw petals from the trees.
The unflowering wall sprouted with guns,   15
Machine-gun anger quickly scythed the grasses;
Flags and leaves fell from hands and branches;
The tweed cap rotted in the nettles.

Consider his life which was valueless
In terms of employment, hotel ledgers, news files.   20
Consider. One bullet in ten thousand kills a man.
Ask. Was so much expenditure justified
On the death of one so young, and so silly
Lying under the olive trees, O world, O death?

1. This poem is one of many Spender wrote about the Spanish Civil
   War in the 1930's. In these war poems, Spender could be bitterly
   ironic. What is ironic in the death of the boy, the "ultimate reason"
   for his death, and the circumstances surrounding his death? How
   does the irony affect the impact of the tragic incident? How are
   the emotions of futility, bitterness, and pity conveyed?
2. This poem illustrates the "coldness" with which Spender could
   "frame and hang" an idea or experience through double-edged
   images, such as the one in lines 1 and 2. Find others which you
   feel contribute to the total effect of the poem.

Dylan Thomas

When Dylan Thomas's poems first appeared, their originality in meter and imagery and their exuberant musical quality made a deep and immediate impression. The reader has to dig for the meaning, but it is always there—even when it is hidden under images which are symbolic in purpose. In his later poems, he expressed what he wanted to say more clearly, but the basic structure remains: compression of symbols and controlled rhythms which give his verse roughness of surface and terrific impact. Finally, however, what one remembers about Thomas's poems is the variety and beauty of musical sounds. He was a man intoxicated with words, who conveyed to others his joyful appreciation of the language.

FERN HILL

Now as I was young and easy under the apple boughs
About the lilting house and happy as the grass was green,
    The night above the dingle° starry,   valley
        Time let me hail and climb
    Golden in the heydays of his eyes,   5

And honored among wagons I was prince of the apple towns
And once below a time I lordly had the trees and leaves
　　　Trail with daisies and barley
　　Down the rivers of the windfall light.

And as I was green and carefree, famous among the barns　10
About the happy yard and singing as the farm was home,
　　In the sun that is young once only,
　　　Time let me play and be
　　Golden in the mercy of his means,
And green and golden I was huntsman and herdsman, the
　　calves　　　　　　　　　　　　　　　　　　　15
Sang to my horn, the foxes on the hills barked clear and cold,
　　　And the sabbath rang slowly
　　In the pebbles of the holy streams.

All the sun long it was running, it was lovely, the hay
Fields high as the house, the tunes from the chimneys,
　　　it was air　　　　　　　　　　　　　　　　20
　　And playing, lovely and watery
　　　And fire green as grass.
　　And nightly under the simple stars
As I rode to sleep the owls were bearing the farm away,
All the moon long I heard, blessed among stables,
　　the nightjars°　　　　　　　　　　　nighthawks　25
　　Flying with the ricks,° and the horses　　stacks of hay
　　　Flashing into the dark.

And then to awake, and the farm, like a wanderer white
With the dew, comes back, the cock on his shoulder: it was all
　　Shining, it was Adam and maiden,　　　　　　30
　　　The sky gathered again
　　And the sun grew round that very day.
So it must have been after the birth of the simple light

In the first, spinning place, the spellbound horses
    walking warm
      Out of the whinnying green stable   35
        On the fields of praise.

And honored among foxes and pheasants by the gay house
Under the new made clouds and happy as the heart was long,
    In the sun born over and over,
        I ran my heedless ways,   40
      My wishes raced through the house high hay
And nothing I cared, at my sky blue trades, that time allows
In all his tuneful turning so few and such morning songs
    Before the children green and golden
        Follow him out of grace,   45

Nothing I cared, in the lamb white days, that time
    would take me
Up to the swallow thronged loft by the shadow of my hand,
    In the moon that is always rising,
        Nor that riding to sleep
      I should hear him fly with the high fields   50
And wake to the farm forever fled from the childless land.
Oh as I was young and easy in the mercy of his means,
      Time held me green and dying
    Though I sang in my chains like the sea.

1. How does this poem reveal the influence of Gerard Manley Hopkins, whom Thomas imitated? Time is the central figure of the
   speaker's reminscence—the ruler of his childhood days. What is
   is the child's attitude toward time? Toward the world?
2. As a grown man looking back, what observation (implied in the
   last two lines) does the speaker make about these early years?
   How do you interpret lines 46-51?
3. What childhood experiences are pictured through the unusual

images in stanzas 1 and 2? What farm activity is going on that in-volves wagons and "apple towns"? In what ways is he "hunts-man" and "herdsman"?

4. How do you interpret lines 19-22 and the several references to "it"? Is each reference different or do all refer to the delights of being young and carefree? What does the speaker, as a child, imagine took place as he "rode to sleep" (lines 23-27)? What image pictures the scene when he awoke?

5. Recalling the shining morning (stanza 4), the speaker identifies it with "Adam and maiden." Point out the meaning and develop-ment of the metaphor in the remaining lines of the stanza.

6. In stanza 5, what images convey the passage of time? What was the attitude of the speaker as a child? What symbolic meaning do you think the oft-repeated words *green* and *golden* might have as they are used in this poem?

7. What Hopkins said of his own work — when you "read it with the ears . . . my verse becomes all right" — is also true of this poem. Even such expressions as " the house high hay" and "spellbound horses walking warm" seems less puzzling. Thomas's purpose is nearly always to create a picture in the mind, to appeal to the senses, or to express figuratively, rather than literally, a thought or feeling. Point out and discuss the words or expressions which seem unusual — even puzzling. Also point out examples of Thomas's extraordinarily keen ear for the sound of words in combinations.

THE HAND THAT SIGNED THE PAPER
FELLED A CITY [1]

The hand that signed the paper felled a city;
Five sovereign fingers taxed the breath,
Doubled the globe of dead and halved a country;
These five kings did a king to death.

[1] This poem may have been inspired by the signing in 1938 of the Munich Pact by Premier Daladier of France and Prime-Minister Chamberlain of England, which allowed Hitler to take over Czechoslovakia.

The mighty hand leads to a sloping shoulder,   5
The finger joints are cramped with chalk;
A goose's quill has put an end to murder
That put an end to talk.

The hand that signed the treaty bred a fever,
And famine grew, and locusts came;   10
Great is the hand that holds dominion over
Man by a scribbled name.

The five kings count the dead but do not soften
The crusted wound nor pat the brow;
A hand rules pity as a hand rules heaven;   15
Hands have no tears to flow.

1. In the first four stanzas, through what examples does Thomas emphasize the irony of the consequences of "a scribbled name"? How do you interpret line 4 and lines 7 and 8?
2. Are the "five kings" referred to in lines 4 and 13 the same? To whom do they refer? What deeper meaning is implied by the figurative language used in the reference?
3. The common meaning of the verb *rule* is "to govern." What meaning is intended in line 15? What general truth do you think that Thomas intends to convey in this line? What relation do you see between this line and the two preceding lines?
4. The last line could be interpreted as both the reason for the signing of the paper and a bitter commentary on war. State your interpretation and give reasons to support it.
5. What is unusual about the pattern of the metrical lines in each of the four stanzas? The poem appears to be traditional in both rhythm and rhyme. Is it? Point out irregularities in the predominant rhythm. What effect does each have on the meaning or movement of the line?

John Betjeman

Since the late 1940's, John Betjeman has been generally recognized as "the most popular poet in England." The reasons for this popular acceptance are easily recognized—his lyrical gift, his overt senti-mentality (carefully controlled to avoid spilling over into bathos), his humor, his ready "comprehensibility," as compared with many contemporary poets. For a time, there was a tendency among critics to dismiss Betjeman as merely a facile and "funny" poet, but he can strike a somber and deeply ironic note, as is shown in the second of the poems given here. Like Philip Larkin, whom he foreshadows, Betjeman combines traditional ("neo-Victorian") poetic forms with content and point of view typical of the second half of the 20th century. Betjeman and Larkin are known to admire each other's work greatly.

INDOOR GAMES NEAR NEWBURY

In among the silver birches winding ways of tarmac[1] wander
   And the signs to Bussock Bottom, Tussock Wood and
                         Windy Brake,
Gabled lodges, tile-hung churches, catch the lights of our
                         Lagonda[2]
   As we drive to Wendy's party, lemon curd and
                         Christmas cake.

                               5

[1]*tarmac:* a kind of road surface
[2]*Lagonda:* a make of automobile

Rich the makes of motor whirring,
Past the pine-plantation purring
Come up, Hupmobile, Delage³!
Short the way your chauffeurs travel,
Crunching over private gravel
Each from out his warm garage.

Oh but Wendy, when the carpet yielded to my indoor pumps
There you stood, your gold hair streaming,
Handsome in the hall-light gleaming
There you looked and there you led me off into the game of
clumps⁴
Then the new Victrola playing   15
And your funny uncle saying
'Choose your partners for a fox-trot! Dance until its *tea*
o'clock!'

'Come on, young 'uns, foot it featly!'
Was it chance that paired us neatly,
I, who loved you so completely,   20
You, who pressed me closely to you, hard against your party
frock?

'Meet me when you've finished eating!' So we met and no
one found us.
Oh that dark and furry cupboard while the rest played
hide and seek!
Holding hands our two hearts beating in the bedroom silence 25
round us,
Holding hands and hardly hearing sudden footstep, thud
and shriek.
Love that lay too deep for kissing —
'Where *is* Wendy? Wendy's missing!'
Love so pure it *had* to end,
Love so strong that I was frighten'd   30
When you gripped my fingers tight and
Hugging, whispered 'I'm your friend.'

³*Hupmobile, Delage:* makes of automobiles
⁴*clumps:* a party game, somewhat similar to "twenty questions"

Good-bye Wendy! Send the fairies, pinewood elf and larch
tree gnome,
  Spingle-spangled stars are peeping
  At the lush Lagonda creeping   35
Down the winding ways of tarmac to the leaded lights of
home.
  There, among the silver birches,
  All the bells of all the churches
Sounded in the bath-waste running out into the frosty air.
  Wendy speeded my undressing,   40
  Wendy is the sheet's caressing,
  Wendy bending gives a blessing,
Holds me as I drift to dreamland, safe inside my slumber-
wear.

1. This poem, of course, is a reminiscence of childhood. Do you
   think that the poet has deliberately chosen a metrical form suit-
   able for this theme? Explain.
2. The poet brilliantly evokes the "magical" atmosphere and excitement of a children's Christmas party. See if you can identify
   specific lines, figures, and words that contribute to this effect.
3. Betjeman is much admired for his ability to use apparently
   commonplace adjectives in a way that yields a special and distinctive effect. Some examples are *"private* gravel" (line 9) and
   "funny uncle" (line 16). Find some other examples in the poem.
   Try to explain why the adjective is so "right" in each case.
4. What is the mood of the last stanza? What effect is gained by
   the three successive lines beginning with "Wendy"?
5. Is the poet making fun of this "childish infatuation"? Or does he
   remember it as an authentic and enriching human experience?

DEVONSHIRE STREET W.1

The heavy mahogany door with its wrought-iron screen
  Shuts. And the sound is rich, sympathetic, discreet.
The sun still shines on this eighteenth-century scene
  With Edwardian faience[1] adornments — Devonshire Street.[2]

[1]*faience:* a kind of earthenware decorated with colored glass, particularly
popular during the Edwardian era (the reign of King Edward VII; 1901-10).
[2]*Devonshire Street:* a street in London where many doctors have their offices.

No hope. And the X-ray photographs under his arm   5
    Confirm the message. His wife stands timidly by.
The opposite brick-built house looks lofty and calm
    Its chimneys steady against a mackerel sky.

No hope. And the iron knob of this palisade
    So cold to the touch, is luckier now than he   10
'Oh merciless, hurrying Londoners! Why was I made
    For the long and the painful deathbed coming to me?'

She puts her fingers in his, as, loving and silly,
    At long-past Kensington[3] dances she used to do
'It's cheaper to take the tube to Piccadilly   15
    And then we can catch a nineteen or a twenty-two.'[4]

1. The first stanza evokes an atmosphere of solidity, placidity,
   permanence. How does the poet do this? In view of the theme
   of the poem, why does he *want* to begin with such an effect?
2. In a very few words at the outset of the second stanza, the poet
   gives you the essence of the situation. What are these words?
   Why does he choose to convey this in so spare and economical
   a style?
3. How does the third stanza express the feelings of the sick man?
   Does he actually speak the sentences quoted in lines 11 and
   12? In what sense does the poet attribute these words to him?
4. In the last stanza, the poem becomes powerful and poignant.
   Yet the words which the wife speaks are utterly trivial. How do
   you explain this paradox?
5. What does this poem tell us about death—and life?

---

[3]*Kensington:* a district of London
[4]These numbers refer to bus routes.

Philip Larkin

Philip Larkin's poetry springs from a sense of emptiness made bearable by a sense of humor. While the informal diction of his poems often slides into carefully chosen slang, it is never sloppy. Larkin's slang always achieves an effect not possible to gain in another way. The tone of his work is sophisticated and intelligent. Such polished verse is not the youthful bleating of a passionate animal, but rather the humane and well-modulated voice of a civilized man.

PLACES, LOVED ONES

No, I have never found
The place where I could say
This is my proper ground,
Here I shall stay;
Nor met that special one   5
Who has an instant claim
On everything I own
Down to my name;

To find such seems to prove
You want no choice in where   10
To build, or whom to love;
You ask them to bear
You off irrevocably,
So that it's not your fault
Should the town turn dreary,   15
The girl a dolt.

Yet, having missed them, you're
Bound, none the less, to act
As if what you settled for
Mashed you, in fact;   20
And wiser to keep away
From thinking you still might trace
Uncalled-for to this day
Your person, your place.

1. What, about marriage (as it is described in lines 5-8), seems to frighten or offend the speaker? What objections does he pose in stanza 2?
2. Lines 14-16 seem to imply that under some circumstances it *might* be one's own fault if the town turns dreary and the girl seems a dolt. Under what circumstances would one have to accept some blame for such things?
3. Who does *them* refer to in line 12? in line 17? What mood dominates the last stanza? How does this stanza differ from the first two? What picture of the speaker emerges from this stanza? Does he seem the same personality who spoke in the rest of the poem? What is the pretense he finds objectionable in lines 17-20? What belief does he warn himself away from in lines 21-24?
4. Where do you find partial or faulty rhymes in the poem? What effect do they have on the poem? Such phrases as *in fact* in line 20, make the tone of the poem chatty or conversational. Do you feel this tone is appropriate, or would you prefer a more formal style? Why?

5. Turn the situation of the poem around. If you could say "This is my proper ground. Here I shall stay," what kind of life and world would you be accepting?

MR. BLEANEY

"This was Mr. Bleaney's room. He stayed
The whole time he was at the Bodies,[1] till
They moved him." Flowered curtains, thin and frayed,
Fall to within five inches of the sill,

Whose window shows a strip of building land,   5
Tussocky, littered. "Mr. Bleaney took
My bit of garden properly in hand."
Bed, upright chair, sixty-watt bulb, no hook

Behind the door, no room for books or bags —
"I'll take it." So it happens that I lie   10
Where Mr. Bleaney lay, and stub my fags°   cigarettes
On the same saucer-souvenir, and try

Stuffing my ears with cotton wool, to drown
The jabbering set he egged her on to buy.
I know his habits — what time he came down,   15
His preference for sauce to gravy, why

He kept on plugging at the four aways —
Likewise their yearly frame: the Frinton folk
Who put him up for summer holidays,
And Christmas at his sister's house in Stoke.   20

[1] *the Bodies:* Mr. Larkin writes, "The Bodies is intended to suggest a firm making car bodies. I hoped the line would have comic overtones."

But if he stood and watched the frigid wind
Tousling the clouds, lay on the fusty bed
Telling himself that this was home, and grinned,
And shivered, without shaking off the dread

That how we live measures our own nature,   25
And at his age having no more to show
Than one hired box should make him pretty sure
He warranted no better, I don't know.

1. What kind of person does a name like Bleaney suggest? Which
   words does the name appear to be composed of? What kind of
   man do the room's furnishings suggest?
2. When the speaker takes Mr. Bleaney's room, what kind of man
   do you assume the speaker is? How are the two further identified
   with each other? What does the speaker seem to think of Mr.
   Bleaney?
3. What dreadful possibility does the speaker wonder if Mr. Bleaney
   thought of? Why, having spoken of this possibility, does the
   speaker end the poem with "I don't know"?
4. How would you describe Larkins's style in this poem? Comment
   on rhythm, meter, rhyme, musical devices, tone, diction, and final
   effect.

About the Poets

Matthew Arnold (1822-1888), the son of a famous headmaster of Rugby School, spent thirty-five years of his adult life serving as Inspector of Schools. Despite the routine drudgery of this job, however, he managed to publish five volumes of poetry. A turning point in his life came in 1857, when he was chosen Professor of Poetry at Oxford, an appointment he held for ten years. Although he lectured on literary subjects, he became increasingly concerned with the great cultural problems of his day. He all but abandoned writing poetry for the vigorous prose of literary and social criticism. His purpose was to change the values of the complacent, middle-class people he called "Philistines" by describing the humane ideals of culture. *Essays in Criticism* (1865) proclaims his high literary standards. *Culture and Anarchy* (1869) contains his most significant social criticism.

Wystan Hugh Auden (1907-1973) became associated, as a student at Oxford, with a group of poets who felt that only the creation of a new order could arrest the decay of middle class society. In 1937 Auden drove an ambulance for the Spanish Loyalists, and in the same year was awarded the King's Poetry Medal. By 1940 he had published several volumes of poetry, a collection of prose fiction, and two anthologies; he had also published three plays, in collaboration with the British playwright Christopher Isherwood. The title of *The Age of Anxiety*, Auden's 1947 volume of poems, provided critics with a descriptive phrase for the 1950's and 1960's. The year after he received an award from the American Academy of Arts and Letters (1945), he became a United States citizen. In 1948 he was awarded the Pulitzer Prize in Poetry and in 1953, the Bollingen Prize.

John Betjeman (1906-   ) has been called "probably the most popular English poet since Byron." Coming from an affluent and cultured family, he was educated at Oxford, and apparently never had the slightest doubt that he would be a professional poet and writer. His first book of poems, *Ghastly Good Taste,* was issued in 1933, and since then he has published a dozen books of verse, as well as prose works, with such titles as *Pocket Guide to English Parish Churches* and *Victorian and Edwardian London.* He has received many honors, including the Queen's Gold Medal for Poetry in 1960, and was knighted in 1969. In 1972, he became the 17th Poet Laureate—a post held by such figures as Dryden, Wordsworth, Tennyson, Robert Bridges, and John Masefield.

Sir John continues to write enthusiastically in both poetry and prose, "celebrating his homeland's unique glories and crotchets." He has also become a popular "personality" on British TV.

William Blake (1757-1827) was a self-educated poet, painter, and engraver. The son of a poor London shopkeeper, he was apprenticed to an engraver at the age of fourteen. His most famous engravings are those for "The Book of Job" and Dante's *Divine Comedy.* Blake's *Songs of Innocence* (1789) and *Songs of Experience* (1794), like some of his other collections of poetry, were published in a manner unusual in both literary and art history. He cut both the verses and the accompanying illustrations in copper plates to make engraved copies, each of which was then colored by hand.

Blake was a religious mystic who saw evidences of God's handiwork in every object and every action. To him the whole world was a rich tapestry of symbols through which he interpreted the meaning of life.

Elizabeth Barrett Browning (1806-1861), writing in the seclusion of her father's home at 50 Wimpole Street, London, where she was confined as an invalid after an injury to her spine, was the most highly respected woman poet in England. Robert Browning, an obscure poet, admired her poems, came to visit, fell in love, and rescued her in 1846 from the gloomy household dominated by her ogre-like father, who never forgave her elopement.

Mrs. Browning's social sympathy was expressed in early poems, such as "The Cry of the Children," and in her later poems treating of Italian political affairs. *Aurora Leigh* (1857), her longest poem, is a romance in blank verse in which she expressed her views on social, political, and economic subjects. Her highest achievement was *Son-*

nets from the Portuguese (1850), a series of love sonnets which she began writing to her husband during their engagement.

Robert Browning (1812-1889) acquired from his well-to-do parents a love for books, pictures, and music. His father provided him with tutors and with access to his own fine library. Even though Browning was not educated at a university, he was one of the most learned men of his time. In fact, Browning's first poems were too erudite to appeal widely to the public. His poetric triumph is *The Ring and the Book*, a succession of dramatic monologues which retell the story of a crime and trial many times, each time from the point of view of a different person as he perceives the truth.

In 1846 he eloped with Elizabeth Barrett, taking her to Italy, where they enjoyed an ideal marriage until her death thirteen years later. After his wife's death, he returned to London, where he became a well-known figure in the society of his day.

Robert Burns (1759-1796), Scotland's greatest poet, was considered an untaught genius because he lacked the formal education thought essential for a poet's training. However, his family, although poverty-stricken peasants, were "reading people," and as a boy Burns became acquainted with the English poets from Shakespeare to Gray. He also delighted in Scottish songbooks, which influenced his talent. After his first volume of poems was published in 1786, he went to Edinburgh, where he became a literary and social celebrity.

After a stormy courtship, Burns married Jean Armour, settled on a farm, where he was constantly beset by financial difficulties. In 1789 he became an exciseman in Dumfries to eke out a living. His last years were devoted largely to collecting and editing traditional songs and ballads of ancient Scotland. His early death at the age of thirty-seven is believed to have resulted from heart disease.

George Gordon, Lord Byron (1788-1824) was an aristocratic rebel whose high-spirited life captured the imagination of all Europe. The son of erratic parents, he attended Harrow and Cambridge, where he was both a good student and an excellent athlete. A deformed foot only increased his determination to excel at everything.

Byron dismissed a political career in the House of Lords after the sensational reception of the first two cantos of *Childe Harold's Pilgrimage* (1812), an account of his tour of Europe and the Near East. This poetical guidebook presented Europe through the eyes of an active, full-blooded, yet melancholy young man with a soul that

loved liberty and adventure. Byron became famous overnight and
was the toast of London society, through which he cut an amorous
swath. Marriage to Anne Milbank, a conventional woman who
wished to reform him, proved disastrous. After their divorce, society
turned against him, and he left England to reside abroad the last
eight years of his life.

Byron was joined by Shelley and other English expatriates in
Italy, where he composed the last cantos of *Childe Harold*, most of
his dramas, and his masterpiece *Don Juan*, an unfinished verse satire.
Aroused by the Greeks' struggle to gain independence from Turkey,
Byron gave both financial support and personal leadership to a company of Greek soldiers. At Missolonghi he contracted fever and died
at the age of thirty-six.

Geoffrey Chaucer (c. 1340-1400) was the son of a prosperous wine
merchant who had enough prestige to gain Geoffrey an appointment
as page to the Countess of Ulster. In her household, Geoffrey gained
an excellent education. Later, he served with the English army in
France during the Hundred Years' War, was captured, and then
ransomed by the King. Sometime within the next seven years,
Chaucer married one of the Queen's attendants who was a sister of
the woman who later became John of Gaunt's third wife. Thus
Chaucer's marriage provided connections not only with the royal
household but also with John of Gaunt—perhaps the most powerful
man in England at this time. In 1374, he was appointed to the first
of several comfortable positions in the customs office, which gave
him financial independence. Though his finances grew more pre-
carious after 1388, when the shifting fortunes of Richard II imperiled
all of Richard's associates, Chaucer produced his best poetry in his
last years. Besides *The Canterbury Tales*, his most important work
is *Troilus and Criseyde*, a long chivalric narrative. Chaucer, along
with Shakespeare and Milton, is considered one of the greatest poets
England has produced.

Samuel Taylor Coleridge (1772-1834), the thirteenth child of a
scholarly minister, came to Cambridge as a scholarship student with
a reputation for astonishing erudition. With several others, including
the poet Robert Southey, he planned to go to America to found a
"Pantisocracy," a community of poets and philosophers. The scheme
failed, but not before he had entered into an unhappy marriage with
Southey's sister-in-law.

His best poems were written during his intimate friendship with

William and Dorothy Wordsworth. In 1798 the two men published *Lyrical Ballads,* often seen as the beginning of the Romantic movement. Coleridge never again wrote poetry equal to the "handful of golden poems" produced within a few months in 1797-98. His productivity was hampered by his addiction to opium, which had been prescribed to relieve the pains of neuralgia. Always a brilliant conversationalist, he gave lectures to earn a living. In his *Biographia Literaria* (1817), he defined the nature of true poetry and set forth criteria for judging works of art.

John Donne (1572?-1631) studied law, traveled on the Continent, took part in several expeditions, and spent his family inheritance before he settled down as secretary to Sir Thomas Egerton. Donne fell in love with his employer's sixteen-year-old niece, Anne More, and secretly married her. For many years they lived in great deprivation, cut off from any financial assistance for their growing family. After a deep spiritual struggle, he gave up the Roman Catholic faith into which he had been born, and in 1615 entered the Church of England. His talent as a preacher was as striking as his talent as a poet. He was soon a favorite of James I and became famous as the Dean of St. Paul's in London.

Most of Donne's poetry, though widely read in manuscript form during his lifetime, was not published until after his death. Recognized now as the leader of the Metaphysical poets, Donne has probably influenced modern poets as much as any writer of the English Renaissance.

John Dryden (1631-1700), soon after his education was completed, turned to playwrighting as a means of earning money. The most famous of his plays, *All for Love,* is based on Shakespeare's *Antony and Cleopatra.* But he was not primarily a playwright; he rose to become the leading poet of his time and, eventually, Poet Laureate of England. He is associated with the eighteenth century because of his influence on younger poets, notably Pope and Gray.

When Dryden converted to Catholicism almost as soon as the Catholic king, James II, gained the English throne, people accused Dryden of being hypocritical about religion. However, he remained a Catholic after the Revolution of 1688, and lost all his public posts and his poet laureateship because of his religion. By this time, though, he had established himself not only as the leading poet, but as the most important satirist and literary critic of his time. Two of his most famous satires in verse are *Mac Flecknoe* and *Absalom and*

Achitophel. During the remaining years of his life he was held in the highest esteem, and was buried in Westminister Abbey.

Robert Graves (1895-   ) was educated at Oxford, served in World War I in the Royal Welsh Fusiliers, and was wounded in France. He has taught and lived in many countries, including Egypt and Greece. Since World War II, he has made his permanent home on the island of Majorca, off the coast of Spain. A versatile writer, Graves has produced everything from critical essays and historical novels, to ballads and lyrics. Some of his best-known works include his autobiography, *Goodbye to All That*, the novel, *I, Claudius* and his books on mythology, *The White Goddess* and *The Greek Myths*. His *Collected Poems* was published in 1959, and in 1961, he succeeded W. H. Auden as Professor of Poetry at Oxford. In 1963 he spent a year as lecturer at the Massachusetts Institute of Technology.

Thomas Gray (1716-1771) was one of the most learned men of his day and remains one of the most scholarly of all English poets. A shy man, he was constantly absorbed in and stimulated by books. Most of his life was spent at Cambridge, first as a student and later as Professor of History. Perhaps because he alone of a family of twelve survived childhood, Gray was preoccupied with death. As a young man, Gray accompanied Horace Walpole on a walking tour of France and Italy, where he took delight in the sublime beauty of the Alps. His keen perception of beauty may account for the demands he placed upon his own verses. He spent six years composing and carefully revising the relatively short "Elegy Written in a Country Churchyard," which he finally published anonymously to escape attracting attention to himself. Today he is one of the most frequently quoted poets because he expressed commonplace sentiments with precision and beauty.

Thomas Hardy (1840-1928) was born in a small hamlet in Dorset, a rural section of southern England which became the famous "Wessex" country of his novels. Here he spent most of his life. During his early years he composed many poems, but when no publisher would accept them he spent the next twenty-five years writing fiction. His early novels, including *The Return of the Native*, established him as a successful novelist. However, although *Tess of the D'Urbervilles* and *Jude the Obscure* were equally distinguished, they were so savagely attacked that Hardy abandoned fiction entirely. He devoted the remaining years of his life to poetry, during which time he produced *The Dynasts*, a three-part verse epic of the Napoleonic era which, like his novels, exhibits the role Fate plays, ruthlessly and purposelessly, in human affairs.

George Herbert (1593-1633) belonged to one of England's greatest families. His mother, Lady Magdalen Herbert, was considered one of the most gracious, intelligent, and devout women of her day. She often entertained such luminaries as the Reverend John Donne, Dean of St. Paul's Cathedral, in the Herbert home. Lady Magdalen is credited with influencing her son George to go into the ministry.

Herbert was educated at Westminster School and Trinity College, Cambridge, where he was considered a brilliant scholar. After earning his M. A., he served for eight years as public orator of the university. In 1630, however, he gave up his promising secular career to enter the church. He and his wife were assigned to a country parish, where most of his best poetry was written. He died at Bemerton three years later, and was buried beneath the church altar. Published after his death, Herbert's poems were immediately popular and influenced a whole school of poets which followed him.

Robert Herrick (1591-1674) was apprenticed to a London goldsmith as a young man. He left London to gain his university education, but apparently returned for ten years to enjoy the kind of life available to one in Ben Jonson's literary circle. In 1648, on Jonson's recommendation, he supervised publication of his complete works, a volume of some twelve hundred poems, entitled *Hesperides*.

When Herrick entered holy orders, presumably for the sake of earning a living, he went somewhat reluctantly to a vicarage in Devonshire, far from the delights of the city. He learned to love the country and his rustic parishioners, however, and enjoyed those rural pleasures idealized by the ancient pagan poets he admired. This pastoral idyll was interrupted for fourteen years when he was exiled to London by the Puritans, but he seems to have enjoyed himself there, too. In 1622 he was allowed to return to his old parish in Devonshire, where he remained happily until his death.

Gerard Manley Hopkins (1844-1889), the eldest of eight children, was born in Stratford, Essex, and attended day school near London.

In 1857 he toured Belgium and the Rhineland with his father, and in 1863 he was matriculated at Balliol College, Oxford. Here, in the academic town he grew to love, he came to know John Henry Newman, first through his writings and then in person. As a result of this acquaintance and of much spiritual reflection, he was converted to Catholicism and, in 1868, entered the Jesuits. Nine years later he was ordained to the priesthood. Thereafter he spent a quiet life in academic and pastoral pursuits, serving as Professor of Greek at the Royal University of Ireland in Dublin from 1884 until his death in 1889. His poems remained unpublished for nearly thirty years. A first edition, edited by his friend Robert Bridges, appeared in 1918. A second edition, which was published in 1930, finally brought his poetry the acclaim it deserved.

A. E. Housman (1859-1936) gained first class honors in the classics while attending St. John's College, Oxford, but he failed to obtain honors in the humane letters. He thereby lost the opportunity to qualify for a fellowship. The effect on his sensitive, defensive nature was so crushing that for ten dreary years he served as a clerk in the British Patent Office in London. At night he studied Latin and Greek in the British Museum, determined to redeem himself in some way for his academic failure. A series of scholarly articles written during this time finally won him recognition in the learned world. In 1892 he was appointed Professor of Latin at London University, where he taught until 1911. From that time until his death, he was Professor of Latin at Cambridge University. In 1896 he published, at his own expense, a small volume of poems entitled *A Shropshire Lad*. No book of verse published in the past half-century has had such popular appeal.

Ben Jonson (1573?-1637), a brilliant and largely self-educated student, worked as a bricklayer, ran away to join the army, but returned to establish himself as actor, playwright, poet, and eventually as the literary leader of London. His admirers made him famous for the lively literary sessions he dominated at the Mermaid Tavern. Constantly embroiled in quarrels, he often provoked attacks through his satirical plays. On one occasion, he went to jail voluntarily to show his sympathy for his collaborators who had satirized King James. Nevertheless, the king later gave Jonson a pension, making him Poet Laureate. Jonson supervised publication of his own literary works, including two volumes of poetry and a volume of miscellaneous comments, translations, and criticism. With no false mod-

✓

esty, he made sure that his writings were preserved in proper form
for posterity.

John Keats (1795-1821), though an honor student, showed no
special interest in literature until he was introduced to mythology
and travel lore at the age of fifteen, the same year he was both or-
phaned and apprenticed to an apothecary-surgeon. By the age of
twenty-one, he had decided to give up medicine and devote himself to poetry.

Keats's first volume, called *Poems* (1817), attracted little attention.
His *Endymion* (1818), a rather formless, overexuberant poem, was
harshly condemned by reviewers. As a result, a legend grew up that
Keats's early death was provoked by harsh criticism. Maturing
rapidly in his poetic skills, however, Keats wrote nearly all his best
poems during the year 1819. Before the close of that productive
period he also learned that he was dying of tuberculosis, as had his
mother and brother. By the time his third and last volume of poetry
was published in 1820, his health was failing fast. He died in Rome
in February, 1821, at the age of twenty-six. He is considered one of
England's greatest poets.

Philip Larkin (1922-   ) was educated at King Henry VIII School,
Coventry, and St. John's College, Oxford. He has held posts in
several colleges since 1943. In 1961 he became the jazz correspond-
ent for the *Daily Telegraph* and in 1965 he won the Queen's Gold
Medal for poetry. His publications include three volumes of poems —
The North Ship, *The Less Deceived*, and *The Whitsun Weddings* —
as well as two novels — *Jill* and *A Girl in Winter*. He is presently
librarian at the University of Hull.

Richard Lovelace (1618- c.1657) is remembered for the two poems
included in this volume. His other poems never reach the point of
excellence attained in these two.

Lovelace was born either in Holland or at Woolwich, England. He
attended Oxford for only two years, but was granted an M. A. at the
request of "a great lady" who attended the Queen during a royal
visit to the University. After his schooling was completed, he became a popular courtier because of his personal charm and his poetic
and musical talent. He participated in the Scottish expeditions of
1639 and 1640. Then he was imprisoned for presenting to Parliament
a petition to restore Charles I's rights. It was during this time that

he wrote "To Althea from Prison." Abroad most of the time between 1642 and 1647, he was again imprisoned in 1648. When released, he found his fortune gone, his King executed, and his beloved court dissolved. Tradition has it that he died poor and heartbroken in London.

Christopher Marlowe (1564-1593) was born and grew up in Canterbury. While a student at Cambridge, he ran afoul of the university authorities because of his involvement in some kind of secret government service. He led a turbulent life which ended with a tavern brawl in which he was stabbed to death by one Ingram Frizer. Today the cause of the quarrel is thought to have been political, possibly related to Marlowe's activities as a spy. The most brilliant of a group known as the "university wits," Marlowe enjoyed sensational success with his romantic tragedies. These included *Tamburlaine the Great, The Tragical History of Doctor Faustus, The Jew of Malta,* and *Edward II.*

Andrew Marvell (1621-1678) was born in Yorkshire, the son of a Puritan clergyman. He gained his education at Cambridge and then briefly held a clerkship at a Hull business house. From 1642-1646 he traveled in Europe and later, in 1650, he became the tutor to Mary Fairfax, daughter of the powerful Lord Fairfax. Despite John Milton's recommendation, he failed to win an appointment as assistant secretary to the Council of State, but later served as a colleague of Milton's in the Latin Secretaryship. He ended his public career by serving during the last twenty years of his life as a Member of Parliament representing his home town of Hull. Though only a few of his poems were printed during his lifetime, his verses were brought together and published after his death in 1681.

John Milton (1608-1674) received from his father, a prosperous scrivener, an exceptional classical education, after which he wrote his early poems. His education was climaxed by a fifteen-month grand tour of Europe. In traveling, he met such leading intellectuals as Grotius and Galileo, and absorbed the Renaissance culture of Italy; but his Protestant convictions compelled him to return to England in 1640 to lend his support to the Puritan Revolution. From 1641 to 1660 he was deeply involved in public life, becoming Secretary for the Foreign Tongues to the Council of State for the Commonwealth in 1648.

After the Restoration of Charles II, Milton was imprisoned, fined, and then freed to write. During the final phase of his life, when he was blind, Milton reached the height of his creative powers. His third wife, thirty years his junior, served as housekeeper while he dictated his mighty epic, *Paradise Lost* (1667), and its shorter sequel, *Paradise Regained* (1671) to his daughters. He also wrote a biblical tragedy, *Samson Agonistes* (1671), a Latin grammar, and a Latin dictionary. Milton is considered, along with Chaucer, Shakespeare, and a few others, one of the greatest poets England has produced.

Alexander Pope (1688-1744), frail and sickly at birth, suffered from ill health and a physical deformity throughout his life. His Catholic faith prevented him from taking a degree, but he was better educated, through his own efforts, than were most men of his day. By the time he was twenty-five, he was recognized as England's leading poet. His translations of Homer's epics, the *Iliad* and the *Odyssey*, brought him a fortune and enabled him to purchase an estate at Twickenham where he lived out his life. Between 1709 and 1738, Pope wrote such major works as *Essay on Criticism*, *The Rape of the Lock*, *The Dunciad*, *Essay on Man*, *Moral Essays*, and *Imitations of Horace*. His poetry, didactic and satiric, has been restored somewhat to popular favor in modern times.

Sir Walter Raleigh (c.1552-1618) was a public figure of considerable importance. Born in Devonshire, he studied briefly at Oxford but soon won fame as a soldier of fortune. He and his half-brother led a fleet against Spanish shipping; on an expedition to Ireland, he was credited with executing some six hundred Spaniards. At times a great favorite with Elizabeth (she profited greatly from his raids on Spanish ships), she once had him put in prison for paying too much attention to one of her maids of honor. Though his efforts at colonizing the New World came to nought, he introduced potatoes and tobacco into England. James I had Raleigh imprisoned in the Tower of London for opposing his claims to the throne. While in prison Raleigh began his ambitious *History of the World*. He wrote one of his best-known poems on the eve of his execution.

William Shakespeare (1564-1616). The facts of William Shakespeare's life that are known with certainty can be told in a few paragraphs. The poet-dramatist was baptized in the Church of the Holy Trinity at Stratford on April 26, 1564, and because baptism ordinarily took place within three days of birth, his actual birthdate is usually reported as April 23. The next date on record is that of his marriage to Anne Hathaway, November 28, 1582, when William would have been eighteen. The baptismal dates of his three children follow: Susanna, May 26, 1583, and the twins Hamnet and Judith, February 1585. No other fact is known of his life up to 1592, when Robert Greene wrote an angry passage, proving that by then Shakespeare was well enough known in dramatic circles to attract the jealousy of a rival playwright.

The next few years provide scattered facts: publication of certain poems in 1593 and 1594; death and burial of his only son in 1596; purchase of New Place, the largest house in Stratford, in 1597 — a fact that suggests how well he was prospering in the London theater; various negotiations and legal actions between 1600 and 1610; finally, the date of his death, April 23, 1616, and burial in the chancel of Stratford Church — a fact which indicates the respect he had achieved at home. Aside from his literary works, the principal document of his life that survives is his will, which leaves no doubt that he died a prosperous man.

Percy Bysshe Shelley (1792-1822) flouted conventionality and asserted the freedom of the individual. He was expelled from Oxford for writing a pamphlet entitled *The Necessity of Atheism*. His *Prometheus Unbound*, based on an ancient Greek myth, attacks tyranny and states that love of humanity is the harmonizing element of life.

A youthful marriage to Harriet Westbrook, who lagged behind him as an intellectual companion, failed. Shelley eloped to the Continent with Mary Godwin, whom he married after his first wife committed suicide. When the courts refused him custody of his children by his first marriage, he left England permanently to reside in Switzerland and Italy, where he was an intimate friend of Byron. Those who knew him agreed that Shelley was thoroughly unselfish and always motivated by the highest integrity. Yet he moved naively through a series of unconventional acts which caused much unintentional suffering. When he was but thirty years old, his sailboat capsized off the coast of Italy and Shelley drowned.

Sir Philip Sidney (1554-1586) belonged to a prominent and powerful family and himself had a brilliant, if brief, career, both as soldier and poet. In his travels, he met some of the best minds of Europe and acquired a broad cultural background. His sister, the Countess of Pembroke and the leading patroness of letters in her day, persuaded him to write *Arcadia* when he was temporarily out of favor with the court. *Astrophel and Stella*, his sonnet sequence dedicated to Penelope Devereux, was written just before he married Frances Walsingham. Sidney was planning to join Sir Francis Drake on an expedition to America when he was appointed Governor of Flushing in Holland and was thereby given the opportunity to fight the Spanish. Wounded in battle, he died twenty-six days later. He was universally regarded as the ideal Renaissance gentleman and was given a magnificent hero's funeral in London at St. Paul's Cathedral.

Dame Edith Sitwell (1887-1964) was the daughter of the famous antiquarian and geologist, Sir George Sitwell. Educated privately, she spent much of her childhood at Renishaw hall in Derbyshire. From her early years she exhibited her enduring interest in the modern movements of art and literature. As soon as she was old enough to gain some independence, she began to write, her early work greatly influenced by Swinburne and the French symbolists.

Dame Edith's career is associated particularly with poetry. She produced ten volumes of verse and also, between 1916 and 1921, edited *Wheels*, an annual anthology of experimental poems. Her accomplishments earned her honorary degrees from the universities in Leeds, Durham, Oxford, and Sheffield. She became a Dame of the British Empire in 1954. Several works in other fields besides poetry were also published by her. She wrote critical and historical works on subjects such as Alexander Pope and the British eccentrics. Her autobiography, *Taken Care Of*, was published after her death on December 9, 1964.

Stephen Spender (1909-   ) is grouped with W. H. Auden and C. Day Lewis as one of the leaders of the "new" English poetry. Frustrated by economic conditions in England in the 1930's, and an ardent humanist, Spender temporarily saw in Marxist Communism the promise of a better world. He was quickly disillusioned by the Russian interpretation of Marxist ideals under Stalin. When World War II broke out, he gave full support to the defeat of Hitler, despite his reservations about "the Chamberlain system."

In 1955 he published *Collected Poems*, which he felt represented his best work. He was one of the founders of the literary magazine *Horizon;* in 1953 he became a co-editor of another literary magazine, *Encounter*. He has edited several anthologies of poetry, translated from the German the poems of Rainer Maria Rilke, and has written critical essays which have won him praise as a writer of permanent value.

Edmund Spenser (c.1552-1599), son of a clothmaker, held a poor boy's scholarship to the Merchant Taylors' School and a kind of working scholarship to Cambridge. He and Sir Philip Sidney later became friends and helped to introduce classical meters into English poetry. Through Sidney, Spenser gained access to court circles, where he had hopes of a career.

Spenser spent much of his adult life in Ireland, where he served as secretary to Lord Grey, Lord Deputy of Ireland. He returned to England to seek favor with Queen Elizabeth by publishing *The Faerie Queene*. Elizabeth was apparently pleased, but Spenser returned to Ireland with a smaller pension than he had anticipated. To Elizabeth Boyle, his second wife, he dedicated *Amoretti*, his sonnet sequence, and *Epithalamion*, his famous marriage poem. He also completed three more books of *The Faerie Queene*. It was while he was in England, arranging for their publication that a revolt broke out in Ireland. He returned to his family but finally fled with his wife and surviving children to London, where he soon died.

Sir John Suckling (1609-1642) grew up around London and attended Cambridge University and Gray's Inn — much like any other comfortably-provided young man of his time — until he inherited his father's large fortune. Then he traveled extensively in Europe and when he returned to England in 1630, was knighted. A soldier at heart, he fought in several important battles; but he excelled equally in the social graces. He was well known at court because of his wit and his wealth. He was notorious for leading a dissipated life and for indulging in extravagant entertainments. Because he was discovered taking part in an illegal plot in 1641, he was forced to flee to France. He supposedly committed suicide there in 1642. Although he wrote four plays, he is chiefly remembered for a few quickly composed lyrics which have lived.

Algernon Charles Swinburne (1837-1909), distinguished himself at both Eton and Oxford by his extensive reading. However, his radical opinions and rebellious behavior caused his stay at both institutions to be brief. After writing two unsuccessful plays, he published *Atalanta in Calydon* (1865), which was praised for its lyrical beauty.

About the Poets **⋙** 501

The following year his *Poems and Ballads* scandalized Victorians, who never forgave him for detesting organized religion and for writing frankly sensuous verses. As a hater of monarchy, Swinburne took up the cause of Italian freedom, writing *Songs Before Sunrise* (1871) and other poems celebrating the Risorgimento. As a critic, he produced monographs on Shakespeare and other Elizabethans. But finally this unconventional apostle of liberty became a conservative man of letters in his later years, defending imperialism and opposing Home Rule for the colonies.

Alfred, Lord Tennyson (1809-1892), the most important poet of the Victorian Age, was born into a clergyman's family of twelve children. He and his two brothers brought out their first book of verse when they were schoolboys. Later, at Cambridge, he belonged to "The Apostles," a club of young poets, critics, and thinkers. He was by then a large, gruff, shaggy fellow, notoriously shy and undistinguished as a scholar.

Tennyson's first collection of verse was *Poems, Chiefly Lyrical* (1830). Two years later, after his second volume received sharp criticism, and after the death of his closest friend, Arthur Hallam, the sensitive young poet entered his "ten year period of silence." During this decade he studied, traveled, and perfected his craft. When *Poems in Two Volumes* appeared in 1842, a popularity began that was to accelerate for fifty years. *In Memoriam*, the elegy to Hallam, reached the public in 1850, the year Tennyson married Emily Sellwood and became Poet Laureate. In 1884 he was knighted by Queen Victoria.

Dylan Thomas (1914-1953) was born in Wales and was educated at the Swansea Grammar School, where his father was an English teacher. His first volume of verse, *Eighteen Poems*, was published when he was only nineteen. He later wrote a tentative autobiography, *Portrait of the Artist as a Young Dog*, in which he tried to explain in prose what he was attempting to do in verse.

After World War II, during which he served as an antiaircraft gunner, Thomas continued his career as a writer. Gifted with a winning voice, he read his own poems, and the poems of others, over the B.B.C. He later traveled throughout England, Wales, and the United States, winning great public acclaim for his poetry readings. *Under Milk Wood*, a drama written for broadcast by the same network, has been successfully produced on the New York stage. Thomas died in New York City in 1953 while on a lecture tour.

William Wordsworth (1770-1850) is credited with beginning the English Romantic Movement when he and Coleridge published *Lyrical Ballads* in 1798. Wordsworth and his sister Dorothy, who was his lifelong companion, shared many convictions with Coleridge. The three of them, for a time "three persons in one soul," visited Germany together at the turn of the century. Upon returning to England, the two Wordsworths took a home in the Lake District, where William later held a government post, which allowed him to devote most of his time to literature. In 1802 he married his sister's friend, Mary Hutchinson.

Wordsworth was an early enthusiast of the French Revolution. With the rise of Napoleon, however, his revolutionary ardor waned, and he finally became so intensely nationalistic that younger writers derided him for his political conservatism. His finest poetry was written during the decade from 1798 to 1808. In 1843 he was made Poet Laureate.

William Butler Yeats (1865-1939), Irish by birth, was educated partly in England and partly in Ireland, spending many summers in County Sligo, in the wildest part of western Ireland. Here he lost his heart to the exquisite scenery of lakes and mountains, listened to family stories, and learned the legends and folklore which survived among the peasants.

Yeats gave up all attempts at a formal education in 1886 in order to devote his time to the writing of poetry. With the publication of his first volume in 1889, he became a member of the *fin de siecle* (end-of-century) group of poets in London. His interests at that time were Gaelic folklore and literature, and eastern mysticism. He called himself "the last of the Romantics."

Yeats was a distinguished playwright, as well as a poet. He also wrote many essays on literature and a series of exquisite and deeply revealing autobiographies of his life in Ireland, which were collected in 1939 as *The Autobiography of William Butler Yeats*. This has become one of the most important literary documents of our time.

After World War I, when the Irish Free State came into existence, Yeats served his country as a senator. At that time he was also appointed inspector of schools and censor of motion pictures. In 1923 he received the Nobel Prize in Literature "for his consistently emotional poetry, which in the strictest form expresses a people's spirit."

Glossary of Literary Terms

aestheticism: a literary movement in the latter half of the nineteenth century, which revered beauty above all things and which adopted the motto, *art for art's sake.*

aesthetics: the science or study of the beautiful.

allegory: a narrative in which objects, persons, or events stand for qualities or things not directly included in the narrative itself. For example, in the allegory *The Pilgrim's Progress,* Christian stands for any Christian man, and his adventures for the perils and temptations that beset such a man.

alliteration: the repetition of a beginning consonant sound, usually in a line of verse or in a sentence:

"Doom is darker and deeper than any sea-dingle."
—W. H. Auden

allusion: a reference to some person, place, or event that often has literary, historical, or geographical significance.

analogy: a comparison of ideas or objects which are essentially different but which are alike in one significant way; for example, the analogy between the grasshopper and the man who lives only for the moment.

apostrophe: a figure of speech in which words are addressed to a person or thing—absent or present—or to a personified idea, such as death, truth, or nature:

"Hail, Holy Light, offspring of Heaven firstborn!"
—John Milton

archaism: a word or phrase no longer used in actual speech:
> "*Eftsoons* his hand dropped he!"
> — Samuel Taylor Coleridge

assonance: the repetition of the same vowel sound accompanied by unlike consonant sounds.
> "Sounding like an overtone
> From some lonely world unknown."
> — Edith Sitwell

atmosphere: the general feeling of a literary work conveyed through setting, mood, and tone.

ballad: a narrative that sprang from unknown sources, was transmitted by word of mouth (often altered in the process), and was designed to be sung.

folk ballad: a ballad which originated with the "folk" or common people. Its authorship is unknown.

literary ballad: a ballad composed by a known author who consciously imitated the stanza form, rhythm pattern, and rhyme scheme of the folk ballad. The story told may have originated with the "folk" and previously have been transmitted by word of mouth.

blank verse: unrhymed verse that is generally written in iambic pentameter:
> "No grief did ever come so near thy heart
> As when thy lady and thy true-love died. . . ."
> — William Shakespeare

cadence: the effect created by the rise and fall of the voice and by the emphasis and pause required by the meaning. In other words, the rhythm is not determined by a carefully planned combination of accented and unaccented syllables, as in traditional verse.

caesura: the main pause within a line of verse to indicate both the rhythm and the sense:
> "To be or not to be: that is the question . . ."
> — William Shakespeare

canto: a major section of a long poem.

characterization: the literary portrait of a person revealed through what he says or does, what others say about him or how they react to him, and what the narrator reveals directly.

classicism: the principles thought characteristic of Greek and Roman literature, such as balance, simplicity, restraint, and dignity. See *neoclassic.*

cliché: an expression used so often that it has lost its freshness and effectiveness.

climax: the point of highest interest or of greatest dramatic intensity. Usually it marks a turning point in the action, since the reader is no longer in doubt about the outcome.

conceit: a fanciful image, especially an elaborate or startling analogy.

connotation: the implied or suggested meaning of a word or expression, or the associations the word arouses.

consonance: the close repetition of the same consonant sounds before and after different vowels; for example, *splish-splash.*

contrast: the bringing together of ideas, images, or characters to show how they differ.

couplet: two consecutive and rhyming lines of verse which are usually of equal length:

> "Had we but world enough, and time,
> This coyness, Lady, were no crime."
> —Andrew Marvell

closed couplet: a couplet containing a complete thought. A closed couplet ends with a strong punctuation mark, usually a period.

open couplet: a couplet which forms part of a thought that is completed in the following lines.

heroic couplet: a couplet whose lines are iambic pentameter.

denotation: the precise, literal meaning of a word or expression.

dialect: the speech associated with a particular region or a class or group of people.

didactic: morally instructive or intended to be so.

dissonance: a combination of harsh and jarring sounds or rhythmical patterns.

dramatic monologue: a poem in which a single speaker reveals his own nature as well as the details (time, place, other characters, etc.) of the dramatic situation.

eclogue: a short pastoral poem, often in the form of a verse dialogue between shepherds.

elegy: a poem of subjective or meditative nature, especially one of grief.

epic: a long narrative poem that deals with persons of heroic pro-
portions and with actions of great significance.

episode: a related group of incidents—or a major event—that com-
prises part of the main plot or, in a long work, is related to the
main plot.

epistle: a letter written in verse form.

epithet: an adjective, noun, or phrase that characterizes a person
or thing; for example, *brave-hearted* William.

euphemism: a mild, inoffensive word or expression used in place
of one that is harsh or unpleasant; for example, "to pass away" is
a euphemism for "to die."

fantasy: a tale involving such unreal characters and improbable
events that the reader is not expected to believe it occurred. Some
fantasies are intended merely to entertain; others have a serious
purpose as well: to ridicule outmoded customs or the stupidity
of certain people.

figure of speech: the general term for a number of literary and
poetic devices in which words or groups of words are used to
create images in the mind or to make a comparison. See *hyperbole, metaphor, personification,* and *simile.*

foot: a combination of accented and unaccented syllables which
make up a metrical unit. A foot may incorporate syllables from
different words, and the foot divisions may cut across words, thus:

"The cur/tains drawn/ upon/ unfriend/ly night."

Some of the most frequently used poetic feet are:

the amphibrach: one accented syllable flanked by two unaccented syllables (convíction).

the anapest: two unaccented syllables followed by one accented syllable (interrúpt).

the dactyl: one accented syllable followed by two unaccented
syllables (dífferent).

the iamb: one unaccented syllable followed by one accented
syllable (abóve).

the spondee: two accented syllables in succession: (shóeshíne).

the trochee: one accented syllable followed by one unaccented
syllable (prómise).

foreshadowing: the dropping of important hints by the author to
prepare the reader for what is to come and to help him to antici-
pate the outcome.

form: a fixed metrical arrangement, such as the sonnet.

frame-story: a narrative setting which prepares for, introduces, and unifies or binds together a story, or series of stories.

free verse: verse which does not conform to any fixed pattern. Such poetic devices as rhyme and regular rhythm occur only incidentally.

hyperbole: a figure of speech employing obvious exaggeration; for example, "His mind was a million miles away."

idiom: the language or manner of speaking that is typical of a particular region or group of people.

idyll: a piece of literature describing the simple pleasures of rural life.

image: a general term for any representation of a particular thing. It may be part of a metaphor, a simile, or a straightforward description. An image may also have symbolic meaning.

irony: a mode of expression in which the author says one thing and means the opposite. The term also applies to a situation, or the outcome of an event (or series of events), that is contrary to what is naturally hoped for or expected.

kenning: a metaphorical or descriptive phrase in Anglo-Saxon poetry, used in place of the name of a person, object, action, or emotion; for example, a ship referred to as a "wave-walker."

legend: a story that has come down from the past and that may have some basis in history.

lyric: any short poem that seems to be especially musical and expresses, in most instances, the poet's clearly revealed thoughts and feelings.

madrigal: a short poem which can be set to music; a song with parts for several voices.

masque: a dramatic entertainment, popular in England during the sixteenth and seventeenth centuries, which combined elaborate costumes, scenes, and spectacles with song, dance, and dialogue.

metaphor: a figure of speech in which two things are compared without the use of *like* or *as:*

> "Life's but a walking shadow, a poor player
> That struts and frets his hour upon the stage
> And then is heard no more."
> —William Shakespeare

metaphysical: designating a group of seventeenth-century English poets, such as John Donne, whose poetry was characterized by elaborate conceits, paradoxes, and intellectual imagery. Their poems were usually expressed in the form of an argument.

meter: the pattern of rhythm determined by the accented and unaccented syllables in a line of poetry. Meter is established by the repetition of a dominant foot; for example, iambic pentameter, a line of verse consisting of five iambs:

> "If music be the food of love, play on."
> —William Shakespeare

metonymy: a figure of speech in which one word is used in place of another word that it suggests, as the cause for the effect, the effect for the cause, the sign for the thing signified, the container for the thing contained, etc.; for example, John Milton used metonymy in the line "When I consider how my light is spent," where he substituted *light* for the related word *vision*.

metrical line: a line of verse composed of one or more feet. The following names are used to identify the most common lines:

monometer: one foot	*pentameter:* five feet
dimeter: two feet	*hexameter:* six feet
trimeter: three feet	*heptameter:* seven feet
tetrameter: four feet	*octameter:* eight feet

mock epic: a long narrative poem written in the manner of the true epic but dealing with persons and actions of little consequence. The grandiose style intensifies the ironical or comic effect intended.

monologue: a long speech by a single character.

mood: the frame of mind or state of feeling created by a piece of writing; for example, a sorrowful mood or a sentimental mood.

moral: the lesson taught by a literary work.

motivation: the cause or reason that compels a character to act as he does.

movement: a literary trend or development; for example the Romantic movement.

musical device: a poetic device involving *sound,* such as alliteration, assonance, consonance, internal rhyme, etc.

narrative poem: a story told in verse form.

neoclassic: pertaining to English literature written between approximately 1660 and 1780. The models for much of this literature were ancient Greek and Roman writings, from which the classical "rules" of restraint, balance, dignity, simplicity, rationality, and correctness were derived.

octave: an eight-line poem or stanza, especially the first eight lines of a sonnet.

ode: a lengthy, dignified lyric poem expressing exalted or enthusiastic emotion, often about some person or occasion worthy of esteem.

onomatopoeia: the use of a word, the sound of which suggests what the word means (*splash, buzz, murmur*). This device enables the writer to express sense through sound.

ottava rima: an eight-line, iambic pentameter stanza rhyming *abababcc*. Yeats uses ottava rima in "Sailing to Byzantium."

paradox: a statement which on the surface seems contradictory, yet if interpreted figuratively, involves an element of truth:
> "The child is father of the man."
> —William Wordsworth

parallelism: the grouping together of similar ideas by the use of coordinate constructions:
> "Had we never loved sae kindly,
> Had we never loved sae blindly,
> Never met—or never parted—
> We had ne'er been broken-hearted."
> —Robert Burns

paraphrase: a restating of the sense of a piece of writing, or approximately the same length as the original but in different words.

parody: a humorous imitation or burlesque of a serious piece of literature or writing.

pastoral: the portrayal of an idealized country life, usually involving the love affairs of elegant shepherds and shepherdesses.

pathetic fallacy: the ascribing of human traits to nature or to inanimate objects; for example, "a stubborn door" or "the skies wept."

pathos: that quality which evokes a feeling of pity and compassion.

personification: a figure of speech in which places, things, animals, or ideas are endowed with human qualities:
> "Swiftly walk o'er the western wave,
> Spirit of Night!"
> —Percy Bysshe Shelley

prologue: an opening section of a longer work, usually a play or poem. It may, as in *The Canterbury Tales*, establish the situation and introduce the characters. Sometimes it states the moral of the work.

pun: a play on words, either by using words that sound alike but have different meanings or by using a word with two different meanings, both of which apply. For example, this pun on "done" and Donne:

> "When Thou has done, Thou has not done. . . ."
> —John Donne

quatrain: a four-line stanza.

realistic: the faithful and factual portrayal of people, scenes, and events as the writer feels they are, not as he would like them to be.

resolution: the events following the climax of a work of literature, sometimes called *falling action*.

rhetorical question: a question that is asked for its dramatic effect and to which no answer is expected.

rhyme: the identity of sounds in accented syllables and of all vowel and consonant sounds following (*beautiful, dutiful*). The term *rhyme* is ordinarily used in the sense of end rhyme, the identity of sounds occurring in words that are at the end of matching lines of poetry.

> *eye rhyme:* the appearance, in close proximity, of two words which, because of their similar spellings, look alike but when pronounced do not sound alike (*heath* and *death*):
>
> > "If this be error and upon me proved,
> > I never writ, nor no man ever loved."
> > —William Shakespeare
>
> *feminine rhyme:* a rhyming of matching lines of poetry in which the accented syllable is followed by one or more unaccented syllables which also rhyme:
>
> > "Lord, confound this surly sister,
> > Blight her brow and blotch and blister. . . ."
> > —J. M. Synge
>
> *masculine rhyme:* the rhyming of only the final syllable of matching lines of poetry:
>
> > "He only fair, and what He fair hath made;
> > All other fair like flowers untimely fade."
> > —Edmund Spenser

internal rhyme: the rhyming of a word in the middle of a line of poetry with another word or words in the line, usually at the end:
"I sift the snow on the mountains below."
— Percy Bysshe Shelley

rhyme scheme: the fixed pattern of rhymes used in a poem.

rhythm: in poetry, the recurrence of accented and unaccented syllables in a regular, or nearly regular, pattern.

rhythm pattern: the basic movement of a line, stanza, or poem resulting from the choice and arrangement of the metrical units (feet). The rhythm pattern of a line containing five iambic feet is iambic pentameter, thus:
"Blame not my cheeks, though pale with love they be."
— Dylan Thomas

romance: a long narrative, either in verse or prose, which deals with chivalric adventures, courtships and loves.

romantic: the portrayal of people, scenes, and events as they impress the writer or artist or as he imagines them to be. A romantic work has one or more of the following characteristics: an emphasis on feeling and imagination; a love of nature; a belief in the individual and the common man; an interest in the past, the unusual, the unfamiliar, the bizarre or picturesque; a revolt against authority or commonly accepted conventions.

rondeau: a fixed verse form usually consisting of 15 lines of eight or ten syllables. These lines are usually printed as three stanzas. The opening words of the first line of the rondeau serve as the refrain of the second and third stanzas.

satire: any piece of writing which criticizes manners, individuals, or political and social institutions by holding them up to ridicule.

scansion: the analysis of the metrical structure of poetry.

sentimentality: a superabundance of emotion in a play, poem, or novel.

sestet: a six-line poem or stanza; especially the last six lines of a sonnet.

setting: the time and place in which the events in a narrative (prose or poetry) take place.

simile: a figure of speech in which a comparison is made between two objects essentially unlike but resembling each other in one or more respects. The comparison is indicated by *like* or *as:*
"O, my love is like a red, red rose . . ."
— Robert Burns

sonnet: a poem consisting of fourteen lines, usually written in iambic pentameter and dealing with a single idea or emotion.

Italian or Petrarchan sonnet: a sonnet composed of an octave (eight lines) followed by a sestet (six lines). The rhyme scheme of the octave is *abba abba;* that of the sestet is *cdc dcd.* Poets frequently vary the scheme of the sestet.

Shakespearean sonnet: a sonnet composed of three quatrains and a couplet. The rhyme scheme is generally *abab cdcd efef gg.*

sonnet sequence: a group of sonnets by a single author, generally having a common purpose or thematic link.

stanza: a group of lines of verse treated as a unit and separated from other units by a space.

stereotype: a character who conforms to certain widely accepted ideas of how such a person should look, think, or act.

style: the distinctive manner in which the writer uses language: his choice and arrangement of words.

suspense: a feeling of excitement, curiosity, or expectation about the outcome of a narrative (prose or poetry).

symbol: an object that stands for, or represents, an idea, belief, superstition, social or political institution, etc. A pair of scales, for example, is often a symbol for justice.

tale: a simple story that recounts a real or imaginary event.

tercet: a three-line stanza.

terza rima: a series of tercets in which the second line of each ter-cet rhymes with the first and third lines of the following tercet: *aba, bcb, cdc, ded,* etc.

theme: the idea, general truth, or commentary on life or people brought out through a literary work.

tone: the feeling conveyed by the author's attitude toward his subject and the particular way in which he writes about it.

verisimilitude: the appearance or semblance of truth; the use of details in such a way that a reader accepts, at least for the time of reading, the most far-fetched or impossible settings and events.